THE BRIDGE PEOPLE

Daily Life in a Camp of the Homeless

Jackson Underwood

UNIVERSITY
PRESS OF
AMERICA

Lanham • New York • London

Copyright © 1993 by
Jackson Underwood

Printed in 1993 by
University Press of America® Inc.
4720 Boston Way
Lanham, Maryland 20706

3 Henrietta Street
London WC2E 8LU England

Library of Congress Cataloging-in-Publication Data
Underwood, Jackson.
The bridge people : daily life in a camp of the homeless / Jackson
Underwood.
p.   cm.
Includes bibliographical references and index.
1. Homeless persons—California—Los Angeles.   I. Title.
HV4506.L67U53   1993
362.5'0979494—dc20   92–38148 CIP

ISBN 0–8191–8961–8 (cloth : alk. paper)
ISBN 0–8191–8962–6 (pbk. : alk. paper)

The paper used in this publication meets the minimum requirements of
American National Standard for Information Sciences—Permanence
of Paper for Printed Library Materials, ANSI Z39.48–1984.

Acknowledgments

A great many people helped in this project. To begin, I would like to thank my first and by far most important teacher: my mother, Emily Russell.

I would also like to acknowledge the help of the late Professor Philip Staniford of San Diego State University, Professor Claude Warren of the University of Nevada, Las Vegas, and Dr. Jamie Cleland of Dames and Moore, San Diego. At various times, all of these gentlemen gave me significant opportunities to conduct research and polish my report writing skills.

My Ph.D. committee at UCLA helped in innumerable ways in learning about psychological and medical anthropology and the social world. Thank you, Professors John G. Kennedy, Lewis L. Langness, Allan David Heskin, and Robert M. Emerson. I especially want to thank my committee chairperson, Professor Robert B. Edgerton for his help and support through the years.

Dr. Paul Koegel lured me into research on homelessness in the first place and generously shared his time and resources with me. He discussed this research with me frequently and provided insightful criticism of this manuscript in its earlier forms. I would also like to thank my colleagues in the Adaptation of the Homeless Mentally Ill Project, UCLA: Dr. Dana Baldwin, Dr. Tom Ward, and Mr. Alex Cohen. Professors Keith Kernan and Jimmy Turner of the Program for Medical Anthropology and Psychocultural Studies, UCLA, discussed a variety of psychological and anthropological topics with me on many, many occasions and thus also contributed to this project.

Molly Thayer helped as computer consultant, sounding board, and informal editor. Most importantly, however, she was an unflagging source of emotional support and encouragement throughout this long project. I would like to thank Sharon Sabsay and Ray Shoemaker for conducting the final editing and layout.

My literary agent, Laurie Harper of the Sebastian Agency, San Carlos, California, offered great assistance and insight in translating this report from "Academese" into English and I would like to thank her very much for that. On many different levels, this book would never have happened without her.

And finally, I would like to thank the homeless people who shared their lives and camps with me. My hope is that this work will ultimately improve their lives in some way.

Funding for this work was partially provided by the California Department of Mental Health Contract No. 90-70044, The Adaptation of the Homeless Mentally Ill, Dr. Paul Koegel, Principal Investigator, and a grant from the Martha Hewes Thayer Trust for Social Responsibility.

Jackson Underwood, Ph.D.
Pacific Palisades, California
1993

Table of Contents

Introduction

On the green fringe of our grey urban lives you may glimpse the camps of the homeless.—Look around the edges of public buildings, at the back of a vacant lot, or in the foliage near the freeway as you sit fuming in frustrating traffic on your way to do something important. This book is about the daily life of a group of homeless people who live in camps under some freeway bridges in downtown Los Angeles. It is what is called a narrative ethnography, that is, it consists primarily of what I said to them and what they said to me.

The research project on homelessness of which this study was a small part lasted for about four years; what is reported here took place over a period of about two and one half years. The ethnography unfolds in chronological order to allow you, as much as possible, to learn about the Bridge People the way I did—one day at a time. My goal was to let you witness for yourselves the sights, sounds, and smells of this particular form of extreme poverty, to provide you an opportunity to gain some insight into the daily lives of these people and how they view their existence and the world around them.

My research among the homeless began in October, 1987, when I was offered a job as ethnographer on a project that an acquaintance, Dr. Paul Koegel, was initiating. He was looking into the lifestyles of homeless mentally ill people in the downtown area of Los Angeles with the goals of documenting how they live and finding out why so many did not use services that were ostensibly set up to serve them. My research job with his Adaptation of the Homeless Mentally Ill Project (or AHMI—pronounced Ah Me, often with a sigh) was to consist of a combination of ethnographic fieldwork and note taking to total twenty hours a week, and I was free to pursue my own line of research the rest of the time. Paul was supportive of my research from the start. He often referred me to important articles, lent me books, and discussed my research with me.

During the early days of the AHMI Project, I found it quite difficult to approach dirty, shabbily dressed strangers and strike up a conversation, as you might imagine. I had to make myself do it by saying to myself it was important work and by pretending to be relaxed, confident, and competent. After many months of this ruse, I realized I had, for the most part, become what I had pretended to be.

When I initially approached people, I told them that I was from UCLA, that I was doing research, and that what they told me would be confidential. If they were interested, I would usually take the time to discuss the project in detail. Then I asked their permission to tape record our discussions. I found that tape recording conversations was the best way to get the verbatim material necessary for the kind of report I wanted to produce. The little tape recorder I used was relatively unobtrusive and people appeared to get used to it quickly. Only occasionally was I turned down (mostly by paranoid schizophrenics and police officers). When that happened, I had to reconstruct conversations from fieldnotes taken shortly after the event. (Details of field methods are discussed in the appendix.)

In the AHMI Project, we developed guidelines against giving money to our homeless acquaintances other than a little change occasionally. We didn't have the money to become financial resources for them and we wanted to develop a special kind of friendship with them that as much as possible did not include dominance, dependancy, or patronage. Instead of giving out money, we took homeless people to lunch or bought food or small personal articles for them. Sometimes I did pay them a dollar or two for allowing me to take their photograph.

My AHMI colleague, Dr. Tom Ward, suggested that since the vast majority of homeless people smoke, and getting cigarettes is a constant problem for them, we could also buy cigarettes and give them to our homeless acquaintances as way of helping. I followed Tom's suggestion and gave away cigarettes, despite the fact that tobacco is by far the most dangerous drug in America, responsible for over 300,000 deaths annually (compared with 100,000 deaths associated with alcohol and only 6,000 deaths associated with all illegal drugs combined [Jonas 1989]). I did this because most of the homeless are dedicated smokers anyway, and it seemed to me and to them that death from lung cancer was the least of their worries.

I also began smoking a pipe when I was in the field to give me something to fiddle with while my homeless friends rolled cigarettes and smoked. It improved rapport in a modest way by including me in the smoking circle. An important benefit that I hadn't anticipated was that smoking my pipe helped mask the very unpleasant odors that I often encountered in the streets and back alleys of Skid Row and in the camps of the homeless.

At home I usually have some dry sherry or cheap white Bordeaux or a couple of beers in the evening. When I was in the field in the company of my homeless friends, I would buy them a like amount of whatever they preferred so that we could drink together. I found it helped build rapport to drink with people if they were drinkers. It also helped distinguish me as an anthropologist from other middle-class people, such as police, psychiatrists, and social workers, who might be quite critical of street people and their values, and who would never sit down and have a drink with them. I tried to fit into their lives as much as was practical and to learn from them as they went about their more or less normal existence. Drinking and smoking with them helped them relax with me and me with them. Social scientists should remember the words of Theognis: "Wine is wont to show the mind of man."

In keeping with the anthropological tradition of trying to protect the privacy of field consultants, I have used pseudonyms throughout this report for most people and locations. In this narrative ethnography, we focus on the lives of Tom Kinkaid and Jerry Michaels, two White, homeless men in their mid-forties. You will also get to know several other people who live under the bridges. I must point out that Tom and Jerry are not "typical" homeless people. They are somewhat more articulate and reflective about their lives than many I have met, which is one reason that I chose to spend my time with them. On the other hand, in my experience their style of life is common, with some variation, among the panhandlers you see on the streets of any large city in America.

The notion of a "typical" homeless person, moreover, suggests that the homeless are a relatively homogeneous group, but that is not the case at all. There is tremendous variability in lifestyles, abilities, handicaps, and backgrounds among the homeless. No single community of homeless people could possibly be representative of "street people" in the United States, just as no single neighborhood could be representative of all the different kinds of "house people" or "apartment people." The existence exemplified by the Bridge People is only one style of life among the very poor in the United States today.

The camps under the bridges are similar to other camps I have seen and visited in the western part of downtown Los Angeles. In other parts of Los Angeles and in other parts of the United States, the demographic composition of homeless camps varies. However, there are thousands of people more or less like the Bridge People camping in vacant nooks and crannies around any urban center in the United States today.

The lives of most of the Bridge People revolved around the use of alcohol, but, as you will see, some of these people drank only moderately. In the homeless population at large, the vast majority report using only moderate amounts of alcohol or no alcohol. In their survey research among homeless people in Los Angeles, Koegel, Burnham, and Farr (1988) found that about 33% of the people they inter-viewed reported abusing alcohol within the last year and about 41% reported alcohol abuse within the past three years. Of course, self-report data on self-incriminating topics like alcohol abuse should be taken, like tequila, with a grain of salt and a squeeze of lime.

When I began this research I did not have many preconceived ideas about homelessness. By virtue of my education, I am prejudiced toward the Enlightenment view of the perfectibility of humankind and the importance of indi-vidual human dignity. I also believe strongly in democracy, a notion revived during the 18th Century in Europe after a long feudal sleep. To me, democracy means that people should have some significant say in all institutions, public and private, that impact their lives. As far as I can tell, democracy is the only honor-able, legitimate, and fair form of managing human affairs. Unfortunately, many of our public and private institutions are still petty tyrannies modeled on feudalism (the divine right of kingpins) or Fascism (might makes right) in which the participants have little or no voice in the conditions of their participation. From a practical point of view, democracy, and its requisite open flow of information, leads to under-standing and cooperation better than any other form of institution, and we Americans very much need mutual understanding and cooperation to live and prosper in an increasingly complex and capricious technological world. My liberal beliefs in democracy and humanism are evident in this report. My respect for the dignity of the individual led me, over the course of the research, to view the people

I studied with compassion as we got to know one another and became friends across our vast socioeconomic differences.

Politically, I consider myself to be a democrat of the Jeffersonian variety and a fiscal conservative. While this might sound somewhat odd, the important political distinction, in my view, is not between fiscal conservative and liberal, but fiscal conservative and spendthrift. Many of those who flaunt the flag of fiscal conservativism today are really militarist spendthrifts below their bunting. Many others are just mean, stingy, and shortsighted. Fiscal conservativism, in my view, means a great deal more than "no new taxes." It means being provident, planning for the future, living within your means, getting your money's worth, and investing the dime of education now to save the dollar of correction later.

I met Jerry on December 2, 1987. The research reported here ended on March 17, 1990. During that time, I was also conducting part-time ethnographic research for the AHMI Project with 14 homeless mentally ill people, most of whom suffered from florid schizophrenia, who spent their lives primarily on Market Street, one of the main streets in the older part of downtown Los Angeles. I was also conducting research, partly supported by the AHMI Project, in a predominantly Black, drug-dominated neighborhood in the dangerous core of Skid Row. Altogether, I spent some 30 nights on the street with various homeless people, half of those nights with Bridge People. I also spent approximately 200 days in the field with various homeless people between the time the AHMI Project began in October 1987 and when its fieldwork was complete in December of 1990. I probably spent something like 600 days transcribing tape and typing up notes, but I didn't keep a record of that.

Being around so much deprivation and misery took a toll on me emotionally. Sometimes, after two or three weeks at home transcribing and typing up field notes, it was quite difficult for me to force myself to go back to the field. The more "the homeless" emerged as fellow human beings with faces, feelings, and beliefs, the more difficult it became. Occasionally I felt quite depressed about the value of doing this work and the values of our great affluent society. Although I was associated with a larger research project, I didn't see my fellow researchers often and frequently felt like a "lone ranger" in a horrible wasteland.

I coped with being around this misery in several ways. In typical American fashion, I often threw myself into my other work as a way of getting my mind off it. I played guitar and wrote songs, many of which were cathartic rantings unfit for human consumption. I also sculpted a great deal, mostly abstract pieces of weathered wood juxtaposed with natural rock, glass, or plexiglas. Since 1970, I have also regularly run, swum, and, to a lesser extent, ridden a bicycle and have found this strenuous aerobic exercise very good for my emotional health. In the winter, I try to utilize as much snow therapy as possible, and during the course of the research, I was occasionally lucky enough to escape to the ski slopes of Mammoth where I would scare the hell out of myself going off The Cornice and various other black diamond runs on Telemark skis. I would also go backcountry skiing in the majestic white silence of the eastern Sierra Nevada. A few times, when the sickness and suffering I was seeing really got me down, I transcended miserable reality the way many street people do—I got roaring drunk.

1. Jackson meets Jerry

On December 2, 1987, at about noon, my colleague Dana Baldwin and I were walking through the Civic Center area of downtown Los Angeles. The sidewalks were crowded with bustling business people, bureaucrats, and attorneys. Here and there you could also see homeless people walking aimlessly, slumped on benches, and lounging on patches of public grass. On one corner, we dropped some change into the cap of a panhandler we had seen in the area before. I wondered if he kept seed money showing, since both times we had passed he had displayed a similar small amount of change in the cap.

We walked back to the panhandler and introduced ourselves. We told him that we were conducting research about homelessness and that we were from UCLA. I asked him if I could tape record our conversation, and he said, "Sure, no problem." I mentioned that we'd seen him there a couple of times. I joked, "Is this your office?"

He replied, "Yes. Hee, hee, hee. This IS my office, but my secretary is out right now."

The guy's name was Jerry. By Skid Row standards, he looked pretty healthy—thin but not emaciated and without the wear and obvious scars that tell of terribly hard miles and poor maintenance. He was dressed in clean faded Levi's, a sport shirt, and a sweater. Capsized on the ground in front of him was a nice looking wool driving cap and in the cap were a few coins.

We sat down with Jerry on a small curb at the edge of a flower bed. At our backs was the cold pink marble of a state building. As we talked to him, he continued to work the pedestrians passing his "office." Most were nicely dressed, middle-class people who apparently worked in nearby offices.

"Howdy ma'am. Howdy sir. You look real nice today. Have a nice day." Jerry gave the couple a warm toothless grin from beneath his bushy red beard. Because of the long beard and moustache, his toothlessness was not very noticeable, but he did talk in soft slurs and whistles. Working on Skid Row, you get very used to toothlessness.

Jerry immediately shifted his attention to the next pedestrian. "Good morning, John. How you doin' today?" The old man in the business suit nodded and smiled as he dropped a couple of quarters into the cap. The pride in the way he carried himself suggested he was an important person, maybe a retired judge, I thought, or army officer.

"Take better care of yourself, Jerry," he said in a voice like Walter Brennan's. Then he continued striding down the crowded sidewalk.

"Thank you, John. Thank you and have a nice day, sir," Jerry said. He looked up and smiled at the next potential patron. "Good morning, ma'am." She marched past without acknowledging his presence. "Have a nice day, ma'am." There was no cynicism or malice in Jerry's voice.

Dana and I asked a question now and then when foot traffic thinned. We didn't want to curb the wheels of Jerry's commerce. I asked about the change in his cap, but he wouldn't admit that it was really seed money. As we sat there, though, I noticed that as coins accumulated in the cap, he would occasionally pick them up and put them in his shirt pocket, leaving only a few nickels and pennies. Once a woman handed him a dollar bill, and his face lit up as he leaned out to grasp it and swiftly stuffed it into his shirt. Dollar bills, it seemed, did not make good seed money.

When we asked Jerry if this was his permanent spot, he said that he might or might not be there on any given day depending on how much money he had made the previous day.

"I'm, I'm only trying to make enough to get by. If I make enough for a little food and maybe a little something to drink, then I'll knock off for the day, you know. I'm not tryin' to get rich and famous and stuff like that. If I have a GOOD day, then I'll prob'ly give myself a day or two off."

"So, how long do you work, on a workday?"

"Oh, it depends, you know. I guess I usually get down here at about ten thirty or so, something like that, and I stay until I get enough to get by. I like to make at least about five or six dollars. A lot of times, I'll give up after that, but sometimes I'll keep at it, if the money is rollin' in. On a really GOOD day, I'll make maybe twenty, twenty-five dollars, you know. But all I'm tryin' to do is make enough to buy food and, and, tobacco for me and Tommy."

"So, what time do you leave the office usually, do you think?"

"Oh, it's sorta hard to say. I guess I usually leave in the middle of the afternoon. Maybe one thirty, two. Something like that, you know."

"Yeah. I see."

Dana asked, "How much of what you make goes towards alcohol and how much towards food?"

"Well, hee, hee, hee, I don't really know, but food always comes first. Food is always first. What I do is, I go down to the Grand Central [Market] after I'm done here, and I buy whatever food I need, you know, and then I buy liquor with whatever is left over. Then I go home and cook it up. I cook a lotta beans, stews, soups. Stuff like that. But I always try to eat right, you know. I cook most every night."

I wanted to believe him. I want to believe everybody, but I'm pretty cynical. I asked Jerry if he used alcohol and drugs to self-medicate. Jerry understood the question and said yes. He said, "Drugs are a way to motivate me to get out from under the bridge. I'm a very depressed person and I don't mind saying it." He added that with his "meds" (medication) and alcohol, he got along okay.

From our brief discussion with him, Dana and I tentatively concluded that Jerry might be suffering from manic–depressive (bipolar) disorder. He mentioned that there were times when he didn't get out from underneath the bridge for four or five days because of depression. There were other times when he had what sounded like manic periods, also lasting four or five days. He mentioned how during these periods, "I have a heckova time sleeping, but at least everything in camp gets cleaned up. Ha, ha, ha, ha."

Summoning up all my sophistication, I blurted, "Do you drink a lot?"

"You better believe it!" he said.

When I asked him what his drug of choice was, Jerry answered unequivocally "Speed," and added that next on his list was wine. He liked anything with an alcohol content over eighteen or nineteen per cent, but his favorite beverage was Thunderbird.

As we all sat on the curb together, Dana glanced down Market Street and noticed a couple of police officers slowly walking in our direction. She asked in a matter-of-fact way if there was a law against panhandling.

Jerry started when he followed her gaze and noticed the police. "You're damn right there is." He quickly shoved his cap out of sight behind him against the wall. He said he'd been arrested numerous times, but not for panhandling *per se*.

"If they want to arrest you, they can. They'll find something to charge you with. They don't usually bother, though, because of all the paperwork involved."

Jerry mentioned that he hadn't had proper identification for five years, so that when he was arrested, he gave them whatever name and social security number occurred to him at the time. He laughed and said, "My worst nightmare, hee, hee, hee, is that I'll accidently give the cops the social security number of a mass murderer or something!"

When it came time for us to move on, Dana and I told Jerry that we'd like to come visit him at his camp sometime. He said, "That would be great! Just give me a little time to tidy up a bit and stuff like that. But sure, that'd be great."

It was relatively pleasant talking to Jerry. He seemed pretty bright and articulate and had a good sense of humor. I was spending most of my field time with homeless people suffering from florid schizophrenia. When I was talking to paranoid type schizophrenics, I always had to wonder what part was delusional. When I was talking to disorganized type schizophrenics, I had to strain to make any sense at all of what they said. Some made sense at the sentence level, but not at the paragraph level. Others could scarcely express themselves at all. In any case, it was quite stressful and demanding work. By contrast, I found that I could relax around Jerry.

There are people that you just instantly get along well with. To me it's a rather ineffable phenomenon. Others have described it as chemistry or vibes. I would describe it as resonating with one another. There are other people that you may like and get along fairly well with, but with whom you lack instant rapport or resonation. Anyway, I felt an instant rapport with Jerry. I felt only a little awkward and out of place sitting there with him as he panhandled, and that was because of the activity and setting rather than because of him.

2. Another day at the office

I saw Jerry a few weeks later at his customary corner. He didn't look as healthy as he had when Dana and I had last seen him. His changed appearance brought home to me how little margin homeless people have. What might be a minor setback for a middle-class person can alter the quality of life for a homeless person in major ways. The results are often visible in their personal hygiene, clothing, and, worst of all, in their eyes. It would take a really major life disaster for a middle-class person to change so visibly.

I asked Jerry how he was doing. He said fine, nothing much had changed with him. I found that difficult to believe, of course, since he looked so much worse. When I asked about his appearance in what I hoped was a diplomatic fashion, he said that when Dana and I had met him, he had just spent the night in "the tubs"—that is, a bathhouse—so he had been exceptionally clean, but that now I was seeing him in his more natural state.

As we sat together on his curb, we talked about this and that as acquaintances will do. Jerry said that he used to be an atheist. Then he came to believe in a God of some kind during the lingering, painful cancer death of his father. "I have come to the point that I don't want to call Him God…but I call him something, something special, you know. I realize—You have to be a very ignorant person alive on this earth and not think there's a superior being. So I just call him Super."

A crippled blonde woman in her thirties, apparently homeless, hobbled past and Jerry glowered.

"I hate her," he said.

"Oh? Do you know her name?" I asked.

"I—No, I have absolutely no idea what her name is."

"Why do you hate her?"

"Because she panhandles right in front of me, that's why!" We watched her approaching people perhaps forty to fifty yards to the north of us on our side of the street. "She hustles in front of me when I'm trying to hustle."

"Yeah, that's a little tacky."

"It's tacky....It's stupid, you know. Give me a break. There's this whole fuckin' street here."

"How close could she come before you would feel that she was trespassing on your turf, sort of, or being inconsiderate? Would fifty or seventy-five feet be okay?"

"No, huh uh, no, no, nope, that's too close."

"How 'bout a block away?"

"A block. Yeah, three hundred fifty feet. It's kinda hard, when you're down here and you're working—A lot of people don't—Like my campmate Tommy, he doesn't realize what it takes to make a dollar. This morning he said, 'Jerry,' he said, 'do you have a couple of bucks?' I said, 'Yeah I do,' but I said, 'but it's gonna be seed. Seed for going on for today.' And he goes, 'Would you bring me back a bottle?' But you know, I have all that on top of me."

"Yeah, you don't need the pressure then, huh?"

"No. Somehow, I got luggage. If I wanted luggage, I'd want Gucci. Hee, hee, hee."

"Ha, ha, ha. Yeah." After a moment I asked, "What happened to your eye? It looks like someone smacked you in your eye."

"Oh no. I had a, uh, I had a seizure."

"An alcoholic seizure?"

"No, no."

"Epileptic seizure?" I asked.

"Epileptic, yeah. And it was bad. It was fifteen stitches."

"Where did this take place?"

"Right here."

"Right in the office?"

"Yep, right in my office."

"How embarrassing. Right in front of your clients?"

"Thank God! It was my clients that called the ambulance."

Jerry continually greeted people as they walked by his office as we talked. He was, after all, at work. A group of three women dressed in office clothing approached. He smiled, they smiled, and he greeted them. He called out to one by name.

"Hi there. Hi Francis."

"Hi there," they all said cheerily, at slightly different times. "How are you?"

The women smiled but continued walking down the sidewalk. When they had gone four or five steps past us, Jerry shouted out in mock anger, "Get back over here and give me some MONEY!"

The women giggled and waved but kept on walking. Jerry turned to me and said they'd probably bring him something to eat or some change on their way back from lunch. He called such people "come-backs."

I was running out of time for the day and said, "Well, Señor, I'm gonna have to take off. It's good to see ya. I'm glad to see you're doin' okay."

"Well, I'm glad to see you. You said you were gonna come up and visit underneath the bridge and you never did."

"That's right. We went by there one time, but you weren't there. And we talked to—I think we talked to Abe, but he was in a real grumpy mood. And real drunk. So we didn't have a real nice chat or anything. But we'll come up and see ya. I want to come up and take some photographs of your camp. I won't tell anybody where it is or anything like that. Would that be okay?"

"Well, let me know so I can...tidy up a LITTLE bit, you know. When you live on the street, that's where you live. I don't have doilies and that kind of crap laying around. My way of life is, 'Stay warm Jerry.' You know, 'Keep warm and then worry about something else. And pull the blanket over your head.'"

"It's reduced down to relatively basic issues?"

"It's very, very basic. And, and a lot of people don't understand that."

"Well señor, I'm going to have to take off. How much have you had to drink today? Had a little eye opener?"

"I've had one short dog, at about seven o'clock."

"Just to keep things goin' huh?"

"Yeah."

"Oh, by the way, what's a short dog?"

"A short dog is uh, uh, one of those little bottles."

"What is that, about a pint?"

"Yeah."

"Well, that should do it. I had my drug this morning. I had a couple of cups of coffee. I get pretty wired on a couple of cups of coffee."

"I went down and had a couple of cups of coffee…and then I went down and had a short dog."

"Is that all you had for breakfast?…Did you have some donuts or something?"

"Nope."

"Liquid diet, huh?"

"Liquid, that's it."

I asked him if he was going to get something to eat today, and he said that he was going to sit there and panhandle and then go to the Grand Central Market (a large open building with small meat markets, fish markets, vegetable booths, fruit sellers, liquor booths, and so on). He said he was going to buy some food and then go to his camp under the bridge and cook it.

While I was trying to say goodbye, a middle-aged Hispanic woman walked up from the direction of the Grand Central Market and offered Jerry and me each an apple. At first I was hesitant to take it. I experienced a touch of panic at the awkwardness of the situation and nearly blurted out, "Oh, I'm not homeless!"

However, I caught myself in time and accepted her gift, smiled, and said thank you. After the kind woman continued walking back toward the Civic Center, I gave the apple to Jerry. He accepted it, but later I wondered what he was going to do with apples since he had no teeth. I supposed that he could roast them over a campfire or give them to some of his campmates or neighbors who had teeth.

3. Going for welfare

Despite repeated attempts, I didn't see Jerry again until the middle of June, 1988. I caught him at his office at about ten thirty and after we had said our hellos, I again sat down next to him while he panhandled. We talked about a variety of things for about an hour and a half. I had an appointment so I had to leave by about noon. Among other things, we talked about the welfare system, known in Los Angeles as general relief, or simply G.R.

"By the time I fill out the papers for G.R. and then I have to go to the hospital, then I have to go to mental health, then I have to do all this other bullshit, and everything else. It's not worth it! Because I can't handle it. I get too nervous. And if they would just take your word for it. But they won't. They gotta have this, they gotta have that. The welfare system—The welfare system is so insulting, degrading, and humiliating, that I would much rather beg one on one than to go down there and sit around all day for the privilege of filling out stupid papers and talking with twisted, mean bureaucrats. They treat you like crap. Let somebody else go for it."

"Yeah, yeah. I understand."

"And even food stamps. Well, I lost my billfold, so I don't have any I.D. at all. I don't even have a Social security card or anything else. I don't know even know how I can get I.D. I went down to Social Security to try to get a social security card and they asked me if I had any I.D. to get the social security card, and—Ha, ha, ha! I told them that's what I'm tryin' to get. And I was going to call my mother to get my birth certificate sent out here. But the last time I called mother, I put the lug on her for seven hundred dollars. Ha, ha, ha. And I went to call her, and she's got an unlisted phone number now. Ha, ha, ha, ha. I said, 'Oh well. The old broad wised up.' Ha, ha, ha, ha. But she's—She's so upset that I'm livin' on the streets anyway."

"Yeah, I can understand that," I said. "Well, Jerry, we'd better get going so you can get to work."

"Oh-key-doke. Nice seeing you again."

4.   The hurt of homelessness

Dana and I continued our fieldwork, sometimes separately and sometimes together. Occasionally we'd stop by Jerry's office to look for him, but without success. Keeping in touch with homeless people can be rather difficult. Basically, you just have to go where you think you'll have a good chance of running into them and keep going until you do run into them or someone who knows them. Toward the end of July, 1988, we stopped by the bridges over Cardenas Street where Jerry lived. According to a couple of his friends and neighbors, Jerry had had a stroke and been taken to County/USC Hospital, but he was now residing in a board and care facility. The guys we talked to didn't know which one he was in or how long he would be there. They did think he was in pretty good shape and not permanently paralyzed from the stroke.

It wasn't until the middle of October that we saw Jerry again. We encountered him at his office at Second and Market, near the Civic Center, at about twelve thirty. Dana and I talked briefly to him, but told him that we had to go to the re-opening of the Golden West Hotel. Formerly a run-down, single room occupancy (SRO) hotel, it had been thoroughly remodeled and was now going to be a board and care facility for homeless mentally ill people. He said that he would walk along with us if it was okay. We said that it was. As a result of his stroke, he was walking very poorly, even with the help of a cane, but we were in no particular hurry.

As we walked along, he told us that a couple of weeks earlier an Hispanic woman had been beaten to death by her boyfriend in a bridge campsite right next to his. He hadn't actually seen the murder, but he did see the events leading up to it. The couple had moved into one of the bridge campsites only shortly before and Jerry hadn't gotten to know them much, but he had seen the boyfriend beat the woman on other occasions. He found the whole affair very upsetting.

Changing the subject, he said that he and a couple of friends had been on a binge for the last few days, during which, he said, he had been consuming about five fifths of white port a day. White port is a fortified wine that is about twenty per cent alcohol. I found it difficult to believe that a person could consume a gallon of it a day for several days and live to tell the tale.

Jerry and his friends were dedicated drinkers, however, and on this occasion he did look a little rough. His eyes were red and bleary, and he was listing a bit to port. On the other hand, it amuses street people to be able to astonish middle-class people like friendly neighborhood anthropologists with tales of horror and decadence. They view themselves as wily tricksters getting by in a game wherein they must play against loaded dice and stacked decks. In this way they can feel some slight sense of self-respect in a world full of suffering and despair. It's a small way of getting back at the greater society which seems to hate them so. Also, street people gain status among their peers by being able to hold their liquor and consume prodigious amounts. Being a good heavy drinker, a raconteur, and a trickster, it seemed to me, was an ideal among many of the street people I was getting to know. I felt that Jerry was one of those who shared this ideal and I suspected that he was probably exaggerating a bit in order to shock, amaze, and impress Dana and me.

As we walked along, Jerry expressed his loneliness and sadness. He said, "It hurts all the time when you live on the streets. Day in and day out. It's, it's not physical pain, but hurt. It hurts when people look at you like you're nothing but a pile of crap. That's when they'll even look at you. Hell, most of the time people won't even look at you at all. Like they wish you didn't exist or something. It sure don't make a fella feel good about himself. So fuck it. So I'm a drunk and I'm a bum, but that's no reason to be so hateful. I don't hurt nobody. I don't take advantage of nobody. I don't cheat nobody. Like, I never sold the Air Force six hundred dollar toilet seats and stuff like that. I don't know why people are so hateful, and that hurts too. So I drink. I drink a lot, and that helps dull the hurt. The disadvantage is that you still have to live with the same hurt when you wake up the next day. 'Cause you're still livin' in the dirt underneath the bridges. And you still got the same problems. And you still get the same hateful looks. And you still got the hurt. So you drink some more, and so, on and on it goes."

We all walked along in solemn silence for a while. Dana and I shared a cheerless glance behind Jerry's back. There didn't seem to be anything to say that wouldn't seem trivial or trite. I was moved by Jerry's soliloquy. I had wondered the same thing about why the well-off seem so mean and hateful toward the homeless and other poor people. It seemed to me an upside-down logic. If one class is justified in being mean and hateful toward another, it would seem to be the poor toward the rich. But I had found very little resentment of the rich among the homeless. The lives of the homeless are brim full of frustration, disappointment, and anger, but it is directed inward and expressed in self-destructive behaviors like alcohol and drug abuse and in hopelessness and depression. However, like Jerry, I had seen plenty of meanness, stinginess, and hatefulness on the part of the well-off toward the poor.

Later, I thought that part of the answer might be that the very existence of millions of homeless and desperately poor people in this great and wealthy country constitutes evidence that challenges our honored beliefs about living in a land of opportunity with liberty and justice for all. What I was seeing seemed like scenes out of *Les Miserables* or *Oliver Twist*. This wasn't the sort of thing I had ever expected to see in the United States. The cream of American society, it seemed, not only didn't care about those below, they hated them for their weaknesses, their handicaps, their failings, and, as Jerry suggested, even for existing. For millions of poor people, the American dream had curdled and seeing it "up close and personal" was leaving me with a foul taste in my mouth.

Dana and I continued to walk with Jerry in silence. After a block or so, we asked about his background. Jerry brightened up and said that he had earned a Ph.D. in English when he was twenty. That really caught our attention, because at the time we were both finishing doctorates in medical and psychological anthropology at UCLA and knew very well how much work a Ph.D was. Jerry said his dissertation had been on the literature of the Jewish holocaust. He mentioned a small private college in the Midwest, but I didn't get the name. When we expressed our astonishment, he said that he had worked very hard, but acknowledged that he had had a drinking problem even then. His mother was an English teacher and she pushed him, he said. The Ph.D. tale seemed like the pathetic wishful thinking of a hopeless Skid Row drunk. It made me quite sad to hear him going on like this, but I made a note to check on his academic career later. It could be true. You hear so many stories on the street and most are either wishful thinking or the grandiose delusions of paranoid schizophrenia, but some ARE true. Of course, wishful thinking and delusions also tell us something about a person's sense of self and mental health, and are valuable aids to understanding in their own right.

At one point Jerry said that he sometimes woke up in the middle of the night crying, but he didn't know why. He had been drinking since high school, and quite heavily since his twenties, he said. He had been hearing voices since high school too. Dana attempted to get a good understanding of his symptoms and the order of their appearance, but Jerry could be an agile conversationalist, and she wasn't able to pin him down.

If the auditory hallucinations had preceded the heavy drinking, then it would seem likely that Jerry was suffering from major depression or possibly schizophrenia. If not, then his diagnosis would probably be organic brain disorder, that is, brain damage from long-term alcohol abuse. Although Dana and I were not psychiatrists, we had undergone a couple of training programs in psychiatric diagnosis (at the Department of Psychiatry, UCLA) and felt pretty comfortable making estimates about mental health.

Jerry again invited Dana and me to visit him at his camp, so we made an appointment to meet him there on Tuesday, October 18, 1988. He explained that he had moved because the recent murder of the Hispanic woman had taken place right near his old camp and it was a little spooky for him to continue to stay there. He was still on Cardenas Street, but now under a different bridge. This was about a mile from Jerry's office in the Civic Center and not far from Chinatown. Cardenas runs more or less north and south, and there are four bridges there where Jerry and his associates camp. There are two high bridges which consist of the east- and westbound lanes of the freeway. These are flanked by two lower bridges which are on and off ramps. The campsites under the low bridges are preferred because they are roomier and easier to get to. The potential campsites are at each end of the bridges on the more or less level ground in front of the abutments. Virtually all freeway bridges in Los Angeles that have a little level ground under them and can be reached on foot provide shelter for homeless people. The foliage around freeways also provides places for very poor people to camp. Caltrans, the agency in charge of highways and freeways in California, is unwillingly and unwittingly one of the state's largest providers of shelter for the very poor.

5. A visit to Jerry's camp

On Tuesday morning, Dana and I decided to walk by Jerry's office to see if he was there before making the long trek to his campsite. We arrived there about ten thirty. There were a couple of White guys sitting perhaps twenty or thirty yards apart near Jerry's customary place. One had almost shoulder length, frizzy hair, the other had over-the-collar straight brown hair. They appeared to be in their thirties. They were both staring off into space and ignoring each other and the passersby. We walked a little further and encountered Jerry sitting on a waist-high marble planter about fifty or sixty yards north of his customary spot.

We greeted him and he said that he remembered our appointment. I was puzzled by that; if he remembered the appointment, why wasn't he in the appointed place? I didn't say anything about it, though. We walked back toward his office where the other two guys were sitting. One of them, the one with straight hair, turned out to be Jimmy Newby, one of Jerry's current campmates. We offered to buy them something to eat and began walking together toward the Del Taco, a fast food place about half a block south. We all approached the counter and ordered something to eat except for Jerry, who had already eaten some food he'd found in a dumpster behind Angelo's Restaurant near his camp. I urged him to eat; he demurred, but did decide to drink some coffee. I paid and made sure I got the receipt, since I was required to turn in receipts to get reimbursed for field expenses. We sat down and ate, drank coffee, and flitted from topic to topic as one does in casual conversation. At one point we got on the subject of the Skid Row missions.

"Such a lovely neighborhood," Jerry said half smiling. When he wasn't too drunk, he sometimes paused dramatically between sentences like Jack Benny. "I don't even go down to the missions anymore."

"Cause it's too dangerous?" Dana asked.

"I'm, I'm scared to death to walk the streets down there," Jerry said.

"Oh, I'm not scared," Jimmy said. "I ain't scared of NOTHIN'. Not NOTHIN'."

"Well, I am," Jerry said. "Yeah, and anyway if you go to the missions, you gotta sit and listen to an—you gotta listen to an ear banging," Jerry said.

We all chuckled at Jerry's expression.

"An ear banging, that's a good way to put it," I said.

"Forty minutes of ear banging and then, you go up…and they give you a bowl of soup," Jerry said.

"You know," Jimmy said, "I don't mind, you know, I like to go to church. But if I wanna go to church, you know I ain't going just to get a bowl of soup."

When we had finished eating and there was a lull in the conversation, Jerry reminded us of our agenda. "Well, shall we get up and walk, kids?"

"Yeah, hold on just a second. Let me go use the bathroom real quick," Dana said.

"Why, that would be a good idea," Jimmy said chuckling.

"Yes, it's better, it's better than ours. Our restroom facilities are, well…," he paused with an almost invisible smile like Jack Benny's, "very open." Dana got up and walked toward the bathroom. After a moment, Jerry looked at Jimmy and said in a lively voice, "Well, we need to get us a jug."

"Yep," Jimmy agreed.

I felt this little exchange was primarily for my benefit. I had told Jerry repeatedly that I wasn't allowed to give him money, although I could buy him food. These were the research guidelines that Paul (Dr. Koegel) had worked out with the UCLA Human Subjects Committee, which must approve any research that, as the name implies, involves human subjects.

I ignored Jerry's implicit request for a bottle and asked about the drinking they'd done the day before. It turned out that they'd drunk three fifths between three people—Jerry, Jimmy, and Jimmy's ladyfriend, Suzi.

"But," Jerry said, "Well, Suzi's got awfully wide lips and a long throat. She's liable to have got a little more than we did." He went on to say that he'd gotten up at about four that morning when Jimmy had come over and woken him up. "And we sat there and we was talking and then my legs got started to hurtin' me. So I told Jimmy, I said, 'I'm gonna get up and go for a walk.' So I left about six, wasn't it?"

"Yeah, about six," Jimmy said.

"And I wandered around and I thought, well, I'll come downtown. I'm bound to run into somebody that has a drink."

I chuckled.

"I couldn't find anybody this morning that had a drink," Jerry continued. "Nobody I knew anyway. So finally I wandered back up to camp, it was about eight o'clock, and went down to Angelo's to check the dumpster out. To see if there was any groceries in it."

I asked about Angelo's. He said it was a nice Italian restaurant located only a few yards south of the southernmost bridge (a low one), separated from it by a small parking lot.

"And I went there, and I was rifling through the dumpster and I couldn't find anything because Moustache Moe had already been there. And so, I go walking up through the parking lot, and the guy, the parking lot attendant—And I was flat broke. I hadn't panhandled, I hadn't done anything. But I wanted a drink. And this parking lot attendant hollered at me. He said 'Amigo!' And I turned around and I looked and he walked over and he handed me three dollars."

"Ho, ho, ho," I said.

"That'll work," Jimmy said with a lopsided grin. The right side of his face was paralyzed, but I really only noticed it when he tried to grin.

"Gee, you didn't do anything? Right?" asked Dana, who had by that time returned from the bathroom.

"He seen me going through the dumpster, and, and so, I go walking up, and I was going to yell at Jimmy to 'Come on, let's go get a fifth.' And Jimmy was walking down the street and I met him right at the hole in our fence," Jerry chuckled. "And he already HAD a fifth. He put the lug on Eddie for a fifth."

"Well, no. I put an argument on Eddie. We went, we went through the motions. I said, 'I'm spendin' four hundred dollars a month in this store, right here. And you tellin' me that you cain't give me a bottle? One little bottle?'"

"Who is Eddie? Is Eddie the store owner?" Dana asked.

"Yeah, he's the store owner. 'Four hundred dollars a month.' He says, 'I'm doin' you a favor.' I tell him, 'I'm spending FOUR HUNDRED DOLLARS a month here, and yore doin' ME a favor?'" Jimmy was reliving the incident and getting quite aroused. "'How the hell you figure this SHIT out?'" he shouted across the table at us. "'Yore out of yore MIND!'"

Jerry continued in a calm voice, "I told Jimmy, I said, 'You go up and start working on yours and,' I said, 'I'm gonna go get another one.' And so I walked up and I got a fifth and came back."

"And Suzi drank jest about three quarters of it. She's good at that," Jimmy said.

"Uh huh," Jerry said, "Suzi's uh, well, she's in pretty bad shape right now. She was drunk the other night and fell down and—"

"She hurt her leg. I been bandaging it up and put ointment on it," Jimmy said.

"How did she do that?" Dana asked.

"She fell down the hill," Jimmy said.

Their camp was on a small level area near the bridge abutment. There was a steep slope of about twenty or thirty yards down to Cardenas Street.

"Yeah, and fell into some glass and gashed her legs up," Jerry explained. Then he said, "Take them napkins and fold them up and put them in your pocket."

"I intend to," Jimmy responded.

"No use wasting good toilet paper," Jerry grinned. "We always save napkins. Of course, we can always go to the Hall of Administration and go into the bathroom there and steal toilet paper," he added. "Well, are we ready? My legs are starting to ache."

Since his stroke, Jerry couldn't sit in one position for too long. Quite a disability for a panhandler who was used to sitting on a low curb for hours to earn his keep.

"Yeah, let's go," Jimmy said.

"Thank you for the coffee, by the way," Jerry said to me as we left.

"You're very welcome."

We continued talking as we walked along. We went through the Grand Central Market with Jimmy leading the way. It's a buzzing, bustling place about the size of a couple of large supermarkets. There are numerous booths with independent purveyors of tacos, burritos, liquor, meat, fish, produce, day-old bakery goods, and so on. While there are numerous liquor stores downtown that carry "snack foods" (at inflated prices), it was the only inexpensive place in the downtown area where one could buy produce, meat, fish, and canned goods. Jimmy and Jerry wanted to buy a fifth of white port with the proceeds of their panhandling from earlier that morning, but they were a little short. I made a small donation and asked them not to tell anybody. I bought a tall can of beer for myself and Dana bought herself a small bottle of Perrier.

As we continued on our way, Jimmy told me that it cost him nine dollars to cash his check at a check cashing service. One can get checks cashed at the Grand Central Market for three dollars, but they require identification and Jimmy didn't have identification. He could also cash it at Eddie's for free, because Eddie knew that Jimmy would spend plenty there. The real name of the store was the Naples Market, but the Bridge People usually called it Eddie's after the owner. It was about a quarter of a mile north of their camp on Cardenas Street.

Jimmy was on Supplemental Security Income (SSI) for physical disabilities. SSI is a federal entitlement program administered by the Social Security Administration for the physically or mentally handicapped. I asked Jimmy what he did when he got his check.

"Well, month before last, I didn't get my check. Well, I got my check, and cashed it, and a dude jerked it out of my pocket and took off running. My legs was all busted up and I couldn't catch him. So he got away with six hundred ten dollars right there."

"My God," I said. "Right outside the check cashing place, huh?"

"Yup," Jimmy said. "And this month, I had to go to my lawyer's office to get it, downtown on Spring Street, but I wouldn't cash it. I brought it all the way back yonder [to Eddie's]. And then he cashed it and I left him with five hundred dollars and then I got the other hundred thirty-five dollars and went and bought some clothes and stuff."

"So how much do you get with SSI? Is it six hundred ten dollars did you say?" I asked.

"Six hundred and thirty-seven," Jimmy said "And, believe me. If you could read my medical charts...." He just shook his head sadly. "I've got more scars than anybody I know of."

I asked about his current physical health. Besides a bad scratch along his fore-arm, he had some cuts on his head as a result of an altercation with a guy over a cigarette. It seems this guy wanted a cigarette and Jimmy had only two, one for Jerry and one for himself, and so he wouldn't give the guy one. He took it rather seriously and broke a wine bottle over Jimmy's head. This had happened several days ago, Jimmy said, and he bent over to show me the top of his head. There was still a lot of glass in his scalp and the top of his head was a bloody mess. He said that he had washed his head, but it continued to bleed.

He went on to explain that his sinuses were "all messed up," and his jaw was broken in a couple of places as the result of a gunshot wound to the head that had almost killed him.

"And how did you get shot?" I asked.

"With a gun. Ha, ha, ha, ha."

"Well, yeah, I could figure that." I chuckled. Jimmy had an insufferably corny sense of humor. "But what were the circumstances?"

"I was trying to burglarize a pharmacy. Well, I was fillin' a prescription at three o'clock in the morning, but the pharmacy wasn't open. Let's put it like that. Ha, ha, ha."

"Oh, I see." We chuckled together. "And who got you, a security guard or something like that?"

"No, the police. And I had a .22 Ruger automatic in my pocket. And I was sit down on him like this." He put both hands together around the butt of the imaginary pistol, holding it at arm's length to indicate a stable, steady shot. "Kicked the safety off, and I was going to shoot him. He come through the window that I had jest kicked out and he was jest about twenty, twenty-one years old. He was jest a kid. And I jest didn't have the heart to shoot him. I said, 'I jest cain't shoot this kid.' I mean, he jest—he was probably more scared than I was. So I kicked the safety back off and stuck the gun back in my pocket and picked up the two paper bags. And I figured he was coming down this aisle and I'll go up that aisle and when he gets back here then I'll go out that way, you know, and I'll hit my truck and I'll jump out."

"Uh huh."

"It didn't work that way." Jimmy shook his head and frowned lopsidedly. "He got behind me, fifteen feet away with a .357 magnum. BLAM!"

"So he shot you in the back? In the back of the head?"

"Shot me in the back of the head. That was my first offense that I'd ever done. I'd never done anything before that, and the only reason I was doin' that was that I was trying to pay off this man that was fixin' to kill me because I wrecked his truck. And that's the first time I ever done anything. But because I knew the officer's name, his name was Curry, the judge, he would not go for probation. Three years. He said, 'In three years, maybe you'll cool off enough so, you know, you won't come back against the cop.' I said, 'I'm not going to come back against him anyway. He was jest doin' his job.' But he didn't have to shoot me in the back, you know. He coulda told me to halt, halt, you know, and all that shit."

We continued walking along together and in a few minutes we arrived at their campsite under the bridge. At the corner of Angelo's parking lot, there was a broken down concrete block wall about a yard high. We had to climb over that and then through a hole in a chain link fence. It was a few steps up the steep slope to the camp proper. Dana and I stood there awkwardly for a moment. We had seen several camps of the very poor before, but had never actually been in one when there were people around.

Suzi was lounging on her bedroll about ten yards away from Jerry's mattress and chairs. There was a young, good looking Black man lounging on a bedroll between Suzi's and Jerry's mattresses, and there were several unoccupied bedrolls spread on the ground beyond Suzi. I had the impression that the population at the various bridge camps fluctuated quite a bit. When we visited, there were four people living at this camp.

The camp was situated on a level area about four or five yards wide along the entire abutment of the bridge. From there, the ground sloped rather steeply down to the sidewalk along Cardenas Street some twenty or thirty yards or so below. There was a six foot chain link fence along the sidewalk. The abutment was constructed of concrete with a vertical clearance of less than two yards at the back. Down at the street, the clearance must have been about three stories.

Dilapidated, dirty couches and chairs were aligned along the back of the camp against the abutment. There was little order to the site and it was, from my perspective, rather filthy. Wine bottles, paper scraps, food wrappers, and paper bags were scattered around the camp. In addition, there were a couple of small piles of trash, evidence that someone had made a desultory attempt at cleaning the place up. In the center of camp was a hearth consisting of two concrete blocks about sixteen inches apart supporting a grate that had begun life as a refrigerator shelf. On the grate was a beat up, blackened pot that looked like it might hold about fifteen quarts. Although the overhead was black with soot, there was a distinct lack of charcoal ground into the dirt floor, which suggested to me that they might not do as much cooking as Jerry would have had us believe. The ground was a greasy brown color, but not much darker than the surrounding soil. It was definitely not the rich, black midden characteristic of archaeological sites I had excavated where a lot of cooking has taken place over many years. What appeared to be groceries were hanging in three plastic bags from a piece of two by four wedged between the abutment and the overhead. This was an ingenious way of storing food and other items out of reach of the rats.

Jerry offered us his best chairs. Dana laughed nervously and said that she'd just sit by the hearth on some cardboard. I took the chair, without really thinking about it. Later, Dana said that she had been concerned about lice. That, I agreed, was certainly a justifiable concern, but it hadn't occurred to me at the time.

It was all rather awkward there for the first few minutes. The huge differences between us clean, middle-class anthropologists and the Bridge People were brought into sharp focus by the experience of being in their filthy, chaotic camp. Dana sat nervously on her square of cardboard sipping her Perrier, ill able to conceal the squeamish revulsion that was all but overwhelming her. I may have felt slightly more at ease, but I'm sure I looked as nervous. Despite her misgivings, she was, however, a professional anthropologist, and she continued talking to Jimmy about what things in camp were used for, where they came from, and so on.

I asked Jerry if I could take some photographs. He said sure, so I got up and photographed the camp and Jerry, Suzi, and Jimmy. The young Black guy didn't want to be photographed. We talked briefly, though. He was from Bakersfield, where I grew up, an agriculture and oil town in the San Joaquin Valley some one hundred twenty miles north of Los Angeles. Then I sat down again with Jerry and Jimmy and finished my beer.

My curiosity was aroused by the sight of some four or five steel hatches spaced along the length of the abutment. These were less than a yard wide by about one and a half yards tall. The hatches opened into small, low storage lockers about the size of the hatches and about a yard deep. The campers kept a few garbage bags of clothing and other personal items in these storage lockers, but during the rainy season the lockers leaked. They were very dark and and getting things in and out of them was very awkward. The lockers had flanges for padlocks, so the campers could have secured some of their belongings in them, but because of the inconvenience, they didn't use the lockers much. They thought that these lockers had been originally intended to hold gardening or maintenance equipment.

Suzi said that the vegetation around camp had been quite full until that summer, when Caltrans had started coming around monthly and chopping it down. Up until then, the vegetation had shielded the campsite from the view of Angelo's parking lot just to the south. The Caltrans crews had spared the half dozen or so thriving sunflower and tomato plants that the campers had planted on the slope between the bridge abutment and the fence along the restaurant's parking lot.

We continued to talk to the Bridge People until about two thirty that afternoon, then we walked back through Skid Row to Gorky's, a Russian restaurant, art gallery, and brewery in the Flower District. It was a pleasant place with a secure parking lot just south of Skid Row that Dana and I used as a place to meet and plan our day's fieldwork.

6. The trials of being a pedestrian

Ten days later, I walked along Market looking for Jerry and found him at his office at about eleven. Jerry and I sat together on the curb. As usual, he panhandled as we chatted. After a while, Jerry announced that he now had proper I.D. He pulled out a pink, official-looking document with his complete formal name at the top. I glanced at it and then looked up to see a mischievous grin on Jerry's face. I looked back at the document. After several seconds realized that it was a property receipt from jail. The grin burst into laughter.

"Ha, ha, ha. They got me for jaywalking again. Ha, ha, ha. I got a dumb ticket because I wasn't within those two wide white lines."

"Oh, so the light was in your favor?"

"Yeah. Uh huh. But it's jaywalking because I wasn't in the crosswalk."

"Oh, gosh. Thanks for the tip," I said, "I didn't know that."

"Oh, yeah, they'll nail you for it. Especially, especially if you look anywhere near a derelict, you know."

"Yeah?"

"You gotta be, you gotta be either an out and out drunken wino or a derelict and then the police will gladly accommodate you any time you even look cross-eyed at something or other."

"Uh huh. You suspect that if you were wearing a suit or something, you wouldn't be...."

"Oh, I know that for a fact. I went down to Third and Main, down to the liquor store down there, Monday. Towards evening. And got a jug for Tex and me and that's not a real nice neighborhood. I don't like to be in that neighborhood. Especially when it's startin' gettin' dark, you know. And so, I—The pedestrian light was flashing with the red hand, you know. But I thought, 'I can make this.' And I didn't even pay any attention. And there was two cops standing right in front of the liquor store. But I didn't look in that direction. I was lookin' to get across the street. And I headed across the street. Got half way across the street and the light turned yellow. And they hollered at me to come back over to them so they could kindly write me a jaywalking ticket. So I got that jaywalking ticket.

"Three days later—I had gone down to the L.A. Mission and taken a shower and got clean clothes and stuff like that. Three days later, I did exactly the same thing, in front of the exact same two cops and they never said a word to me. The only thing they said was—They met me over across the street, they let me cross the street, but they hollered at me to wait and they came up and they said, 'Sir, don't you realize that you could, you know, get hit by a car by doing that?' And they just gave me a polite little lecture and it was purely because I was all cleaned up. I had my beard trimmed and everything else. And so, if you look civilized and stuff like that, you get the lecture. If you look like you're down and out, and don't have a penny, you get the ticket. The ones who could afford to pay the ticket, never get the ticket. But if you can't afford the ticket, you get the ticket. That's just another little thing that doesn't make sense in my book."

"Yeah, I hear ya. I hear ya."

Jerry told me about trying to get his cane back when he was let out of jail. As I mentioned before, his recent stroke had damaged his legs. At first he couldn't walk at all, and although his legs were getting better, he still needed his cane.

"I went to go get my cane. They took my cane away from me when they took me to jail. They let me keep my cane for a while, but then they decided that it was a lethal weapon and so, they came and took my cane away from me. But I go down to claim it, and I walk in. And they send me all the way down to this property room that's down in the basement some damn place. So I hobble down there and I stood there for an hour. And nobody, and I mean NOBODY, even talked to me for an hour. There was about eight people workin' the windows, but they were getting all of the stuff for police officers. And finally I asked one guy, 'Isn't anybody gonna'—there's me and this lady standing there—'Isn't anybody gonna work these windows over on this side?' He goes, 'As soon as we're done with the police officers.' And I said, 'Well, you wait on one and three walk in,' I said. 'We're liable to be here, you know, for a week.' And he goes, 'Well, we gotta get them out first because they have to go to court.' And finally one guy came by and he said, 'When were you arrested?' And I said, uh, 'On the twenty-sixth.' And he goes, 'Oh! Well,' he said, 'Your property's still upstairs in the jail.' So I go ALL the way upstairs, find out how to get to the jail, and I walk out to the jail, and this lady was there IMMEDIATELY. She looked at my papers and she goes, 'Oh, yeah.' She said, 'Just a second.' And I was there for maybe about three minutes."

"Isn't that amazing."

"But they had me standing down in that stupid room for an hour and wouldn't even talk to me. Couldn't be bothered to tell me I was in the wrong place. You come and go someplace and you try to get one thing accomplished, you know. And they, they give you the run around, and the run around, and the run around, and finally you end up so confused that you forget what you were there for to begin with."

"Yeah, really," I chuckled. "Really. Is that why you don't wanna apply for G.R. and that kind of stuff?

"I, I can't handle, I can't handle the paperwork."

"Yeah?"

"It's too much for me. It's a—You go there, Jackson, you go there and they hand you enough paper, that if it was tissue paper, you could wipe your ass for three years on it."

"Ho, ho, ho! Really!"

"And it's all these dumb, dumb, dumb questions. And some questions, that I don't even, I can't even remember the answer. Like, what was your last job? I, I have no idea what my last job was. I've, I've completely forgotten. That, that segment is, is just blank."

"You've erased those tapes, huh?"

"Yeah, yeah. Beam me up Scotty, and get me outta HERE. And I, uh, uh, and other stupid questions. And then if you don't have, quote, Proper I.D...."

"Yeah, a jail receipt probably wouldn't do it?"

"Well," Jerry's eyes brightened, "I'm hoping it will. Uh, I was gonna go up and talk to uh, Don and find out the name of that lawyer that he goes to. The same one that Jimmy has. And, uh, she's supposed to be able to help you get, like a social security card, and...."

"Yeah." Although I was conducting research and, of course, shouldn't have done anything to affect the outcome, I told him of a couple of other people that I knew that also helped with legal problems on Skid Row.

We continued to talk about this and that as he panhandled. At one point he described the time a friend of his, Mack with the Cans, got hit by a bus. Among street people, I often heard first names used with epithets like this. For example, among the Bridge People, besides Mack with the Cans, there was Dirty Mack, Moustache Moe, Big Joe, and Little Joe. Nicknames were usually based on some behavioral or physical trait, like Pee Wee, Sleepy, or Weasel. I even knew a guy on the street nicknamed Skeletor because of his resemblance to the cartoon character. All the nicknames I knew of had been conferred on the person by someone else.

Nicknames were used in both address and reference. That is, they were used in face to face interactions to address the owner of the nickname and also to refer to somebody who might not be present. Epithets, like "with the Cans," however, were usually just used to identify someone not present. Among the Bridge People, last names were seldom used, and were only occasionally known to fellow campers, somewhat like the way middle-class people are with middle names.

"Yeah, Mack with the Cans was run over by a bus. And the bus stopped and everything else. Paramedics came. And here Mack had a broken arm and a broken leg. But he wasn't bleeding, so the paramedics wouldn't take him to the hospital. And they said, 'Take a bus.' So I go up to the bus driver that hit him, because that bus just so happened to go by County Hospital. He said, 'No.' He said, 'I can't take him.' He said, 'He's too hurt.'"

"Oh, that's great!" I said.

"So then, I went out and I panhandled. Mack just laid there. He couldn't move, you know. And I went out and I panhandled enough to call a taxicab. And I took him to the County Hospital in a cab. Now, is that crazy or is that crazy?"

"A really nice system, huh?"

"Oh, yeah," Jerry said with thick sarcasm. "Well, poor Mack with the Cans doesn't have great luck anyway. He got out and finally got out of his cast after about, oh, six weeks to twelve weeks. Somewhere around in there. And he was standing down on the corner right up over here on First and Market. Standing there minding his own business, and he got the walk signal. Well, a guy come along on a 10-speed bicycle and ran over him. Knocked him down. Re-broke his arm. And then, it was a hit and run. The guy just kept right on going down the street. But he was stopped. And then we had to go—Tex and I went out and panhandled money to get Mack on the bus at least, to get him out there to the hospital. It was crazy. The way these people drive. And here you are a simple pedestrian, TRYING to make it across the street with your life.

"Oh, I guess while I was in jail there was a big hoo doo underneath the bridges."

"Oh really?"

"Yeah, there's another old bum that comes up there called Whispering Bill, and that's what he does. When he's sober he whispers; you can hardly even hear what he says. And then the drunker he gets, the louder he gets."

"Oh, so you gotta give him a bottle or something to get his volume up, huh?"

"Yeah, yeah. Either that or turn up your hearing aid. One or the other. But him and um, Moustache Moe were over with Johnnie and Leonard and Dirty Mack. And they were having a good time talking and I guess they were waiting for a ball game to come on the radio or something or other. And all of a sudden, Whispering Bill calls Johnnie a nigger, and uh, Leonard was a bastard, and I forget if he called Dirty Mack anything. So then—Oh, Sam Robbins was there too. And so Moustache Moe readily agreed that one was a nigger and the other was a bastard.

"And so Johnnie got up and told them to leave camp. He said, 'This is our camp, you're not welcome here.' You know, 'Three of us live here. And that's it. Goodbye.' Well, old Moustache Moe wouldn't leave. So Sam Robbins got up. Hee, hee, hee. And politely threw him down the hill. Well, then he decided to leave. Well this morning I wake up, and I'm walking down, and I meet Moustache Moe on the sidewalk and he's still fired up and juiced up to boot. And he starts yelling at ME about what happened. And I said, 'Moe!' I said, 'I was in jail!' I said, 'I wasn't even here. I don't even know anything about it!"

"You were away on business, huh?"

"Yes, yes, I was on a business trip. Ha, ha, ha, ha. Well, then he started yelling something, calling me names so I had to politely threaten him with my cane."

"Ah ha!" I said with a grin. "So the police were right, it IS a deadly weapon."

"Yeah. And well, I did whack him across the shins, you know."

"Oh," I said sadly. I realized that somehow I wanted all these poor people to get along well together. Like a modern Rousseau, I wanted to see noble savages in the post-industrial slums, but being forced to live in savage, inhuman conditions didn't necessarily make these people noble.

"Well, I had to make a believer out of him," Jerry said.

"Yeah."

"But, I guess that was uh, uh, quite a little upsetting deal. And of course, Johnnie is Black. But Johnnie is far from a nigger. Johnnie is very nice and civil."

Later I thought about the process of getting to know these people. As I've said, I really wanted them to get along with one another and the conversation with Jerry had underscored this feeling. It's impossible to interact with people a great deal, as an anthropologist does, and not form some strong feelings about them. I noticed myself trying to maintain some emotional distance, in the interest of self-preservation, but at the same time I was trying to get close to understand them. I tried to keep things on a positive note. Spending a great deal of time with people is a lot easier if you can find at least something to like about them. Anthropologists usually try to present the other's point of view and, if anything, err on the side of romanticizing the other. Sometimes, however, people's inhumanity to one another can plunge the researcher into deep despair. This was demonstrated, for example, by Colin Turnbull's reaction to the Ik, a starving, dying people in East Africa.

Working with the Bridge People and others, I had noticed that some sense of camaraderie usually developed, deriving in part from just spending time together. Part of my feelings for the Bridge People arose from my appreciation of their working with me and allowing me into their lives. Primarily, however, such feelings of comaraderie had more to do with my becoming increasingly aware of their basic humanity. As I was allowed to become a part-time member of their group, I began to understand, in small, subtle, and largely ineffable ways, how they defined their existence. We began to speak a common language and I began to understand their culture—the values, attitudes, and beliefs that form the foundations and buttresses of behavior.

It is remarkably easy to scapegoat some powerless group of people like the homeless and blame them for their own plight, or for this or that problem in society. The dominant society can gradually define the group as sub-human and do to them things they wouldn't do or couldn't do to "real" human beings. After the group is defined as sub-human, it's a small matter to erect barriers so that one rarely or never actually has to interact with them. In the absence of interaction, ignorance and fear can fester into cruelty. Knowledge is the first step toward justice.

Anthropologists work against this dehumanizing process by living for a time among groups of people who are poorly understood, or misunderstood, and by describing their way of life. These descriptions should be written up, I feel, in a way that lets a reader get to know some individuals of the group and through them learn what the life of the group was like. I thought that what I was doing was worthwhile because it was fleshing out the increasingly familiar statistical outlines of homelessness. There are perhaps two million homeless people in the United States: about a third of them suffer from substance abuse; about a quarter suffer from major mental illness; and about a third are veterans. I was providing readers a (safe) way to get to know a few homeless people and to learn about their day-to-day realities.

So I wanted the Bridge People to get along well together. I wanted them to be noble, kind, and just, but I didn't really expect it. I realized that as I spent more and more time with them, they would reveal themselves as complex human beings with a dark side too. These people were deeply flawed. They were, after all, the rejects, culled from the assembly line of American life.

So I continued to sit there on the curb with Jerry. A moment later I asked, "How's business when it's real foggy like this?"

"It's lousy. Um, people, people just aren't in the mood to uh, stop by when, when it's hazy and stuff like that. Now bright sunshiny days, you know, people are in a better mood."

"That picks it up, huh?"

"Yeah. And that, that's the best time to really be out and about. But, uh, these dreary days, well, people are in a down mood."

"Well, I tell ya, I don't mind fog for a while, but I guess it's been a couple of weeks since the sun came out, you know, and it is a drag. So the weather has an effect on the, uh, on the panhandling business, huh?"

"Oh it definitely does. Definitely. Except there's one, there's one kind of day, and it's amazing a lot of people don't think about it. But there's one time, when dreary weather improves panhandling and that's when it's raining. Sit out and look pitiful and soaking wet and uh, that's when you start getting the paper. Paper starts rolling in real, real fast. But the only problem of it is, is that by the time you make enough, you have to make extra money to go to the laundromat so you can dry your clothes out. Ha, ha, ha, ha."

"Yeah. Ha, ha, ha....So uh, do you modify your uh, your appearance in order to look more pitiful?"

"I have done it."

I told Jerry about another street person I knew who got clothing at the missions that was several sizes too big and said that I suspected that he did it on purpose to make himself look even worse off than he really was.

"I have definitely—I have done it. I, I don't think there's a probably panhandler that hasn't done it. But, it's like old Dirty Mack, he'll sit and brag that he has not had a shower in two years."

"Wow!"

"That he has not washed in two years. Period. And he does it on purpose. 'Cause he's got a sister that lives out in Pasadena someplace. Or Covena. And about every two, two and a half years, she'll come down. She drives a great big, ole huge car like a Cadillac or Oldsmobile or something. Nice car. And she'll gather him up, dump him in the back seat—she won't let him sit in the front seat. Hee, hee, hee—and takes him on home and keeps him for two or three days. Gets him all cleaned up, takes him to the barbershop and gets him all trimmed up and everything else. And brings him back down. And the very first thing Mack'll do, is he'll go out and, you know how dusty it is, you know, at home?"

"Yeah." Underneath the bridges, the soil never received any precipitation or other moisture except the occasional spilled food, wine, or urine.

"Well, he'll start rolling in the dust, just like a dog."

"Oh, no! Ha, ha, ha, ha."

"Gettin' re-dirty so that he can go back out and go back to work."

"So he couldn't, he couldn't really panhandle very well when he was all cleaned up like that."

"No, he looked too good. He panhandles the pedestrian tunnels from the Music Center into the mall there. That's where he panhandles." The Music Center is an upscale facility with several large theaters for opera, symphonic music, musical comedy, and live theater. The nearby mall is surrounded by the County Courthouse and county offices.

We continued to chat as Jerry worked. He told me that he and his campmate Jimmy and some others got mail and cashed checks at Eddie's Market.

"Yeah. Eddie, Eddie always treats us VERY decently. Uh, and every once in a while, uh, when you get home with your sack of goodies, you start going through it and there's something in there that you know you didn't pay for. But that you— Maybe a small can of Spam or something or other. He'll throw something in on you, stuff like that. So he's, he's been AWFUL nice to us. And then, of course, letting us use his address. Stuff like that. That's a godsend to begin with."

"Yeah, so you use it as a mail drop and a bank?"

"Yeah."

We continued to talk about his recent experiences at the general relief office while he was trying to get food stamps.

"So you went to the G.R. office to get food stamps and the woman wanted to convince you to take a hotel voucher and you didn't want it."

"Well, she wanted me to sign up for G.R. and all that other stuff. And I said, 'No, that's too much paperwork.' I'd already done the food stamp paperwork, that's all I could handle. If I had to do the G.R. paperwork on top of that? Uh, NO WAY! Maybe if she let me take the papers and take them home with me and fill them out at my own speed. But you can't."

"You just can't handle the stress in that kind of office?"

"No. No. It's way too much. And why they have to know my mother's maiden name to give me food stamps I will NEVER understand that one."

"Yeah. So you think there are a lot of questions on there that are just kind of punishment, huh?"

"Yeah, I think they want to discourage people…from applying for it. And one way to discourage anybody from doing it, especially anybody like me, is uh, to hand them an inch and a half stack of papers and say fill these out."

I asked Jerry if he had explained to the caseworker why he didn't want to be in a voucher hotel.

"Well, I told her first off, 'I've never been in a G.R. hotel that wasn't infested with roaches.' You get the room key and your ration of roaches right in one fell swoop. And then, the majority of them are dingy. There's nothing in them for you to do, except to sit there and look at four walls. So there's nothing. Even if they had piped-in music that you could listen to. Anything. Some noise, because you're in there by yourself. You can't have no company. If anybody comes to visit you, you've got to go outside and meet them. And so why not be out on the street to begin with, if I'm gonna have to live my life on the street. I might as well. The only thing that room is good for is a bed for me to sleep in. Well, I've got a bed to sleep in [under the bridge]. You know, I don't need that either. And I, and I thought I was doing the county a favor, by saying, 'No I don't want this.' Because the county has to pay for it. I, I—But she just couldn't understand why anybody would rather live on the streets.

"I said, 'At least this is entertaining.' Lookit. I got all this entertainment walking by, you know. And I'm a great people watcher. I love to watch people. Because you see the darndest things. And uh, since I've been down here so many years, I know people, you know. And they'll stop by and say hello. And how ya doin' and everything else. And so, I don't know, my friends are out here. And more than likely, they would either shove me in the Weingart, either that or they'd shove me into some hotel way the heck out in Hollywood someplace."

"So if you were going to design a facility for street people, you'd make it, maybe, with a big lobby where people could hang out, you think?"

"Yeah. Have a dayroom that would have a TV set in it. And uh, uh, I'd even have piped-in music to the rooms. It wouldn't take that much to do that."

"Yeah….It looks like you took a hit in the eye. Did someone smack you?"

"No, no, I did that. I had another seizure. I went down. I had a big old gash up here and a scrape down here. And then this eye got all black and blue and everything else. And I thought 'Well, that's the end gate of the situation,' you know."

"When did this seizure take place?"

"Just shortly after you guys were up." That had been ten days before. "I went around looking like a raccoon for about three or four days. It's just getting now to where it's barely noticeable."

"Yeah, it's not bad at all."

"I'd give it about three more days, MAYBE. And it'll be straightened out. But that was a weird seizure."

"How's that?"

"Well, I remember bein' over at camp, then I got up and I had gone over to Angelo's, to the dumpster. And I had all this extra food. Beef, ham, and stuff like that. So I thought, well, Tommy's always hungry. So I thought, well, I'll take some over to him. 'Cause, there's way more than we would ever need, before it went bad on us. So I loaded up a sack and I took it over to Tommy's [perhaps seventy-five yards away]. And I had crawled over the side of his bridge and I was walking along the side of his bridge to get to his camp because that's easier for me than climbing that hill up there.

"And uh, Tommy said—I, I don't remember any of this. I remember climbing over the railing, but from then on, I don't remember anything. But he said I made it right to the corner to get underneath his bridge. And he said I just did a nose dive. And went halfway down the hill. And he jumped up and come down after me and stopped me before I got down into the glass and stuff. Because there's a whole bunch of glass."

"Down by the fence?"

"Yeah, 'cause that's where we used to throw our wine bottles. And so there's a BUNCH of broken glass down there. BELIEVE me. And Cabin Still bottles, and vodka bottles, and gin bottles. You name it. And uh—Say, didn't that look like a beer she was drinking. That looked like a beer, didn't it?"

He had seen a nicely dressed, attractive young woman walking by with some kind of canned beverage in a brown paper bag.

"Gee, I didn't notice." I had noticed HER, but not what she was drinking.

"Now, if I walked down the street with a beer like that," Jerry said, "I'd be right back to the Glass House." (The jail in Los Angeles, a modernist, Mies van der Rohe style cube of glass and steel, is known on the street as the Glass House.)

"Yeah?" I asked.

"Yeah. But anyway, I guess I went down. And they called the paramedics. And the paramedics came and got me. And the next thing I remember, I woke up and I was in the hospital. And they were bathing my face with peroxide and I had

an I.V. in this arm and an I.V. in this arm. And then they shot me full of something or other and knocked me out for a few hours. Then, when I came to, they
give me a prescription for my seizures."

He said he had been taking Dilantin, but that it made his hallucinations worse,
both visual and auditory, so he'd quit taking it. He said he had been following the
directions about no alcohol and still it had made his hallucinations worse, so he quit
it. I suspected that the fact that he was supposed to refrain from drinking was a
major factor in his decision to forgo the medication.

"When you quit drinking did you have withdrawal symptoms?" I asked.

"I never do. It's real strange. Uh, I can make up my mind to quit drinking and
I'll just quit drinking. That's it. And people will say, 'How do you do that?' I, I
never have hangovers, either. I've never woke up in the morning with a
headache."

"That's REALLY amazing." (I can get really dreadful hangovers from even
rather moderate drinking.)

"Well, I figure that's part of the reason that I'm such an alcoholic. Maybe if I
did have them symptoms, I'd slow down a little bit. But seein' as how I've never
had it, I've never experienced it. To me, drinking is just drinking, you know. You
get up and start it all over again. That's all there is to it. But now, like Jimmy,
Jimmy quits drinking and he turns into a mess. I mean, he can't roll a cigarette, he
can barely get a cigarette up to his mouth if you roll it for him, cause he's shakin'
so bad and everything else. And then he has hellacious headaches and everything
else. I told him one time, I said, 'Jimmy, why do you drink if all this is happening
to you?' He goes, 'Because I'm a drunk.' I said, 'Well,' I said, 'You're
punishing yourself,' you know. Maybe if I had them symptoms, maybe I could—I
doubt very much if I would stop drinking completely, but I probably would slow
down."

"Yeah....Yeah."

"But I can, I can go and just get BLITZED and wake up and feel fine. Of
course, I always make it a point, I always eat. A lot of these fellas that you see
down here, that are in real bad shape, their idea of eating is, is going and getting a
six pack, you know. Well that's not FOOD food. You gotta have something,
something solid in you. For your body to function on. I like to eat a lot of fresh

fruit. Because that, like uh, bananas give you your potassium, which alcohol burns out of your system very quickly. And, then oranges give you your vitamin C back, or tomatoes, you know, anything of that nature. And I always make it a point to do that. You're a fool if you don't. Maybe if I didn't do it, maybe I would get them symptoms."

"Yeah."

A few moments later the talk turned to Suzi. She had gotten another bad cut on her leg. She wouldn't take care of it, so Jerry and Tom tried to.

"Well, that gash got infected. And I went out and bought some peroxide. Went back. We disinfected it and stuff like that. Then I got a pair of tweezers and there was some proud flesh in there. So I pulled that proud flesh out and then we— Tommy had some ointment and so he gave that to me and we put that ointment on there and re-bandaged it. So now the gash is healing, but her foot is just all swollen up. Puffy. Funny looking. Stuff like that. And I tried to get her to go to the clinic. [Reedy falsetto voice] 'Oh no. I'll be okay.'"

I decided to move on and I told Jerry that I was going to walk back down Market Street. We decided to walk along together. He had made a few dollars panhandling and was going to stop at the Grand Central Market to buy some food and wine. Then he was going to walk home. Jerry appeared to be walking a lot better than he had a week and a half earlier. "Are your legs feelin' better?" I asked.

"Well, I've been up getting some exercise. As long as I can get some exercise, I can keep loosened up. It's when I sit too long that I have problems."

I said so long to Jerry near the Grand Central Market. I considered what he'd said about eating and exercise. I wanted to believe him of course, but I felt he was patronizing me a bit. He was an articulate fellow and did seem to have a pretty good grasp of basic nutrition and the value of a balanced diet, but I wondered if he was just telling me what he thought I wanted to hear—he knew I was a marathon runner, a triathlete, and a quasi-vegetarian. Maybe bridge reality would be divulged in the days and weeks to come, I thought.

7. Outdoor life and County Hospital

In early December on a Sunday, while having breakfast with my mother in Hollywood, I realized that in spite of repeated passes by his office on Market Street, I hadn't seen Jerry for something like three weeks. My impression was that he didn't work on weekends, so checking for him underneath the bridges on a Sunday seemed a good tactic. Since I was nearby, I decided to drop by and see if I could make contact.

At Cardenas Street I rode along slowly and looked to my right and noted that Jerry's camp was gone. He had had a fairly extensive camp, complete with a couch, some chairs, cooking utensils, mattresses and bedding, and so on. As I rode by, I saw that all of this material was completely gone. I got to State Street, where Angelo's Restaurant was, made an illegal U–turn, and slowly rode along again staring at the former campsite. I couldn't quite believe it was completely gone and I wondered what to do next.

There was a young Black man climbing through a hole in the chain link fence on the east side of Cardenas (the side I was now on, opposite Jerry's old camp). He was dressed in an old khaki Army shirt with PFC stripes. I hailed him, introduced myself, and asked him his name. He said that he was John. Jerry had mentioned the name John on a couple of occasions, but at the time I didn't remember that and I asked him if he knew Jerry. He said that he did. About that time I saw two figures struggling up the steep embankment to the camp behind John. These lower campsites were four or five yards above the level of the street and back about twenty or thirty yards on a level area that forms the support for the bridge abutments. It was relatively dark under there and difficult to see the camps clearly from the street. One of the figures, a big, middle-aged man dressed in a dirty flannel shirt, Levi's, and work boots, had his arm around a shorter, frail-looking man and was half carrying and half dragging him up the hill. Just when I was about to ask John if he had seen Jerry lately, I realized that the frail guy WAS Jerry.

I blurted out something like, "Oh, there's Jerry now." I made another U-turn and parked my motorcycle just a few yards away at a legal parking spot. After taking off my helmet and gloves, I walked toward the hole in the fence. John had climbed up to the camp by this time and he yelled down to me, directing me to the hole. Jerry was sitting in an easy chair in the camp and weakly yelled his greetings to me. I could hear him tell his comrades who I was as I scrambled up the hill to join the group in the camp.

Several thoughts flitted through my mind as I scrambled up the loose and very dry clay embankment. I had not come prepared for fieldwork. I was wearing a Hawaiian shirt, off-white pants, and my leather flight jacket. This costume was not as off-putting as a suit and tie, but it did accentuate class and economic differences that I would have preferred to keep muted during fieldwork. Then there was the BMW motorcycle. Mine was actually their smallest, least expensive model, but BMWs are something of a status symbol. There were also functional matters—I didn't have my tape recorder or even note paper.

By the time I had joined the others, I had resolved these issues by saying to myself, "Oh, what the hell. Here goes!"

Jerry was a picture of immanent death. His eyes had the red, unearthly glow of high fever. His face was tired, thin, and deeply lined, and the skin around his eyes hung in grey folds like an old, limp sail. He had lost a lot of weight since I had last seen him. His health had been in gradual decline since I'd met him about a year previously, and on that day he looked as if he would not make it more than a few months longer. He gave me a goodhearted, toothless grin and said that he was glad to see me.

Jerry was dressed in a clean pair of grey, light canvas field pants that were currently in fashion, a raspberry-colored velour pullover, white sox, and nice oil-tanned deck shoes. I immediately noticed that he was shaking violently and was so weak that he could barely sit in his greasy, tattered easy chair.

I stood there awkwardly for a moment, thinking about the off-white pants I was wearing and the greasy dark dirt of the camp floor. Normally, when I went to the field, I wore olive drab field pants or Levi's and didn't hesitate for a moment to sit on filthy Skid Row sidewalks, curbs, or the ground. John rescued me by providing me with a grey plastic milk crate to sit on. He introduced me around.

Big Joe, the guy I'd seen helping Jerry up the hill, was a forty-three year old man with a Southern accent. He was a fairly muscular six foot three or four, with dark brown, over-the-collar hair. His sidekick, Tiny, was dressed similarly, but was a little taller and thinner. Tiny's straight, dishwater blond hair was cut shorter, especially on the sides, revealing ears that stuck out noticeably. Both of them had teeth. I later learned that they had been bumming around together for five years. Tiny raised the possibility that we had met before. I didn't remember him, but said that it was possible, since I had been around Skid Row for over a year. Later I talked to Dana about it and she remembered that we had met Tiny while looking for Jerry when he was in a board and care facility.

A grizzled, balding old man was lying silently on a dirty mattress at the northern perimeter of our circle. He raised himself up on one elbow and said hello flatly when Jerry introduced him to me as Mack. Jerry had told me about two different Macks, so I asked, "Is this Dirty Mack or Mack with the Cans?" Jerry said, "This is Dirty Mack." Dirty Mack acted as the camp alchemist, buying cheap whiskey and mixing it with various sodas or fruit juices. He had a bottle of whiskey in his hand virtually the entire time I spent in camp.

Suzi was the only female in camp. She was still in possession of her upper and lower incisors, but no longer had any other teeth. Her face had the wrinkled, puffy look of a serious, long-time alcoholic. Her puffy cheeks and prominent incisors made her look somewhat like a squirrel. Suzi had been Jimmy's ladyfriend the last time I had seen her. Now, it seemed, she was Big Joe's. They sat or reclined together on a mattress about two yards south of Dirty Mack's. My impression was that Suzi got passed from man to man in a fast-paced serial monogamy. On the few occasions I had seen her, she had been significantly separated from her surroundings by a thick alcoholic fog. I got the impression that she was like that virtually all the time.

The camp we were in belonged to John and Dirty Mack, with Big Joe, Suzi, and Tiny staying there temporarily. Jerry made it clear later, not in front of the others, that he didn't live there because of the noise and constant bickering. He now lived on the east side of the northern-most bridge, in a low camp like the one we were in. His current campmate was once again the guy named Tommy, whom I had yet to meet although Jerry had spoken of him several times.

Tiny, John, Jerry, Suzi, Big Joe, and I sat and lounged in a sort of circle while we talked. Dirty Mack was a couple of yards north of us. According to Jerry, Big

Joe and Tiny had been up drinking Night Train (a cheap fortified wine) since about four in the morning. By the time I arrived, at about ten thirty, they had begun to get loud and repetitive as people often do when thoroughly bombed. Big Joe in particular seemed to like to dominate the conversation. He often confused the volume of an utterance with its value.

Big Joe and Tiny periodically announced how much they cared about Jerry and what good buddies everybody in camp was. They may have been trying to impress me, but of course this kind of behavior is quite common whenever friends or associates get drunk together.

John, the young Black man, was the only one in camp who didn't appear to be thoroughly sloshed. He was calm and considerate. He urged Jerry to eat something. He said that he too had been suffering from dysentery for a couple of days, but that last night he had made some lima beans and that they had made his stool solid. He still had some of the beans left and repeatedly urged Jerry to have some, but Jerry refused. John and Tiny urged me to have some. I pleaded that I had just had a big breakfast with my mother. They persevered. It's tough debating with drunks on a toot. They don't hear what you have to say and make up for their inability to comprehend by shouting.

Somebody put a spoon in my hand. I felt more than a little squeamish about eating out of the fire-blackened, beat-up old pot, but I felt that I had been cornered. Had I seriously questioned the hygienic qualities of the food or refused, I would have endangered the delicate rapport that was taking shape between us. I get food poisoning often and easily, but beans keep pretty well and, I reasoned, they had just been cooked the previous night. I took a few bites. The beans were a bit salty for my taste, but pretty good.

"Not bad," I said, looking up from the dirty pot to meet the eyes of my expectant audience. "Not bad at all," I said through a beany grin. They chuckled and grinned back. I had a few more mouthfuls for the sake of diplomacy and then set the pot back on the hearth. They seemed quite pleased that I had actually sampled their fare, and I felt like I had passed a test.

Jerry said that the last thing he needed to eat was beans. He had just been to Eddie's earlier that morning seeking Kaopectate. Eddie didn't carry that, but he did have Pepto Bismol. Jerry had downed a bottle of that just before I arrived and said that he thought he should try to let it take effect. He had been suffering from dysentery for three or four days by that time. He had not slept the night before. He had not eaten or taken significant amounts of liquid (other than wine) for a couple of days. Of course, this had resulted in dehydration and temporary malnutrition. He had spent the previous night, he said, "shitting my brains out."

Since his latest seizure, he had again had problems walking. The circulation in his legs was very bad and getting worse. He now shuffled along with steps only about a foot long. He rarely left camp without his cane and often needed help getting up the steep slopes of his camp and those of his neighbors. He complained of severe cramps over the last few days that had kept him from resting or sleeping.

To make matters worse, he had an infected boil on the back of his neck just above the hair line. Despite my protestations, he insisted on showing it to me. When he leaned over toward me and pulled back his matted red hair, I winced. An area at the base of his skull almost the size of a golf ball was a mass of dried blood and puss. It looked very painful, but unfortunately, it was the least of Jerry's troubles.

As we chatted, a bottle of Night Train was being passed around. I took the bottle as it came my way and without reservation (which surprised me) I tilted it up for a little swig. I don't know exactly why I wasn't concerned about the hygienic quality of the wine and was about the beans. I guess it's because I've gotten sick a lot of times on bad food, but never on bad booze. The Night Train tasted something like overly sweet Kool-Aid spiked with vodka. The syrupy sweetness hid the burn of the alcohol, so it slid down my throat with a warm, friendly glow unlike the hostile fire of cheap whiskey.

Jerry was not in the Night Train drinking circle because he was working on his own fifth of Thunderbird, another sweet fortified wine. It was about half gone when I arrived. His shakes visibly calmed down as the minutes ticked off. When Jerry's bottle got low, Dirty Mack got off his filthy old mattress and shuffled over to Jerry's chair. He silently held out a greasy, half-full bottle of cheap whiskey.

I was struck by how dirty and bony Jerry's hand was as he held up the bottle and said in a reedy, shaky voice, "Thanks. Thanks a lot, Mack. This'll help straighten me out."

Around our circle, we continued to talk. Big Joe, Tiny, and John actively argued with Jerry and each other about his best chances for recovery. Eventually they came to a consensus that Jerry should go to the hospital. They all agreed that he looked very bad. Of course, they all had witnessed his suffering for the last several days. At first Jerry didn't want to go, but eventually he capitulated—swayed not by their indisputable logic, but by the decibel level and unity of their urging.

Once a general strategy had been decided upon, we talked about the various possible ways to get Jerry to the hospital. It was stated and unanimously agreed that the paramedics would not pick up a person who was still on his feet. John suggested that he could go call the paramedics and tell them that Jerry had had a seizure or something and Jerry would then have to go lie down on the sidewalk. They all agreed that that tactic would probably work, but somehow it didn't have much appeal.

Without warning, Tiny, who was sitting next to me, turned and solemnly looked me right in the eye for a second. I was transfixed by his bloodshot, bleary gaze, startled as I often am by the impact of looking deeply into the eyes of another human being. It was as if I could look deep into his spirit for a mystic moment, and he could look into mine.

"Jackson, would you take Jerry to the hospital on your motorcycle?"

"Uh, well, I...." I was taken aback by the question and looked away to collect my thoughts. I had wanted to keep a rather clean distinction between my research, my life, and theirs. In part, I had wanted to avoid getting involved in order to preserve the pretense of research purity. That is, I didn't want to be a factor in their lives because that would ultimately distort the research results. But I realized that I didn't want to get involved mostly because I didn't want the responsibility and the hassle. Of course, I couldn't really say that, because it would endanger rapport. I was there in their camp asking them to share their lives with me, but I found myself reluctant to do something that involved only a little inconvenience to me, something that would probably be of real benefit to Jerry. I was rather surprised and disappointed at myself.

"Sure, Tiny," I said, looking at him again. "No problem....I wonder if he can hang on."

A lively discussion followed about how Jerry should be aware of his balance, how he should lean into the curves, and so on, as if we were about to begin the Baja 1000. I told them that at the low speeds we would be going, there would not be much leaning and that all Jerry had to do was to stay in the saddle. There was a long discussion about whether or not Jerry was strong enough to ride the two or three miles to the County/USC Hospital. This was not a trivial concern. In my mind it was questionable whether he was strong enough to sit up on his own for the ten minutes or so needed to get there. I could just picture him tumbling off like a sack of cement in the middle of some busy intersection.

Jerry was too sick to take much part in the discussions, but I think he was listening most of the time. He slumped in the chair, his feverish eyes red coals behind half-opened lids. Occasionally he'd tilt up the greasy bottle and take a couple more hard swallows of whiskey.

In the midst of this discussion of motorcycle technique, he looked up and said in a shaky voice, "Well, you know, I've never been on a motorcycle before, but I'll give it a try."

That made me a little concerned. Although being a motorcycle passenger doesn't require skill, it could be disastrous if the passenger couldn't sit without wobbling.

"I'll give it a try, but you've got to let me finish my whiskey first," he croaked. "The whiskey, the whiskey is calmin' down the damn shakes and stuff like that. I'm startin' to feel a little better. Hell, by the time I finish the whiskey," he managed a weak smile, "I'll be feeling so good, that I'll want to go dancing instead of goin' to the damn hospital."

Everybody chuckled at that and then a drunken discussion ensued about the health benefits of whiskey. What they said had some merit in their case: alcohol was one of the only things available to them that could help suppress physical pain and psychological distress. However, it relieved these things only temporarily and at great physical and social cost to them in the long term.

Everyone eventually agreed that when Jerry finished his bottle, he and I would ride the motorcycle to County/USC Hospital.

As I've said, Jerry was silent throughout much of these discussions. Twice he had to get up to shuffle over to the bushes to "take a dump." He was in serious trouble because the diarrhea struck swiftly, but because of his weakness and his damaged legs, he could shuffle along only slowly. Once he made it to the bushes at the edge of camp without incident; the second time he wasn't so fortunate.

Necessity struck as he was getting to the bottom of his bottle of whiskey. He got up and began shuffling rapidly with very short steps toward the bushes. He reminded me of a child playing at being a steam locomotive.

"Oh, I hope I can make it," he wheezed. "Oh, this is going to be close. Oh! Oh! Oh!"

We all just sat there transfixed and helpless, silently urging him on with our eyes. When he was just short of the designated latrine area, he began furiously fumbling with his belt and pants buttons. "Oh! Damn!" he growled.

"Oh shit," somebody said.

"Ain't that the truth," Jerry said, grinning weakly. He pulled his pants down a few seconds later. Runny, pale feces bathed his skinny, pink legs.

John jumped up and looked through a plastic bag near his tent, coming up with a half-roll of toilet paper. He took it over to Jerry. Tiny and Joe stayed seated, but asked Jerry if he was okay. He protested that he was. John began looking through a large green plastic garbage bag where he kept his laundry for another pair of pants for Jerry. After a few minutes he found a pair of filthy, stiff Levi's. As dirty as they were, they were certainly more serviceable than the nice grey pants that Jerry had just ruined. When he had finished with this latest episode, Jerry got up from his squatting position and began wiping himself off. It was a tedious task and he was at it for several minutes. Then, shaking and unsteady, he pulled on the pants John had offered him.

At another point during the morning, Dirty Mack got up to defecate. There was a plastic milk carton sitting about three yards away from our circle, where the vegetation began. Jerry had pointed it out to me earlier when I asked him if there was a designated latrine area and where it was. It was in plain sight and smell, of course. Mack went over to it and sat down facing away from us as if there were nobody within miles. Through the open lattice of the milk create it was hard not to notice the feces dripping and plopping into the crate. The minor gas explosions that accompanied this were, of course, plainly audible and the aroma occasionally rolled over us like foul surf. It was quite unpleasant for me. I fired up my pipe and puffed away furiously in hopes of covering up the odor a little. I noticed that nobody else noticed it, so I tried to ignore the revolting sights and smells too, but I was on the verge of gagging each time the smell surged over us.

The conversation in our circle resumed. Beginning to feel a little better toward the bottom of his bottle, Jerry told me a story about Jimmy Newby, the guy who had been shot in the head by the police officer. One day a couple of weeks before, Jimmy and Jerry had decided to make eggs Benedict for breakfast. Jimmy was making the hollandaise sauce in a sauce pan over an open fire. As sometimes occurs even under the best of conditions, the sauce curdled. Jimmy flew into a rage. He hurled the sauce pan down the hill. Then he plunged his bare hands into the flames and seized burning boards and flung them all around the camp, setting it on fire. Most of the campers' belongings and all of the camp furniture were burned. Jimmy's hands were a mass of blisters and charred flesh. Jerry tried to talk Jimmy into going to the hospital, but he refused. He was unwilling to even wash his hands, so they got badly infected over the next couple of days. Then Jimmy disappeared; no one had heard from him since. Since the camp furnishings had burned, Jerry picked up what he could salvage and moved across the street and north a half block to live with Tommy again.

While Jerry and I were talking, he was steadily working away at the bottle of whiskey that Dirty Mack had given him. Eventually he tilted his head way back and drained the last dregs from the upturned bottle. With a loud sigh, he announced that he was now ready to go. He slowly got to his feet by pushing himself up shakily on the arms of his easy chair. Once on his feet, he began shuffling down the hill. Big Joe rushed up to help. He walked in front of Jerry while Jerry placed his arms on Joe's broad shoulders to brace himself. John told Joe to remember his arms and Joe complied by putting his arms straight out horizontally on both sides of him. This was to catch Jerry if he started sliding to one side or the other as they slowly negotiated the hill. They were all familiar with this maneuver, as if they frequently helped one another down the hill in this way.

John and I walked on ahead. I told them that I would have to get ready. I put on my helmet and gloves and got on the motorcycle while they approached. With the motor purring and my feet braced wide apart, I gave Joe and John the thumbs up and, one on each side of Jerry, they picked him up and put him into place behind me. He didn't seem to have very good control of his legs and they got a bit tangled as he was suspended above the seat. A couple of seconds later, he was sitting securely behind me with his hands around my abdomen holding on gingerly. I was struck by how easy it was for John and Big Joe to lift him aboard, but then sadly realized that though Jerry stood almost six feet tall, he probably didn't weigh more than a hundred and forty pounds. Joe, Tiny, John, and I all gave Jerry brief instructions, in our own ways, about how to hang on.

As Jerry and I sat there on the motorcycle, Joe, Tiny, and John tried to give me directions to the hospital, but John wasn't too sure about where it was, and Big Joe and Tiny were quite drunk. The resulting directions were pretty crazy. Jerry said that he thought he could recognize the proper turns when the time came, but then he had just polished off at least half of a fifth of Night Train and half a fifth of whiskey. After a couple of minutes of listening to their drunken directions, I got disgusted with the drunkenness and incompetence and thanked them, revved up the motorcycle, and slowly pulled away. Jerry proved to be able to navigate AND sit up, and the trip was uneventful.

When we got to the hospital Jerry wasn't sure where the emergency entrance was because, as he said, "I'm always in the back of an ambulance when I'm brought in, and I've never seen where you come in."

We pulled up to a kiosk with a security guard. He directed me to where I could drop Jerry off and also told me where I could park the bike afterwards. The emergency room entrance was at the top of a ramp that went up to the third floor in a big sweeping left turn. There was space for perhaps eight or ten ambulances at the top of this ramp, but there were only a couple parked there then. I dropped Jerry off at the door and told him I'd be back to help him get checked in. We both thought that they probably wouldn't keep him since he could walk. Because of a very lean and mean budget, the overcrowded hospital tends to be rather cavalier about discharging the sick and wounded.

After parking the bike, I walked back up the long ramp to the emergency room entrance. I had never been to County/USC before. It was a huge structure with cavernous hallways. The interior was mostly an institutional off-white that had yellowed over the years. In the hallways there were many places where splotchy paint and patched plaster testified to a history of cheap, make-shift modifications.

(Since I used to be a remodeling carpenter, I find my eyes drawn to such things.) Signs were posted on doorways and in the junctions of hallways with arrows to direct stray souls like Jerry and me. On the floor in the center of the halls various colored stripes about two inches wide lead the lost from place to place.

Over one of many doors I noted a sign declaring, "All Emergencies Check In Here." I went in. The triage nurse there said that she had noticed me on the motor-cycle dropping Jerry off, but he hadn't come in to the E.R. I went into a waiting room for trauma patients to look for him, even though he hadn't suffered any trauma. He wasn't there. I walked back out and was beginning to feel a little relieved, assuming that he had gotten into the signing-in process on his own and my responsibilities were at an end. Just then, I bumped right into him. He had received directions to go to another processing room for non-emergencies. We headed in that direction, but had a small emergency on the way trying to find a restroom.

When one of Jerry's bowel rushes struck him, it was without much warning and Jerry couldn't hold it off for long. On this occasion, we were able to get to the facilities in time. In the processing room, I filled out the paperwork for Jerry. He told me the things to put on the form, of course, but I knew some of it already. One thing that surprised me was that the date of birth that he told me to put down was 1948. That would make him forty years old, but he had told Dana and me earlier that he was forty-six.

One part of the signing-in process was determining the patient's ability to pay. The form demanded to know about current employment and income, place of resi-dence, and so on. In filling in these things for Jerry, I found them both ludicrous and sad at the same time. Filling out the form only took about ten minutes, then we just sat in the waiting room with other sick and wounded people. After about an hour, we got through this phase of the processing and were told to go off to another office to see another triage nurse and, eventually, a physician. For several minutes we followed a black and white colored stripe on the floor through various hallways and found the room, but just as we were approaching, Jerry said that he had to find another bathroom fast. We asked around and found one not far away, but it was being cleaned. We scurried back to the area we had come from and, after asking around again, found another bathroom, but it was out of order. We were really getting desperate by this time. We joked about having to head for the parking lot, but realized that we didn't even know which hallway to take to find it. We eventually found our way back to the area near the Emergency Room. I asked a sheriff's deputy hanging around in the hallway if he knew where a restroom was and he replied, "I have no idea, buddy. I don't work here." We thanked him anyway and hurried into the E. R. We did have an emergency this time. The triage nurse directed us to a restroom through a doorway that led us back out to the hall only a few yards from where the sheriff's deputy was still standing. Jerry rushed into the bathroom just in time. He stayed for quite a while, perhaps ten minutes.

I passed the time in a small waiting area nearby that was filled with rows of cheap, mismatched plastic chairs. A television set, bolted high on a wall, was blaring a football game. The antiseptic excitement and well-staged pageantry of the game made a stark contrast to the dreary, sick poor people and the shabby hospital. While I waited for Jerry, the deputy we had asked about the restroom casually walked over and went into it. I wondered if he had known where it was all along.

When Jerry came out we backtracked to the proper waiting room and he checked in with the receptionist. We waited and waited. He was called to see the nurse. She took his temperature with a paper disposable thermometer. He rejoined me and we waited. And waited. At about two o'clock, after we had been in that waiting room for about an hour and a half, I decided that I needed to go take care of some other business. I told Jerry that I would have to go. He seemed a bit distressed, but he said he understood.

"I, I wonder if they give out bus tokens somewhere around here?" he asked no one in particular as he twisted around in his chair and looked anxiously around the waiting room. "One time I was here and they discharged me and I didn't have bus fare. Of course! I had to walk all the way home and it took four hours. I was sick as a dog, too. Not a real fun time, I'll tell ya. Especially if you're sick."

Of course, I didn't know if they gave away bus tokens either. I gave him a few dollars and wished him well. As I walked out through the maze of hallways, I had plenty of time to think about the harmless act of giving a poor person a few dollars. According to the terms of my job with the AHMI Project, I was not supposed to give homeless people money. We were allowed to buy people food, cigarettes, or small personal items, but not money and certainly not alcohol. I was never completely comfortable with that and did violate the rules from time to time. I wasn't completely comfortable with that either, of course.

I reasoned that it was my professional duty as an anthropologist to spend great amounts of time with a group of people, to live right with them if possible, so that I could find out what their lives were like. I needed to try to understand their values and beliefs and to respect them regardless of how they might seem to the powerful pillars of United States society. I had been taught over years of graduate study that this is what leads to a more than superficial understanding of a group of people. I deeply believed it too. I resented the fact that the university would forbid me from giving extremely poor people money, because, I supposed, they were afraid they would spend it on alcohol or drugs. From my anthropological training, I believed that if you had resources, you should try to give people what THEY want and try to understand the basis of their wants and desires rather than imposing your values on them. I wondered if the university was afraid that I might be leading people astray. Perhaps they envisioned headlines: "Anthropologist Buys a Drunk a Drink! Neo-Victorians Riot!"

We had been at the hospital for about three hours by the time I had to leave. Jerry had been interviewed by three different triage nurses, a couple of receptionists, and a bookkeeper. The only "treatment" he had received so far was to have his temperature taken. (He had a slight fever.) Together we had trudged the hallways considerable distances to three different waiting rooms and Jerry had suffered three bouts of diarrhea. The nurse in the last waiting room assured me when I left that he would be seeing a physician soon.

I later checked a map and found it was just over three miles from the bridges to the hospital. When it took Jerry four hours to walk home, he did so at approximately three-quarters of a mile per hour. A reasonably good walker would have made the trip in an hour.

Much later, I read about a study of waiting times in emergency rooms in hospitals for the poor, conducted at the Los Angeles County Harbor/UCLA facility in Torrance (one of six hospitals for the poor in the county, similar to County/USC) and San Francisco General Hospital. The study found that many patients left before getting care because they were in too much pain or discomfort to wait. The average wait at San Francisco General was 3.5 hours, with waits up to 17 hours.

Patients who had left Harbor/UCLA Hospital had waited an average of 6.4 hours (Wielawski 1991).

8. A short visit with Dirty Mack

About a week later, toward the middle of December, 1988, I again sought out Jerry at his campsite. As I approached the bridge at about eleven forty-five that morning, I noted that there were a couple of guys in Jerry's old campsite. I wondered if he had moved back there, but then I noticed people in the camp where I had last seen him, so I continued toward that side of the bridge and climbed up the short hill. There was a person sleeping in a dirty sleeping bag on a pile of cardboard. I could see a filthy hand sticking out, but couldn't see a face. There were some women's shoes nearby, so I guessed that it was Suzi. There was a sleeping form huddled under a dirty grey blanket in the beat-up old easy chair. Big Joe was sprawled on a dirty mattress to the south. His snoring was clearly audible from some ten yards away.

Dirty Mack was lying on his filthy mattress. He sat up when I approached, the only one conscious in camp. I said hello. He remembered me and said hello. He got up and sat on an old grey plastic milk crate, motioning for me to sit on another a couple of yards away. He pulled a pack of cigarettes out of a grimy denim jacket pocket and lit up with a shaking, filthy hand. I fumbled with my pipe and eventually got it going. We sat and smoked together in silence for a few moments, then I asked if the person under the blanket in the chair was Jerry. He said that it was. At that point, there was a stirring in the chair and the blanket shifted a bit to reveal part of Jerry's face and one closed, baggy eye. Slowly the eye opened. It was red and bleary. The eye and blanket gave me a barely perceptible nod in recognition. Then the eye slowly closed again, the blanket shifted, and the eye was gone.

When he was sober, Dirty Mack was rather reserved, so although I intended just to make casual conversation with him for a while, our interaction turned into something more like a formal interview. I would ask a question and he would make a curt reply. Then there would be silence and I would try to wait him out. In an old introductory psychology text I had at home, there was an account of Carl Rogers waiting over sixteen minutes for a reply from a psychotic patient. I didn't

9. Jerry on social justice and social research

In the middle of January, 1989, I again tried to visit Jerry at his camp under the bridge. It was almost eleven o'clock in the morning when I climbed through the hole in the chain link fence and scrambled up the slope. John, Tiny, and Big Joe were there lounging around. They said that I had just missed Jerry. He had just left to go panhandling and I could catch up with him easily.

John, the young Black man I had found so helpful and likeable, was busy around camp, apparently tidying up. Joe and Tiny were a different story. I felt uneasy around them. There seemed be an undercurrent of violence about them. They had a friendly and jocular manner, but I felt a hint of something ugly under the joking, like maybe they were waiting and watching for a weakness to exploit.

I thanked them for the information, wished them a good day, and headed off through the ivy on the trail that they had said Jerry had taken. It led from under the bridge, around one end of the abutment, through the general latrine area, and up along the offramp to the surface street, a distance of some fifty yards. All along the trail through the ivy, on both sides out to a distance of a couple of yards, and occasionally right in the trail itself, there were piles of feces. There were dark piles. There were light piles. There were piles decorated with wads of toilet paper or scraps of brown grocery bag paper. There were unadorned piles. There were old, crumbling desiccated piles. There were fresh, moist piles with squadrons of flies darting and diving through the aromatic air.

I threaded my way quickly through the ivy, puffing madly on my pipe and being very careful where I stepped. I caught sight of Jerry within a couple of minutes. I was astonished that he had not gotten further. When I realized that it could only be because of his poor health, I was suddenly saddened. As I got closer, I could see that he could only hobble along very slowly with the aid of his walking stick.

When I hailed him, Jerry's face lit up in a toothless grin and he said he was glad to see me. I asked how he was doing and he said he was doing much better, thank you.

"So your dysentery finally cleared up, huh?"

"Ah…basically. Ah…since you've seen me, I've been in jail again."

"Uh huh."

"I got picked up for uh, uh, panhandling. And I spent uh, five days in jail."

"Five days for panhandling?"

"Yeah."

"How many times have you been arrested for panhandling?"

He gave me a rather theatrical look of mock disgust for a couple of seconds. "If I had a nickel," he paused dramatically, deadpan, "for every time I've been arrested for panhandling…I could retire a wealthy man."

"But they don't usually put you in jail for it do they?"

"It just all depends on the cops, you know. Some of whom are good, some of whom are bad."

"So what do you feel about getting arrested for panhandling? I mean, there are some people that suggest that homeless people think it's pretty nifty to go in and get a clean place to sleep and a shower and all that stuff."

"Oh, no. It's not fun. It's not fun at all. But, especially when you walk around, when you have to deal with the jailers. They are not uh, pleasant people. They walk around like they're little Napoleons. And they have this attitude. And they treat you like you're—Oh, how do I want to say it? They treat you like you're a turd-ball."

"A turd-ball, huh?" I chuckled.

"REALLY! You are NO GOOD. And uh, here you are just tryin' to survive. And you're being belittled."

"So you don't think what you do is damaging to society?"

"Well, you know, it's awfully hard on the street. Because everybody thinks…that you have no morals. And, and, they have to sit around…and make morals for you. Well, that's stupid!"

"So you don't think it's a moral problem?"

"It's social. It's economic. Uh, uh, I mean, after all, look at me. I go out panhandling. I mean if I, if I was economically stable, I wouldn't be doin' this. I mean, that's, that's just a simple fact. But I'm not economically stable and so I HAVE to do SOMETHING! If I want to have a hamburger on the table tonight, God damn it, I better get up off my duff and try to make it. And, and, it's not fun."

"So do you think what you do is more responsible than collecting welfare?"

"I don't want to do that. I don't want to go through all that paperwork and bullshit and everything else. Oh no. Huh uh. I, I, I'd rather just try to do it myself. Because, you know, there's a, there's a—Oh I don't know. In the back of my brain, in the back of my brain—I don't know what you want to call it. Whatever. But if I, if I make it myself—You know what I'm talkin' about?"

"Oh you mean like individualism, or independence?"

"Yeah. Yeah. Independence, there you go. And, aaah, I don't know."

Some middle-class Japanese people approached. The men wore dark business suits, the women dark dresses. There were perhaps a half dozen of them talking together in a small group. Jerry stopped on the sidewalk, whipped off his dingy baseball cap, and went to work.

"Good morning, sir. Could you spare some change?" He bowed at the waist and held the cap out in front of him. He got a quarter from one of them.

After they passed on their way down the sidewalk, I said, "Those were very nice looking people."

"Ha!" Jerry scoffed, holding out his grimy hand and scowling at the lone quarter in it.

"What? They weren't that nice, huh?" We had a little chuckle.

"Just a quarter." Jerry put the quarter away. "I'm going to have to teach you how to panhandle."

"Yeah. That'd be nice. That'd be nice. Lord knows, I don't make much money. I could use it."

"Johnnie, Johnnie made uh, uh, thirty-two dollars yesterday."

"WOW! That's great. Where was he? Around here?" We were approaching the mall near the Courthouse.

"And...he made it in an hour and a half."

"Whoa. That's not bad."

"That's what I told him. I said, 'Fuck it, Johnnie,' I said, uh, uh, 'It beats minimum wage!'" Jerry laughed quietly.

"Yeah. I should take lessons from Johnnie, not you." We laughed together.

"Well," Jerry protested, "I went out for forty-five minutes and made twelve dollars."

I figured later that John had made about twenty-one dollars and thirty-three cents an hour on that remarkable day, and Jerry had made sixteen dollars an hour. Of course, panhandlers only talk about the really remarkable days. We middle-class people are the same way, talking only about the great deals we got or big sales we have made, and only rarely about the regular grind or the grim days. Everyone likes to feel competent and we all tell stories that put us in a favorable light, both for our audience and for ourselves.

Jerry walked with very short steps, putting the walking stick down firmly between each step for support. Shuffle, shuffle, thunk. Shuffle, shuffle, thunk. Shuffle, shuffle, thunk. When we got to the stairs, he showed no signs of pain but went into slow motion and carefully took each step as if it were a small individual challenge.

"Just like the Alcoholics Anonymous slogan, Jerry. One step at a time, ha, ha, ha."

He gave me a sour look, "Really, Jackson. You shouldn't mention THEM in the presence of a dedicated drunk. It's, it's like farting in church. Ha, ha, ha."

"Yeah, ha, ha, ha." After he had negotiated a few more steps, I asked him about his panhandling technique.

"When I'm walking, I'll ask for change. But when I'm down at my office, very, very seldom will you ever see me ask for change. I'll say, 'Good morning. Hi. How are you?' And, uh, the money just comes. But, uh…those are people who know me."

I had thought he was working this mall, but he told me that he was back to his old office at Second and Market at the State Building. While panhandlers like to establish a regular "office," most in my acquaintance worked in several different places, since, for example, security guards or police might tighten control at a particular place for a while, or other panhandlers might arrive to work the area first. Business might fall off in one place and pick up in another, due to changes in traffic flow caused by construction work. I was learning that in order to stay alive on the streets, people learn to keep on the lookout for changing opportunities and to stay flexible.

"I gotta get something to eat today," Jerry said as we walked along.

"Yeah? Did you not eat yesterday?"

"No."

"Did you go all day without having anything to eat?" I wasn't sure he understood my question.

"Yeah."

"Was that a liquor diet you were on? Or a liquor fast?"

"Well, Johnnie come back with a bottle. And the only thing of it was that it built up my sugar content. So I didn't FEEL that I was starving. But I've been hungry. Oh, gosh DARN, am I hungry."

As we walked along, we came upon a wooden pallet, the main source of firewood for street people. Jerry told me that he hadn't been able to get much firewood lately in his neighborhood. He said he couldn't carry the pallet to the bridge because it was too far, but that he could if he had a tramp truck.

"What's a tramp truck?"

"A tramp truck? That's what we call a grocery cart. That's what you haul all your wood and, and, uh, trash and everything else in." After several seconds of shuffling along, Jerry asked about the tape recorder. "Is it still going?"

"Yeah. You've gotta say something profound," I said.

Jerry cracked up. " HA, ha, ha, ha, ha, ha! If I knew something profound, I would certainly say it."

"Well, the tramp truck was pretty good. I mean, that's the kind of stuff anthropologists like."

As we approached his office, I asked Jerry about it. He said that he worked the mall early in the day. Later in the day he worked his regular office at Second and Market. This schedule was dictated by the ebb and flow of foot traffic in these areas.

Although he had said before that he usually didn't ask for money when he's sitting down at his office, as we sat there together I observed him several times ask people things like, "Could you spare some change today, ma'am?" I would estimate that he actually asked for spare change every third or fourth interaction. Overall, this ratio varied on the basis of how hungry or thirsty he was and today he was very hungry. He really did function more as a greeter than as an overt panhandler, although his cap lay overturned on the sidewalk in front of him to remind the passersby of his need for financial support.

I asked him about his cane. The police had taken it away again, and this time he was not able to get it back at all. Johnnie had made his current walking stick for him by cutting a branch from one of the trees near camp and trimming off the twigs.

"It's idiocy. I mean, there are people that are going out and about, jackrolling and, and all this other bejesus. And here I am, I'm, I'm just sittin' here, stupid. And I get harassed. But I'm, I'm not hurtin' anybody. I'm not drinkin' any wine or anything else. So what is it? It's, it's..." Jerry sputtered in exasperation. "Jackson," he said, "it's stupidity. That's what it is."

Jerry explained to me that now he and Suzi were living back in his old camp across from Big Joe and Dirty Mack, that is, in the southwest low camp. He mentioned again that he didn't want to live with Big Joe and the others across the street because of the constant bickering. Later, I reminded him that I still wanted to come stay with him under the bridge some time.

"Well, you're MORE than welcome. Live out on the streets and find out what it's REALLY LIKE!"

"That's just what I want to do, find out what it's really like," I said.

A cluster of middle-class people came by and Jerry had to work for a few moments. After they passed, I prompted, "So you were saying something about reading articles about homelessness or something?"

"Yeah. And I get, I get frustrated when I read them. Because the assholes, that write the articles, they have no more been on the streets than the man in the moon. Uh, they go, uh, they go and they interview a couple of people, and all of a sudden they have a, quote, quote 'article.'"

"Well, sometimes they'll go interview lots and lots of people. What do you think about that?"

"Unless you've been there—You've got to be there first. Interviews are like— Well, it's like you and me talking. I can tell you about my feelings and stuff like that, but you, you don't feel them. You're going to have to feel them first to see what it's like. You've got to see what it's like.—Hi ma'am, how are you doin'? Hi girls, how are you doin' today?"

"Has anybody ever come up to you and asked you why they should give you some money?"

"Oh, some people come up to me and, and say,'Get a job!' And I just turn around and look at them and I say, 'You got a job to give me?' And they say, 'No.' And I say, 'Well then why are you tellin' me that? If you don't have a job to give me, leave me alone. I'm doin' the best I CAN!' You know, like I said, I don't harass people. It's uh, uh, people harass me."

"Yeah, yeah, that's really true....Why do you think people harass you?"

"I don't know whether it's a—I really don't know why. Uh, here I am sittin' here. And I don't know why...if it's because I'm sittin' here, or some other reason. I, I, I, really don't know, Jackson. Honestly. I, I, I've sit here for, for twenty years and I've thought about it. And it happens every once in a while. And I don't know, honestly. It's like a chandelier. It just hangs over you. And it sways. It sways when the sway hits. So, uh...I could understand it if I was an harassing person. I could understand that.—Hi girls, how you doin'?—But I'm not."

"Why do you think they say, 'Get a job!'? Do you think they resent, uh, your luxurious way of life?"

"Yeah, MY luxurious way of life? Thank you!" Jerry gave a Bronx cheer lasting a couple of seconds.

"They do seem to resent something. I mean, some of them do. I wonder why?" I asked.

"Yeah, yeah....I have no idea. It's so hard. It's so hard. Well, when you come down to live with us, you will find out how hard it is. I mean, every waking moment you have, you're either going after food, drink, tobacco, water—I mean EVERY moment."

"Yeah. It's basic survival, huh?"

"Yeah. It's, it's, it's a survival thing. And until you get your survival things— Hello ma'am!—Until survival things are done, that's the way it goes.—Hi, how are you doin' today?" An old gentleman placed some change in Jerry's capsized cap. "Thank you," he said, smiling and giving him a little sitting bow.

A moment later, Jerry continued to expound on social science methodology. "If you come down here with cash in your pocket, you're not learnin' nothin'! That's no lesson. That's NO lesson! The lesson is, is when you don't have a goddamned cent in your pocket. And you're hungry. And that's when you learn. That's when you learn to hit the dumpster. That's when you learn to panhandle. That's when you learn to do all this bullshit. And that's basically what it is—bullshit. You know, the harder you work, the behinder you get."

"Even on the street, huh?"

"Even on the street. And bullshit, that's the name of the game. But there's no other game in town, so, this is the one that you play."

"Yeah."

"Isn't it sad?" Jerry asked.

"Yeah, it is," I agreed. A lone songbird chirped in the background as Jerry and I sat in silence. A while later, I gave Jerry a couple of more cigarettes. "I gotta go, Jerry," I said.

"Okay, Jackson."

"All right, sir, have a good day," I said.

"I hope so."

"Looks like things are going okay," I said.

"Yeah, not bad, fifty-one cents."

I gave him a dollar and began walking south down Market. Apart from the money I had given him, he had made fifty-one cents an hour this morning so far. There was incredible variability in the rate of income from panhandling.

10. A visit with Luke Broder

After repeatedly trying to find Jerry at his office with no success, I headed again for his camp under the bridges early one morning toward the end of April, 1989. I noted as I approached that Jerry's camp had become quite elaborate. I didn't see any sign of life and I didn't feel quite right about wandering around in the camp uninvited. Jerry had told me that the camp had burned down again, some time ago, and had been cleaned up and refurnished. I just stood outside the fence and described the camp in its new configuration into the tape recorder. Just on the other side of the fence from me were several large orange plastic bags, the kind Caltrans uses to pick up litter along highways, that looked like they were full of trash.

The main camp furniture consisted of a big, broken-down old couch, a brown vinyl easy chair, and a grey and green striped cloth easy chair. In front of the couch there were a couple of ragged, sagging mattresses with tangled, dirty bedding on them. Nearby were several medium sized cardboard boxes apparently containing personal belongings and food and a huge clear plastic bag of clothing standing about a yard tall and almost a yard in diameter. For firewood there was a wooden pallet and a medium sized cardboard box containing broken boards. In the center of camp there was a hearth consisting of a pile of ash and charcoal about sixteen inches in diameter with a concrete block on each side. On these blocks was a grate and on the grate were a couple of blackened, beat up pots made of spun aluminum. Near the hearth were three white plastic water jugs that looked like they held about five gallons each.

As I was concluding my description of the camp, standing on the sidewalk talking to the tape recorder, I was startled by someone sitting up on one of the mattresses. It was a man who looked to be in his fifties with blond, shoulder length hair and a long moustache. He just stared at me. While there was no overt hostility in his glare, I felt like I had been caught with my hand in the cookie jar.

"Howdy!" I shouted. "Have you seen Jerry?" The old guy said something, but I couldn't make it out. "Does Jerry still live here?"

Again the old man said something unintelligible to me. I decided to climb through the hole in the chain link fence and go up to the camp. I walked back the few yards to the hole in the fence. First I had to climb over the concrete block wall almost a yard tall. Then I had to crawl through the hole in the wire that began about a foot above the ground and continued up about two feet. It took me a few seconds to get through the hole because my clothing caught on the wire in a couple of places.

The old man had gotten off the mattress while I was negotiating the hole in the chain link fence and was now sitting on the couch. He was wearing a clean, light blue oxford cloth shirt tucked into what, in a more stylish neighborhood, might be called fashionably faded Levi's. He had no belt and his feet were bare. I was somewhat startled to see that they were pretty clean.

When I got a couple of yards away, I introduced myself. He offered me a seat. We sat across the cold hearth from one another and had a nice chat. His name was Luke Broder. He was of Dutch extraction and had grown up Amish, but in Indiana I think he said, not southeastern Pennsylvania. His nickname was Dutch. He had joined the Navy when he was seventeen and had served for eighteen years, attaining the rank of E-9. When he had only two years to go before retirement, he was on a cruise off Vietnam and took a 50 caliber hit in his left forearm. When he recovered, he was found to be unfit for further service and discharged. He now received a small disability check, but it went to his retarded daughter. He had completely lost out on his retirement benefits after eighteen years of service and was quite bitter about it. Talking to him reminded me that about a third of the homeless are veterans. For a society that seems so proud its ability to wage war and so fond of war as a way of solving problems, we sure don't take very good care of our ex-warriors, at least not since the end of World War II. Luke felt that society just tossed people like him aside like empty shell casings, which, he pointed out, is not very smart, because ex-GIs are trained killers.

"If push comes to shove, they WILL fight back. People will only put up with so much, you know. Someday it could happen. Right here." He did not mince words. "This society STINKS!" he said.

Of course, the push of poverty had almost come to the shove of revolt at other times in this country, but Luke, like most of us, didn't have much knowledge of history. In the early days of the depression of the 1930s, several thousand veterans and their families camped out in Washington demanding early pensions and relief.

President Hoover sent in tanks and troops with tear gas and fixed bayonets to disperse them. Before that, Coxey's Army of the Unemployed had descended on Washington during the depression of 1893 (Katz 1986).

Luke was forty-nine years old. He seemed much more together than most of the people I had met on the street. For one thing, he had I.D. He showed me his passport. It was a couple of years out of date, but it served as good I.D. nevertheless, he said. He also showed me the scar on his forearm from the bullet that had ended his military career.

Like Luke, most street people seemed anxious to document their accounts where possible with physical evidence. On the street, people heard so many stories, scams, and hustles that they took everything with a dash of cynicism and a large grain of salt. Accounts were more or less accepted at face value, but kept at arm's distance, as if to say, "Sure. Anything you say, Buddy." Producing evidence or a corroborating witness was necessary to close some of the distance and win more than a tepid acceptance of a story.

Luke spoke with a slight accent reminiscent of a Southern drawl, although he wasn't from the South. His was the generic, working-class drawl that you run into all over the West. He seemed to have a reasonably full complement of teeth, but had a slight whistle when he spoke.

He said that the best time to catch Jerry was in the afternoon at about four or four thirty. Jerry was canning these days and was out working all day. ("Canning" means collecting aluminum cans and turning them in for cash.) He usually left camp around nine o'clock in the morning. Luke was on a different shift. He said he pans (a street abbreviation for panhandling) in the afternoon to catch the people in the Courthouse area as they get off of work.

Luke complained about some Mexicans that had moved in across Cardenas Street and under the last bridge to the north. They were young fellows who made a lot of noise day and night, he said. They also occasionally broke into cars parked in the vicinity. He was worried that eventually they would cause the police to come and arrest or run off everybody under all the bridges.

I asked him how Jerry was doing, if he was pretty healthy.

"Naw, I wouldn't go that far," he said. "He is able to walk around better now, though."

"Is Jerry over his bout with dysentery?"

"Yep. He's doin' okay there. You know, that dysentery can be real serious. Real serious. I knew a couple of men that died of it. Livin' on the street, you know, eatin' outta dumpsters. It can kill ya."

I asked about Tiny, and Luke said that he had left town. He'd applied for general relief, gotten one check, and hopped a freight. Big Joe had had some kind of falling out with Tiny and didn't go with him this time, although they usually traveled together.

While we talked, Luke had put on some dark socks and old, tan Wellington boots. While well worn, the boots seemed to have quite a few miles left in them. The socks appeared to be clean and in good condition. He got up and walked three or four yards to one of the white plastic five gallon jugs.

"I need a little drink of water," he said. "That's all I got, wet-wise. Gotta go down to Angelo's to get water, 'bout ever' other day. Five gallons."

The campers got the water jugs from Angelo's. Cooking oil came in them, and the campers used whatever dregs of oil remained and then washed them out with water heated over the campfire. If they had soap, they would use that too, but often they didn't have soap. The jugs were made of a heavy grade translucent, whitish plastic with heavy duty screw on caps, as good as anything I've seen in a camping store.

I asked Luke about the orange plastic bags piled by the fences. He said that Caltrans had come by.

"We done bagged up all that there stuff. They're supposed to come and get that stuff."

"Oh, you guys bagged it up, huh?"

"Yep."

"So they came by and dropped off the bags?"

"Yeah. And now they're supposed to come get it. They were supposed to get it a good while ago. I hope they do come and get it because the rats are gettin' bad."

"Are they?"

"Yeah, oh, I've seen rats." He held up his hands about a foot apart, scowled, and nodded his head as if his archetypical rat fit nicely between his hands. "Of course, they don't have too much problem across the road over there [Big Joe's and Dirty Mack's camp], 'cause they got cats over there. They've got a mama cat over there and she kills them as fast as they come into their camp. She's got a litter of kittens. She's got five kittens. Three of them pure white. Purdy cats."

"You know, when Caltrans came here and dropped off those bags, did they ask you guys to clean the place up? What did they say?"

"They said they probably won't bother the people that's here as long as, as long as we keep it clean. It's purdy clean." He looked around approvingly.

"Sure, it looks pretty good to me." It did look like they were making a good effort to keep the camp clean.

"But those Mexicans over there are makin' it, are makin' it bad for us. Look at all that trash they throwed down the hill over there." He pointed across Cardenas Street and about seventy yards north of Big Joe's and Dirty Mack's camp. "You see it?"

"Yeah."

"And they're all illegals. Ever' one of 'em. You otta hear 'em at night. You otta come over here at night and turn your tape recorder on. You could, you could really get some good stuff. Some gal went up there the other night. You otta heard that. At first, I heard her, she was yellin', 'Po-leese! Po-leese! Po-leese!' Then I heard one of those Mexicans yell out, rattled off something. Purdy soon it was kinda quiet. I guess they gangbanged her. I seen her when she come down outta there. She was purdy. She was a purdy girl. I seen her come down offa that hill and I don't know what she was wired up on or anything, but when she come down off of that hill over there, she walked sprattle-legged. So I guess everbody that was up there got a little of that pussy."

"Uh huh."

"See the mouse! See the mouse!" Luke pointed excitedly to where a mouse had run between the back of the couch and the bridge abutment. "We got a lot of mice around here."

Luke said that he'd travel up to Utah or Montana after it had warmed up a bit more. He said that he averaged about forty dollars a day when panhandling (about a hundred dollars a week) but he added, "I never have nothin', 'cause I drink it up." I asked how much he drank and he said three or four fifths of wine a day.

His story had a hollow ring to it. He ate with Jerry and Suzi much of the time and said he didn't spend much on food. A pack of cigarettes a day would come to about twelve dollars a week. The hundred dollars that he estimated he made per week, minus, say, twenty-five dollars for tobacco and food, would buy about thirty-two fifths of fortified wine per week. From his neat appearance and his competent comportment, it seemed very, very unlikely that he drank nearly that much. He did not seem in the least hungover or drunk and he lacked that puffy, pasty look of a career alcoholic. I asked him if he had enough to get himself something to drink that morning.

He said, "I tell ya what I got." He fished in the front pocket of his faded Levi's and came up with some change. He stared solemnly at the coins in the palm of his hand. "I got a total of thirty-four cents."

"Hum. How much does it cost to get a short dog? A dollar?"

"A dollar. Yes, a dollar. I feel better if I, if I drink a little bit before I go up that hill. I can, I can face people a little better if I've got a little buzz, you know."

"Yeah," I chuckled, "I hear ya." I could plainly see that begging didn't come easy for this ex-Navy Petty Officer. I gave him a dollar.

Luke said that a couple of weeks before he had been jumped by "crack heads" (people who abuse crack cocaine). The attack had damaged his kidneys and he was in pretty bad shape when he came up to live with Jerry. He didn't go to the area around the missions any more because he thought it was too dangerous. This was in the heart of Skid Row. A lot of people I talked to felt the same way about that area, including Jerry.

Luke had said something about living outside, so I asked him what it was about it that he liked.

"You're, you're independent, not indebted to anybody. You understand what I'm talkin' about. I, I don't want to be indebted to anything that pertains to this society. That's the best answer I can give you. Because, like I said, as far as I'm concerned, this society stinks. I can't say it any plainer than that. I gave them almost twenty years of my life, in the service. What kind, what kind of glory did I get? They stopped me up there. They stopped me up there, from panhandling, and pulled me up on the rug. Took me in and they checked me out. They found out about my war record. Said, 'A guy with your background? What are you doin' on the streets?' I said, 'I was pushed on the streets!' I said, 'When I went to get help, different agencies, Veterans Administration is supposed to he'p ya. I didn't get nothin'.' I feel, I feel I paid my dues. Understand what I'm sayin'?"

"Yep. Yep."

Luke paused for a moment. "Well, I laugh at them. We'll have a shakeup here one of these days, in this country right here, it's the best thing that could happen. They gonna have war right here. I got that feelin'. Maybe not in my time, maybe not in yours, but it's gonna happen. This country's movin' too fast. You're either rich or dirt poor. Always scrapin' for a dollar.

"Oh, I have run into good people. You know, there's a mail carrier. Ever' day, when he comes by my corner, just like clockwork, long about two thirty in the afternoon, he comes up and picks up the mail and he'll hand me three dollars. Ever' day, he just puts three dollars in my hand."

It was getting late. Luke wanted to get to work and I was getting tired. I thanked him for talking to me and wished him well.

I fumbled around in my haversack and found a pack of Camels. "You want some cigarettes?"

"Sure. You bet!"

I tossed him the pack.

"Camels, huh. I used to smoke Camels. They were my old brand. When I could afford to have a brand. Ha, ha, ha. Well, thanks. Thanks a lot."

I also gave him some Winstons to give to Jerry. He thanked me again and said that he would see that Jerry got them. I wondered if that were true, but it was no big deal anyway. I got up from the chair and gingerly picked my way down the short, steep slope to the little hole in the fence.

11. A smoke with Luke and Big Joe

About a week later, I again tried to catch Jerry at home. When I approached from the south, at about nine thirty in the morning, I noticed that the orange Caltrans trash bags were still piled along the fence. As I climbed through the little hole in the fence and trudged up the hill, I could see that no one was home at the camp. Although I knew that Jerry and the others wouldn't mind my being there, as always I felt a little uneasy, like I was trespassing. Nevertheless, I took a moment to pace off the length of the abutment. It was about sixteen yards across. As I've said, the camp furniture and mattresses were arrayed along this abutment facing the street, but well inside the edge of the bridge, so the maximum width of the camp was somewhat less than that of the abutment, something on the order of twelve yards. The number of people who lived at this camp and the others varied quite a bit. I estimated that the camp could hold about eight or nine people, perhaps more, depending on the way they arranged their mattresses and other furniture. However, this camp typically held only three or four people. The one across the street at the other end of the bridge occupied by Big Joe and Dirty Mack usually had between four and six inhabitants, but was the same physical size.

I decided to go across the street to see if Big Joe and Dirty Mack were home. I chuckled to myself at the irony of going to see if my homeless friends were at home, but that's the way they referred to their camps too.

There were two figures sitting up the hill. As I approached I realized that they were Luke and Big Joe. Joe was sitting with his back to the street while Luke was facing north. Between them was a small campfire about a foot in diameter. They were burning small pieces of pallet that they had broken up. Usually there are no axes or machetes under the bridges so the campers just jump on pieces of wood to break them into small pieces suitable for the fire. I said hello and we exchanged pleasantries. Big Joe was making coffee. He had a dented, fire blackened two quart pot heating on a grate over the small fire. The little fire felt warm and friendly on this cool morning.

I tossed them a pack of cigarettes and we settled down to smoke and talk. Both Big Joe and Luke said that they thought it was a bad development that cigarette taxes had just gone up. Big Joe said, "Smokers will smoke. I don't care if they drive the price up to five dollars a pack. People will smoke 'em if they want to smoke 'em." Luke and I nodded in agreement and said "Yep," almost in unison. I thought to myself, "You could say the same about various other drugs," but said nothing. We reminisced about how cheap cigarettes used to be. I told them that when I was in the Army, cigarettes were nineteen cents a pack in the PX. Luke, who was a little older than Joe and I, said he remembered when you could buy Wings for nine or ten cents a pack.

A lot of conversations around campfires or over a bottle go like this. They consist of a friendly, unspoken game of oneupmanship. One guy tells a story, then the next guy says, 'Hell, that ain't nothin', let me tell you about what happened to me....' Then the next guy will say, 'Well, you shoulda seen what happened at such and such.' This conversation about cigarettes went like that. Luke, being the oldest, won this particular game, and then the conversation turned to other topics. Of course, it's not the winning or losing that counts, and it's not the information that's exchanged. The game is about conviviality, friendship, and fraternity.

Luke said that when he'd gotten up that morning, Jerry and Suzi were already gone. They'd been getting an early start canning . Last night they were sober and broke, he said, and that might have motivated them to get with it.

Joe tended the fire absent-mindedly while we talked. Luke was mostly quiet. They both maintained fairly good personal hygiene despite their difficult living circumstances. Luke was better in that regard, and if I had encountered him on the street, I would have never guessed that he was homeless.

I asked Big Joe a bit about his background. He said that he was from Alabama. He had been in prison several times, mostly for armed robbery. The time before last he was in the penitentiary for seven years. Easter before last he was in prison for murder, but he got off. He had been in San Francisco and three fellows had jumped him. He had a big knife and killed one of them. Joe got stabbed in the throat. "All Ah had was four dollars! Can you believe all this happened over four dollars?" He shook his head and looked away. "That's all Ah had," he said in a cracking voice. "Four dollars."

He was silent for several seconds. When he looked back at me, his eyes were wet and red. Then he brightened up and said, "Ah was surprised that the judge believed my story, with my record and all, but he let me go. Ah ended up serving a couple of months before the trial anyway, but, hell, that ain't nothin' compared with murder one."

Big Joe said that if you're traveling around alone, you're really asking for it. You need a buddy so you can watch each other's back. He doesn't carry a knife anymore, though, he said. He didn't feel like he needed one where he lived now, because he was with friends.

Dirty Mack had gotten up that morning and left for work by about eight thirty. He still panhandled around the Music Center and the Court House, according to Big Joe, but he wasn't sure exactly where. Big Joe himself wasn't panhandling or doing anything for support just then. He said that his friends were taking care of him. He hadn't panhandled for about a month. Mack made twenty to twenty-five dollars a day panhandling and Larry, another campmate, had a regular job sweeping up somewhere. They'd been feeding him, Big Joe said. When Big Joe mentioned Larry's regular job, I remembered reading that some twenty to thirty per cent of the homeless have regular employment but are still unable afford rent.

"I'm trying to get off the alcohol. If I get a holda some money, I know jest what I'm gonna do with it," he chuckled. Sheepishly he added, "Mostly I jest been hangin' around camp."

He felt a little embarrassed by his lack of work. Rugged individualism reigned among the Bridge People and everyone was expected to take care of him- or herself. Begging was considered legitimate work. Luke found it a little bit humiliating, but he was the only one who did. As Big Joe's account illustrated, there was a great deal of interdependence among the Bridge People, but it was an embarrassment. It was not often acknowledged as a potential source of strength, an economic advantage, or even a fact of daily survival.

I had just dropped in to see if they knew about Jerry and didn't want to spent a great deal of time there, so I said that I had to be going and scrambled down the steep hill to Cardenas Street.

12. Food, drink, and smoke

A few days later, I tried again. I wanted to make sure I caught Jerry before he left for work, so I arrived at the bridge at about six thirty. The camp was asleep when I arrived. Jerry was on a pile of mattresses stacked three deep. He had a couple of tangled grimy blankets over him and was sleeping in his clothes. At the end of his bed, his feet, with socks on, stuck out from under the blankets. Suzi was on the brown vinyl couch sleeping in an old burgundy sleeping bag. Her couch was right up against the bridge abutment, while Jerry's pile of mattresses was about a yard and a half in front of her, just close enough so they could pass cigarettes and bottles back and forth. There were another couple of sleeping figures on mattresses a few yards north of Jerry and Suzi. I couldn't tell who they were, but assumed that one of them was Luke.

I walked quietly up the hill toward the foot of Jerry's bed. I looked around again to make sure everybody in camp was asleep. I am really reluctant to awaken somebody. Perhaps it's all those times on guard duty in the Army getting rudely shaken out of a sound slumber to go stand in the German snow. Anyway, I felt I had to wake Jerry up, so in a stage whisper, I said, "Hey Jerry, wake up!"

He awoke quite suddenly, startling me slightly. He rolled quickly to see who it was and when he recognized me, he relaxed and said, "Hi Jackson. Sorry I missed you the other day. Big Joe told me that you were around looking for me. We've been going to work kinda early these days."

A few seconds later Suzi stirred on her couch stirred. She had also been sleeping in her clothes. She and Jerry had only to sit up to be ready to entertain guests.

We began talking about food. Jerry said, "Well, we have people that walk by us when we're dumpstering, and they cannot BELIEVE that we're taking food out of somebody else's garbage and making a meal out of it. But, well, like Angelo's, and places like that, they throw away unbelievable amounts of good food. The roast beef in the summer time, if you get roast beef, you do have to use it that night, because by the next morning," he shook his head and made a very sour face, "Ooooh!"

Suzi pointed out that timing is important, noting that Angelo's caters a lot of parties and she and Jerry had learned to be around when the catering trucks returned.

"Tell 'em about our big find that somebody else found on us," Suzi urged.

"Oh yes," Jerry said, sitting up a little taller in his bed. "Well, we went up to The Four Dumpsters, this regular place on our route, and we found all this stuff in the dumpster. It was all canned goods. There was clam chowder, there was split pea, cream of potato, tomato, beef gravy, you know, the kind that comes in a can, pinto beans, baked beans, beets, peas, green beans, corn. It was so much stuff that we had to get a shopping cart. And we loaded it down. We had big bags full of nothin' but canned goods. And we didn't take 'em all. You know, you can only eat so many cranberries. And so we left some cranberries, and we left some garbanzo beans, we only took a couple of them. But, it was all there. I'm not kiddin' ya, we must have had thirty or forty dollars worth of canned goods. An' so we go up by this school up here on State Street. An' we usually sit there and we take a cigarette break and if we've got anything, we'll munch on it and things like that. And so there's bushes all along there. And Suzi said, 'Why, we'll stash it here!' And so we got it all together and we stashed it. And we were so proud of ourselves. We must have had—Well, I know we had at least six cans of New England clam chowder. And Lord knows how many cans of all the other stuff. And uh, so we stashed it up underneath the bushes and we was, uh, lookin' to make sure you couldn't see it from the sidewalk and stuff like that, you know.

"Well, lo and behold, it just so happened that that one day somebody had to go to the bathroom. And they went back behind the bushes to take a crap, and guess what they found? Thirty, forty dollars worth of canned goods. Because they were gone when we got back. And ALL DAY LONG, on our route, we were plannin' meals. Oh, we had a menu made up for a week on nothin' but canned goods."

"And it was too far from camp to bring it back?" I asked.

"We should have just come back. No, it's not that far, it's only up the hill about six blocks. But, everybody has 20–20 hindsight. You know. But I told Suzi, I said, 'The good Lord wanted us to find them…and deliver them to the person that He wanted to have them.' That's the way I figure it."

"You got a good story out of it, anyway," I said.

"Yeah, ha, ha, ha. Ain't that the truth! We all had a good laugh." Then Jerry continued. "But oh, it was disappointing. But it, it sure made our day. It give us something to talk about the whole time. We was gonna fix up a great big ole huge thing and, and have EVERYBODY over and have this big meal. Something like that. Just have a fun time. Which we haven't had for a while. We haven't been able to afford it."

"Do you buy canned goods sometimes?" I asked.

"Oh, we have a little bit of stash. We keep canned goods for emergencies. Stuff we find, though. Because, you know, canned goods don't go bad. And the rats can't get them. And so, we have stuff that we stash back and we got some canned fruit and a can of salmon. That is our emergency stash. Ha, ha, ha, ha."

After a while, one of the other sleepers aroused himself and came over to join our conversation. It was Tom, Jerry's longtime campmate.

I had heard a lot about Tom, but had never met him before. He was a pleasant looking White man in his early forties. He was about six feet tall and quite heavy, with over-the-collar length, dishwater blond hair (like mine but a little dirtier) and a full but wispy beard. He was wearing a fairly clean, sage green workshirt and matching workpants. His personal hygiene was fairly good, considering the living conditions. His hands and face, while a little dirty, lacked the shiny black patina of true filth that I'd seen on some street schizophrenics. Tom came over and sat down. Jerry introduced me. Of course, Tom had heard at least as much about me as I had heard about him. He sat quietly as Suzi continued her story.

"When we got those canned goods," Suzi continued, "I got a shopping cart and brought it and we turned it over, and he stood on it to climb into the dumpster. I wasn't sure I could get in. And he said, 'I hope to hell I can get out!'"

"I didn't know if I could make it out," Jerry said. "Oh, and then while I was in there getting the cans, this little Nissan or Toyota pickup pulls up and it stops. And Suzi's on the outside and she's lookin' in at me and I'm bent over and we're all excited and not payin' any attention. And WHACK! something hits the side of the dumpster. Suzi hollers and I stood up to look. And just as I stood up another water balloon comes flying and WHACKO! It gets me smack in the face. It was like a guided missile. And here's these kids in the back of this pickup truck and they're throwin' water balloons at us. And they're just havin' a great time."

Suzi said, "He ended up soaked!"

"I don't mind takin' a bath, but at least give me time to get my clothes off! Either that, or smack me with a couple of water balloons, let me get a bar of soap, lather up and then drive around the block and come back and smack me again to rinse me off, you know. But they were havin' a blast. But, you know," his voice became quiet, "I, I think it's a pretty sad state of affairs where you are so bored that the only thing you can do is fill up water balloons and then drive around and pick out two grubby street people to throw them at. I mean really. If that's your idea of fun, I'm sorry.

"The only thing I was worried about," Jerry went on, "was that I had a bunch of snipes in my pocket." Snipes are cigarette butts, also known on the street as shorts. Snipes were Jerry and Suzi's main source of tobacco. The longer ones they smoked as is, the shorter ones they crumbled and re-rolled.

The Bridge People had been concerned for some time about the declining quality of life in their neighborhood. "We had no problems underneath this bridge or any of the bridges until the Mexicans started coming in. Then things started disappearing," Jerry said.

"They ran two guys off that used to live over there that live over here now," Suzi said. "They ran him off." She nodded toward Tom. I had a little trouble figuring out what Suzi meant sometimes because her talk was pretty disorganized. She seemed to have suffered some brain damage from long term alcohol abuse.

"Naw, they didn't run me off, I left," Tom said a little defensively.

"Well, literally, you wouldn't have left if it wasn't for them," Suzi said.

"They're crazy over there," Tom conceded.

"They've got guns," Jerry said.

"This one guy gets drunk and takes a hatchet and he's up there chopping down the trees. One guy's got a .22 and they sit there and just fire them off," Tom said.

"Really?" I asked.

"And I called the police," Jerry said, "and they didn't do nothin'. They said to call Immigration."

"The thing is, they said that it's state property, so they don't have any jurisdiction. This is Caltrans," Tom said, waving his pudgy arm to take in the area around the bridges.

"But just wait 'til something serious happens. Well, like when that girl got murdered. It was city property then. Caltrans never came to investigate it, the city police did," said Jerry.

The topic of food came up again, and Jerry told me about a supper they had had a couple of nights before. He had found a gallon of Italian red sauce in a plastic bag in a dumpster on their canning route, and then later, at Angelo's dumpster, they had found a bunch of veal and some mushrooms. They combined this in a pot and had a sort of veal cacciatore.

"We may not be able to afford to go INSIDE Angelo's, but we can improve on their menu, underneath the bridges. It's fine with me." He looked heavenward with a twinkle in his eye. "Keep it coming Lord, watch out after us." He grinned as he looked back at me. "The Lord looks out after Bridge People, and fools, and drunks. And I hit all three categories. Ha, ha, ha, ha." We all chuckled.

I thought it was interesting that he used the terms Bridge People and drunks to refer to people like himself. At one time I had thought about using the anthropological term "troglodytes" (people who live in caves) for Jerry and his friends. I had asked them about it, and they said they didn't want to be called troglodytes. After hearing Jerry use the term Bridge People on several occasions like this, I decided to use the term too.

I asked Jerry why he had started canning instead of panhandling. "I keep gettin' arrested," he said. "I mean lately there's no need to go down there. You know, they arrest me for drunken in public and I ain't even had a drink yet. But they get ya and they slap ya in the paddy wagon or they call People in Progress and you end up down at the Weingart. And you've got to sit there and drink a couple of cups of coffee. Give them a break. I think I hold the record for being arrested for drunk in public. I got arrested three times in an hour and a half. The first time, I hadn't even had a drink. But I made enough money and I was THINKING about going down to the Grand Central Market to get a drink. That's when I got arrested the first time. They took me down to the Weingart. People in Progress took me, and if they take you to the Weingart, you don't even have to go in. And so I just started walking back and I hit Ike's Liquor Store, and I thought 'Dammit, if they want me to be drunk, I WILL be drunk.' And I bought myself a short dog and three cans of beer, which I proceeded to drink before I made it up to the State House."

Weingart Center is a huge private facility on Skid Row consisting of a mental health clinic, an alcohol and drug detoxification center, and a welfare hotel. People in Progress is an outreach program that, among other things, chauffeurs alcohol, drug, and mental health casualties to the Weingart. It's about a mile from the Weingart Center to the State Building where Jerry had his panhandling office.

"Why a short dog AND beer?"

"Because it gets you loaded quicker. Especially if you drink it fast fast. You drink one beer and you drink half a short dog in one fell swoop. Put the cap back on that and open up the other beer. Drink it. Then you drink the other half of the short dog. And then you polish it off with the last beer, for a chaser. That'll get your glow going real quick."

"Is that called anything special, when you do that?"

"Gettin' drunk. Ha, ha, ha. I don't know what you call it, but it works. But I made it back up to the State House, and I sat down, made another two or three dollars. And lo and behold, the same two cops that got me the first time pulled up and got me again. Off to the Weingart I go again. Well, I never even went in. I just turned around and went back up to Ike's and bought another short dog, another three cans of beer, polished 'em off on the way to the State House and set down there and made another two or three dollars and WHACKO, two other cops got me. Third time. All in an hour and a half."

Suzi asked, "Jerry, was that the day the guy said, 'Drink it up Jerry, you're goin' for a ride?'"

"Yep. He said, 'Finish your wine.' You know when I sit there, you don't want to sit there with a wine bottle. 'Cause those people are kinda classy and they don't want to see a bottle. So I had it stashed behind me and I had my coat over it. I thought that nobody knew that I had a bottle of wine. And the cop come up and was writing up my ticket to go to detox and he called People in Progress and he turned around and looked at me and he said, 'Well, Jerry, finish up your wine. You're going for a ride.' I said, 'Oh well, why not?' and I just reached behind me and I polished it off."

"So he knew your name and everything?"

"Oh, yeah, they all know me down there. And then, Fisher, down in Chinatown, knows me. He probably knows my mother's maiden name, even."

"His beat is over in Chinatown, huh?" I asked.

"HIS Chinatown! That's exactly the way he puts it, too. The last time I was down there, he told me, he said, 'I want you to stay out of MY Chinatown.' And he's not even Chinese. Hee, hee, hee. How he became sole owner of Chinatown, I'll never know."

Jerry looked over at Suzi and asked, "Do you have a crutch over there?" She looked around her on the table made of a piece of dirty cardboard on top of a capsized milk crate. She found a piece of rolled up matchbook cover and leaned over and handed it to Jerry. The matchbook cover was rolled around the end of a cigarette butt. The "crutch" enabled Jerry to smoke the butt down to the last few millimeters without burning lips or fingers. I thought that the lowly crutch was an efficient recycling device for turning refuse into a resource.

"Well, you know, tobacco does come hard on the streets," Jerry explained as he lit the snipe.

The use of a crutch reminded me of marijuana smokers, who also use them. I asked Jerry if he ever smoked marijuana.

"No, I don't. It's mostly economics. A joint [a marijuana cigarette] of fairly bad weed costs five dollars on the street. For the same five dollars I can go and I can buy two fifths and a short dog and I can get a buzz goin' that's gonna last and it's gonna knock my socks off all night long instead of a couple of hours. The marijuana high is nicer because you don't feel sluggish and stuff like that afterwards. But, give me the booze. It's a little harder on your body, too, you know. One of these days, my kidneys and bladder are gonna get up and move, probably. But, if I smoke, well I do smoke tobacco. Lungs? It's the same difference."

His assertion that a cannabis cigarette cost five dollars led me to think that perhaps he had never really bothered to look into it. Other street people I knew had said that a joint cost only a dollar on the street and one of the reasons they smoked marijuana was because it was cheaper than a short dog and, as Jerry had suggested, had less deleterious side effects. I supposed there were great variations in price and quality of marijuana on the street, but I hadn't really looked into it. It didn't seem too important. Not many homeless people I knew used it, and it wasn't a big deal in the lives of those who did. Many people on the street thought that marijuana was truly a healthy habit because it helped you put on weight. That was important in an environment where getting enough to eat might be a problem, and where people saw their friends abuse alcohol or cocaine, lose a lot of weight, and get sick.

From my experience on the street, it seemed to me that the current War on Drugs was a ridiculous red herring. Cannabis, at least, is a comparatively mild, benign substance. It doesn't cause kidney disease, brain damage, and some 100,000 deaths per year in the U.S. like alcohol does, and it doesn't cause lung and other cancers or the 300,000 deaths per year that tobacco does. In fact, all illegal drugs put together are now thought to cause only some 6,000 deaths per year (Jonas 1989). I had smoked plenty of weed in the 1960s and I knew that it didn't cause poverty, it didn't cause joblessness, and it didn't cause housing shortages. Substance abuse (as opposed to use) may result in Mr. Jones' becoming homeless instead of Mrs. Smith's, but whether there are a couple million homeless people on the street or virtually none, seems to me to be a function of the number of low-cost houses and hotels that are available, and that number is determined primarily by public policy.

When I smoked cannabis, it just helped me relax and enjoy music. The worst problem was the occasional attack of the chocolate munchies, hardly a threat to society worthy of a drug war. People can use almost any substance or activity to abuse themselves, but the results should be seen as health problems, not police problems. In my experience, substance abuse seemed primarily an idiom of distress, a cry for help like a half-hearted attempt at suicide, a symptom of deeper problems of the person and of society. Substance abuse, it seemed to me, ought to be looked at rationally, based on empirical evidence regarding social and environmental costs and benefits. In those empirical, rational terms, the most serious substance abuse problem in the world is gasoline addiction: there is growing evidence that it is destroying the planet. It seems the addictions of the powerful, no matter how destructive, are twisted into virtues; those of the powerless are demonized.

Big Joe came lumbering up the slope to join us. He had a rolling gait like a big friendly bear. We all said hello. Jerry and Suzi kidded him about being so drunk the night before. Big Joe grinned, "Well, if you say so. Ah don't remember. Ah don't remember! Ha, ha, ha, ha! Ah woke up this mornin', Ah said, 'What am Ah doin' with this?'" He held up a fifth of Night Train that was about three quarters full. "Ah'll be okay when Ah'm done with this one, ha, ha, ha."

Big Joe's flirtation with sobriety had been short lived. I wasn't surprised. Substance abuse is deeply woven into the fabric of people's lives. To really change, the life must be unraveled to a large degree and rewoven into another, healthier pattern and, of course, that would be very difficult for the Bridge People.

Big Joe and Jerry talked about the kittens that now resided in Jerry's camp. They were quite small, perhaps six inches long, and had just been separated from their mother. Suzi had two kittens now; Tom had found a third of about the same age in Chinatown a few days before and brought it to camp. We watched the three kittens scramble around the boxes and furniture and roll in the dirt. One would climb up on a box or the arm of a chair and stalk its pals for a couple of seconds and then pounce. Then they all would roll in a batting and biting tangle for a few seconds until one became attracted to something else and went scampering off. Jerry said that even though the kittens were too small to hunt, the rats had been gone since they had appeared.

I asked Jerry about their canning route and he described it to me and reckoned that they walked about ten miles per day. He added, "It's good for me. It keeps my legs from stovin' up on me."

"It keeps his legs limber," Suzi agreed. "We both come home completely exhausted and achy, but at least it keeps your body healthy, you know."

I think they were saying that partly for my benefit. Later I checked my street atlas and estimated that their route was really more like six miles. If they did a good deal of winding around that I didn't know about it might be seven. Jerry did get much more exercise, however, than when he was primarily a panhandler. Then he probably walked a little over two miles per day; it was less than a mile from camp to his office in front of the State Building.

The conversation drifted back to one of the few things that provided a little purpose to life under the bridges—drinking. The reason I say that drinking provided purpose in their lives is that they were always talking about drinking, scheming to get something to drink, begging, borrowing, and stealing something to drink, and, of course, drinking. I also could see that extreme poverty wasn't very entertaining, and drinking was their only diversion. Needless to say, the Bridge People couldn't go shopping to cheer themselves up like we middle-class people do. They couldn't take a vacation from poverty or even get their minds off of it for long. But drinking helped. Social drinking took the place of television, movies, theater, spectator sports, dining out, counseling, and other aspects of "normal" American life, including the New England town meeting. The bridge life had generous helpings of rich social interaction, but much of it was quite soggy.

"Ah was up way before daylight," Big Joe said.

"Well, why not," Jerry said, "you went to bed way before nightfall. Ha, ha, ha."

"Ah woke up," Joe continued, "and Ah got to lookin' around. Ah says, 'Ah know they's some drink around here someplace.' Ha, ha, ha." We all had big chuckle. "And Ah had about fifth and a half left."

"How'd you manage that?" Jerry asked. "I thought he polished—"

"But he went out [passed out]," Suzi interrupted. "You remember, he went out. When you sleep, you don't drink, you know," she said, capturing a profound fact of bridge life rather succinctly.

"Yeah, yeah, oh, yeah," Jerry acknowledged.

"Ah wish Ah could remember it," Big Joe said with a big grin.

I learned that Jerry and Larry had played euchre and pitch the day before, while Big Joe had devoted himself more seriously to alcohol. Jerry said that while he was on his route, he had found a "whole bunch of slugs." Slugs are the small discs that electricians punch out of junction boxes when wiring a building. Slugs will work as coins in some vending machines—in newspaper machines for example. As incongruous as it might sound, Jerry and the others liked to stay up on the affairs of the day and he had especially wanted to read a five part series on Lucille Ball that had been running in the *Herald-Examiner*.

"I went out and slugged the paper machine yesterday morning, and I'm sorry," Jerry said with a smirk, "it was my day off, but I could not help it, I had to hit the dumpster. I hit the dumpster and I come back with fourteen of the nicest meatballs. Then I found a bunch of spaghetti, a gallon can of spaghetti, and then I come back to camp and then went over to Big Joe and Larry's. So then I got politely drunk and Big Joe had to walk me across the street. I could not make it down the hill.

Actually, I could have made it down the hill, but whether it would have been on my feet or on my back, I didn't know. Joe come and he waltzed me across the street. He wouldn't even let me cross the street because he said, 'You can't even see the traffic.' And he was drunker than I was. Hee, hee, hee, so it was the blind leading the blind. So I comes over here, and I rummaged around and put spaghetti on and made up a sauce with our ketchup and mild taco sauce and barbecue sauce and all this other left over sauce and threw the meatballs in. So we had meatballs and spaghetti last night."

"Those little envelopes of taco sauce?" I asked.

"Yeah, those little packet things."

Jerry and Suzi find numerous little packets of ketchup, taco sauce, relish, mustard, and so on from fast food joints in trash cans and dumpsters. They usually have a large selection in camp, stored in a paper bag.

"The way we figure," Jerry explained, "the good Lord does look out for us. We have a very varied menu. You know, it's not like going down to the Harbor Light [a mission] and, you know, beans for breakfast and beans for supper. Beans and bread and beans and bread and beans and bread."

"When you found that spaghetti over at Angelo's, how did you carry it home?"

"In a gunboat."

"Oh, I see....What's a gunboat?"

"It's a big tin can, you know." He held his hands up to show that it was about gallon sized. The term, he thinks, is Navy slang and alludes to the shell casing of the large gun on a gunboat.

Big Joe spoke up from the couch where he and Suzi had been counting change, "Hey Jerry! Yawl, yawl about forty-five cents short?"

"I don't know. She's got the bank roll," Jerry answered, nodding at Suzi.

"I got a dollar eighty," Suzi said.

"Ah got an extra forty-five cents. Ah'll let yawl have it to get a bottle," Joe said.

"Oh, all right!" Jerry said, with a new lilt in his voice. "Is it eight o'clock yet?" Eddie's liquor store opens at eight.

"Yeah," Joe answered. His interest in procuring more wine was driven by the fact that he had come to the bottom of the fifth he had brought with him.

"Oh, well now, Suzi must be going. Hee, hee, hee, hee, hee," Jerry said.

"It's not, it's not, it's not really eight yet," Suzi said, holding up her wrist. She had a nice looking plastic watch. I complemented her on it, and she said that a lady friend whom she had gotten to know in Angelo's parking lot had given it to her.

Later, Suzi complained about not being able to get her social security checks mailed to her. In the same vein, Jerry said he needed to get his birth certificate and was in a quandary about where to have it sent. I suggested having it sent to Eddie's liquor store and Jerry said that Eddie didn't like that anymore. He had been letting people use the liquor store as a mail drop, but now he was afraid of getting involved in welfare problems. Tom said that he got his mail at the Hippie Kitchen (a soup kitchen) or the L.A. Mission, but Jerry didn't like that.

"But the only thing of it is, is going all the way down to the war zone to get your mail and you never know how long it's going to take. If I knew, when I sent off for my birth certificate, that it would be there one week later, to the day, then I would venture back down into the war zone for that one trip. But I'm not going down there for the fun of it."

"You can't get nowhere without a mailing address. You're up a creek!" Suzi said.

"Why don't you have it mailed to my office?" I suggested.

"Ooooh, there's a dandy idea!" Jerry said.

I gave Jerry my business card and told him to have it sent in care of me. I also said that he should send it to the project office at the Veterans Adminstration Medical Center, because if it were sent to the Department of Psychiatry at UCLA, I might not see it for a long time. Jerry cracked up laughing at the notion that UCLA wasn't up to the task of sorting mail. It's been cracking me up for years. (None of the Bridge People ever bothered to have mail sent to my office, but other street people did.)

I asked about the huge plastic bag of clothing on the south end of camp. Jerry said they were dirty clothes and at the bottom were ones from when he and Suzi were sick with dysentery. Outhouse clothes, Jerry called them. He didn't know if he was going to "toss 'em or wash 'em," although there are some clothes in the bag that he wanted to keep. Acquiring clothing was not much of a problem, Jerry said, and that squared with what other homeless people had told me.

"People come and bring us clothes," Jerry said, "but they bring us clothes that are, well, like for Suzi, they're light pink, or white, bright yellow. How long is that gonna stay clean when you're livin' in dirt? You know? They're worthless. When you're diggin' in dumpsters? And stuff like that. What good is that gonna do us? You know, you CAN wear it. Sure I can put on a white shirt. I've got white shirts, but in an hour or two you look really horrible. What we need are really work clothes, you know, brown, tan, dark colors, not Easter dresses and white shirts."

Suzi had slipped away to the liquor store several minutes earlier and now she returned with a couple of fifths of wine to the applause and hurrahs of Jerry, Joe, and even Tom, who didn't usually even drink wine. I decided to leave at this point, since it was getting late and I wanted to touch base with some other street friends. I left their camp at about eight thirty.

13. Outdoor adventures of Tom and Jerry

About three weeks later, at the end of May, 1989, I visited the bridges again. I walked across the parking lot behind Angelo's Restaurant and climbed through the hole in the fence that leads up to Jerry's camp. I could see that Jerry and Suzi were gone. The hill only takes a few steps to ascend, but it seems larger, partly because it symbolizes the transition zone between vastly different ways of life. It's like stepping through a class barrier. But it's a time membrane, the threshold between the clean, well lighted, middle-class life of the Civic Center and the dark, dirty life of the poorest of the urban poor. It takes but a few steps and a shrug to get from the high technology of jet, cellular phone, and fax to the stone age technology of hauling firewood on foot for light, heat, and cooking. Where every drop to drink, cook, or wash with is brought to camp on foot. Where there are usually no machines at all and the only domesticated animal is the camp cat. With its scavenger economy and its rich social life, life under the bridges was similar to that of stone age hunters and gatherers. It was worse than stone age with its drunkenness, despair, sickness, and violence. That this was taking place in the center of one of the biggest, richest cities in one of the most affluent countries in the world was a major paradox.

Tom was lying on his mattresses and waved to me as I approached. He said that Jerry and Suzi had left at about eight o'clock that morning. I asked how he knew the time, and he explained that he could hear the chimes from the Music Center.

"While I was panhandling down in Chinatown, somebody gave me a cheap, two dollar digital [watch]. I didn't think I had much use for it, so I gave it to Jerry. Jerry gave it to Larry. Later on I started thinking and decided that it would be kinda nice to have a watch, so I asked Jerry about it and Jerry said I should talk to Larry. When I went to see Larry about the watch, it turned out that he had sold it to somebody for a buck."

So goes commerce and exchange among the Bridge People.

When I first found out that Jerry had left, I felt like just packing it up for the day, but Tom was pleasant and willing to talk so I stood there at the foot of his mattresses and we chatted.

It was common practice under the bridges to sleep on conventional mattresses or cast-off couches to get up out of the dirt. Mattresses were not difficult to obtain, and at that point there was even a pile of spares in the south part of camp. Occasionally people drove by the bridges and dropped off mattresses, couches, and chairs, and the Bridge People also found such things from time to time near dumpsters. At that time, Jerry slept on a very broken down full size box-spring and mattress with an additional sheet of foam, Tom slept just on a mattress placed on a couple of sheets of cardboard, and Suzi slept on a decrepit couch.

I asked Tom if I could tape his comments and he said no. That surprised me, but I said, "Fine. No problem." I put the tape recorder back in my pocket immediately. His uneasiness about the tape recorder didn't seem to chill the conversation and he still seemed to enjoy talking to me. He knew that I was an anthropologist and that I had been taping conversations with Jerry earlier. I pulled up a milk crate and sat down and we continued our conversation.

Tom said that Jerry and Suzi had been sick again, just a few weeks ago. "Jerry and Suzi had the shits so serious that for four or five days they just lay in their own shit. They were too weak to even move. Suzi was on her couch and Jerry was on his bed. It was bad, man. Really funky. Jerry got thrown out of Tiny and Big Joe's camp for doin' the same thing. He'd just shit on himself sittin' in that chair over there." Tom got a very sour look on his face. "Ohhhhh! It was bad, man. Joe and Tiny just got tired of trying to help Jerry.

"See, Jerry wouldn't do anything to help himself, so they just got tired of it. He wouldn't go to the hospital and he wouldn't eat. He just wanted to drink his goddamn wine. I don't blame them at all for running him off.

"Jerry has been very nice to me over the years, but honestly, he can be a royal pain in the ass too, you know. Two or three times he's gotten the shits like that, really bad, and I had to call the paramedics to take him to the hospital, but when they got there, he would refuse to go. Can you believe it? He wouldn't go. The paramedics finally said, 'Fuck it, man. We've got more important things to do than to try to help a worthless drunk who doesn't want to be helped.' I don't blame them, either. Let's be real, they DO have more important things to do. These days the paramedics won't come down here anymore unless you really plead with them.

"Check this out. One time Jerry was vomiting blood and had the shakes and everything. He was really bad off and me and Suzi tried and tried to get him to go to the hospital. Well, eventually he gave in and asked me to go call the paramedics. Okay? So I gotta walk to Eddie's where the nearest pay phone is. This is about a quarter mile away, you know. I wasn't about to go through this routine with Jerry refusing to go once the paramedics showed up, so I made him walk to Eddie's with me. I'd have to really sweet talk the paramedics to get them to come down here and I didn't want to go to all this hassle if he wasn't going to go. So I thought if I could get him to walk down there with me, it would show that he was serious, you know. So Jerry and I start walking down to Eddie's. And he's so sick he can hardly walk. It takes us FOREVER to get down there and it's not that far, really.

"So when we get there, what does he do? He goes in and buys a short dog and a bottle of Pepto Bismol. He downed them both, one after another, while I was on the phone convincing the paramedics to come pick up Jerry. I thought he was being a self-destructive asshole, but that's Jerry. I'm not his babysitter, you know. I care what happens to him, but there's only so much I will do, you know. I'm not his father. There's only so much a friend can do, you know. So anyway, I didn't say anything, 'cause we'd already been bickering about his attitude, and all that, and I didn't want Jerry to get REALLY hateful. Jerry was still saying that he didn't know if he really wanted to go to the hospital or not. I was a little pissed, but I just said, 'Fuck it. It's his problem. Let him deal with it.'

"Well pretty soon the paramedics came. Just as they got there and got out of the van and we were talking, Jerry doubled over and gagged. I turned around and there was a huge pink wave of wine, Pepto Bismol, and blood splashing all over the sidewalk. It was great! I cracked up. Ha, ha, ha, ha. It was like something out of the movies. Ha, ha, ha, ha. So then, Jerry went to the goddamned hospital.

"Jerry's basically a very self destructive guy, you know. Like for instance, take his diet. Basically, Jerry and Suzi don't eat, they drink. They just drink wine, nothing but wine. They virtually never drink water. For the last three days Suzi has not eaten anything at all and Jerry only ate a little. Jerry will talk about his great menu and varied diet and all that, but it's bullshit. He DOES like to cook, but most of the time he gets so drunk that by the middle of the afternoon, he doesn't know what he's doing. I've seen him a lot of times, when he did manage to get something cooked, he'd pass out right into his food. Just look at him. If he ate right, he wouldn't be that skinny. He's lost maybe thirty pounds in the last three or four years on his wine diet. And he wasn't all that robust to begin with, ha, ha, ha. I'm just afraid that one of these times, he'll be trying to cook when he's really drunk and he'll catch himself on fire when there's nobody around to put him out."

At that time, Jerry and Tom were sharing cooking facilities and duties, but Tom said he usually got the pallets for firewood and broke them up so they could be used in the campfire and fetched the water. Jerry usually did the actual food preparation, but he only cooked irregularly. Jerry and Tom had no formal agreement on this, and it was a source of quite a few arguments between them. Suzi also cooked sometimes. Most of the time Tom got his own food and ate alone.

"See, I don't really like to cook. I just don't need the hassle. And I don't mind cold food, you know. I can get by fine with sandwiches from the church and cold food from the dumpster. If it was up to me, I wouldn't bother with hauling firewood, hauling water, making a fire, cleaning up afterwards, and all that crap. I just don't care about it, you know. I just don't care."

After a while, Tom suggested we walk over to Chinatown so that he could panhandle. I said sure. He rummaged in the trash around the head of his mattress, found some old dirty court shoes, and pulled them over his dirty bare feet.

He grinned, "I don't bother with underwear or socks anymore. I guess I've gotten life down to bare essentials. Ha, ha, ha." We trudged down the little hill to the street and walked slowly toward his "office."

Jerry was having seizures more frequently these days. Tom said again that Jerry had lost considerable weight in the last couple of years and generally seemed to be in physical decline. It was something that upset Tom, he said, but he didn't feel there was anything he could do about it.

Jerry often got violent and abusive when he got drunk, Tom said. Suzi and Jerry fought constantly, and these fights occasionally ended with Jerry beating Suzi up. Tom tried to maintain order, he said, by threatening to smack Jerry. He tried to intervene in arguments and saw himself as something of a peacemaker. I had always thought Jerry was a pretty mellow, jolly drunk, but according to Tom, this was definitely not the case. The drunker he got, the more abusive, argumentative, and violent he became, like he was letting out a little of the misery and pain of many years on the street.

Tom usually woke up at first light and lay in his bed reading until about ten o'clock or so. Then he walked north on Cardenas Street, past Eddie's liquor store, and up a small hill to a Croatian Catholic Church on the edge of Chinatown. (Los Angeles isn't a melting pot, it's an ethnic salad.) He knocked on the door and someone would answer and hand him a sandwich or two. He said that they made up about sixteen sandwiches a day and they ran out about noon, so he liked to pass by during the late morning. He then walked on toward Chinatown. In the center of Chinatown, on Market, the main street, there was a bus stop where he panhandled about four days a week, he said. He usually stopped after he made six dollars or so. He said that he didn't need much to get along because he didn't mind eating sandwiches and he bought material to make sandwiches at the Grand Central Market very cheaply. Of course, usually he also got a sandwich or two every day at the Catholic church in Chinatown.

"The biggest difference between me and Jerry, is that I don't have that much of an alcohol habit. Jerry and Suzi drink two or three or four fifths of wine a day, you know. That adds up. I usually get myself," he said with a twinkle in his eyes, "a little half pint of vodka and two or three cheap beers. Vodka costs a buck sixty-five and the beers are only sixty-five cents each. That's at Eddie's. If I go to Grand Central, it's cheaper, but I usually don't bother. It's kind of a long walk. If I have a good day panhandling, I get grand and I get a sixpack. Ha, ha, ha, ha. I've gotta buy a package of Tops too [a package of loose tobacco and rolling papers] and they cost eighty-five cents. Jerry and Suzi smoke snipes, but I can't handle that. I snipe around my bed when I'm desperate though. Ha, ha, ha. I've gotta have my tobacco. That's my main vice, I'd say, is my cigarette smoking. So anyway, I can get by fine on about four fifty. But Jerry and Suzi, they're serious wine drinkers. A bottle of wine is about two bucks. I'm not really sure," Tom said with some disdain, "'cause I don't drink wine. So they need to make something like six or eight bucks each to get their daily drinky-poos. Now, that was no problem when Jerry was panhandling, but with canning it's much harder. A lotta days, they'll only make four or five bucks and that's only enough to buy a couple of jugs and that definitely cramps their style. A good day for them would be drinking three or four jugs, but frankly, they're much easier to get along with now that Jerry's canning. They're not around as much and they can't afford to drink as much. So they don't fight and fuss as much. That's what I don't like, is the constant bickering and fighting."

We continued to talk and after a while Tom mentioned that he had tried to commit suicide once. I asked how he did it.

"Well, I bought a jar of muscle relaxants and a pint of vodka. I planned to take the pills and drink the alcohol and then, when I got mellow, I would slit my wrists. I was living alone in a small apartment at the time in the Valley [the San Fernando Valley, just northeast of Los Angeles]. I wasn't particularly sad, just tired of life, you know. Things weren't disastrous in my life, just lifeless. I was down. I was definitely down. Anyway, I locked myself in my room and drank the vodka and then I took a single edged razorblade and slit my right wrist." He winced. "I was SHOCKED," he said dramatically, "at how much it hurt. Well, immediately my right hand went completely limp. That surprised me. I didn't think about that. So then, I couldn't use it to slit my left wrist. I had to put the blade in my teeth and then I sawed away at the left wrist. Eventually got it slashed, but it was a mess," he said making a sour face. "Really a mess. Ha, ha, ha, ha. See. Look here."

He showed me the scars and, indeed, the right wrist had a thin, neat line, while the left had multiple, ugly hack marks.

"Well, then I laid down on my bed to bleed and watch television. I felt relaxed and good for the first time in weeks. But then I realized that I had forgotten to take the pills. That made me feel like an incompetent shit, I tell ya. So then I tried to get the childproof cap off the bottle, but of course, my hands wouldn't work. I had to put the bottle between my wrists and try to get the cap off with my teeth. It was ridiculous. I mean there I was dripping blood all over the place and I, I couldn't get the cap off the bottle. Ha, ha, ha, ha. It was a disaster. After a while, a LONG while, I finally did get the goddamn cap off. Those goddamn childproof caps are murder. And then I was able to take the pills and wash them down with water. After that I felt better about the whole thing. I kicked back and mellowed out again and watched the tube. I thought about my final, last sleep and felt good about it. You know, rest in peace, brother.

"Well, I tell ya, I felt like shit when I woke up. At first I felt really weird and I couldn't figure out where I was or what was going on. I thought maybe I was in heaven or hell or whatever, you know. I couldn't see clearly. For a while, it was just swirling images, you know, and people talking, but I couldn't understand what they were saying. Eventually I was able to get my eyes focused. The people leaning over me turned out to be paramedics. I realized I was alive. I just thought, 'DAMMIT! What a bummer!'"

Tom went on to explain that his wrists had become inflamed and swollen from the cuts, and this increased pressure caused the bleeding to stop. The paramedics told him that this is a relatively common outcome of wrist slashings. If the wrists are slashed parallel to the forearm instead of perpendicular to it, the aspiring suicide victim is usually successful, they said. I wondered why they would tell someone who had just tried to commit suicide how to a better job next time.

Tom and I got to his office—a bus bench on Market Street in the heart of Chinatown. We sat together and chatted while Tom panhandled. He asked almost everyone who came by in a soft, staccato voice, "Can you spare some change today? Spare change? Can you spare some change today?" He didn't work with a cup or cap, but rather just held out his hand. He said he likes to begin work with seven or eleven cents in his hand for good luck. I dug into my pocket and came up with a dime and a penny, which I quietly dropped into his hand.

"Thanks, Jackson, thanks a lot. That'll get things goin'. Ha, ha, ha."

"You're welcome, Tom. No problem."

In the past he had had various lucky coins that he carried with him and held in his outstretched hand.

"You know, I only half-heartedly believe in luck," he said, "but then what the hell, I only half-heartedly believe in anything, ha, ha, ha."

On two different occasions, passersby gave both Tom AND me change. I responded by saying, "Thank you, sir," then, as soon as they had passed, I gave the change to Tom. By this point in the research, this had happened to me before, but it still made me feel quite strange.

While we were sitting on the bench, a police car quietly pulled up in front of us. The officer in the passenger side leaned out of his window a little and said that we couldn't just sit there, that we had to be catching a bus. Tom replied that he was being interviewed.

"Yes," I said, "that's right, officer." I got up, walked over to the car, and handed him my business card. I didn't bother getting out my picture identification badges (from UCLA Medical Center and the Veterans Administration Medical Center), but I did carry them with me. Push can come to shove on the street. He stared at the business card for a moment, then looked up. "Well, Doctor Underwood," he said in a gruff, but courteous voice, "you'd better move along pretty soon anyway."

"Certainly officer," I said and tried to summon up a friendly smile.

The policeman nodded to me with a wooden face, then he nodded to his driver. With a low growl the car eased into traffic.

Tom told me that the officer was the notorious Officer Fish, or Fisher, nemesis of the panhandlers of Chinatown. Tom wasn't sure of his name, and I'd neglected to ask when I introduced myself. Tom told me that he was a vile tempered, mean little guy who liked to hassle panhandlers. He didn't seem mean to me, but I had demonstrated to his apparent satisfaction that in spite of my somewhat rough appearance, I was not a panhandler. It did seem like he was quite prepared to get mean, however.

After Officer Fisher (or Fish) departed, Tom and I continued to pan for another hour or so, but Tom's heart wasn't in it. He had made about four dollars by then and decided to leave. He was fearful of seeing Fisher again, but he never did come by. On our way home, Tom stopped by a liquor store and, true to his word, purchased a package of Tops rolling tobacco, a half-pint of vodka, and a couple of cheap beers.

I was getting tired and wanted to get home to write up my notes, so I continued down Market while Tom continued his slow circuitous route home.

A couple of days later, I parked in the lot that surrounds Angelo's and arrived in camp at about eight thirty in the morning. I chatted with Tom, Suzi, and Jerry for about a half hour and then I went to work canning with Jerry and Suzi. Tom stayed in camp. I had discussed camping there with Jerry before and I had come prepared to spend a few days with them.

We walked slowly north on Cardenas Street toward Eddie's, chatting as we went. Suzi complained again about how Caltrans had cut down the trees between the bridge and Angelo's parking lot. They had effectively shielded the Bridge People from the view of the parking lot and vice versa. Vines had grown on the bridge itself, hanging down from it on the sides, so that the only place passersby had an unobstructed view of their camp was from directly in front of it in the street or on the sidewalk. Jerry and Suzi wondered what reason Caltrans could have had for chopping down the trees and poisoning the vines.

"The people walking or driving by sure as hell don't want to see us, and we don't want them to see us. So why chop down the trees and stuff?" Jerry complained.

I had no answer for him and wondered the same thing. Suzi's explanation was that it was a stupid reaction to a couple of killings. She told me that a woman's body had been found up behind the camp a while ago.

"I didn't even know about it. The cops came about two thirty in the mornin' and I got a shotgun in my face and this guy sayin' 'Wake up!' And I don't know what the hell is goin' on. And they said, 'What are you doin'?' And I said, 'I think I was sleepin'.' Ha, ha, ha. You know? I mean, Lord have mercy! And they said, 'Well somebody got killed over on the side.' And I said, 'Well, I don't know anything about it. I didn't even know it.' But later, the investigators found out that she was killed someplace else and the person dragged her and put her over there."

"Things like that can give the neighborhood a bad name, huh?" I joked.

"Yeah. We that, quote, live here, we don't cause any trouble," Jerry said. "You know, like the old maxim is, 'You don't eat where you shit and you don't shit where you eat.' That's it. But you have these, like these illegals coming through, and like that murder case that I'm involved in, stuff like that. They just showed up here under the bridge one day and a week later he killed her. They were only here for a week. Not like us, who have been livin' up here for years. So that's where our trouble comes from."

"Yeah," I said, "it looks like those Hispanic guys across the street are really trashing that hill. Eventually...."

"Eventually, Caltrans will come. Well, we've talked to Caltrans about it. And, Suzi and I, they said, 'Well, you guys keep your place neat. No trash around. Stuff like that.' 'But,' I said, 'those Mexicans, somebody's gonna drive by and make a complaint and then we're gonna lose out, because of them.'"

A moment later, I asked about collecting bottles, and Jerry said that they were "too heavy, way too heavy."

"And you only get two and a half cents a pound," Suzi chipped in. "Hee, hee, hee, hee, hee."

"So that means," Jerry said, "that you pick up two hundred pounds of bottles and...you get five dollars. An' that's a lot of weight to lug up and down hills, I want to tell ya."

Jerry said that when he had a day or two off from canning, he got stiff from his arthritis and rheumatism. "One good thing about it," he said, "is that we always know when it's gonna rain. My knees ache, her elbows ache, ha, ha, ha, ha, and my back and so on."

"Oh, you've got a built in barometer, huh?"

"Yeah, ha, ha, ha."

"Do you think canning is healthier than panning," I asked, "'cause of the exercise you get?"

"No, I would rather panhandle."

"We did beautiful one day last week," Suzi said.

"Yeah, we went canning that day, and I told Suzi, I said, 'When we get to the bingo place, if we don't have enough, we're gonna go pannin'.' And we didn't have enough, and we turned around and went back down. And I made thirteen dollars in, in two hours." (An income of three dollars and twenty-five cents an hour per person.)

"That was panhandling back at your old place?"

"Uh huh. Yeah. I reopened the office. I was a little bit afraid about it, but...."

"Maybe it's not so bad when you haven't been there for a while," I asked.

"Yeah, if I, if I can stay away and just kinda dip in and dip out, that's the only way to do it. Any other way, I'm DOOMED!"

We approached a dumpster and Jerry and Suzi picked through it. I saw them pass up pieces of aluminum foil. I asked if the "can man," their term for the recycling place, would take it.

"Yeah, they will, but why bother with it?"

"It's not really worth anything, huh?"

"Well, thirty cents, thirty cents a pound, which is okay, but good God, you'd have to have two garbage sacks full of it, you know."

"Yeah, it's pretty light stuff....So you mainly focus on pickin' up cans, huh?"

"Uh huh."

"And then other useful things, that you could wear or eat or something, huh?"

"Right. We're liable to find anything. Like yesterday we were bombarded with food. We had Oriental. We had Mexican. We had turkey, ham, and then we found that whole box of Kentucky Fried Chicken. Hadn't even been opened up! Somebody threw it out, so we had chicken."

A rule they followed was that they never passed up condiments. They found many of the small packets of sugar, coffee creamer, salt, pepper, mayonnaise, hot sauce, ketchup, and so on that are given out with fast food orders and, as I've noted before, had an extensive collection at home.

Jerry normally leaned over the dumpster, picked around in it with his stick, and handed cans to Suzi, who put them on the ground at her feet. They would both smash the cans with their heels, then put them in her bags.

"You always squish the cans. It makes them a lot easier to carry. There's not near the bulk. Smush them down good and flat," Jerry said. He used the heel of his shoe to get maximum leverage. He thought smashing cans was more important than Suzi did and was better at it than she was. He was currently wearing some very nice Florsheim oxfords in an English tan. He had found them on the canning route. For as long as I'd known him, Jerry had somehow managed to keep himself in good footwear.

They carried their cargo in plastic grocery bags they found among the trash, but it seemed to me that a daypack would have enabled them to carry more. "You guys don't ever use a backpack or anything?"

"I had a backpack, but I gave it to Tiny," Jerry said.

"Oh. How come you didn't keep it?"

"Well, he was going back to Fargo [North Dakota], and he needed something to carry his stuff in, so I thought 'Might as well give it to him.' Plastic trash bags work okay for us," he said, "and they're always available. We can always pick one out of a dumpster."

As we continued walking along their canning route, they made a pretty good haul of beer cans out of a dumpster at an automobile repair shop. "I was a mechanic for a while," I said. "I worked on helicopters when I was in the Army, and in my experience it always required the consumption of great quantities of beer. Ha, ha, ha."

Jerry chuckled, "Yeah, well we do get a lot of beer cans behind garages. Ha, ha, ha. There's a couple of 'em on our route."

The other day, in a dumpster behind an apartment house, they had taken a hundred cans out of one dumpster. I suggested that it might be the apartment house where the mechanics who worked in those garages lived. Jerry laughed.

Dumpsters in that part of town were frequently piled very high, sometimes as much as a yard above the top. Occasionally you encountered veritable towers of trash, with the dumpster serving only as a foundation. These over-full dumpsters posed a problem for Jerry and Suzi because they could touch off an avalanche. They generally just poked around the surface of these dumpsters and left them largely unexplored because of the labor involved in putting the material back if an avalanche occured. Jerry said he believed it important to leave the area clean.

"If we don't keep it clean, then that's when the dumpsters start getting locked up...and so we'd like to be tidy. Is that a redundance of words? Being tidy digging through garbage?"

"Well, it is paradoxical, but I guess it's what you have to do," I said.

"Well, you know something? Jerry and I get angry when we come to garbage cans where the people dump the shit all over on the ground. They, they ruin it for everybody else," Suzi said.

I observed Jerry and Suzi going through numerous dumpsters as we continued along their canning route, and they were as good as their word, leaving the areas as clean as they had found them, cleaner if the area had had aluminum cans lying around. As they pointed out, however, some people who scavenged through dumpsters did throw trash around and leave a mess.

Jerry and Suzi could tell just by looking at a dumpster whether or not anything had changed there since the last time they'd been through it. If there had been no significant additions, they'd pass it by.

Their route passed behind a medical clinic. The dumpster there required extreme caution, Jerry said, because the trash contained bare used syringes "infected with Lord knows what kind of God-awful diseases." Later I learned that broken glass and disposable diapers full of baby feces were among the other hazards they encountered going through dumpsters.

Jerry and Suzi utilized what they called canning sticks to help them in their work. These sticks were segments of broom or mop handle about one and one half yards long. In one end they had hammered a box nail (six or eight penny) with about an inch left sticking out. The nail was bent over at about a forty-five degree angle to catch the opening in the top of the cans. The head of the nail helped keep the snagged can from falling off, they explained. A finish nail wouldn't work as well.

Much of the garbage in the dumpsters was in plastic garbage bags and the canning stick was also used to beat and poke these bags to determine if there were aluminum cans inside. Jerry and Suzi had developed an ear for the subtle differences in the sounds of steel and aluminum. The latter crinkled, while steel cans gave off a more melodious, lower pitched clang. Jerry and Suzi generally just thwacked and poked the bags; they didn't open them unless the thwack-and-poke test suggested there was an aluminum can inside.

The canning stick was also used to help push around garbage in the dumpster so they could see what was there without having to climb in. Jerry and Suzi could only reach a small percentage of the material in a dumpster with their hands. The canning stick extended their reach by over a yard and that was enough to reach virtually anywhere within a typical dumpster. The top layer in a dumpster was usually examined for useful things in addition to cans—food, clothing, tools, and things that could be used as tools.

At times, Jerry or Suzi would also use the canning stick to prop up the lid of a dumpster while Jerry rummaged around in it with his hands. Since he was taller, Jerry was usually the one that leaned over and really got into the work. Finally, the canning stick also functioned as sticks have since the Pleistocene. Before the domestication of dogs, sticks were man's best friend and, like Pleistocene hunters and gatherers, the Bridge People used their sticks to threaten opponents, to defend themselves, to lean on, to fiddle with, to serve as a prop in storytelling, and, of course, as an aid in walking. However, Jerry and Suzi didn't seem to have much emotional attachment to their canning sticks. They didn't name them, talk to them, stroke them, or talk about them.

We came to a place with small, two story apartments set behind a large parking lot. In the lot were a couple of dumpsters. A middle-aged Black man dressed neatly in slacks and a sport shirt came out of a commercial building next door and walked over to Jerry, smiled, and silently put a dollar in his hand. When the guy walked away, I asked Jerry if he owned the place and Jerry said that he was the janitor. He gave Jerry and Suzi a dollar every day if he was in the area when they passed through, they said. In my research on Skid Row, I saw more poor working people give money to beggars than building owners and other wealthy people. I wondered why.

We continued to trudge along the canning route. Suzi said that they usually made their rounds a little later on weekends.

"People party and they sleep late, so they get up later and they throw the garbage out later. So on Saturday and Sunday, if you go out early, you don't get nothin'. If you hit these dumpsters at about eleven, twelve, one o'clock, then everybody's thrown their garbage out. See, during the week, the women are goin' to school, takin' the kids to school, and they dump the garbage on their way out. So it's early. But on weekends, it's different."

A bit later, I asked what a good day of canning would bring and they said about eight dollars. Suzi explained, "There's too many people cannin' now, because they're payin' eighty, eighty-five cents a pound. When it was thirty or forty cents a pound, nobody was doin' it. I had people that used to give me cans. And they used to save them for me. Now, they haul them down and get eighty-five cents. I don't blame them."

Suzi's analysis of the worsening situation for canners, understandably, fails to take into account the steadily worsening economic situation for the poor in general, which leads people toward economies of makeshift, like canning, or returning their cans for refunds. Another important factor is competition. The number of people living on the street is growing constantly and canning is one of the major ways they have of supporting themselves. Finally, there are more and more people, like myself, who are motivated to recycle more by concern for the environment than by the money. The increased price of aluminum is an important factor, but only one of several which might explain the growing scarcity of aluminum cans that Suzi was bemoaning.

California had recently passed a deposit law which was largely responsible for the higher price paid to canners for aluminum cans. The recycling companies receive the deposit on the cans (at first, one cent per can, later two and a half cents) as well as the market price of the aluminum, so they can offer over twice as much as the market price of aluminum alone. This accounts for the big difference between the price paid for aluminum foil and aluminum cans. There are about twenty-eight cans (twelve fluid ounce capacity) per pound and when the price of aluminum paid to canners is around eighty-five cents per pound, each can is worth approximately three cents.

At some places on the canning route, Suzi and Jerry had different tasks. They split up to investigate different trash cans or dumpsters at locations such as the junction of an alley or a place where there were two or three different dumpsters in different parts of a large parking lot. Sometimes they discussed who should go visit which dumpster, and sometimes they did it automatically and silently.

Jerry usually didn't carry any of their bags until Suzi got really loaded down. There was almost no discussion of this division of labor, Suzi just accepted it as a given. I neglected to ask why the labor was divided this way, but it probably had something to do with the trouble Jerry had walking as a result of his strokes. It would have been difficult for him to carry bags and use his canning stick as a cane at the same time.

By mid-morning we had gotten to a little Hispanic grocery store that Jerry and Suzi called the Six O'clock Store, because it opened at six A.M. and closed at six P.M. These early hours enabled them to get a bottle first thing in the morning. Eddie's didn't open until eight, and that was rather late for Bridge People. Jerry went inside and bought a fifth of Thunderbird and I got a diet Pepsi. He had said earlier that he intended to get a short dog, but they had gotten the dollar from the janitor, so he had enough for a fifth. There was little discussion that I was aware of. It was a simple algorithm: if you had enough for a short dog, that's what you got. If you have enough for a fifth, you got that. How much alcohol they consumed was directly and almost exclusively dependent upon how much money they could muster.

We walked north for a block to a construction site where we sat to take a break. The apartment building being constructed was about finished and we sat to one side on an empty planter made of concrete block. A small deciduous tree provided us shade. On the side away from the construction site, there was a nice lawn. It was a very pleasant place to take a break.

The manager of the construction project came to an upstairs window and smiled and said hello and watched us silently for a moment, then went back inside to continue his work. Jerry and Suzi had been taking breaks at this location for several months and were well acquainted with him.

Jerry had been canning off and on for twenty years, he said. When he started, he said, aluminum was fifteen cents a pound. Suzi said that she had started a few years ago and it was thirty-five cents a pound then, but she was able to get twenty-five pounds a day or more. She lamented the passing of those good old days. I later calculated what she would have made then, and it came to eight dollars and seventy-five cents, a bit more that what she said would be a good day now, and there were more good days then. Of course, these estimates were very rough. Her perception was probably more important than her figures. Certainly her expenses had gone up. Tobacco and a bottle of "T-bird" cost more then than they had a few years before, so her standard of living and the quality of her life, from her perspective, had undoubtedly fallen.

She said that people who got to the canning route ahead of them were called "cross walks." Jerry called it getting short-stopped.

"It's like panhandling down at the Courthouse. I have my spot. My one spot that I sit at. Then the next thing you know, I got a guy off to my right and I got one over to my left and I'm gettin' short-stopped. The ones coming this way are gettin' hit by that one, and the ones coming the other way are hit by the other."

"The good part of it is that Jerry's got regulars," Suzi said.

"Yeah. If I didn't have my regulars, I wouldn't have shit." A regular is somebody that a panhandler has established an relationship with. It is someone who goes by the panhandling place regularly, says hello, and usually gives the panhandler something.

Later, Jerry and Suzi groused a bit about Tom (Jerry and Suzi called him Tommy, but he called himself Tom, so I called him Tom too). A woman had driven by and given Suzi a five dollar bill. Tom had been lying on his mattress and had seen it. He had asked if it was appropriate to share such tips. Jerry said that he had wanted to establish a policy.

Suzi said, "Policy, policy. The policy is that the bridge is ours! Come on now. People know me and they know Jerry and they come over. Like we have this Black gal that has a Cadillac and she's a good hit for ten dollars. And if she spots me, she'll either give it to him [Jerry] and she'll say, 'Share it,' you know. And if she gives it to me, she'll say, 'Share it.' And like that gal on Friday, that Oriental gal, she gave a dollar to him and a dollar to me and she said, 'Share it.'"

"Do you interpret that to mean to share with Tom too?" I asked.

"No, no, no! Tommy's on his own," Suzi said. "He don't bring nothin' in for us. We bring him food. EVERY DAY! I swear to God, I don't think there's a day that goes by, we don't bring him something to eat."

"There will be no chicken left when we get home, because he asked me, he said, 'Can I have a piece of chicken?' And I said, 'Yes, you can have A piece of chicken.'"

"He's starin' at that pot. He was sittin' on that chair starin' at that pot. You know that pot's gonna be empty when we get home," Suzi said.

"And what was in the pot? Is that where the chicken was?" I asked.

"Yeah. Half a chicken," Suzi said.

"But wouldn't it have gone off by the time you got home anyway?"

"Oh no. No, it'd still be good because it was warm when we found it," Jerry said.

"So fried chicken lasts pretty well, then, huh?"

"Oh, sure. It'll last a couple of days. Any other thing we find, if it's raw, or packaged, or out of a can, usually when we get home, if we want to save it, we immediately cook it. And if it's cooked, then it'll last."

Suzi said that the other day they'd found five pieces of Domino's Pizza which they'd brought home to Tom, who'd eaten it all in ten minutes. "He eats so fast, that's why he's so fat, because he eats too fast and he eats too much because he never lets his body tell him when he's full. That's his problem. That's why most people are fat. 'Cause they eat too fast and they don't let their body tell 'em, 'Hey, you've had enough.'"

The issue of sharing food is a major dilemma for the Bridge People. Tom said he didn't really want their food, that they forced it on him to some degree and so he accommodated them. He asserted that Jerry and Suzi brought him food they found on their canning route because they wanted to, not because he asked them to. On the other hand, Suzi and Jerry saw it as their duty to bring him food, because in their eyes, he would starve if they didn't. While it was a source of irritation to Suzi that Tom was fat, she kept providing him with food. Since he weighed in at about two seventy-five or so (he was six feet tall), there was only a slim chance that he'd starve any time soon.

Eventually, Jerry and Suzi finished their fifth of Thunderbird, and we had to get back to work. I didn't get a precise time, but I would estimate that we spent twenty to twenty-five minutes in the shade chatting and drinking. As we walked along, I asked Jerry about the surplus of mattresses at camp.

"Early in the morning this guy walked by and he looked up at us. Then he went back by again and he looked again and then the next thing I know, he shows up with this pickup truck. Him and two other guys. And he said, 'Can you guys use some mattresses?' And we said, 'Oh, well, yeah.' And they threw all them mattresses over the fence. And then he turned around and he reached in his wallet and handed me fifteen dollars and APOLOGIZED because it was only fifteen dollars. I said, 'That's PLENTY!' Good Lord a mercy! Here I got eight mattresses and fifteen dollars in one fell swoop? Good God! And it just so happened that we had a lousy day canning that day…and so it was a real windfall."

As we walked along, Jerry stopped occasionally to pick up snipes. As you might imagine, sometimes the snipes have been stepped on or run over. If that was the case and there was a cut or tear in the paper that prevented the cigarette from drawing properly, Jerry either crumbled it up and saved the tobacco or applied what he called a band-aid—a scrap of cigarette paper that he licked and applied over the wound.

I asked if he preferred smoking shorts to rolling his own.

"Well not necessarily, but, when there's free tobacco layin' on the ground, and we both smoke, so uh, sometimes we come up with an abundance of them, and then other days, you don't get quite enough. But uh, there's our tobacco…and we don't have to buy it. So the only thing we have to worry about is booze."

At one point on the route we came to a one story brick building with a chain link fence around a paved parking lot big enough for six cars or so. Unlike most of the commercial places in the area, it was very neat. Inside this fence there was also a dumpster. One day, Jerry told me, he had been investigating the dumpster and a guy came out and ran him off.

"All we want is cans. I don't give a SHIT what goddamned paper they throw out there. Matter of fact, there is no sign on this building, I don't even know what in the hell they do in there. But he, he got real nasty, 'Get OUTTA that dumpster!' And the only thing we were doin' was lookin' for cans. Matter of fact, let's go up there right now. With Jackson here, I'll work this fuckin' dumpster!"

Jerry marched off toward the dumpster like a drill instructor. It made me a little uneasy and I tagged along reluctantly. I didn't want to confront some angry businessman about his right to his garbage. When we looked into the disputed dumpster, we saw only a few hundred sheets of computer paper in the bottom and no cans. We had no reason to stay around and were able to leave as quickly as we had come. I was relieved about avoiding a confrontation and so were Jerry and Suzi.

"There's no reason for me to have gotten upset about it. I mean it IS private property. And so I just said to the guy, 'Have a nice day.' To myself, I said, 'Be an asshole if you want to be an asshole.' And he was TOTALLY one. And he had two rotunda women with him, too. And they were scowling at us like we were dirt underneath their fingernails."

"Yeah, a threat to Western Civilization, huh?"

"Yeah."

We came to an alley and turned into it. Behind a chain link fence there was a dog that looked like it was mostly golden retriever and a smaller, short-haired black dog of indeterminate ancestry. The dogs began barking and prancing on the concrete driveway behind the wire. Suzi and Jerry said, "Hi dogs! Hi you guys. How you guys doin'?" The dogs paced back and forth and grinned as Jerry and Suzi talked to them.

Jerry smiled at Suzi, "Well, what have we got for them today?"

"Hot dogs, remember?" She fished around in one of her plastic grocery bags and came up with a hot dog for each of the animals. She and Jerry had found the hot dogs on their route the day before and cooked them (so they wouldn't spoil) especially for the dogs. She leaned over as she gave the hot dogs to them and, reverting to a rhythmic baby-talk, she said, "Now, this one's for you...and this one's for you."

The dogs bolted the hot dogs in two or three bites and then sniffed and licked the concrete where the food had been. Jerry and Suzi said goodbye to the dogs, Suzi picked up her bags, and she and Jerry resumed walking up the alley. They tried to bring something for the dogs every time they passed by, they said.

I noticed that when Jerry met somebody in a parking lot, alley, or around a dumpster, he usually was cheery and friendly. He would say hello and wish them a good morning. He usually took the initiative in these encounters, and, of course, since he was usually very dirty and haggard, sometimes people would only scowl in return.

He said that when he was nineteen years old, he had had his teeth straightened. Just after he'd gotten the braces taken off of his teeth, the dentist discovered he had cancer in his jaw bone. They'd had to pull all of his teeth and much of his jaw was removed at that time as well. He'd had dentures in the past, but not for many years.

We took another break near an elementary school. We sat on a curb across from a fenced abandoned lot. They smoked their snipes and I smoked my pipe.

We sat there for perhaps fifteen minutes. This break is customarily shorter than others on their route because it is usually without refreshments.

I noted that they skipped some dumpsters that were right on the route so I asked how they knew which dumpsters to check.

"If you go by two or three times and you don't find nothin', and then it's not even worth it," Suzi said.

Eventually we got to the can man where Jerry and Suzi exchanged their cans for money. The can man parked his truck at the same place every day, so all the various canners knew where to find him. The truck was a van a little bigger than a UPS truck. It wasn't particularly shabby, but it wasn't new either. When we arrived, the driver wasn't there, so we found some shade across the street and sat on the curb and smoked. The driver showed up a few minutes after we arrived. He conducted business from the back of the truck. The whole back of the van opened by means of a steel door that rolled up into the roof. There were stacks of cans and pieces of scrap aluminum along the sides of the van and in the center, near the tailgate, swung a scale of the kind you used to see in the produce sections of supermarkets. The can man took the cans, put them on the scale, made some calculations to determine how much he owed Jerry and Suzi, then handed them some cash.

I borrowed Suzi's bag of miscellaneous collectibles and weighed it on the can man's scale. It weighed ten pounds. We began walking back toward their camp. They told me they have a little jingle that they said to themselves that guided their actions when they found something of possible value—"Eenie, meenie, minie, moe. Shall I take it or let it go." They said that what they brought back to camp was influenced by how heavy it was and by how far from camp they found it. They didn't mention it, but I knew Jerry and Suzi weren't really strong enough to carry much. Their walking pace during the morning's work was pretty slow, on the order of two miles per hour. A serious strider, by contrast, can do about four miles per hour on fairly flat terrain.

We had left camp at about nine o'clock that morning and we had turned in our cans at about one in the afternoon. We had taken perhaps an hour in rests along the way, so we had worked about three hours, not counting the time it would take them to get back to camp. We turned in six pounds and made four dollars and eighty cents. That worked out to be about eighty cents an hour each for Jerry and Suzi. This amount was fairly typical for a day of canning, but their income from canning could range from as little as three to as much as eight dollars, they said.

On our way back, the topic of firewood came up. I asked how far they had to go to get wood, and Suzi said, "Well, we have to go all the way up to, well, the Six O'clock Store [about a half mile]. And we gotta lug it all the way down there. He lugs skids [pallets]. I lug skids. One day he lugged a skid and put it right outside our gate. And the son of a bitches from across the street come across and took the skids." Then she nodded at Jerry, "And he had drug it all the way down. And he's disabled and he's luggin' wood and tryin' to walk with a cane and drag all that skid down. And he drags it to the opening, and he says, 'Suzi, I got a skid by the door [actually the hole in the fence].' And I said, 'Well, that's all right.' I said, 'Well, leave it there, we don't need it tonight. I said—"

"I drug two down," Jerry broke in, "you drug one up and you left the other one down by the fence."

Suzi continued. "I said, 'I'll bring it up tomorrow morning. But son of a gun, they come over, and, and, and then they turn around and brag about it! It was Wally that done it."

"Sheeesh!" Jerry said. "Now I don't want to say anything bad about anybody, 'cause I'm probably just as bad as they are, but...THOSE ASSHOLES! Ha, ha, ha, ha."

"Yeah," I said, "Ha, ha, ha."

All was not harmony under the bridges. After a moment, I asked Suzi how they got coffee.

"When we go cannin', there's a couple of dumpsters at the top of Ruggedy Hill," her name for a place on their route, "they have Columbia and Yuban coffee that they use, in the things."

"In the filter bags," Jerry said.

"So I usually find a cup or something, and I accumulate, you know, the old grounds, and then we put it in a sock and tie it up and we put 'em in a pot and fill it full of water and let it boil and...we got coffee. Because coffee, that one time it goes through—"

"Coffee is expensive," Jerry interjected, "it's five and six DOLLARS a can!"

"Wally was—The last time, he brought us that jar of instant coffee. And it was five dollars for just that little bottle about this high," Suzi said. She held her hands up in front of her. The imaginary jar that filled the opening between them was about five inches tall. "It was Yuban and it was, it was EXPENSIVE!"

"It was delicious, but uh, that would be one full day of canning! For one jar of coffee," Jerry said.

Actually, the Bridge People seldom drank coffee. It was simply too expensive, either in cash or in time and trouble. The conversation lagged and I had a chance to think about the situation with Wally and the coffee and the pallet. In it you could see the kinds of active exchanges that went on among the Bridge People. Like everywhere else I'd been, I found no unblemished saints and no unredeemable sinners under the bridges. Wally brought them instant coffee, a rare luxury, and he was a great guy. On the other hand, a short time later, he stole a pallet and then he was "an asshole." Such extreme swings were common here. I thought it had to do with the immediate relevance of these small villainies and charities. Under the bridges, if someone took your firewood, you couldn't cook. If someone took your bottle, you were dry. These little acts directly and significantly affected a person's comfort, quality of life, and standard of living. The Bridge People had frequent opportunities to do these relatively important good and bad things to each other because they lived in such propinquity. They had been brought up on the myth of the frontier and rugged individualism, but were living an urban, interdependent existence that required reciprocity and social skills. I thought they did a pretty good job most of the time, considering the very difficult living circumstances. But there were usually several simmering misunderstandings between people and these occasionally boiled over into arguments and even physical confrontations.

A little later, Suzi and Jerry talked about Big Joe and reciprocity. Jerry said, "He comes around and wants favors. 'Do you have a drink?' 'Do you have a cup of coffee?' 'Do you have a sandwich?'"

"'I didn't find anything to eat at Angelo's.'" Suzi took up Jerry's litany in a sing-song satire of Big Joe. "'Do you got anything to eat?' And I said, 'No, we don't have nothin' to eat.' I had bags of food, but I'll be damned if I'm gonna give it to him."

"And he doesn't reciprocate?" I asked

"No! Never! Never!" Jerry said.

"Bullshit! Bullshit! That's what we get from Big Joe!" Suzi said. "I found 'im dungarees. I found 'im shirts. I find 'im pants. I found 'im sneakers. ALL those guys over there. We find 'em sneakers, shoes, pants, everything else. And they never, never reciprocate."

"Well, there was that piece of rotten roast beef. It was rotten when we got it. That's why I didn't bother with it. It was rotten when we got it. And when I can smell it—It smells raunchy, naw, I ain't gonna deal with that shit," Suzi said.

"So you sniff it pretty well to make sure it's okay?"

"Oh yeah. Definitely! You have to," Jerry said.

"When you find a piece of meat," Suzi said, "all I gotta do, if I'm wondering about it, all I gotta do is give a piece of it to the cat. If the cat go like this," she gestured, "tryin' to cover it up, then you KNOW!"

"That's a clue, huh?" I chuckled.

"That's definitely a no-no," she said. "Don't even bother with it. I just throw it down the hill for the rats. Let the rats eat it. I hope it kills them. Hee, hee, hee, hee, hee."

On the way back to camp we stopped again at the Six O'clock Store, where Jerry and Suzi bought two fifths of Thunderbird with the proceeds of their day's labor.

When we got back to camp, Tom was there in a somewhat agitated state. He said that two cars of police (six officers) had come by and told him that Caltrans was coming by later to clean out the camp. We all speculated about whether or not it would happen. I remarked that their camp wasn't likely to be a high priority with Caltrans, since they didn't seem to be able to pick up even the piles of trashbags at the foot of the hill. The bags had been there for a month, I thought, but Tom corrected me, saying that it had been four or five months. Caltrans had come by a couple of weeks before, but had picked only up half of them. There had been enough room in the truck for all of the bags, he said, and he couldn't figure out why they had taken only half of them.

Tom hadn't known any of the policemen. Officer Fisher had not been among them. Tom said he wasn't sure if the Officer's name was Fish, Fisher, or Fishe.

"Oh," I said, "maybe it's Fish-ah, rhymes with militia."

"Yeah," Jerry said. "No, really it rhymes with three days in jail."

We all chuckled. They said that if they were forced to abandon the bridges, they would go somewhere else for a few days and then come back and start over. Tom recounted what the police had said. "They just came in and said, 'You're all evicted. Caltrans is coming with a truck, and what you take is yours and what you leave behind is going to be loaded up on the truck.'" Tom and Jerry said that the times that Caltrans had shown up, they had just come by themselves. Police officers had never preceded them.

"If they come, they come," Jerry said fatalistically. For very poor and power-less people like Tom and Jerry, it was too painful to give a damn about much of anything, including themselves. Life was more bearable for them if they just didn't care, because to care invited disappointment, defeat, and failure, and their lives were brim full of that. To care required emotional investment and energy and they had none left after bare survival was assured for another day. By not caring they maintained distance from their miserable existence. Apathy was the most effective painkiller readily available to the poorest of the poor, even cheaper and more effective than wine. It's often seen among people in highly stressful, powerless positions.

We sat around chatting for a couple of hours while Jerry and Suzi sipped their Thunderbird. Jerry spent most of the time sitting on his bed. Suzi sat on the brown vinyl couch that served as her bed. I sat on the nearby armless easy chair that I often used when I visited the camp.

Tom joined us for part of the time, but most of the time he spent on his bed reading paperback novels. He read constantly. His main interest in life, he said, was reading and smoking cigarettes. Some books he got from the Goodwill, a second hand store. He also traded with the fellows across the street for some. Occasionally Jerry and Suzi found books and brought them home to him as well.

By about three that afternoon Jerry and Suzi were quite intoxicated and nodding. Their speech and thinking were both significantly slurred. I decided to take a turn up and down Market to see my other street friends.

15. A night under the bridges

I was back in Angelo's parking lot by about eight thirty that evening. It was dark by that time. It gets dark a bit earlier under the bridge, and of course, except for the long, slanting rays of the sunrise and sunset, it was always in deep shade there. When I trudged up the hill, I found Suzi and Jerry were asleep. Tom was awake and told me that they had fought with each other most of the evening, but had passed out fairly early, about six he thought. He said that Jerry had hit Suzi in the head with a pair of vice grips during their drunken argument.

As I've already mentioned, I had come to the bridges this time with the intention of spending a few nights there. Earlier that day, I had asked Jerry if I should sleep on the spare mattress next to Tom, and he'd said sure. I thought that mattress would be best, because it was already laid out. There were other spare mattresses, but they were in a stack. Also, a week or two ago, I had noticed that that was where a guy who was just passing through had slept, so it was where a "normal" visitor would sleep.

Tom and I sat on our mattresses. Since I normally have a sip of sherry in the evening, I had brought a bottle of cheap, dry sherry with me from home. It is a little less potent than Thunderbird, seventeen per cent alcohol compared to eighteen per cent. I asked Tom if he wanted some. "Just a little," he said. He searched in the trash around his mattress and found his large plastic coffee cup and held it out. Beginning to catch on to the code, I filled it about three-quarters full. That's a lot of sherry. We sat and smoked and sipped. I drank directly out of the bottle. He finished his cup before I had had more than a couple of nips. I refilled it. I certainly didn't want to drink half a bottle of sherry by myself, so I didn't mind that he was drinking much faster than I. A few moments later it occurred to me that even though Tom had a reputation as one of the lighter drinkers among the Bridge People, he could still really put it away. And he didn't even particularly like sherry.

It was peaceful there talking quietly to Tom, despite the constant rumble of freeway traffic just a couple of yards above. It eventually faded into the background like distant surf or the roar of rapids.

Under the bridge, opening a bottle presupposed finishing it almost immediately. With Tom's able assistance, we did just that. By the time we had finished the bottle it was late. Tom eased back on his mattress to go to sleep and I set about making my bed.

I chuckled to myself as I reflected that since I had been an Eagle Scout and was an avid backpacker, I was eminently prepared for homelessness. I'm sure that's not quite what the Boy Scouts of America had in mind when they urged us squeaky clean kids to "be prepared."

I had decided against bringing a sleeping bag. I owned a couple, but they were down bags that I used for backcountry ski camping and much too warm for L.A. Jerry had said that he had extra blankets, but I must admit I was a little leery of lice. Instead, I had brought an ancient, patched down parka for my upper body and a pair of side-zip windpants for my lower. In the blue-green spill light from the freeways, the mattress glistened with grime. I was reluctant to lay my head on it, so I spread my field jacket over the part of the mattress where my head would be, careful to get the pockets well off to the sides. They were full of things that wouldn't be improved by my sleeping on them. I zipped on the windpants, put on the parka, and headed off to the bushes just to the north of my mattress to use the latrine one last time before retiring.

I thought about the fact that this was my first night sleeping out with homeless people. The light from the freeway above filtered down through the trees at the edge of the bridge. The color reminded me of being under water. It was like being in a kelp forest instead of in a eucalyptus grove on the edge of a freeway. The rumble of the freeway was like the roar of bubbles from a scuba regulator. There was a calm, eerie beauty to this bucolic scene in the heart of the bustling megalopolis. I walked back to the mattress, sat down, and took a big drink of water from my canteen to help ward off a hangover. It must have been about nine thirty, very late by bridge standards, when I nodded off.

I was awakened at about one A.M. and looked down slope to the street. I saw a California Highway Patrol car and a tow truck near a Mustang that had been abandoned on the street just below our camp. The red and blue lights on the highway patrol car were blinking nervously. A loud, garbled voice occasionally hissed and crackled over the police radio. The yellow beacon lights on the tow truck twirled around the top of the cab. I had been awakened by the tow truck operator as he banged around trying to hook up with the Mustang. After a few moments, the highway patrol officer slammed his car door and left. A few minutes later, the tow truck driver eased the front of the Mustang into the air. He got back in the cab of the truck, slammed the door one last time, and roared away in low gear with the Mustang dutifully tagging along behind.

Sleep patterns under the bridges were not like sleeping in a house. There were freeways above and Cardenas Street below, so a few times during the night an extra loud vehicle rumbled or rattled along to wake us up. Sometimes when they were awakened, the Bridge People sat up and began smoking cigarettes and chatting quietly. Jerry and Suzi hunted around to see if there was a bottle left with anything in it. If there were, they would have a couple of big pulls from the bottle. (Since they often passed out in the evening, they seldom had a clear idea of their current inventory and were sometimes astonished at how much or how little wine there was.) After a couple of minutes, people finished their cigarettes and nodded off to sleep again.

16. A morning under the bridges

I slept well in spite of the disturbances and awoke at about first light. I looked around at the awakening campers. Out came the cigarettes. Then Jerry and Suzi looked for wine left over from the previous night and made "breakfast" of it. I anticipated a morning cup of coffee with an addict's relish. (I had made them a gift of a jar of instant coffee, more because I didn't want to do without coffee than for altruistic reasons. From experience, I knew that if I went a morning without my dose of caffeine, I would have a nagging headache by afternoon. Coffee, or at least the caffeine in it, is definitely an addicting drug, though most of us who drink coffee wouldn't want to admit it.)

Tom got up and walked over to the hearth. He crumpled up some newspaper and pieces of cardboard and lit a fire. At this camp, they used a piece of heavy steel pipe for breaking up the pallets for firewood. Pieces of wood too big to break, typically four by fours or four by sixes, were burned by gradually feeding one end into the fire. As the end was burned up, the board was scooted a little further into the fire to expose a fresh part to the flames. This seemed like a very convenient method, but it did have the disadvantage of leaving big butt ends sticking out of the fire to trip over.

Jerry got out of his bed long enough to fill a beaten up, fire blackened pot with water and put it on the young fire. Then he resumed his position on his bed. As I've said, water was hauled up the hill in five-gallon plastic jugs that the Bridge People get from Angelo's dumpster. They drew their water from a couple of hose bibs on the outside of Angelo's building. Jerry and Suzi had a pair of vice-grips that they used to turn the water on and off. Suzi also had an aluminum handle that fit one of the hose bibs. They had found both of these tools while canning.

From his bed, Jerry directed me to a dish drainer full of dishes and flatware which sat on one of the numerous milk crates that constituted general purpose furniture under the bridges. I looked in the dish drainer for a cup and recoiled for a moment. Everything in it had a rather rich patina of grime. I thought, "Oh, what the hell," and grabbed the cleanest filthy cup and a spoon. Jerry got up and poured me some hot water and I spooned coffee into the cup. He offered me sugar and cream from their large collection of packets in a dirty brown paper bag. The bag had been handled so much that it had taken on the appearance and feel of dark brown felt. I drink my coffee black, so I didn't take any of the offered condiments.

Tom got up and joined us, and soon Big Joe lumbered over from across the street. All five of us sat around drinking instant coffee and smoking. Breakfast usually consisted of wine and cigarettes but since I had brought instant coffee, a rare and memorable luxury for the Bridge People, everybody indulged in it.

At times throughout the morning, various people got up and went off into the bushes for a few minutes to relieve themselves. I did likewise, but once, instead of going to the bathroom, I secretly ate a couple of granola bars that I had brought with me. Since I'm a runner, I find that I need some carbohydrates rather frequently. Also, if I don't have something to eat first thing in the morning, I tend to get an upset stomach from the black coffee. I would have felt awkward eating in front of my fellow campers, since I didn't have enough to go around. They often ate and drank in front of one another without sharing, one of the exigencies of life here, but I didn't feel right about doing it. Of course, as an anthropologist, I also wanted to minimize the impact of my presence on their ordinary routines in order to find out what "typical" days and nights were like.

I also used these trips to the bushes to brush my teeth and clean myself up a little using some "towelettes" (the small, moist paper towels in foil envelopes given away at fast food places like Kentucky Fried Chicken and El Pollo Loco). There is also a minor tradition in cultural anthropology and sociology of taking fieldnotes in the bathroom when you don't feel good about taking them in front of the people you're with. I fell right in with this tradition and taped notes to myself about people's appearance, my cynical and theoretical asides, and so on, things that would have been awkward and disruptive to do in front of the campers.

Food was a problem that I hadn't thought much about before. When my research had just consisted of day trips to visit with various homeless people, I could always eat before or after going to see them. Also, I was working downtown amid many cheap cafes and fast food places and I would often take homeless acquaintances to lunch so we could talk in relative privacy and comfort. While that kind of food is hazardous to your health in the long term because of the salt and fat, it is at least prepared under fairly sanitary conditions and probably won't give you dysentery or salmonella poisoning. Among the Bridge People, however, I knew that I had to be very careful about what I ate or I'd end up having to ask Jerry to give ME a motorcycle ride to the hospital. I have a fairly delicate digestive system and in the last couple of years had gotten food poisoning from some *dim sum* in Chinatown and from some *churros* from a Mexican place on Market Street.

Most of the Bridge People get a fair amount of their calories from alcohol, of course, but though I often had a few beers or some sherry with them in the evening, I could hardly use alcohol for a major source of my calories and remain conscious enough to do my work.

Eventually, I returned to the hearth area and the discussion turned slowly to the fine points of panhandling.

"You never ask for an amount when you panhandle," Jerry said. "You ask for spare change. Because, if you ask for a quarter, and they don't have a quarter, then you don't get anything."

"It wouldn't occur to them to give you maybe the nickel or the dime or whatever," Tom said.

"It's liable to turn out that you would get more than the quarter. They'll reach in their pocket and look for a quarter and not find one and put all the change back in. Uh, uh, there's liable to be uh, fifty or seventy-five cents worth of change there that you don't get," Jerry said.

The conversation meandered, as casual conversation will, and eventually came around to the topic of violence and danger on Skid Row.

"It PAYS to carry something down there," Big Joe said. "Ah won't even go down there unless Ah got a knife on me. Ah'm gonna tell ya the truth. Big as Ah am, Ah will NOT go down there unless Ah got me a knife."

"At LEAST a knife," Jerry said.

"Yeah. Listen, they got Gomez and Sanchez down there one day. Sanchez went out and bought one of those imitation Buck knives, but he took it down to a knife sharpener place and he had them really sharpen it up. And he always carried it open, in his pocket. And he would NOT hesitate to use it. He got jumped once, and that was it," Tom said.

"Yeah, I think a lot of people on the street carry knives," I said.

"Yeah. A lot of people carry screwdrivers," Tom said.

"Yeah, a lot of people carry screwdrivers," I agreed. I had seen several people on Skid Row carry them. They sharpened the tips. Police didn't usually confiscate screwdrivers, since they were ostensibly a tool not a weapon, but I'm sure they knew why they were carried by street people, who, after all, had no screws to drive. I had also seen people carry pieces of pipe, heavy chain, and big wrenches. Of course, if it came to hand to hand combat, as it occasionally did on the street, almost anything could be used as a weapon. Skid Row at night was an unbelievably violent place and, from my experience, the police seemed primarily interested in keeping the violence contained there and in calling the paramedics to haul away the bodies.

The campers kept drinking and telling war stories about violence on the street, but I didn't collect any more of them. They had an endless supply and the situation on the street continually generated new ones. While we were sitting there, we heard what sounded to me like small caliber pistol shots. That lent an air of authenticity to the stories. The campers said again that it was fairly common to hear someone touch off a few rounds. I, too, had heard shots frequently at night during other research expeditions down on Skid Row.

17. Jerry and Suzi go panning

At about six thirty in the morning, Suzi was dispatched to the Six O'Clock Store to purchase a bottle of wine. By seven thirty, she and Jerry were fairly well impaired. The sun came out and it looked like a beautiful day was in the offing. We finally got started canning at about eight o'clock. I had thought we weren't going to leave for work at all, considering their condition. Jerry checked Angelo's dumpster, while Suzi and I went to one of the hose bibs to fill our canteens. Suzi carried a plastic bottle that had once contained a fashionable mineral water. I had a plastic Army surplus canteen. I took the opportunity to splash water on my face and hands and clean up a little while water was available. I was a little surprised that Suzi didn't wash up a little too. It didn't even seem to occur to her. She just stood there watching me like I was a bird in a fountain. This was a rather busy corner near the Civic Center with many bureaucrats and business people walking past. I was surprised that I didn't find it at all embarrassing to take a little bath in this busy, public setting, but I didn't.

We rejoined Jerry and, as we walked along, he talked about Luke Broder. Luke had said that he made twenty or twenty-five dollars every day, but he'd never pitched in to buy food or wine. "Well, that was like Big Joe over here. He said he never ever made less than...it was eighteen dollars a day. I could clock it. Eighteen dollars a day. Well, now hold it. Anybody that makes eighteen dollars a day, EVERY day, panhandling, I just can't buy it. It sounds a little bit fishy to me."

"Yeah. He doesn't reciprocate much either, does he?"

Jerry and Suzi just began to giggle and look at each other.

"That's a little joke, huh?" I asked, feeling a little left out. "So he doesn't share tobacco with you guys, or food or anything?"

"We might be lucky if he gives us a cigarette," Suzi said.

"We might be able to go over and get some rolling papers from him, something like that. He might have that."

Later I thought that this was a good example of the difference between what people say and what they do. One of my pet peeves concerning social science is its overemphasis on information obtained using questionnaires and interviews. In this case, had I been content with an interview I would have gone away with the notion that Luke and Big Joe made eighteen or twenty dollars a day, but by "hanging out" with Jerry and Suzi, doing what we anthropologists call participant observation, I had learned that things were a good deal more complex than they had first appeared. The best thing would have been to go panhandle with Luke and Joe on several occasions as I had with Tom, Jerry, and several others.

While Jerry and I were crossing the street, with the light, in a crosswalk, a guy in a van pushed the light and careened through a left turn just missing Jerry. "Get outta the street, you fucking WINO!" I was a few yards behind Jerry, taping some notes to myself. Jerry yelled something back at him like, "Oh, go to hell, ASSHOLE!" The driver yelled something else at Jerry that was completely unintelligible to me, and Jerry yelled back, "Yeah, sure come on back here! I'll take care of ya!"

"To call somebody names," Jerry said a moment later when I rejoined him, "that's ridiculous. I'm not hurtin' a soul. And all of a sudden, they yell 'fuck' at me. I don't appreciate that at all. That is one word that is not in my vocabulary. I don't use that word. To me that is the most derogatory word. They can say shit, they can say anything else, bitch, bastard. At least they mean something. Fuck is a non-word."

I found this soliloquy on foul language more than a little hard to swallow. Jerry himself used only moderate amounts of profanity, but he was certainly around massive doses of it day in and day out, and I had certainly heard him use the "F word" on many occasions. It made me feel a bit sad that he would try to feed me such nonsense, but I didn't say anything about it. He was quite upset, and I tried to calm him down a bit.

Poor, powerless people constantly try to shrug off all the bad things that happen to them, and I suppose in a way it's a good adaptive strategy, but the frustration and anger just builds up unnoticed in their souls and from time to time they run out of shrugs and something finally touches them off. When that happens at the same time to a whole lot of people, you have events like the storming of the Bastille, the Boston Tea Party, or the recent Los Angeles uprising.

We found a few hot dogs in a dumpster early in the canning route that morning. And four or five pounds of perfectly serviceable sweet potatoes. Suzi took a couple of pounds of them for dinner and left the rest. She and Jerry arrayed the rest of the useable food on the top of the dumpster so that others could easily find it. They said they typically do this if they find more food than they can carry or use. Of course, I didn't know it that was true or not, but I'd like to think it was.

We found an electric waffle iron and Jerry salvaged the teflon-coated cast iron plates for use back at camp. I asked how they would be used and he said that he would use the griddle sides for warming up food. The plates could be placed directly in the flame. The one he had now used to have a plastic handle, but it had long since melted off.

"One time," Jerry said, "Suzi and I got up and we were both about half drunk, hee, hee, hee. And we started coffee. And we had a fire going, I mean, we had a FIRE fire. And all of a sudden, I turned around and looked at the coffee pot and the handle was on fire. And I told Suzi, 'Suzi! The handle's on fire!' And she jumped up and went over and she went to pick up the pot with the handle and the handle come right off! Ha, ha, ha, ha! She just threw it back in the fire. That was it. Oh shit," Jerry sighed, "you know."

Jerry and Suzi said that they keep their eyes open for pots and pans that have metal handles, because they can be used over an open fire. They had found such a pot the day before.

We found a sixteen penny nail which could be used to improve Suzi's canning stick. Jerry saved it. The nail was a bit too big, but, as Jerry said with a grin, "Beggars can't be choosers." The end of her stick had shattered, but Jerry said that we might find some tape to repair the stick and then attach the nail.

"I got some tape at home," Suzi said. "I don't have no more electrical tape and don't have no more silver. Electrical tape would work real well."

"Luke used up the silver tape. He used silver tape for EVERYTHING," Jerry said in exasperation.

"He taped up his bag. There was a rip in it and he taped up his bag with it. He taped up his sleepin' bag. He used all of it. And that silver tape's not cheap," Suzi said.

"Did you guys find it in a dumpster?"

"Yeah, I found it and then—I know a full roll is worth about eight or nine dollars. It's expensive stuff. But it's good stuff. Well, he taped up his sleeping bag with it."

As we walked along and I watched Jerry and Suzi work, I thought about the vocation they call dumpster diving. Of course, it was a dirty occupation. As if digging around in garbage and filth weren't enough, most beverage cans had a small amount of liquid left in them, so frequently, when Jerry smashed them with his heel, sour beer or syrupy soft drink squirted out and splashed on his clothing— or on Suzi's or mine if we were within a couple of yards or so. The liquid sometimes dripped all over Jerry and Suzi's hands as they handled the cans, both before and after smashing. The sticky liquid attracted dirt, of course, and soon they were really coated with grime.

As we walked along, we encountered a Hispanic woman and her little girl. Both were rather fat, their clothes shabby, their personal hygiene poor. Suzi and Jerry knew them and said that they lived nearby. On one of her wrists Suzi was wearing a number of the bangles that she found occasionally in the dumpsters. When she asked the little girl if she wanted one, the little girl's face lit up in anticipation. Suzi struggled to untangle one of the bangles from the others. After a few seconds of fumbling that must have seemed like hours to the little girl, Suzi smiled, leaned over, and gave her the bangle. The woman smiled warmly and the little girl beamed. "¡Muchas gracias! Thank you! Thank you very much!" Suzi and Jerry smiled back and said "You're very welcome," almost in unison. We continued on the canning route, and the woman and her child walked in the opposite direction.

"It's amazing how just a little thing like that will brighten up things for somebody," Jerry said. "Like the bracelet and the little girl. That made her day. It'll make her day for a month. And it didn't cost us one penny, we found it in the trash. But the mere act of giving...I love to give. Of course, we don't have much, but whatever...."

When we got near the Six O'clock Store on State Street, they found a cold beer in a bag on the sidewalk. Then they went inside to buy a short dog. The store was in an Hispanic neighborhood, and I often saw unemployed men hanging around the streets in this area drinking from bottles and cans thinly disguised in tiny brown paper bags. Many of these bags and other packages littered the sidewalks and gutters. In these heavily littered areas, Jerry and Suzi would sometimes spread out, one on the sidewalk, one in the gutter, in order to give each discarded bag or package a thwack or poke with their canning sticks.

When we got to the construction site, we sat again on the concrete block wall that forms the edge of a flowerbed. It was about ten o'clock. We sat and smoked and chatted. Jerry was discouraged about the way the canning was going, and he and Suzi discussed the pros and cons of continuing. Jerry finally decided that it was fruitless and that they ought to go panning down at the Civic Center instead.

Jerry said that you can often feel who is going to give you money. Suzi described it as "vibes." I wanted to know who gave money to panhandlers, so I asked Jerry if he could describe the characteristics of a good panhandling patron.

"No, no, no," he said. "There is no description to it. It's an impossibility. Because you never know. When I was going down to the State House, I've had State Police give me money. And then, of course, I've had other State Police come and run me off. But you never, ever know. You never know."

He went on to tell me about how Dirty Mack had taken care of both him and Suzi when they were sick with dysentery. Mack had come over every morning and brought them scrambled eggs or ravioli or grilled cheese sandwiches. All prepared with butter and lots of salt.

"Salt?" Jerry said. "I could open up a mine. But bless his heart, he'd bring us a pack of cigarettes, and he'd give us a jug. Always a jug and always some cigarettes. And he'd ask, 'Suzi? Jerry? Are you okay?' And we were so sick, throwin' up and shittin'. That was the time when I was so sick I couldn't even get out of bed."

Eventually we began walking very slowly east on State Street toward the Civic Center where Jerry was going to panhandle. Jerry panned as we went along, as kind of a warm up he said. Suzi was ahead of us by several yards most of the time. Jerry had traded his white visor for Suzi's navy and white trucker's cap, because he preferred to use a cap when panning. Suzi, as a rule, did not pan. When a prospective patron approached, Jerry held the cap in front of him and bowed slightly. "Excuse me sir, do you have some change you can spare? Hi, how are you doin' today? Could you spare some change today?"

On our way, we came to a recessed doorway that was fenced off at the street with metal grating. The holes in the metal were about three-quarters of an inch in diameter. Behind the grating was an aluminum can that we had passed the day before. It had been tempting Jerry for several days, he said. He had tried to fish it out with his stick, but the stick wouldn't fit through the holes in the grating. There was a gap at the bottom of the grating, so today, without hesitation, Jerry laid face down on the sidewalk and fished around under the grate with his stick. There were several large deposits of pigeon feces on that particular portion of sidewalk, which would have made me hesitate. Jerry extended his arm under the grating, adding its length to the length of the canning stick. After a full minute of angling, lying face down in the filth, he was finally able to get the nail into the opening in the top of the beer can and pull it toward him. As he got it near his body, it tipped and fetid beer flowed down his arm. A small puddle of beer and pigeon feces formed around his chest as he lay on the sidewalk still fishing for the can. He did succeed in getting it after about two minutes work and some detriment to his personal hygiene and appearance. This, for a can worth about three cents.

"I got it!" Jerry said with the proud grin of a successful fisherman. "It was one of them cans that just sits there and stares you in the face," he scowled. "It's been mockin' me for days. There's another one like that down the street JUST out of my reach."

It was a difficult for me not to chuckle at this scene. "So you'd be better off if the stick was another foot longer, huh?" I said trying to keep a straight face.

"Well, yeah. But then they'd just throw the cans another foot further. The whole thing of it is, I don't know how to explain it. You know, you went out with us yesterday. Goin' after cans, is goin' after CANS. I don't know. That one can that I dug for, laid in the pigeon shit and everything else for, that might be the one that tips the scales over to the next dollar."

It's Suzi's and Jerry's belief that people throw cans into fenced areas, and away from the fence, just to make them hard to get. But Jerry's overriding response to this, as to most everything, was a sardonic fatalism.

By ten forty we had made it back to State Street and Cardenas, where Angelo's is. Jerry pointed out that we had been up since five thirty and that it had already been a long day. They usually finished canning in the early afternoon, between one and three. If they had had a good day, it took longer.

It was rather surprising to me that Jerry had such a good command of the time, since he had no watch or clock and was almost never inside a building where there were clocks. Part of the answer, I thought, was that from his camp under the bridge, one could plainly hear the chimes of the Music Center. It was my impression that these only peal during business hours, however, so how he knew that it began to get light at five thirty was quite a mystery to me—until I remembered that Suzi had been given a watch by a woman she had met in the Angelo's parking lot.

Jerry talked again about being a witness for the prosecution in the trial for the murder that had taken place under the bridge about a year before. The incident still bothered Jerry. He told me about another murder that he had witnessed a couple of years earlier. He and Tex, his panhandling partner at the time, had been across from the *Los Angeles Times* building in State Park, a respectable area in the heart of the Civic Center area. They had seen a young woman come running around the corner, shrieking and crying for all she was worth. There were two men chasing her. They caught up with her right in front of the *Times* building and one of them clubbed her in the head with a length of steel reinforcing bar. Jerry started to run across the street to help her, but Tex grabbed him and said, "No! No, don't do that or you'll get yourself killed!" The woman collapsed to the sidewalk and the two men jumped on her and began stabbing her. Horrified and helpless just across the street, Jerry and Tex watched as the men stabbed her, and stabbed her, and stabbed her. After about a minute, they ran off and Tex and Jerry went over to see if there was anything they could do. The young woman was crumpled up in a big pool of blood. She was quite dead.

"You just can't do anything," Jerry said. "You just can't. 'Cause you'll get killed. I don't feel good about it, but that's the way it is."

"Yeah," Suzi said. "You really can't interfere or you'll be dead yourself."

We continued toward the State Building. As we passed near the Hall of Administration, a big Black parking attendant hailed Jerry and told him that he had something for him. He went behind his kiosk and brought out an armful of clothing. Jerry thanked him graciously and handed the clothing to Suzi. Suzi said to me, "I feel like a goddamned truck!" In addition to the clothes, she was carrying two bags containing all of the cans they had collected and her walking stick. When we got out of hearing range of Jerry's benefactor, Jerry said again that people were always giving them clothes, but not the kind that they needed.

"You don't really need clothes, huh?" I asked.

"Yeah, well, we need work clothes and very dark colors."

"Black, blue, green, brown," Suzi said.

"Look at this. What am I gonna do with a white shirt?" Jerry asked.

He said that he liked long sleeves because of the tracks (scars from injecting drugs) on his arms. I was surprised that that would be an important consideration. He showed me his arm and the veins were indeed ugly streaks of scar tissue. He had told me on several occasions that years ago he had been a heavy user of methamphetamines and had injected them several times per day, but because the story had lacked internal consistency, I hadn't altogether believed him. After looking closely at his arm, I did.

Jerry kept a couple of dark shirts and left the rest of the clothes on a bench in the plaza between the Hall of Administration and the Courthouse. He said that he was sure somebody would come by and pick up the rest. We walked slowly over to a bench right in the middle of the square and sat down. It was about eleven o'clock.

"We live strictly day to day," Jerry said. "Heaven help us if I ever make enough money to live two days. Because then we are on a downhill drunk for two days. That was like the last time I went to court, and I got the money. Or the last time I went panhandling and made the thirteen dollars, I said to Suzi, I said, 'We're gonna get FIVE jugs.' And then we walked all the way up to the Six O'clock Store, and they were out of fifths, so we had to buy ten short dogs. Hee, hee, hee. So we politely sat there and polished them off for two days. For two days we were drunk, and then we still had three dollars left over."

Jerry talked about the problems of panhandling. "The cops come and they type my name up on their little computer that they have in the car, and bingo, three or four warrants. Jaywalking, blocking the sidewalk, publicly drunk, begging… Oh, hold it, I've got five. Oh, well, I just take the tickets home and I start the wood with them. What am I GONNA DO? Here I am. I'm destitute to begin with, and I can pay a fifty-eight dollar ticket? BULLSHIT!"

"Which ticket is fifty-eight dollars?"

"Jaywalking is fifty-eight dollars. Public begging is a hundred dollars. Well, the last time I was in court, I told the judge, I said, 'I have to go out and beg for five days to pay this ticket!' And the judge just looked at me and said, 'Oh, case dismissed.' I said, 'I live underneath a bridge, where am I gonna get a hundred dollars?'"

Jerry said that he had to go back to court for the murder trial on June 20th. He said that he doesn't mind going to court, since he got an eighteen dollar witness fee, but the problem was that if he didn't have anything to smoke, he went out into the hall and picked up butts out of the ashtrays and people looked at him. "They look at me STRANGE, like I've got scales and a horn growin' out of my forehead. But," he said brightly, "that's the only bad part. I try, basically, to keep clean, but," he chuckled, "the last time I went to trial, I had on white corduroy pants and I picked up the coffee pot off the fire and I had all that charcoal on my hands, and I wiped my hands on my pants and it was, it was just black. It was ridiculous."

He and Suzi had found a pair of black pants with a bunch of zippers on them that he intended to wear to court the next time, but he laughed about looking like Michael Jackson.

There were a couple of electronic bank tellers across the plaza from us. We commented on all the people going to get money, and I was suprised to discover that Jerry didn't know that the machines dispensed only twenty dollar bills, but as he pointed out, "Well, how would I know?" It's easy to talk about empathy and trying to understand what other people go through, but it's quite difficult to do. In a different culture or subculture, lives can be so different in so many details that we take for granted in our own daily grind.

At about eleven thirty, Jerry and Suzi headed toward the State Building to panhandle. I decided to see if I could meet an attorney friend of mine, Gary, who was in court. We had made a tentative lunch date. I was feeling fairly dirty and stale by this time, so when I went into the Courthouse, I put on my UCLA Medical Center badge. All kinds of people, including jurors, wear plastic badges there and I thought it might help keep me from being hassled or thrown out. I did find Gary. He was suited up in his grey pinstripes; I was in my dirty olive-drab field jacket. I felt funny since we were each in our career costumes and they were so different.

We strode across the plaza, through the underground garage, and hopped into his immaculate BMW. We drove to his office to pick up some papers and then had lunch in a health food deli in a fashionable area west of downtown. The contrast between the life of affluent attorneys and the life of the Bridge People was stark, of course. Though they both frequented the Civic Center, they occupied very different orbits. I felt like a space traveler with rocket lag when I got back to the plaza area. I learned later that Gary had won a $600,000 judgment the next day.

It was about one fifteen when I got back to the plaza. I decided to go over to the Grand Central Market to buy some cigarettes to give to my street friends and to see if I could run into anybody I knew on Market Street.

When I got back to Jerry's camp, around a quarter of three, Jerry, Suzi, and Tom were there. Jerry and Suzi sat in their usual places chatting. Tom was lounging on his mattress reading a paperback book. Jerry and Suzi had made seven dollars and change panning. They had left Jerry's old office around two, perhaps a little earlier. That meant that they had earned seven dollars in about two and a half hours or about a dollar forty a person per hour.

Suzi said that a State Police Officer had come up to them and said, "Mr. Michaels, would you politely move your body." It was prime panning time, and Jerry was making what he called good hits on many of his old regulars. At lunch hour, he got what he called "comebacks." These were people who passed him on the way to lunch and said, "I'll take care of you when I come back." On the way back to their offices, they often took care of Jerry very well with both food and funds.

I asked Tom about his day and he said that he had gone to the kitchen of a nearby broadcasting school for lunch. It was less than a quarter mile away. The head cook, he said, got very upset if he saw somebody going through the dumpster, so he had told street people to come around to the kitchen door after lunch hour and he'd find them something to eat. Tom said that not many street people knew about this, but that he ate there a lot. I had the feeling that he did not exactly spread the word and that was understandable. He didn't want to spoil it for himself. Several other Bridge People did know about it, however.

As the afternoon wore on, Jerry and Suzi began slurring their words rather badly and were in imminent danger of passing out. Suzi had been sent to the Six

O'Clock Store upon their return to camp, where she had bought three fifths of Thunderbird, but no tobacco. Jerry and Suzi knew they could freely bum cigarettes from me and they had gotten a good supply of snipes in their day's travels.

Jerry and Suzi began yelling at each other. They were so drunk that the fighting was almost comical. It was playing at full volume, but in staggering, slurring, slow motion.

I retreated to the adjacent bridge for a few minutes to have a granola bar and get some peace and quiet. This site seemed preferable to the one Jerry and friends occupied, even though it received more freeway noise. It was high above Cardenas Street, well above the other bridges, and more enclosed by vegetation. The ledge near the abutment was much narrower, however, and you would have had to arrange your bed parallel to the abutment instead of perpendicular to it like at Jerry's. It would accommodate only a couple of campers, whereas Jerry's site could handle eight or more. The approach to the upper campsite was quite steep and that probably accounted for its lack of popularity among the Bridge People. It would be a bit difficult to negotiate while tipsy. No one was currently living there.

After a few minutes to myself, I went back to the bridge and lay down on my mattress. Jerry started a fire, but in his drunkenness he forgot why and passed out. When someone first lit a fire, there was a lot of smoke. As it rose under the bridge, it piled up in the low overhead and billowed along in soft fluffy puffs, like small cumulus clouds, but faster. It reminded me of the time-lapse pictures of clouds you sometimes see on TV weather reports. I lay on my mattress, daydreaming and watching the smoke for a while. At about a quarter after four, a busboy from Angelo's came to the hole in the fence with a tray of food in his hand. He yelled, "Hey! Hey!" Jerry and Suzi were too drunk to be aroused from their stupor, but Tom snapped upright in his bed, slipped on his delapidated shoes, and hustled down the hill to the camp entrance to receive the food. The busboy gave him a steam table tray, about a foot wide, eighteen inches long, and four inches deep, completely full of Mexican food—enchiladas, black beans, ground beef, *salsa fresca*, and rice. He also gave him two glass bowls, about seven inches across, one full of guacamole and the other full of sour cream, and said that he wanted the tray and dishes back.

Jerry and Suzi woke up as Tom returned to the hearth area with the food. Tom relit the fire to heat the food. The campers had some flat circular, aluminum trays about a foot in diameter, somewhat like cookie sheets, and I suggested to Tom that he put a couple of them under the stream tray to keep it from becoming blackened and scorched from the fire.

"Wind it up tight!" Jerry yelled, directing Tom to make sure he built the fire with properly twisted newspaper.

After a few minutes, Tom and I grabbed a couple of the cleanest dirty plates and forks from the dishdrainer. I wiped mine off a little with my bandana, but I tried to not make a big deal of it. I didn't want to attract attention to my squeamishness. Tom was really focused on the food, however, and paid little attention to me. Like many very heavy people, he really likes to eat. We had quite a feast. There was enough for perhaps half a dozen very hungry people, but it had arrived too late to be of any use to Jerry and Suzi.

Suzi had passed out again on the brown vinyl couch. For some reason, this exasperated Jerry so he sat on his bed, more or less paralyzed by wine, and attempted to shout some sense into her. He was so drunk that he could only occasionally get out an understandable word, let alone convey a thought in something like a sentence. His complete lack of teeth was more than a slight handicap in this effort, as he slurred and whistled a bit under the best of circumstances.

Bobbing and weaving, for several minutes he sat cross-legged in the center of his bed trying to make up in volume what he lacked in coherence. He slurred, slobbered, and ranted at Suzi, but she couldn't be roused. This continued for only a few minutes, then Jerry keeled over too. I couldn't comprehend enough of his slurred shouting to understand what the argument was about, but in a sense, Suzi had won Jerry over to her position.

After Jerry had joined Suzi in slumber, Tom told me that Jerry hallucinated quite often. I couldn't get him to say how often. Jerry occasionally yelled at people on the street below for no reason and had even at times rushed down to the fence to confront somebody when there was no one there at all. I hadn't seen anything like that personally, but I did once see Jerry yell angrily at a couple of nicely dressed Black children who were walking along the street in front of camp, minding their own business. He appeared to have imagined some insult. I didn't think it was simply racism, because I'd never heard him make racist remarks, though I did hear them occasionally from a couple of other Bridge People.

One of the things I was interested in was the actual alcohol consumption of the Bridge People. Heavy drinkers, street people and others, often talk about how much they drink, but self-reports on such value laden topics are notoriously inaccurate. People seem to either over-report out of braggadocio, or under-report out of concern for respectability. However, since I had been with Suzi and Jerry most of the day, and had later conferred with Tom, I was fairly confident that I knew how much they had had to drink that day. They had consumed about three and a half fifths, a short dog, and a couple of pints of beer between the two of them. That meant that they had each drunk the equivalent of two fifths of fortified wine and a pint of beer, which had been sufficient to get them to the point of passing out and still leave one fifth in reserve. They had eaten nothing all day, but, according to Tom, that was hardly unusual.

Now Jerry and Suzi are dedicated, serious alcoholics. Seasoned professionals. If they were completely put out of action by a little over two fifths each over the course of an entire day, as I had just witnessed, then the self-reports of drinking five or six fifths, rather common among street alcoholics, should be viewed with extreme caution. Eating something along the way would certainly have helped increase their ability to tolerate alcohol, but heavy doses of alcohol do tend to deaden the appetite. It is conceivable that, with some diligence, they could go through two cycles of drinking and passing out per day, so they could perhaps drink three or four fifths in a very long day of serious drinking, but that was quite rare for Jerry and Suzi, at least according to Tom.

At about five o'clock I left the camp to go make some phone calls and to check on some of my other street friends. When I got back to camp, about eight, I talked to Tom and we shared a couple of beers that I brought back with me. I asked if he had seen Jerry and Suzi eat anything that day. He said that all that Jerry had eaten was a cup to a cup and a half of the beans and rice from Angelo's. He had come to for a few minutes, eaten a little, and then passed out again. Suzi had awakened too, but didn't eat anything.

As I said before, the Bridge People usually went to bed rather early. No one had lanterns, and the only source of light was the campfire. Since it required a lot of work to haul to camp on foot, firewood was precious and was not usually burnt frivolously. Nighttime campfires were infrequent. Most often, when it got dark, they went to bed. When it got light, they got up. In the summer, this meant that they went to bed around 8:30 P.M. and got up at about 5:00 A.M.; in the winter, they went to bed at perhaps 6:00 P.M. and got up at 6:30 A.M. They spent something on the order of twelve hours a day in bed during the winter and this meant that they got an excess of sleep, but not a huge excess because of the frequent disturbances during the night. The hour the Bridge People went to bed seemed to fluctuate quite a bit from night to night since it also depended on social events in the various camps and how much alcohol was available, and that in turn depended primarily on the return from panhandling or canning, which varied wildly. The time that they went to work varied quite a bit too, depending upon how much wine had been consumed the night before and how much wine (or money to buy wine) was available for breakfast.

Tom and I sat together quietly. While lights from the freeway above cascaded down through the trees on either side of the bridge, it was quite dark under the fire blackened bridge itself. He had a couple of cigarettes and I puffed my pipe. We didn't say much, just finished our beers and then turned in. It must have been about nine thirty, late for him, but quite early for me.

18. A day in camp with Big Joe

I awoke the next morning feeling rather rested and paid careful attention to the morning's activities. Early morning was a time for socializing. The Bridge People, like many other campers, hikers, and trekers, slept in their clothing, so it wasn't necessary to dress in the morning. Suzi had a few incisors, and Tom had most of his teeth, but they didn't brush them. Jerry had no teeth to brush. They performed virtually no morning ablutions. The usual procedure was simply sit up, roll a cigarette, light it, and look around in the early morning grey. As people became aware of others being awake, quiet conversation started. Sometimes, in these early morning hours, guys from the other side of the street came over to chat, smoke, and drink. The residents seldom made coffee or ingested anything except wine. When they had visitors, they would all sit around and chat until Jerry and Suzi left for the day's dumpstering at about eight o'clock.

During the morning socializing, people slipped away one by one to the bushes that served as the camp's latrine. When people had to get up to urinate during the night, the practice was to go about to the drip line. (A drip line is an archaeological term. It's an imaginary line on the floor of a cave or rockshelter marking where rain can drip off the top of the entrance. Within the shelter, behind the drip line, the ground is always dry; beyond it, the soil is exposed to precipitation and vegetation can grow.) Under the bridges, people placed their mattresses a couple of yards behind the drip line because wind could blow rain in a little ways.

The first subject usually broached between Suzi and Jerry upon awaking was the state of the wine supply. If there was wine, drinking began immediately. If there was money but no wine, Suzi was dispatched to the Six O'Clock Store, to be there when it opened. Suzi ran a lot of errands for Jerry, presumably because he had had difficulty walking since his series of strokes. Suzi is certainly a much faster walker than he. Sexism was a factor too, though. All the men ordered her around to some degree, and seemed to do so because, in traditional American society, and especially among the working class, women are expected to wait on men, and the vast majority of street people came from working-class backgrounds.

If there was no wine and no money, drinking couldn't begin until they could get some money. On the canning route there was the possibility of running into the janitor who usually gave them a dollar. That was the first opportunity to get some money. If that failed, it might well be noon before they got a drink, because it took that long to cover the canning route and get to the can man.

Jerry and Suzi existed at that time as a corporate entity in as much as they consistently and thoroughly pooled their resources. Tom was independent. He didn't drink as much and didn't socialize as much with the more dedicated drinkers. While the other Bridge People in various camps frequently went in together on a bottle, Tom very rarely joined in. He received food from Jerry and Suzi, but seldom reciprocated. He asserted that he didn't really want their food, but accepted it when offered and felt little motivation to return the favor, since he defined it as a non-favor. So, while the shared compulsion to drink fueled the lives of the dedicated drinkers and infused their existence with a modicum of meaning and sociability, Tom was outside of their drinking circle most of the time.

(Tom frequently said that he did not drink wine, but he certainly shared in my sherry and even consumed the lion's share—for which I was quite thankful the next morning. Jerry said that Tom asked for a drink of his wine from time to time too, so I think Tom protested a bit too much about his disinterest in wine.)

While I was lying on my mattress, a white four wheel drive pickup with big mud and snow tires drove by. There was a steady flow of commuters on Cardenas Street in the morning, but the mud and snow tires on this truck made a loud distinctive brrrrrrr sound and roused me from my reverie.

"Oh, there goes seven thirty," Jerry noted. He said that there was a six thirty, a seven thirty, and an eight o'clock truck. The knobby tires made so much noise and such a distinctive sound that Jerry began using them to tell the time. I was reminded of the way farm folks used to check the time by the passing trains.

The previous evening, while I was gone, Suzi had told a middle-aged Black woman that she should park her car near the camp, in the Angelo's parking lot, and Suzi would watch it for her. The woman had done as Suzi suggested and this morning she came over to the fence and shouted up to Suzi to come down. Suzi did and the woman tipped her five dollars. That was what Suzi and Jerry called "a major hit." (Remember that their canning route typically netted only four to six dollars and took five to seven hours of walking and digging into dumpsters.) I suspected that a major hit like that might completely alter their day's agenda.

On this occasion it caused a bit of an argument about how much wine to buy. No other options were entertained. When they had some money, the question for Jerry and Suzi wasn't, "What should we buy?", but only "How much should we get?" They discussed it at some length. Suzi got me chuckling when she yelled at Jerry in disgust, "God dammit! Would you make up my mind?"

In the middle of this conversation, Suzi told Jerry to change his shirt because, in her view, it was filthy. Jerry didn't want to. She had the five dollars and she was going to go fetch the wine, so she had an enviable bargaining position. She said, "Jerry! You change your shirt, or you ain't gettin' any wine!" In the face of such a dire threat, he did, in fact, reconsider his position.

"Ah, well. If you're gonna get nasty about it, all right, I'll change my goddamned shirt."

Jerry succinctly expressed the *raison d'etre* of the Bridge People when he said, "Cash is for wine." Ultimately, they decided that they would get two fifths and a short dog.

I continued to use the classic field worker's gambit of going off to the latrine to take notes. As at Big Joe's camp across the street, the latrine areas here were roughly defined areas, not a formalized site or feature. There were two of them, one on each edge of the bridge, back past the abutment and behind camp. They began only about five yards behind each side of the bridge and spread over a considerable area, maybe five by fifteen yards. On the north side, where Tom and I were, there was a little trail past the latrine area leading to the high bridge campsite. Along it, there was quite a bit of vegetation (tansy, mustard, pyracantha, scrub oak, tall eucalyptus trees, and various ruderal annuals and grasses). Sometimes I just sat down on the trail for a few minutes, and sometimes I went up to the high bridge campsite.

Sometime during the morning the topic of God came up, and I encouraged Suzi to express her views. She said that a woman she had met on the street recently had asked her if she believed in God.

"I said, 'Yes, I do.' I said, 'I believe in God.' I said, 'If it wasn't for God, I wouldn't be here.' 'Cause the Supreme Bein' watches over all of us. And He takes care of us. And we wish for things. Jerry and I walk down the streets, and we'll wish for something. Like I was wishin' for him for a new pair of shoes, and this lady come out and asked us if we wanted some lemons, and what did she do when she came out with the bag? She came out with a pair of boots for me and a pair of shoes for him." It seemed to me that Suzi had confused God with Santa Claus.

As the conversation continued and the wine flowed, I excused myself and went off to a service station near Eddie's to make a phone call. When I got back about eight forty it was apparent that Jerry and Suzi were not going out canning that day. The five dollar hit that Suzi had made first thing that morning was clearly the cause.

Sam Robbins and Big Joe had come over at about eight thirty. Sam said that wine was great medicine. He said that it'd cure headache, backache, toothache, depression, loneliness, anything you've got. He chided Jerry for his morose mood that morning and said, "Like Red Skelton used to say, if you take life serious, you'll never get out of it alive." Sam was a short White man whose white hair reached over his collar. A jocular, affable guy in his early sixties, he appeared better educated, more articulate, and healthier than many street folk, but he had a reputation of being one of the worst drunks in a subculture of hopeless drunks.

Jerry, Suzi, Big Joe, Sam Robbins, and I sat around for most of the morning. Tom and I drank instant coffee while the others drank wine. Tom didn't hang around or participate in the conversation much. Mostly he relaxed on his mattress reading a paperback book. By about nine thirty Jerry and Suzi had passed out. Between them they had consumed the short dog and the two fifths, less the amount that they had shared with Big Joe and Sam, so, again, their pass out point was at about two fifths. Big Joe and Sam Robbins wandered off separately. Joe had brought a bottle of his own to start things off. He preferred Night Train to Jerry and Suzi's Thunderbird, but I wouldn't make too much of this distinction. Bridge People didn't often turn down an offer of anything alcoholic.

I told Tom I had to go see some other people and headed off toward Market. When I got back to the bridges in the middle of the afternoon, everybody was having a siesta or just lazing around. An Hispanic guy came down Cardenas pushing a shopping cart and picking up glass. Jerry roused himself and gathered up the half dozen or so empties that were lying around his bed and Suzi's couch. I handed him a couple of empty sherry bottles that were in my area. He took them down the hill to the guy. Suzi, Tom, and I didn't help.

Shortly afterwards, Big Joe came back over to our camp from across the street. He lumbered up the hill like a bear and came over to sit on the edge of my mattress. He was pretty drunk and quite pleased with himself, saying that that he had made fifteen dollars panning near the Courthouse. Having talked with Jerry about him, I suspected that Joe rarely made that much. His behavior seemed to confirm my suspicion to some degree. If it had been a routine accomplishment, he wouldn't have brought it up.

Joe had been working with Sam Robbins. "Sam Robbins, ever' time he makes a quarter hit, he wants to leave. Ah said, 'Fuck you! We're gonna sit here and we're gonna make some money.' Ah got Camel cigarettes too! Hummmmm." He held up the Camel he was smoking and smiled at it as if he were posing for an ad.

Tom, lying a little over a yard away and apparently deeply immersed in his book, looked up with interest at the mention of cigarettes. "Speaking of which," he said, "may I borrow a smoke?"

Big Joe gave him one. I suggested that we go talk to Jerry, since he had been asleep all day. "I ain't been asleep all day! God dammit! I been out here workin'!" Jerry shouted.

"Jerry's been asleep all day," Tom said flatly.

"Ah want to talk to Jackson. Ah want to talk to anybody who makes sense," Joe said.

"Oh, well, then you're in the wrong place," Jerry said chuckling.

"Ah know this! Ah know this. Ah know this—Sam Robbins done run off, and everybody else done run off. So Ah thought I'd jest come over here and draank."

"Where'd Sam go?" Jerry asked.

"Ah don't know. Ah told the goddammed stupid son of a bitch, Ah said, 'Sam!—'"

"Now!" Suzi cautioned Joe.

"Shut up! Now Suzi!" Joe said.

"No, no, no, no, no, no. Be polite," Jerry said.

"He's pretty smart. I mean, he can pan very well, so don't call him no stupid son of a bitch," Suzi said.

Jerry and Tom said something at the same time, so I could understand neither. That happened from time to time in these drunken discussions. People lost the ability to take turns talking.

I got up and moved over to the hearth area where most of the interaction in camp took place and Big Joe followed. I didn't want to disturb Tom, who was reading. There were plenty of chairs and milk crates to sit on there, and it was the public area, whereas the beds were quasi private space. Tom joined us after a moment, probably in hopes of bumming another cigarette from either Big Joe or me.

"We made purdy good money today. Ah made most of it. Sam just set there and looked like he was stupid. Of course, he does that if he's just settin' anyway," Joe said chuckling.

"He does very well," Suzi said.

"Yeah, but you know what? Hey, you know the reason he don't make more? 'Cause immediately after he makes a small hit, he gets up and runs. You gotta set there all day and make yore money. We made, we made fifteen dollars. Ah did. AH did. Sam? Ever' time he made a quarter hit, he'd come over to give it to me and he'd say, 'Let's go.' 'Naw,' I'd say, 'get your ass back over there and sit down, God dammit!'"

"Were you guys sittin' together or were you sittin' apart?" I asked.

"No, no. I'm settin' on one side of the steps and he's settin' on the other," Joe said.

"It's an impossibility, it's an impossibility to panhandle together," Jerry said. "One has to be in one spot and one has to be in another spot and, and,...."

"See, what it is, Sam is a little bitty guy, right? Ah cannot stand up. Ah'm too big. Ah cannot stand up and get in these people's face. They'll look at me and say, 'Well God damn.'"

"You're hovering over them," Tom said.

"Naw, what I'm sayin' is that it scares them. That's the reason Ah sit down and hold my little hat. Ah nut up. Ah nut up." He drew in his arms, rounded his shoulders, and brought his knees up under his chin. The effect was indeed to make him look smaller, just as he wanted. He was making a good point; he was six foot three or so and his weight varied between two hundred fifty and two hundred seventy-five pounds.

"You get little, huh?" I asked.

"Hey, Ah'm serious. Ah'm serious, Ah tell you the truth. If you big, you cannot panhandle and get in somebody's face. 'Cause they think you gonna rob them."

I thought he may have been projecting a little here. After all, he had been in the armed robbery business some years ago. "How far apart do you have to sit from Sam?" I asked.

"Well, you know where the Courthouse is? Well, they got two ways when they come out. Ah put Sam over there, and Ah get on the other side. Anything that flows this way, Ah get it. Anything flows that way, he gets it," Big Joe said. Then he suddenly changed the subject. "This is really what I'd like to do," Joe said. "My dad. Ah don't know. Ah haven't seen him in twenty-seven years. He lives up there in Fremont [a town in northern California]."

"Well, why don't you just go up there and go see him?" Jerry asked.

"Ah don't want to see him. But I've got little brothers and sisters up there that Ah haven't seen since they were like this." Big Joe held his hand about a yard off the dirt. "Ah got a brother that's only twenty-three years old."

"How old are you?" I asked.

"I'm forty-three," Joe said.

"You're forty-three? We're the same age."

"Well, you've probably got more sense than Ah got too," Joe said.

I grinned sheepishly, not knowing what to say. I thought that if I agreed it would sound like a put down; if I disagreed it would sound patronizing. I was about to say something profound like "Aw shucks."

"Well, that wouldn't take too awful much!" Jerry commented and everybody laughed. I felt relieved to be off the hook.

"Last time Ah seen my dad, it was twenty-seven years ago. Before that Ah hadn't seen him for fifteen years."

"Yeah, that's right, you were raised by your grandparents," Jerry said.

"Yeah, my grandparents raised me. My grandparents raised me. Ah sat over there and talked to you guys about it one day," Joe said seriously.

Suzi said, "He was in tears, one day. He was in tears and he just sat there and us...."

"SHUTUP! Ah don't want to talk about it," Big Joe said.

"Well you did it," Suzi continued, "and you were glad when you did it 'cause it made you feel better because you had to get it off your chest. You have to get that stuff out."

"Ah was tellin' you guys somethin' that Ah won't tell nobody. Ah was tellin' you guys somethin' that Ah won't tell nobody," Joe said, looking down. Then he looked up at me and said very solemnly and quietly, "My grandparents died when Ah was in the joint, Jackson. Ah was in a lock-up cell. Ah was in a lock-up cell. Ah went crazy. See, that's the only family Ah ever knew. My grandparents. Ah went stoned-ass nuts. Ah guess Ah've been stoned-ass nuts ever since then."

"You're stoned ass nuts now," Jerry said chuckling.

"No he ain't!" Suzi said earnestly, "No he ain't." Sometimes, when Suzi was somewhat sober, she demonstrated a sense of caring for whomever she thought was currently getting picked on. It was something I admired.

Jerry pulled out an almost new pack of Tarrytons. I asked if he had bought them, since I thought they would only buy non-filter cigarettes. He said that I was right, he wouldn't buy Tarrytons, but the glass man who had come through that morning had given them to him.

A few moments later Big Joe said that he was mad about the Mexicans that live a couple of bridges to the north among other things. "Hey Jackson! Jackson, can Ah ask you a question?"

"Sure."

"Have you ever been sick and tarred of bein' sick and tarred?"

"Yeah, I have. When I was in the Army. I understand."

"Then you know what I'm sayin'. Does that make any kind of sense to ya?"

"You betcha."

He continued in a serious tone, to himself more than to anyone else, "I'm sick and tarred of bein' sick and tarred. I'm just sick and tarred of bein' sick and tarred." His puffy face sagged like a basset hound's, a picture of mournful dejection. After a couple of seconds, he suddenly looked up and grinned, slapped his leg. "Good God! We made some money today! Ha, ha, ha, ha."

Big Joe's returning over and over to the subject of how well he had done that day panning made me believe even more that a fifteen dollar day was quite rare for him. As I've mentioned, he'd told Jerry that he had eighteen dollar days all the time. Apparently he exaggerated to give the idea that he was a more competent panhandler that he actually was. I think this kind of exaggeration was common among panhandlers I've met, but it worked against the Bridge People who did it because, even though their campmates only half believed each other's stories, they resented the fact that the exaggerator did not reciprocate and share more. This may have been the case with Luke Broder as well. He told his campmates that he always made twenty or twenty-five dollars a day, but he'd never reciprocated by extending offers of food or drink to his campmates and had been thrown out of camp after a few weeks. In reality, he may have made only enough for a bottle of wine and a pack of cigarettes with nothing to spare. I know the old Navy Chief was greatly embarrassed by having to beg for a living.

The campers related an incident which had happened about year before, when Big Joe, Rubio, Jerry, Suzi, and, Tom had been sitting around drinking and, for some reason, Rubio had been waving around a machete. He slapped Joe on the side of the face with the machete and cut his nose badly. Joe then tried to take it away from him and almost got his thumb cut off. Joe was very drunk at the time, as was Rubio. Jerry pushed Big Joe down, quite an undertaking, since Joe outweighed Jerry by well over a hundred pounds. Then he got on top of him and told Rubio that if he wanted to kill Joe, he would have to kill him first. Tom took off to call the police. Rubio decided to calm down.

"I'll never forget that. He saved my life. Jerry saved my life… Ah was so damn drunk Ah could hardly walk," Joe said.

"And I was so drunk, I did it," Jerry said and everybody laughed.

The campers really didn't like Rubio. He had later cut another guy with the machete and then gotten his own throat cut, but he had recovered from his wounds. The consensus was that Rubio liked to pick on people when they were too drunk to fight back. He had been put in prison for a while for his latest machete misadventure, but was thought to be out by now.

There was great respect among these folks for physical strength, independence, and assertiveness. Rugged individualism was idealized despite the obvious importance of cooperation in their lives and the fact that they were extremely dependent economically. They constantly borrowed, loaned, and shared what little they had with one another. Begging, the epitome of dependency, was by far the best paying "job" available to them. This paradox between the mythic individualism and their actual dependence and interdependence permeated the existence of the Bridge People.

Joe asked me how I liked living under the bridge. Again I was embarrassed and didn't know what to say. I hadn't thought about the research in terms of liking the way they lived. I thought to myself, 'Well I could think of a few hundred places I'd rather camp.' I finally just said, "Oh, well, uh, I like it fine. No problems."

He said, "Yeah, it ain't too bad, but you know Jackson," he was suddenly serious again and looked me right in the eye, "it's a hard life. It's a hard life." He looked down for a moment, then he leaned back and took a big drag on his cigarette then let it out a huge sigh.

"This is it for me. Relaxation." Joe said, "A good cigarette. Ah got a packet of tobacco Ah got hid over at the camp right now, plus Ah got some more in my pocket. That's the only thing that bothers me. Ah don't worry about a drink when Ah wake up. Ah worry about something to smoke. First thing Ah want to do when Ah wake up in the morning, is to smoke a cigarette. That's why Ah come over here this mornin'."

The discussion turned to food. Joe had found a whole pizza and a pound and a half of Canadian bacon in Angelo's dumpster earlier in the day. "Hey, we live good around here!" Joe said. "Ha, ha, ha, ha."

"That's what he said," Suzi said, referring to me. "He's been livin' here for four days, and he said, 'Man, you guys eat good!'"

"Have you been eatin' the same thing they been eatin'?" Joe asked.

"Well, some of the time," I said. I was beginning to realize that Big Joe, in his drunkenness, had a knack of asking me embarrassing questions. Actually I had been eating very little of their fare, mostly the perfectly serviceable fruit that Suzi had found in a dumpster and the Mexican food that the busboy from Angelo's had brought over. When I went off to check on other homeless friends, I usually grabbed a bean burrito at an inexpensive Mexican place on Market Street. And, of course, I sneaked off and ate granola bars from time to time. Fortunately Joe was too drunk to be very critical of my answers.

"Let me cook a stew!" Joe proposed. "Hey, Ah can cook. Tell 'em Jerry. Let me cook a stew sometime and you eat some of that."

"Yep! He's a good cook. And beans. I want your beans," Jerry said.

"Ah'm a bean cookin' son of bitch, ain't Ah?"

"Boy, can he make the best pot of beans. I'll be constipated for a week, but I will eat a lot of beans," Jerry said.

Joe and Jerry decided to go in together on another jug, and Suzi was sent off to make the run to Eddie's. While decision making was up to Jerry, Suzi actually carried and counted the money. In essence, she had been ordered to make the run by Joe and Jerry.

They were all pretty drunk by now. The conversation drifted from topic to topic. Joe said that he had a couple of Indian friends up in Portland that used to mix Lysol with milk and use it as a cheap drink. He said that it was a common practice on the Portland Skid Row. They only sold fourteen percent wine there, not fortified wine at twenty per cent like here in Los Angeles. You would have to go outside of the Skid Row area to buy fortified wines and they cost almost three dollars for a fifth instead of two dollars, so people had concocted this Lysol and milk beverage. Joe didn't know what it was called, but someone told me later that this concoction was called a White Knight.

Jerry told me about the "Green Lizard," a drink made of Mennen aftershave and Seven-Up. Joe said that Mennen is forty-five per cent alcohol and that Green Lizards would "git you as drunk as you wanta git!"

They also mentioned that vanilla extract and Nyquil were used as substitutes for fortified wine. All of these were really novelty drinks for the people under the bridges, and they virtually never resorted to them except as topics of conversation. If push came to shove, however, they would drink them.

Joe and Tom talked about paperback books. Joe told me that every time Sam Robbins went to the Five Points, a second hand store about a mile west of the bridges, he'd buy one and steal one.

"He always gets great books," Tom said. Larry, Joe, and Sam all read paperbacks to some degree, and they passed copies around. Tom was by far the most avid reader. In fact he read as much as anyone I've ever met. They all liked mysteries, adventure, and the less bizarre science fiction.

"Ah like readin' shit like that, you know," Big Joe said. "Well, you know what it does? It gits my mind off my ever'day problems. Hey Jackson, I'm serious. I'll sit there and read, and it gits my mind off things. And it makes me happy for a while, so what's wrong with it?"

"Not a thing Joe, not a thing," I said. It seemed to me that reading light fiction, even trashy light fiction, was a very good way to get your mind off your problems. I thought this was especially true for homeless people: They lived less complex lives than middle-class people, and their problems, while rather basic, were really much more serious and essential. Everybody needs some way to get their mind off their troubles. Drinking was the main way the Bridge People did this, but that took a heavy toll on their health and on their relationships. Reading was one of the very few activities that wasn't linked to drinking.

Joe and I continued to talk. He said that he had a candle that he sometimes used to read at night. He was the only one of the Bridge People who had a light of any kind. Then he talked for a while about a couple of his current campmates, Larry and Tiny.

Larry worked from time to time as a handyman and gardener for a rich guy who had a mansion in East Los Angeles. The rich guy paid him five dollars an hour. He came and got Larry in a car and took him out there for a few days at a time. This took place infrequently and sporadically. Larry also made pretty good money, by Bridge People standards, by cleaning up a parking lot several times a week, and he received food stamps most of the time (ninety dollars per month). He didn't panhandle.

Tiny had supported himself by panhandling while he was in camp, but he'd wanted to go ride the rails again, so he'd applied for G.R., gotten one check, and then left town again. He had only been in town for a few months this year.

Big Joe talked a bit about his past. "Jackson, I'm tellin' you the truth. Ah used to rob. Ah used to rob banks. Ah used to rob banks, for real. It's been ten years ago. Ah don't do it no more. Ah don't do that shit. And Ah wish they'd quit breakin' into these little funky-ass cars around here, 'cause, what the hell are they stealin'? A little bitty radio or a battery or something? Don't let your car get stopped right over here, 'cause it'll git stripped. That motherfucker WILL git stripped."

"That yellow Mustang that was over there, and we sat up here and watched," Jerry said, barely getting in a word.

"They got the battery, the radio, and the front end. They done pulled the front end out of the motherfucker, 'cause he hit the post right over there. See all the oil over there. And they pushed it over there and they stripped that son of a bitch. They got ever'thing but the tires. They got ever'thing out of it. And Ah ain't gonna say nothin'. It ain't none of my business. They come and ask me somethin' and they want to know? I'm layin' up there asleep, Ah don't know nothin'. Ah don't know nothin'. That's the way you're supposed to be. Jackson, you git hurt out here. You WILL git hurt out here. Unfortunately. Hey man, you don't see nothin'. You don't see nothin' and you don't know nothin'. It ain't 'cause you're scared, though. You just don't want to get involved."

"You know, that's a sad part of society," Jerry said, "when we have gotten down to that stage of the game where you don't want to get involved. Because involvement is the essence of the game. I mean, if I see somebody stabbing you, stuff like that...."

"Well, now that's a different story. If Ah see somebody hurtin' somebody, Ah'm gonna do somethun. Ah'm gonna do somethun about it 'cause uh—"

"Joe, where do you draw the line?" Jerry asked.

"That's where Ah draw the line. Ah'm talkin' about takin' things outta cars. Ah look the other way. Ah look the other way."

Conversations in camp were sometimes difficult to follow. As the campers got drunker, they sometimes talked all at once and no one would be listening except the poor anthropologist. As this condition worsened, the loudest, most aggressive speaker tended to hold the stage. In this instance, it was Big Joe. Since she didn't have a loud voice, Suzi had lost out early.

"Ever'body's got their own beliefs. Ah don't put nobody down. Ah don't put nobody down. Ever'body's got their own beliefs. You know what Ah believe in, though?" Joe asked. He leaned toward me and fixed me in his bleary gaze. "Me," he said quietly. "Me. Ah know me and what Ah know and that's all. Anybody else?" He shook his head, looked at the ground, and fell silent for a moment. Solipsism is a retreat to a very lonely outpost.

My campmates were getting thoroughly intoxicated and more than a little incoherent. It was fairly pointless to be around them in that condition, so I decided to walk around downtown and Skid Row to see if any of my other street friends were out. I left camp that evening at about six forty-five and returned at about eight thirty. The camp was quiet. Tom was awake, lying on his mattress. No longer able to read, he was just staring at the soot blackened ceiling. Jerry and Suzi were asleep. I had a smoke with Tom. We didn't talk much, though he did tell me that Big Joe had killed three people, all on different occasions; all in self-defense, according to Joe. It was about nine when we turned in.

During the night, about three thirty or so, three fire engines came roaring and screaming down Cardenas Street with bright red beacons flashing. They were separated by about fifty yards as if they were playing tag. It was a rather spectacular way to awaken from a deep sleep. The shriek of the sirens was deafening as it ricocheted off the asphalt street, the concrete bridge abutments, and the underside of the concrete bridge itself. As I have said, screaming fire trucks, growling ambulances and police cars, rumbling trucks, and backfires were common at night, so no one slept the whole night through.

I awoke at about five thirty. Jerry and Suzi were already up and talking with Big
Joe, who was sitting near Jerry's stack of mattresses and Suzi's couch. I got off
my mattress, shuffled over to them, sank into the sagging easy chair, and joined in
the conversation. I had been sleeping in my clothes, like a real Bridge Person, so I
needed no time to get ready to entertain visitors. Joe began talking about his
sleeping gear.

"I sleep under one blanket, over there," he said.

"Yeah, it wasn't too cold last night," I said.

"I sleep with just a tee shirt and one blanket, even when it's cold."

Jerry said, "I sleep under, well, remember when I was sleepin' with you guys,
I was sleeping under ten blankets and a sleeping bag. And I was still cold."

"I got a sleeping bag, now. Will left his, so I'm gonna take it," Joe said.
"There's a couple of them, one of them won't zip up though."

Joe said that Dirty Mack had moved back under the bridge. He had moved out
and into the bushes a couple of days earlier when the police said that Caltrans was
going to clean out the camps. At that time, Big Joe was camping with Dirty Mack,
Will, Sam Robbins, and Larry.

Out of the blue, Joe said, "My mom and dad both was alcoholics. Both of 'em.
So, uh, where does that leave me?"

Jerry said, "Yeah, that makes things pretty tough."

"Yeah," Suzi said, "You didn't have much of a chance."

Joe said, "Speakin' of hopeless drunks, I seen Jimmy, Jimmy Newby, the
other day. That reminds me, Jackson, I never told you about this. I damn near—I
started to beat him to death one night. I had one blanket. Here we are, we were
stayin' across from the courthouse on that little corner. I had one damn blanket and
we were both about half drunk and I lay down to go to sleep and I wake up and I
feel somethin' wet on me. The son of a bitch pissed on me, on my blanket and
ever' damn thing. I said, 'Jimmy! I ought to kill ya. You son of a bitch, I ought
to kill ya.' Boy that made me mad! It did. But he cain't he'p it though. He cain't
he'p it. They's somethin' wrong with him."

"Yeah, there's something wrong with him, that's for sure. There's something wrong with all of us," Jerry said cheerfully.

Jerry was right, I realized. All of the Bridge People were flawed and handicapped in some way. They were the losers in a society that glorifies winning. Losers were the side-effects and by-products of an economy where you have to compete for everything, including a place to live and something to eat.

Jerry, Joe, and Suzi all began talking about how much they didn't like drug users. Jerry brought up the notion that wine and tobacco were drugs too, but the Bridge People, like American society in general, usually excluded tobacco and alcohol from the category of drugs.

I asked Joe if he considered tobacco a drug, and he said, "No, but it's habit formin' though. I know, I been smokin' since I was fifteen years old. I quit one time for a week and I was clawin' at the walls."

Jerry said, "Well it definitely is [a drug]."

At about seven thirty, Suzi was sent to get a bottle for breakfast, and I decided to talk to Tom for a while. I wasn't sure whether Suzi and Jerry would go canning that day or not, since they'd seemed to be getting a little tipsy already and it was still pretty early.

Tom had been sick the day before. He'd had a bout with food poisoning and had had diarrhea every half hour or hour. He didn't go to work. There was really no place to relieve yourself in Chinatown, he said, and that could be a real problem if you had the runs. I asked him if he felt better today, and he said that he did.

I asked Tom how often he thought Suzi and Jerry went canning and he said, on average, five days a week. That agreed with my observations, and contrasted with Jerry's report of six or seven.

"The thing that would keep them from going canning, say like Larry had twenty dollars and had ten jugs over there and he invited them over. That would be it. Or like Suzi got that five dollar hit yesterday, plus they had money left over from the night before. Suzi still has five dollars, she'll go and get two bottles and uh, a lot of times they will still go canning, but later. Just like me, if I have tobacco, I don't go panning," Tom chuckled. "Today would be a good day to panhandle, 'cause it's nice and overcast. Day before yesterday, it was HOT! And especially since it's been three days since the cops saw us sitting there. They don't like the fact that I'm always there on that bus stop. I may go today, I don't know."

"Is that why some guys have that roaming around technique?"

"Yeah, there's a lot of guys who walk. Constantly walking. They zig-zag in those little arcades and they're moving constantly. The police never really notice them that much. It's just if you stand in one spot, then you're really obvious. John had a problem with that in Chinatown, 'cause he's Black. He really stands out in a crowd. And then, I'm so tall. Six feet's not all that tall, but by comparison with the people in Chinatown it is, and then being White, and weighing over two hundred seventy-five pounds, I truly do stand out.

"I used to stand right there on the corner and panhandle, you know by the fence [on a busy corner in the heart of Chinatown]. And then one day, I had a cramp and I had to walk off this cramp in my leg and it took about five minutes. And I noticed that there was no one sitting down on the bus stop. This was when the police never bothered me, about a year ago. And I used to stand there on the corner for three or four hours. And after a while, you get tired. I've had spinal surgery and my back would start bothering me. And so, I said, 'Try sitting down and panhandling on the bus bench.' So if I'm sitting on the bus bench maybe the cops will just ignore me and I have a phony shopping bag with me and stuff.

"I learned everything by accident in Chinatown. Something would happen and I would figure a new way to do it. I used to panhandle at Lee's, that liquor store right there at Oak and Market?"

"Yeah."

"And I'd sit on the bus bench, 'cause it was nice, and I'd ask people for change, and I wasn't making a great deal. I was making two or three dollars in maybe two hours. I thought, 'Well, that's not a lot, but I didn't have anything to begin with.' So I'd rush right into Lee's and get cigarette tobacco, you know, the minute I'd get sixty cents, 'cause this was before the tax on cigarettes went up.

"Well, one day, you know, these two Black guys got off the bus and they were roaring drunk. And they had bedrolls and each of them had a bottle of Thunderbird and they sat right down on my bench. And they started panhandling, not very seriously. And then they were starting to make rude remarks to some of the young girls. And I said, 'Christ! There it goes,' you know, so I was sitting there, and there's this guy that always gives me a dollar, and I was waiting for him to cross the street. And he's an older guy, he must be in his seventies, and it takes him a while. I thought, 'Once I get the dollar from this older guy, I'm gonna split and go somewhere else.' And, um, two of the chicks that these guys got rude with went in and told Lee. And I saw Lee come out of the store and look, and there was a cop coming down the street, and Lee did his whole thing in Chinese to this Chinese cop. So I thought, 'Well, it's time for me to leave.'" Tom chuckled. "So I was just getting the dollar from the older Chinese man who always gives me a dollar when I see him, and so I didn't want to be around there, so I walked all the way up to Beech, 'cause there's no other cross streets. And I was standing on the corner of Beech and Market and I said, 'Well, look at all these people.' I stood there and panhandled and I made something like fifteen dollars in about two and a half hours [six dollars per hour]. But it was miserable. It was hot. It was like eighty-five, ninety degrees and there's no shade there at all. So, uh, eventually I started sitting on the bus bench there, after I got the cramp.

"I've only been hassled by the police, in two years, about four times. I've never been arrested. I've never gotten a ticket. One thing I learned from Jerry: Have your money on you. Sometimes they take the money out of your hat, if you use a hat. I don't panhandle with a hat. Jerry, they've arrested Jerry and took his hat and dumped the money in the street." Tom paused for a moment. "That's kinda rude of the cops to throw your money away."

"Yeah. But I always thought that Jerry just put a little seed money in his cap."

"Yeah, but Jerry—See, Jerry panhandles and then when he makes a dollar, he'll go buy a short dog. Then he'll wait for two dollars, and get a jug, so Jerry drinks a third of his money that he ever takes in. So by the time Jerry is finished making his ten, fifteen, or twenty dollars in a three hour period, he's plastered. So he doesn't realize he's got all that money in his cap."

"Oh, I see, so he just spaces it out."

"Yeah."

20.   You walk up to it and take a deep breath

Jerry and Suzi did finally decide to go canning, so I joined them. It was about eight when we began trudging along the canning route. I asked if they usually just had wine for breakfast and Jerry said, "Ah, yes. And an occasional cup of coffee, if we have it. Yeah, that's it."

He told me of a time a while back when they had found six dozen eggs and had had three egg omelettes every morning for a while. They gave a dozen each to Mack, Joe, and Tom. They found a couple of pounds of bacon once, too. I doubt that they eat anything in the morning very often, though.

Before Jimmy burned the camp down, there were salamanders in camp. Jerry observed that they had voracious appetites and kept all the bugs under control. There was no problem with ants, flies, or roaches at all, he said. Since the fire, however, the salamanders hadn't been around. I hadn't noted any problem with insects.

Suzi explained a summer technique for checking out dumpsters. "Literally, you walk up to it and take a deep breath and look. And if you don't see anything, you let it go. Wait 'til you see July and August," she said as her face wrinkled in disgust.

"Oh, yeah, it's REAL lovely," Jerry said smirking.

I asked if they lost money by starting late on their canning route. "Well, if we start off late, we got interruptions," Suzi said. "We got other people hittin' our dumpsters and you go to a dumpster and you look and see the bags are all turned over and everything else, you say, 'Hey! Lord have mercy.' You can pretty much tell."

On this morning, despite what Tom thought, Suzi and Jerry had no money to get a short dog for their customary break. It was a quarter to nine by the time we got to the Six O'clock Store, which is a steep six tenths of a mile uphill from their camp, but we had arrived by a flatter, more circuitous route after checking dumpsters. We must have walked almost a mile. I noticed that Suzi was carrying an extra bag and asked Suzi and Jerry about it. They said that they take along some of their food.

"We take a certain amount with us," Jerry said, "because when we show back up at home, lo and behold, there Tom is, sitting there belching, and, and the food's gone. And he plays so nonchalant about it. You know, like, 'Oh, well, I don't know where the food went, BURP!'—Oh did you hear Joe this morning? He accidentally killed a cat."

"Oh no!" I said.

"Last night when he went home, and he was drunk and stuff like that, and he was gonna heat something up, I forget what the heck it was."

"Oh he got some pizza," Suzi said.

"Oh yeah, he was gonna heat up some pizza. And he started breakin' up a pallet, and the cat was underneath the pallet."

"Oh no."

"And next thing you know, poor little Tiger is dead. Used up all of his nine lives in one fell swoop."

"Yeah. That's a shame," I said.

"Yeah. But he felt so bad about it this morning. It, it's literally the closest I ever seen him come to tears. Joe is uh, Joe is uh...well, Joe has been around," Jerry said.

After a moment I brought the conversation back to the topic of food. I asked what kinds of food they take and what kinds of food they leave back at camp.

"The thing is, Tommy will not cook," Suzi said "Anything that's cooked, he'll eat. He will polish it off. Hee, hee, hee."

Suzi carried whatever fresh food they didn't want Tom to eat in a plastic grocery bag that she called her junk bag. It also contained some belongings that she didn't want to get stolen. In another plastic grocery bag she carried any cans that they found on their route. Jerry didn't carry anything, except his canning stick, but he did do most of the reaching into dumpsters.

As we walked along they gave me an idealized account of their work habits. "Even if we have a good day, the next day we'll still go out. It's almost like a force of habit."

"Really?" I said.

"No, the thing is, like Jerry will say, 'Well, we got enough money to get a fifth.' And I'll say, 'Well, let's just finish off the route and we'll save the other couple of bucks in case we have a bad day,' you know," Suzi said.

This did not agree with what I had seen, of course. They did not manifest great tenacity. If things weren't going well on the canning route, they turned to panning, as they had a couple of days before. If they had a great day, they bought almost exactly as much wine as they had money for and didn't work again until it was gone. If it took two or three days of constant drinking, so be it. They might not buy all the wine at the exact time of their "big hit," but, eventually, almost all the money went for wine. I wondered who they were trying to deceive, me or themselves? Most likely both.

We continued walking their canning route and arrived at the Five Corners at about nine thirty. Five Corners is Jerry's and Suzi's name for the junction of five streets. There, Jerry and Suzi fed wieners to the friendly dogs again. They also sometimes scattered stale bread or cakes that they had found in the dumpsters for the birds.

As we walked along, Jerry picked up snipes and put them in his breast pocket for re-rolling later.

"What was it Tommy said the other day?" Jerry said. "He was sayin' something about he'd re-smoked his tobacco three or four times and it was still rejuvenating. Re-sniping." Jerry and I talked about the term crutch, which, as I said before, referred to a piece of matchbook rolled to make a crude snipe holder. He used the term and his friends used it, but he didn't know if it was universal among street people.

"Suzi, did you ever call them anything else?" I asked.

"Naw."

"Well, she didn't even know how to do it until I showed her," Jerry said. "And living on the street. Hah! And you call yourself a bum? Hah!" Jerry and I broke up laughing. At times, he has a sharp sardonic wit, but Suzi was a little offended.

"I'm a decent person. I might not look clean, but I'm decent. And I'm respectable and I don't hurt nobody. I don't start no fights. I don't cause no problems. I don't hit nobody on the head with a two by four."

That got Jerry talking about violence. "I have an awful hard time understanding violence," Jerry said. "After all, everybody was put on the earth to alleviate pain. What more can you do? How much more humane can you be. I mean, we are called humans, that's a joke, but uh, why would anybody ever want to hurt somebody else? Of course, I have an awful hard time understanding murder. Suicide, I can understand."

Of course, Jerry had never seen himself drunk and violent. On the subject of violence, Suzi suggested that it is irresponsible for the government to take fellows into the military and train them to kill people, and then just set them loose when they were done with them. Soldiers should go into another boot camp for a few weeks, she thought, to learn how to be a civilians again. She and Jerry knew several guys who were still damaged from the Vietnam War, and she thought they might have done much better if they'd had some retraining about how to fit back in to society at the end of their tour of duty. These are not her exact words, but they express essentially what she meant. I thought it was a great idea.

At an empty parking lot near some union offices, we took about a twenty minute break. We sat down right in the middle of the lot and had a smoke. At the school where we'd stopped a few days before, we took another break for about ten minutes. Jerry investigated a couple of trash cans down the alley, then came back and Suzi hit a couple of dumpsters down the same alley. In other words, they split the break at this place. Both the union and the school rest stops were dry. The breaks were separated by only about twenty or twenty-five minutes of work. It may not seem like much, but this kind of work is taxing, and Suzi and Jerry weren't healthy nor did they have much endurance.

Actually, the school break was not entirely dry. Suzi found a warm bottle of beer that was about three-quarters full. Jerry yelled to her to smell it. "Well, ya have to smell the beer bottles, because, because sometimes guys will piss in beer bottles and leave them around. I guess it's their idea of a big joke. VERY funny."

Suzi told me about a small portable TV that they had had under the bridge for a while. It was designed to operate on eight D batteries, but it also had a plug that fit a cigarette lighter on a car, so the campers got a receptacle for a cigarette lighter and wired that directly to a car battery that they had found. They could get the battery charged once a week at the nearby gas station for three dollars. The D cells wouldn't operate the TV for longer than a couple of days and would have cost about ten dollars to replace. I was impressed with their ingenuity.

The TV had been stolen when Suzi went to the hospital. I asked her what had happened.

"I fell down the hill and I got cut on my leg. And I was tryin' to take care of it by myself, but livin' in the dirt, I didn't have the facilities to take care of it. If I'd a had epsom salts and stuff like that, to soak my leg, I probably woulda got better."

"So it got infected, huh?"

"It got infected, my leg got swollen, and, matter of fact, the doctor, when I went to the doctor—They got the paramedics, and made me go," she nodded at Jerry. "I couldn't hardly walk."

"She couldn't walk!" Jerry said. "She couldn't get up to go take a piss! We had to help her up and over to the side in the bushes so she could go to the bathroom. I said, 'This is IT! We're GOING to the hospital now.'"

"So I went to the hospital and I got there, emergency, and the doctor took one look at my leg and said, 'Miss, how long have you had this?' I said, 'It's goin' on three weeks.' He said, 'Lord have mercy.' He didn't say nothin' else. The next morning he said to me, he said, 'You know,' he said, 'Suzi, if you hadn't come in when you did, we'd probably woulda had to cut your leg off at the knee.' It was that bad."

"Well," Jerry said, "she had gangrene, and, and the stuff was running out of her sore. And then she got blood poisoning. And that's when I freaked."

"Oh, I was in the hospital for eighteen days, and they were feeding me intervenously [intravenously] and I got very poor blood vessels. And I'm tellin' ya, I felt like a pincushion, because they were constantly—And they were diggin', diggin', diggin'. And my veins roll, so they couldn't get the needle in there."

While she was in the hospital, Jerry had also gone to the hospital and that left only Jimmy Newby at camp. He got an SSI check and he brought a couple of fellows back to camp with him. He got drunk and passed out and his guests rifled the camp and took the TV and a variety of other items.

"They [the hospital people] didn't want to let me go, because I didn't have any place to stay. I said, 'I DO have a place to stay.' 'Oh, no! Livin' under the bridge isn't good enough!' So they put me in the Shepherd, Good Shepherd."

Jerry chortled, "That didn't last too long."

"I stayed there five days. I put up with it, let's put it, for five days—And I've been tryin' to get on G.R. and tryin' to get my birth certificate and all that stuff. Come to find out, my stupid caseworker, he's tryin' to get my birth certificate under my married name. It's impossible."

"There is no such person, huh?"

"No!"

"What was it about the Good Shepherd you didn't like?"

"Because, it was mostly Blacks and Spanish women in there, and all they do is argue. Every meal there was an argument. Constantly arguing. Kibbitz, kibbitz, kibbitz. Over and over and over. Arguing over 'You gonna drink your coffee?' 'No, I ain't gonna drink my coffee.' 'Can I have your coffee?' 'No, you can't have my coffee, it's my coffee.' I mean crazy, little, stupid things."

A few moments later she continued, "I was tryin' to get on G.R., and the reason I was tryin' to get G.R. was so that I could get my birth certificate and get my social security card. 'Cause without a birth certificate, I can't get a social security card. And that's what I was tryin' to do. And so, right away, the sisters called up G.R. And Mr. James was there within an hour. And I was workin' for almost six months tryin' to get to his face. And he was always constantly busy, or blah, blah, this and that, and he was gone to Chicago for a vacation and some damn thing. He went in there, and he, he was in there exactly a half an hour, and he sat there and he filled out all the papers that were necessary to fill out, turned around, went back to the office, and came back in the afternoon and paid those sisters a hundred and sixty-eight dollars. And gave them money for food stamps, and all I got out of it was twenty dollars. All the rest went to them for room and board. And boy, he came lickety split. And then after that, I said well, what about my birth certificate, and he gives me the paper and shows me, he says, 'See, they sent it back, as if there's no—' I says, 'That's impossible, how can it be me,' I said. 'My name is Lanski. I was born Lanski, not Boncini.' So he was going to send away for it and everything, and I was supposed to go back over there. Just sit there for hours and hours and, and,—

"Just like the time we was down in Chinatown and he [Jerry] was pannin'. We didn't do no good canning, so he says, 'Well, we'll go down Chinatown and pan.'

So what'd we do? The cops bring us over to the Weingart. They said we were drunk. We hadn't even drank. Matter of fact we were thinkin' about gettin' a bottle, but we hadn't even drank. So we were disturbing the, oh, how do you put it?'

"Obstructing the pedestrian thoroughfare," Jerry said.

"Yeah, obstructing the pedestrian thoroughfare. He had a legal weapon, his cane, which they threw in the dumpster."

"That was a weapon, huh?" I asked.

"Yeah, that was a legal weapon," Suzi said

"Lethal weapon, oh yes," Jerry said, "a lethal weapon. I guess, I guess, if you walk around with a cane, you have to go get a license."

"I think that's called harassment," I said.

"Yeah, that's Fisher. The one that harasses me all the time," Jerry said.

"Anyway, we went down to the Weingart, and Jerry and I sat there. We drank four cups of coffee and this gal is makin' us fill out all these damn papers. And she says, 'Well, you can come back Monday.' This was a Friday. 'You can come back Monday,' she says, 'and you can get your social security card.' I said, 'I can't get it without any I.D.! I know, I tried it before!' 'Oh, no, no, no,' she said, 'with these papers, you can go.' So Jerry and I, like two little kids, we walk all the way down to Social Security Office and they said, 'Well, you got a birth certificate?' And we said no. 'Sorry. We can't help you.'" Suzi sighed, "I mean, Lord have mercy."

"So, it gets, it gets to the point, where, where you're damned if you do, and you're damned if you don't," Jerry said.

"It's damned disgusting," Suzi said. "And she said, 'Well you can get a job.' And I said, 'No I can't get a job. I can't get a job without a social security card.' I can give them my number, but I gotta have that card."

Talking about identification led Suzi to rummage around in one of her plastic grocery bags and show me what she called her wallet. It turned out to be a dirty and tattered small manila envelope. She kept what few documents she and Jerry possessed in it. She carried it with her in her "junk bag," since things were not at all secure at camp. I gave her one of my business cards and told her again that she could have her birth certificate mailed to my office if she wanted to.

We continued along the route, chatting as we went. It hadn't been a big day canning. We arrived at the can man's location by about eleven forty-five. We had collected only five pounds, which amounted to four dollars in cash. After cashing in the cans, we began trudging back to camp. Just up the street, Suzi found a tire weight in the street. Tire weights are made of lead and, she pointed out, can be slipped in with the cans to boost one's can weight. Jerry said that sometimes the can man checked the cans with a magnet but, of course, lead is not detectable with a magnet.

We took a little break at Tammy's, an abandoned taco stand just up the street from the can man's, on the way back to camp. After that we walked slowly but steadily until we reached the Six O'clock Store where Jerry was able to purchase two fifths of Thunderbird. Since he was a little short, I helped by paying the sales tax. I was surprised that he didn't open one of the jugs on the spot.

"You're going to postpone gratification until you get back under the bridge, huh?" I asked.

"Oh yeah." Jerry answered.

"Not me," I said taking a big swig of the cold beer I had just bought. Jerry laughed heartily.

Usually, if Jerry and Suzi had made a little more money, they'd stop at a store near Tammy's and buy a short dog for the trip home. Today, they didn't feel that they could afford it. A short dog there costs a dollar twenty-five, and a fifth costs two fifty. If they bought a short dog there and they only had four dollars or so left, they couldn't get two fifths later, at the Six O'clock Store, where fifths sold for two dollars. They opted to be patient and buy the two fifths later in their route. Jerry said that he didn't want to crack one of the fifths now, because they still had a little more work to do. They had the dumpster near the Six O'clock Store to check and then the one at Angelo's. I was fairly sure they didn't demonstrate this delay of gratification just for me. They seemed capable of planning and delaying gratification if there was a compelling reason to do so (if they were reasonably sober to begin with). However, compelling reasons for delaying gratification were largely lacking in their lives.

I asked if Jerry and the others had conflicts about who had access rights to Angelo's dumpster, since it seems to be THE major resource for all of the Bridge People and other homeless people in the area too. He said, "No, we share."

Just down from the Six O'clock Store, there is a dumpster next to the house where the people who own the Six O'clock Store live. Since the Six O'clock Store is mostly a produce market, this dumpster is a good place to find fruits and vegetables, Jerry said. Evidently the family processed a lot of the produce at home and then took it to the store. Suzi checked the dumpster and found some good nectarines.

"It's the best little dumpster," Suzi said as she smiled and gave it an affectionate little pat.

It was one o'clock or so when we made it back to camp. We had been gone for about five hours. They had taken various breaks which amounted to about an hour, so they had worked for about four hours. They had made four dollars, which came to about fify cents an hour per person for the day.

When we sat down back at camp, we chatted for a few minutes. I told them that I had to be going. I had a few dollars on me, so I gave Tom a couple of bucks and Suzi and Jerry three bucks and a couple of cans of kippered herring that I had brought with me for emergency rations. I explained they were a small gift for having put up with me for a week. I thanked them for their hospitality. We all shook hands and said so long.

As I walked toward my motorcycle, I was struck by how much difference in their lives just a couple of bucks makes. Most of us hold a simpleminded notion that a dollar, by God, is a dollar. I wondered if a Jerry Michaels dollar has any relationship at all to a Donald Trump dollar or a Michael Milken dollar. For Jerry and Suzi, a four dollar day is pretty grim, but a six dollar day is really okay, especially if they find a fair amount of food and snipes. To improve their lives, according to their own views of their needs, seemed to take very little.

21. Big Joe's flame out

Almost three weeks had passed before I went back to the bridges. It was on a Thursday in late June at about seven in the evening. Tom, Suzi, and a guy I didn't know named Art were present. Jerry wasn't there when I first arrived, but Suzi and Tom told me that he was "hitting" the Angelo's dumpster and would be back shortly. The big news was that Big Joe was no longer around.

Suzi said, "Big Joe got pissed at us and he went on a drunk and he started making Molotov cocktails—"

"Where did he get the wine bottles?" I asked.

"There's hundreds of wine bottles over there," Tom said soberly.

"That's a joke! That's a joke, you guys!" I chuckled. Tom and Art laughed too, somewhat out of duty, no doubt, but it went well over Suzi's rather alcohol-fogged head and she earnestly continued her narrative without pause.

"And he went over to the gas station and got gas and he started one and he got mad at me and Jerry and he was gonna blow us up over here, and he blew himself up."

"Oh, he hurt himself?" I said sadly. I liked Big Joe in a way. I always felt that he was potentially dangerous, but I could also sense that he was a lonely, sad outsider, even under the bridges and he couldn't quite understand why.

"You know, he had those two king sized mattresses on top of one another, and they were sitting on top of six of these milk crates. Everything burned down on him. You see that burned stuff on the hillside?" Tom asked.

"Yeah, I saw that ash over there," I replied.

"The fire department came," Tom said. "And so he took off, and—this was about four days ago, and he hasn't come back. The fire department said they consider it arson. You see, he was throwing bottles at Eddie's store. He'd light them, but he didn't make them well enough so they didn't explode."

"He was BERSERK!" Suzi said.

"So he's never come back, and we're happy about that," Tom said. "Plus he stole some money from Suzi."

We moved on to other news. Suzi showed me her latest acquisition. She had found a little radio, about four inches tall. It was a cute caricature of a lion made of yellowish brown plastic. She called it Leo. She and Jerry operated it on AA cells that they frequently found in the trash. People evidently throw batteries away when they still have enough juice to run radio Leo.

I had brought them a few cans of beef stew, fruit cocktail, chili, and spaghetti and meatballs for their starvation kit. I had also brought a pack of Camels for Suzi, Jerry, and Tom, and, since I would be arriving at the cocktail hour, a fifth of sherry to sip while we talked. Everyone took a modest sip and then passed the bottle on. I was surprised at how dainty their sips were. It seemed that despite the considerable time I had spent with them, they were still somewhat on their good behavior with me. I found that somewhat disappointing, of course, as if I hadn't been quite accepted.

We sat around daintily sipping sherry while they caught me up on the rest of the news. Tom was occupying himself these days by reading the six Reader's Digest condensed books that Suzi and Jerry had found while dumpstering and given to him. Suzi said that they now had six kittens, since Dirty Mack had said that he didn't want the one that Big Joe had left at their campsite. Caltrans had finally come by a couple of weeks before to pick up the pile of garbage bags by the fence. There had been no hassle about moving the camp. The trash was removed by general relief workfare people, supervised by a couple of Caltrans personnel.

"You remember that burned mattress that was down there?" Tom asked, pointing to the bottom of the hill by the fence. "When they picked it up about thirty rats came running out of it. The guys FREAKED! They just freaked! A couple of them refused to pick up any more trash down there. Ha, ha, ha."

Jerry returned from his foraging with about five pounds of veal. He said that he had barely scratched the surface, that there was a lot left.

Jerry was dressed in Madras print shorts, a bright yellow surfer's tee shirt, clean white socks, and his Florsheim oxfords. He looked like a tourist from the Midwest, which he was—it had just been a very, very long tour.

The murder trial in which Jerry was a witness had been continued again. While he was on the subject, I asked him what he did with his canning stick while he was in court. He said that he took it to court, and the bailiff took it away from him.

Then he had to stagger over to the bailiff and get it back every time he wanted to go out into the hallway to have a cigarette. When he came back, he had to give the stick back to the bailiff. He mentioned that the policeman in Chinatown, Officer Fisher, had now taken four canes from him on the grounds that they were lethal weapons. John found the last one that Fisher had confiscated in a dumpster and brought it back to Jerry.

"He pays attention to me now when he sees me panhandling," Tom said matter-of-factly.

"Yeah, he's got a nose on Tommy now," Jerry said.

"Oh really? I wonder if that's 'cause he saw me with you that time?" I asked. I was pretty sure it was.

"Yeah. Well, he used to see me sitting there all the time, you know. Every day I'm waiting for a bus, but it takes me two hours," Tom chuckled.

I asked Jerry about how he felt about Big Joe. "I don't think there's anybody that wants him around here anymore."

"We, we, we, just tolerated him, you know," Suzi said.

"It was a good toleration type situation. Basically that's it right there. Nobody ever liked Joe. I don't know of anybody," Jerry said.

"We was always afraid of what he was gonna do," Suzi said.

A few minutes later, I asked Jerry how many years he had been panhandling.

"God, I don't know," Jerry chortled. "Twenty, off and on, maybe, right around in there."

"How long have you been under these bridges?"

"This is going on—Underneath this bridge?"

"Well, if you count all these bridges as a unit, how long?"

"As a condominium?" Jerry chuckled. "We're going on four years here. And I was two years down at the City of Hope, a year and a half at Martha's Kitchen, three years, about three years, at State Park."

After a while, Tom took his book and a blanket and shuffled a few yards away from our group to the north of the bridge. He spread the blanket in the tall Bermuda grass and lay on his stomach reading. The kittens would occasionally climb up on top of his large rump and play king of the mountain, tussling at the top and then rolling down off Tom and into the deep grass. The kittens were only four or five inches tall at that point in their lives. (For comparison, the fat, full-grown cat that reigns at my house is about ten inches tall). The small kittens could virtually disappear in the rangy grass. One would lurk, sneak, and then bound upon a brother or sister as it came creeping past. This victim would often be, in turn, stalking another brother or sister or it might be creeping up on one of those very real and bewitching things that only cats can see. Occasionally I would look up and see kitten stalking kitten stalking kitten.

While Tom was the peak attraction of this kitten arena, he was deeply immersed in his reading and seemed oblivious to them and to his campmates talking a few yards away.

"Look at those kittens on Tommy," I said.

"Oh yeah. Well, it's like climbing the Alps, you know. Look at that!" Jerry chuckled. Suzi cackled.

"I've taken care of Tommy SO many years..." Jerry began solemnly.

"How many years?" I asked.

"Oh, God," Jerry said. "Since we've been to Martha's Kitchen, or before even then. At State Park. And I feed him, and everything else. And I'll be the first one to admit, and, Suzi is always yellin' at me about it, that, she says, [in a raspy witch's voice] 'Tommy's takin' advantage of us! Takin' advantage! Takin' advantage!' But I, I just feel, I just feel like his brother. For two solid years, every night I went down to the City of Hope for beans and I took this Tupperware thing that I had, until Caltrans came through when I was in the hospital and stole it, but it was uh, a nine by thirteen cake pan with a lid on it. Tupperware. It was good. And I had them fill that up full of beans. And I brought it home every night for two solid years and fed Tommy. Tommy never moved out from underneath that bridge, the high bridge, unless he was going to go to the bathroom. That was the only time he moved for six months."

"And to go do Benny's laundry," Art said.

"Yeah, Benny's laundry on Tuesdays."

I asked Jerry about Eddie's liquor store and he said that Eddie was a rip off. He said that Eddie's sign said that he opened at seven thirty, but it was usually more like eight o'clock or later before he actually opened. "I see, so that's why you guys wait until eight until you get your morning jug?"

"Uh, no. We go to the Six O'clock Store. They're open," Jerry snapped his fingers, "on the beam at six o'clock."

"One time I was here and you waited 'til eight for something."

"That's what we were doin'," Suzi slurred. "We were waitin' to go to Eddie's."

"Oh, so sometimes you do go to Eddie's."

"Yeah, well, but not any more," Jerry said. He had had an argument with Eddie. Eddie wouldn't allow Jerry and the others to collect their mail there any more. He also used to allow Jerry credit on a bottle or two, but he had recently refused to do that anymore. Eddie also charged twenty-five cents more for a fifth than the Six O'clock Store did.

"That's half a pound of cans," Jerry said. (It was really less than a third of a pound of cans.)

"Or twenty-five per cent of a short dog," I added, "or a third of a pack of Bugler."

"Definitely," Jerry agreed.

"That's as far as I can go with that," I chuckled.

"Yeah, my arithmetic doesn't go even that far."

"But the Six O'clock Store closes at six in the evenings," I said, "and you have to go to Eddie's after that, huh? So you probably shouldn't make any rash judgments about Eddie's, 'cause one of these days you're gonna be thirsty, and it's gonna be six-thirty."

"I know. I know," Jerry said in mock gloom. Jerry is a witty, articulate guy, and that makes him a good field consultant. And he is reflective too, about many things. On the other hand, he is not above embellishing a story, and he is not always a keen observer of his own behavior, motives, and so on.

Events like this one have led me to believe that people are often not competent to accurately generalize about their typical behavior, their motivations, and so on. Of course, some are more honest (with themselves and others), accurate, and reflective than others. This is a difficult interpretive issue for ethnographers, who spend months or years getting to know the people they study, and a disaster for those social scientists depending on questionnaires and interviews.

I visited the Bridge People again a week later, at the end of June, 1989, as it was beginning to get dark. I parked in the lot to the west of Angelo's at about eight o'clock, and walked over to the bridge to see who was home. Jerry, Suzi, and Tom were there. Art had cut Jerry's and Tom's hair and they now wore it quite close cropped on the sides, about a quarter of an inch long around the ears, but about two and a half or three inches on top. The cut was very much the style those days in Los Angeles, but it didn't appeal to me. Jerry had also shaved off his long red beard, leaving a bushy full moustache; Tom was clean shaven. He wore the same clothing that he'd been wearing about a month before—tattered and dirty gray work pants and a gray pinstriped work shirt. He looked like a service station attendant who had fallen on very hard times. Suzi's hairdo had not changed. Her hair was a greying medium brown, shoulder length and wavy.

Jerry and Suzi had red, unfocused eyes. As usual, Jerry was sitting on his bed and Suzi on her couch. Both swayed very slightly as if on the deck of a boat in a calm seaway. The harsh, sharp edges of life under the bridge had been significantly softened for them by wine.

"So are you going to shpend the weekend with ush?" Jerry asked.

"Yeah," I said, "if that's okay."

"Oh, that'll be great."

I sat in the easy chair next to Suzi's couch. Tom got up from his mattress and walked over and sat directly across the hearth from me with his back to the street. I tossed him a pack of Camels. He caught them smartly and said thank you. I tossed another pack to Jerry. It bounced out of his heavy hands, but landed within easy reach on his bed. I had again brought a fifth of sherry to sip before retiring, so I cracked the bottle and passed it around. Jerry and Suzi were too far gone to be very interested in the wine, but the four of us formed something of a drinking and smoking circle as we chatted. They all lit cigarettes while I fumbled with my pipe. The beauty of pipe smoking, I thought, was that it afforded a major outlet for nervous fiddling, with a minimum of actual smoking and no inhaling at all. And, of course, pipe smoke smelled much, much better than other things that came wafting in on the breeze.

Jerry told me that Sam Robbins was sleeping on the mattress that I had slept on the last time I was there, but said that they would make a place for me. Sam had been sleeping up in the bushes near where the Mexicans were camped, and Jerry and Suzi were afraid that he would be hurt or rolled by them. They had gone over and helped him move his few belongings into Jerry's camp and he now had my old spot. I glanced over in the dim light and there he was, apparently asleep, but perhaps passed out. I was surprised that I hadn't noticed him before.

The latest news was that Big Joe was now on G.R. and staying in the Weingart Center. Jerry said that it was scary that he was still so close. They were worried that he might come by again and that he might have learned how to make a proper Molotov cocktail. Jerry and Suzi were convinced that Joe didn't like them. He was violent and unpredictable, they said. When I asked if they thought that was because he drank too much, they said no, he just didn't like them or anybody, even himself. Maybe especially himself. Rubio was like that too, they felt. The rumor was that Big Joe would wait around and do his work project until he got his first relief check, and then go back up to Portland, Oregon.

Tom told me that somebody had tried to break into a Corvette that had been parked nearby and was caught by the owner. The owner had chased the guy down the street. On a different occasion, a battery had been stolen out of a car that was parked on the street.

"The guy came up, and, you know, he was really rude about it. He says, 'You know anything about a battery out of a car?' I said, 'Naw.' He said, 'Well, you're lookin' awful innocent.'" Tom chuckled. "You know? Like we go around stealin' batteries out of cars. What in the world would I want with a battery?"

"You know, the good thing about Angelo's," Suzi slurred, "is that they know that we are not a part of that crap. And they know that we go over there and we report if we see anybody. We report them. They don't, they don't, you know, they know we are not a part of that, that bullshit. 'Cause we, we just take care of ourselves. But these son of a bitches, they come like, after eight o'clock, between seven thirty and nine o'clock, these son of a bitches come along up and down the street."

"They're bold on Sundays," Tom said calmly. "It's all the people who go to the Music Center."

"Don't they have an attendant here on Sundays?"

"Oh, not on weekends," Tom said. "It's like a free park. A lot of people park there who are going to the matinee on Sunday at the Music Center."

"So it's also open house for the burglars, huh?"

"Yeah," Tom said. He sometimes spoke in a languid manner that made me think he was in imminent danger of bursting into a yawn.

Jerry had pulled himself together when I first showed up, but by now he was on the verge of losing consciousness. He sat cross-legged, swaying uncertainly on his bed. He and Suzi had lapsed back into another of their perpetual, pointless fights. They were loudly slurring and slobbering. The softness of their syllables seemed to cushion some of the harsh, cutting comments. In the background, radio Leo was playing oldies in a thin, tinny voice.

Tom and I ignored all this and continued a quiet conversation.

"Fisher ran me out of Chinatown the other day twice. And I came back the third time. I went to Olvera Street and was sitting there for about an hour, you know, and I found a newspaper in the trash can, so I was reading that. And I thought, 'Well, I'll go sneak around the back way, and do something on Dale Street.' There's really not that much business on Dale, 'cause it's mostly big banks, it's not the little shops and arcades, you know, further up. I had just sat down on a bus bench, who comes out of the parking lot right there: Fisher! He said, 'This is the third time! Out!'"

Tom suggested that we take a walk down to Chinatown. I agreed, and we stood up to go. The next day was the first of the month, a good day for panhandling, and I wanted to see Tom at work, so I decided to go panning with him in the morning instead of canning with Jerry and Suzi. I told Jerry and he said fine. I said good night to Jerry and Suzi who were barely conscious at that point, and Tom and I shuffled down the hill to the fence. At the hole in the wire that functions as a gate, Tom pointed out a bush almost a yard tall with bright, five lobed, red flowers, which he identified as four o'clocks.

We heard what sounded like a couple of pistol shots not too far away as we were climbing through the fence. They didn't whistle and hum in our direction, so

I wasn't too concerned. Tom commented that it was common to hear gunshots around there, and I remembered hearing gunshots the last time I'd stayed under the bridge. We went past the Angelo's and down State toward Chinatown, talking as we walked.

Tom had had serious back problems. Although he rarely talked about it and I didn't get the impression during the time I spent with him that it bothered him much, he'd had a couple of surgical procedures done on his back which had affected his walk. He leaned forward from the pelvis as if he were carrying a heavy, invisible backpack. He had a large rump, made to seem larger by this tilt in his walk. When joking around, Jerry occasionally called him "the hips of death."

Tom said that a couple of nights ago, he and Art had gone down to Chinatown. Tom had wanted to panhandle for a while to make enough for a pouch of tobacco. Not a single Oriental person had given him money; all the money he got was from Hispanics. This was in marked contrast with his normal daytime experience. Usually the Oriental people gave him money and the Hispanics (and Whites) didn't. My experience was leading me to conclude that panhandling was usually quite unpredictable, the amounts panners collected and the kinds of people who made contributions varied widely.

That evening, as Tom went across the street to begin panhandling at Lee's Liquor, a familiar looking Oriental guy had come out. As he got closer, Tom realized that the man was Officer Mitchell, the Chinese policeman. He was wearing a sweatsuit and carrying a little bag. Tom said, "Oh, hi there!"

Officer Mitchell asked him what he was doing, and Tom told him that he was waiting for his friend who was making a phone call. Art was actually on the phone at that time, so it looked good, Tom said.

"He said, 'You won't make any money tonight,'" Tom chuckled. "He knew what I was doing."

Tom and Art had gone to Chinatown together the previous morning as well. Tom usually went to panhandle there at around ten thirty or eleven, but the preceding day he had arrived at nine thirty; he hadn't expected that it would be good for panhandling, but admitted that he'd done "reasonably all right ". It was the end of the month, and he hadn't been sanguine about his prospects, but he'd been pleasantly surprised. Tom was concerned about working too many hours at a location, because the longer he stayed the more likely it became that the police would see him. He said he liked to get to work and then get out of the area in a couple of hours. My impression was that it usually took him two or three hours to take in what he felt was his minimum daily allowance (my term).

He'd made about three dollars and fifty cents in about three hours. "And then this one guy was walkin' down the street, this Chinese guy, I guess he was about fifty years old. And I asked him if he could spare some change, and he gave me this filthy, hateful, dirty look! And he had on some of those old fashioned pants from the '40s that have the pleats and the cuffs and the slash pockets. And out popped a pack of Marlboros and the box had never been opened. And he kept on walking. I got up and scooped it off the sidewalk. It's worth a dollar seventy, so I traded it in at Lee's against what I was buying, plus the change that I had."

"What were you going to buy?" I asked.

"Oh, I bought a half pint of vodka and some roll tobacco. Tops." He added dramatically, "I mean, I wasn't going to smoke THOSE cigarettes. They're too expensive. A dollar seventy for a pack of Marlboros? I mean, for a dollar seventy you can get two packs of roll your own tobacco and have a great deal more."

"Yeah, that's right."

"Lee just raised the price of Tops to ninety cents. It used to be eighty five," Tom said.

For the day, in cash and merchandise, Tom had made about six dollars, he said, in about three hours. He felt pleased with this return. With the help of additional food from Jerry and Suzi, Tom could stretch that amount to cover a couple of days.

Tom told me about a couple of new bus lines called DASH. The buses travel from Chinatown through the Civic Center and the Financial, Flower, and Garment districts, and the fare is only a quarter. The buses drop people off at the bus stop where Tom worked. I asked if it had helped his business.

"No, I never ask them, 'cause you never get anything from White people," Tom chuckled.

"Yeah, but some of these guys that work the Courthouse say they make pretty good money."

"Yeah, there you do, but in Chinatown, it seems like you never get anything. And then I say 'I'm never gonna ask a White person again,' and a week will go by and I'll ask somebody, and I'll get fifty cents. So now I just ask everybody. And then," he sighed, "sometimes I don't."

"Yeah, that's what I hear is the best policy, just ask everybody," I said. I found it interesting that Tom considered fifty cents to be a pretty good hit.

"Yeah, ask everybody. Tomorrow is the first of the month so it should be very good....I want to panhandle tomorrow since it's Saturday and everything. Hopefully, I'll be able to make enough to coast through Sunday. Yeah, this is the first Saturday in the month, and it also falls on check day, so the way that that works out is that I'll have two good weeks and then things slow down."

Tom said that he was thinking about going down to LAMP, a drop-in center on Skid Row, to get cleaned up so that he could go to welfare to get signed up for food stamps.

"I hate going downtown, to tell you the truth. I don't mind dirty clothes, but I just refuse to walk into welfare being this dirty. Living under a bridge and panhandling on a bus bench is one thing, but sitting in an office, you know. It's different. It's gonna take hours. It's gonna be, oh, probably five hours. So I wanna be clean. And I'm going to take a couple of Reader's Digest Books with me," he chuckled.

Tom said that Larry, the guy who'd been camping across the street with Dirty Mack, had gotten on general relief a couple of weeks ago, but all the voucher hotels downtown were completely full so he'd been sent to 88th and Central, about nine miles south of downtown. This story surprised me, since the conventional wisdom is that homeless people migrate like sunbirds, south in the winter and north in the summer. In as much as this was summer and there were no vacancies in the downtown voucher hotels, it may be that too much is made of this seasonal migration pattern. There are at least a couple of other explanations: It may be that the county has figured another way to intentionally discourage the poor from applying for entitlements, that is, by offering them accommodations several miles from the downtown area where the other services they need are located and where their friends are. Or it may be that there are simply so many people without a place to live that the voucher system is overwhelmed. The voucher system seems a very poor approach to the housing problem anyway, since it creates no additional housing units. It places a still greater bureaucratic impediment before these disaffected people, by producing a *de facto* limit upon their access to even the rooms that are available.

Tom said that if he did apply for general relief, it would take longer than for food stamps, and they might want to give him a voucher for a hotel way out of the downtown area, which he considered unacceptable. If they gave him a voucher for the Weingart Center, which is in the heart of Skid Row, he probably wouldn't stay there either, he said. But he would accept the voucher and go sign in and out and probably "grab a shower" there once in a while. He preferred to live under the bridge and just get the food stamps. The Skid Row hotels are dirty, depressing, and dangerous, he said. As bad as most of these single room occupancy (SRO) hotels are, many street people do occasionally rent a room for a night, or a few nights, so they can get a shower. But generally they don't consider them viable options, primarily because of the expense.

While some panhandlers make wild claims about how much they make, the people I've spent time with, Bridge People and many others, made approximately five to fifteen dollars a day on average, amounting to, perhaps, one hundred fifty to three hundred dollars per month. The income of most of those I knew lay in the lower end of that continuum. By comparison, general relief provides about three hundred dollars a month. Rooms in Skid Row hotels cost around two hundred fifty to four hundred dollars a month. Some rooms are cheaper, but these are rarely available. Prices for the safer and cleaner rooms are on the high end of this spectrum. In these Skid Row hotels, safety is a serious problem. Among the several I stayed in, one had gained a reputation for having people thrown out of its tenth story windows every month or so. I was also told by some of the long term residents that sometimes when you got off the elevator, a gang of thugs would be there to "help you to your room." The bathroom doors often don't have working locks, so when someone's taking a shower, people sneak in to steal their pants. I didn't have any problems when I was there, but off and on all night I heard rats running in the walls and people yelling and bottles, thrown out of the windows, shattering explosively on the pavement far below.

We walked and chatted. Tom described how things had been going at camp. After a while, I asked how much Jerry had had to drink that day.

"Sam Robbins bought him a short dog in the morning. He gave Jerry sixty cents. And then Art bought Jerry a bottle that Suzi doesn't know about, and he drank that."

"A little one?"

"Yeah, a little one. And then they had two big ones when they came back from canning. Then Sam Robbins came over, and Suzi grabbed his bottle and killed that off after Sam passed out. And then Sam gave Suzi some money, and she came back with a big jug. And her and Jerry polished that off 'cause Sam was just playing with the cats and not keeping track of the bottle."

I figured that Jerry's share in all of that added up to approximately two and one half fifths of wine for today, a bit above his theoretical pass out point.

When we got to Lee's, Tom asked me if I could buy him a cold beer. I would have liked one myself, but I didn't have any money with me and told him so. It was really hot and humid. If it weren't for the lack of mosquitos, I'd have sworn I was in the tropics.

"Well, you know, I'm not really in the mood to panhandle. After all, I've got smokes," he said grinning. He was referring to the Camels I had given him earlier. We stood on the corner for a few moments watching the traffic, then he said, "Oh, well, we might as well head back."

The possibility that I might buy him a cold beer may have been a factor in Tom's wanting to walk to Chinatown. However, he does take an evening stroll over there on his own from time to time. I think he just likes to get out of camp in the evening when Jerry and Suzi get sloshy. In any case, he didn't express much disappointment about the beer.

The lives of homeless people that I saw were suffused with disappointment: they limped from the cumulative weight of it. But on a blow by blow basis, they shrugged it off, sometimes bravely, sometimes with a dash of humor or a shot of wine. Always, just below the surface, there was a sort of sad detachment from life, as though they were just doing time. They showed very little hostility, hatred, or anger, although those feelings were certainly justified by their circumstances. They manifested, instead, a heaviness of spirit, a suffocating demoralization—an emotional callous developed over a lifetime of rubbing up against a harsh reality. They wore their apathy like a bullshit-proof vest.

We turned around and walked back toward the bridge, this time going up Buena Vista Street. There are several blocks of vacant lots where mansions once stood. Two and three yard tall retaining walls built of large round river cobbles line the sidewalk. Broad concrete stairways lead up to weedy patches of dirt surrounded by huge, old date palms, fig and pepper trees, and leggy shrubs in what were once yards. In one front yard, near a huge old fig tree, is a tiny chapel constructed of cobbles. Since it's at the top of a two yard retaining wall, it's pretty well out of the sight of passersby on Buena Vista. I didn't measure the chapel, but I estimate it to be only about two by three yards. Tom said that a homeless woman, "a psych case," lived there. Other homeless people camped back from the street here and there under trees.

23. A night in the upper camp

We arrived back at the bridge around nine thirty. The camp was quiet. Tom said that it was very late for him and that he was going to go to bed. Since Sam Robbins had my old sleeping spot, I had told Tom that I'd sleep in the upper camp. He pointed out the trail to it as we walked by. I was surprised that he had showed it to me, since I had been at their camp so much and knew very well where it was. I wished him a good night. The trail from Cardenas to the campsite is steep and goes straight up the fall line. Like most steep fall line trails, it is badly rutted by erosion. I gingerly picked my way up the hill.

There was no longer a mattress at the campsite. Tom had told me that the Mexicans across the way had taken it to their camp. There were, however, several pieces of corrugated cardboard. Since this is a standard mattress for street people on Skid Row, I thought it would be a good idea to experience at least one night on cardboard. I found that a couple of layers of cardboard was only a little harder than a thin Ensolite backpacking pad. Neither is very comfortable.

The upper bridge is much noisier than the lower bridge. I could look down on the zooming cars and trucks through the trees and bushes. The din was deafening. I was surrounded by shrubs and eucalyptus trees on either side of the bridge in something that looked like a bucolic, peaceful setting. Yet maybe only twenty or thirty yards to either side and slightly below me roared one of the busiest freeways in L.A.

It was a still tropical night. Perspiring after the short climb up to the campsite, I arranged my cardboard and lay down. I decided not to go get my down parka and windpants out of the motorcycle saddlebags, because it was so warm I thought they would be unnecessary. After listening to the roar of the freeway, I gradually drifted off to sleep at about eleven o'clock.

I was awakened from a deep sleep by what I thought was a minor crash on the freeway. It sounded as if someone had drifted into the guardrail and slammed a fender, but maintained control of the car and driven on. I pushed the tiny button on my watch and the little light came on. It was one fourteen.

A few minutes later, there was a minor accident on Cardenas below and a bit to the south of my camp, toward Angelo's. It was about forty or fifty yards away from my perch on the ledge. It involved what looked like an old Pinto and an American van. The Pinto had evidently suffered a thoroughly bent fender and the driver and passenger tried to bend it back out so they could proceed. A small Japanese car stopped as well and the people in it got out to help. They fiddled with the bent fender for some time and then drove off, evidently to summon help. Soon there were a couple of other cars there with several people talking and trying to fix the car. It looked like a group of actors or musicians on their way home from the Music Center. Soon the drama began to drag, so I drifted back off to sleep.

I awoke again at about two o'clock. Cold had begun to seep in and stiffen me. I lay there, tense against the chill, lazily pondering the option of getting up and walking over to the motorcycle to get my parka, a distance of only about a hundred fifty or a hundred seventy-five yards round trip. I thought about the two or three million homeless people in this great country, many of whom were probably sleeping out that night too, but without a parka to put on if they woke up from the cold. I lay there half asleep, wondering if I should try to tough it out just to see what it was like. I reflected that I had slept cold occasionally on pack trips or ski mountaineering trips, so I already knew very well what it's like to sleep cold. Or rather, to lie awake cold. I don't really sleep if I'm cold, I just lie there with my body tense and my mind spinning like a bald tire on snow. Eventually I concluded that I wasn't going to be able to work very well the next day without some sleep, so I got up, and took the trudge.

It was very quiet and eerie walking to the motorcycle. Downtown isn't really dark at night. It's lit with various bulbs and tubes that give off sickly shades of blue and green. The light gives things a ghostly cast. Places that you are accustomed seeing in warm sunlight, bustling with people, are always eerie when seen deserted in the silent dead of night.

After I got my parka, I slept warm and well and the rest of the night was more or less peaceful. I awoke at about five thirty as it was getting light, but just lay there on my narrow ledge thinking for a while. I could faintly hear the people under the lower bridge as they talked among themselves, so I knew they were awake. They would be lounging around, still in bed, smoking cigarettes. If I hadn't been along to provide a supply of "ready-made" cigarettes, they would be rolling or rerolling some Tops or Buglers or smoking snipes with crutches.

I went back to sleep for a while, then at about six thirty I got myself together and brushed my teeth as I sat on the cardboard watching the cars down below on Cardenas. I wiped off my face and hands with a towelette, then I gathered up my parka and windpants and picked my way down the trail to the lower bridge campsite.

When I got down to the lower camp, Jerry and Suzi were sitting up in their respective sleeping places talking, and Tom was lying on his mattress reading. It appeared that Jerry had slept in his shoes last night. I had thought that he normally slept in his clothes, but not his shoes. I had slept in my shoes also. When you sleep out in an urban setting, it's safer to leave your shoes on. It makes them more difficult to steal, and, should the need arise, you are better prepared to repel boarders. These are reasons other homeless people have given me for sleeping in their shoes. I neglected to get Jerry's comments, but my guess is that he had just passed out wearing his.

I sat around chatting with Jerry and Suzi for about half an hour. Tom said that Sam Robbins had "hit the road" at first light to go panning. He had had "the bad shakes" that morning and was fairly desperate for a bottle, Tom said. I reminded Jerry that I had decided to go panning with Tom that day, and told him that I would like to go canning with him the next day. He said that would be fine. I asked Jerry and not Suzi because he seems to set their agenda. I had told him about this the night before, but he had been pretty drunk, so I didn't think that he remembered it. He didn't.

I had to make some phone calls and put away the parka and windpants, so I excused myself at about seven. I walked over to the motorcycle and locked the things in the hard, plastic saddlebags. I then headed down to Market to see if I could find any of my other street friends to hang out with until about ten or ten thirty when Tom normally left for Chinatown.

When I got back to the bridge, Tom was lying on his mattress reading, as usual. No one else was in camp. We chatted while he got ready to go. According to Tom, Jerry didn't remember that I had given him a pack of cigarettes the night before. Suzi had seemed just as drunk then, but had somehow ended up with the cigarettes and had hidden them. When Jerry had asked for a cigarette that morning, she gave him one of the Camels without showing Jerry that she had a whole pack. "She's dispensing them," Tom chuckled.

Tom reported that they had all had a nice breakfast while I was gone. I asked for details.

"Well Jerry and I found a ten pound box of miniature hot dogs. Cocktail hot dogs. They were frozen solid in the dumpster at Angelo's. And there's nothing wrong with them and Jerry found about two pounds of Mozzarella cheese and Suzi found about four pounds of assorted vegetables: zucchini, celery, and carrots. And they boiled that up. There's a one pound piece of pepperoni, Gallo pepperoni, like they put in the pizzas. They cooked that up like corned beef with all the veggies in it. We had a cantaloupe.

"The cats had five pounds of roast beef, which they ate already, from yesterday. Now they're finishing off some ricotta and spaghetti and ravioli. They like spaghetti. That's just the way they are. If you gave them cat food or dog food, they wouldn't eat it. They're spoiled. And you see that bunch of stuff down there on the walkway?"

"Yeah."

"That's crab legs. They had that the day before yesterday. There must have been about three pounds of meat on it."

I commented on a pair of new shoes near Jerry's bed. Tom said that they were Sam Robbins's. "He found them and doesn't need them, so he thought that some of us could wear them. But I'm a ten and a half or eleven and Jerry's a nine. Plus, Jerry's got two other pairs of tennies. For the first time in three years, I now have two pairs of shoes."

"Yeah, those look like nice ones, the ones you have on there."

"Yeah, they were expensive when I got them. But they're slowly starting to fall apart. There's still some tread left."

Tom dug around in some bags of belongings amid the trash behind his mattress and after a moment came up with a pair of nylon and leather hiking boots. They weren't new, but seemed to be in very good condition. Tom was understandably very proud of them.

"And they fit me! I wore them once. When these wear out," he said, referring to the dirty, tattered court shoes he was wearing, "I'll switch."

"Yeah, those are great. They're just what you need for around here, 'cause you get good traction climbing up the hill."

Tom finished lacing up his court shoes over his bare feet and we were finally on our way. He also carried what had formerly been a trendy mineral water bottle as a canteen. He typically filled it at a hose bib on the side of a house on his route to Chinatown.

"I usually try to get down to Chinatown by about eleven. Well, in the summer I like to get down there a little earlier because the older people want to avoid the heat, so they go early. It's especially important to get down there around the first of the month, when they get their disability and social security checks. I'll say that seventy-five per cent of all the money I make comes from senior citizens. Come the end of the month, my income really goes down. Now, since school's out, I'll be picking up more, 'cause there's a lot of kids, high school kids. They're pretty good too, you know, they come through for me."

"Yeah, come to think of it, one of the times I was down there with you working, you got a couple of scores from high school kids. Little Oriental high school kids."

Tom asked me if I had any access to clothing. He needed some shirts, he said. He was down to two shirts that fit him. He wore an extra, extra large. "Jerry gave me a whole bunch of shirts, and so did Joe, but they're only extra large and they're made in Korea, and I can hardly squeeze into them."

As we walked along, Tom told me that he'd once gotten on general relief, but had been terminated after nine months because of a bureaucratic mixup and had just said "to hell with it."

"So I moved back to living in State Park. I'd go to the missions and eat. I could panhandle enough to come up with some tobacco. And then Benny said, 'You wanna do my laundry once a week?' So there was five bucks. Richard wanted his laundry done, and that was five dollars. Then I could make ten dollars every Thursday unloading the truck at Mack's Market. The grocery truck. So I had twenty a week, which kept me in roll your own cigarettes."

"Do you smoke more than one of those packets a day?"

"I could if I had them, but I cut it down 'cause I can't afford it."

"Uh huh. So now how much do you smoke, maybe one a day, something like that?'

"No, about three quarters." He coughed a couple of times, which added a nice touch of irony.

I fished around in my pockets and came up with a couple of packs of cigarette papers, which I handed to Tom.

"Oh, thank you. I'll give one to Suzi and Jerry."

"Okay." I had intended to ask him to give them one and was pleased that he had offered. "Jerry said that he'd been livin' under the bridge now for four years. Is that right?"

"No, he's crazy. No. I lived here—All right, this coming Christmas will be our second Christmas. Two years. That's all. And then Jerry was gone for six months and I lived by myself."

"When he had his stroke and was in the hospital?"

"Naw, naw. He was just on a drunk downtown. See, we were there for four days on my food stamps from January and February and then I gave Jerry my last five dollar food stamp and he was going to the Grand Central and bring back a loaf of bread and whatever, some food. And then he never came back. So he was gone for three weeks and I went and found him. And he said, [old man's raspy voice] 'I don't want to live up there. I want to live down here with Tex. We're panhandling, makin' ten, fifteen dollars every day.' And they were sleeping with the Justiceville people [a short-lived homeless activist group] in the tunnels [at the Music Center] for a while. And I spent most of January and February by myself and then one day Jerry came up. I was flat broke. The next day I was going to do Benny's laundry, so fine, I had something to look forward to. And Jerry had two shopping bags and he was drunk. I mean, as a skunk. And he sat down, and he says, 'I'm movin' back in!' I said, 'Okay. Your shit's still here. What's left of it, that hasn't been stolen.' And he said, 'Okay.' The big sleeping bag was there and that's all he cared about. And I said, 'Well, what clothes you had, the Mexicans stole.' He says, 'I got a few things somewhere else, I'll go get them later.' So Jerry hands me a fifth of Thunderbird. 'Oh, well thank you, Jerry.' He handed me a six pack of beer and a half pint of vodka. And he threw me two packs of cigarettes. He said he'd panhandled forty dollars in two hours at the State Building.

"So then the next morning, I told him, 'Well, I've got to go do Benny's laundry and make my five dollars.' He said, 'Well, you have to hurry right back, 'cause I have to go panhandle and you have to watch the camp.' I said, 'Well, I'm going to come right back, anyway.' You know. So I did that, and the next day after that I says, 'I've got to do Richard's laundry.' So I went and did it and came back and the next day, I told Jerry I was going to get it together to go panhandling in Chinatown, which everybody's been talking about. 'Cause Jerry's panhandling the State Building and doesn't need any competition. And he says, 'Naw, that's all right, we have so much stuff now.' 'Cause Jerry had gone out the very next day and bought pots and pans and he'd dug a firepit. And then one of his customers brought three shopping bags full of dishes, we got a dish drainer, an egg flipper, all this old stuff that she had in her garage, camping equipment type stuff.

"And so Jerry said, 'They'll steal it.' He says, 'You just stay here and I can panhandle enough to bring you back a couple of beers and a cheap half pint.' And I says, 'Well, I'd rather have the tobacco, but Jerry, I can go out and get it on my own.' He said, 'No, no, that's all right! I make SO MUCH, Tommy. It's NO problem.' Well it was like that way for about two months. And I would leave to go do Benny's laundry, Richard's laundry, and do Richard's dry cleaning, and once a week I would unload the truck. I'd bring back Jerry's wine. When I'd do Richard's laundry, or Benny's, I'd just throw in our clothes with theirs." He chuckled, "Of course, I wouldn't say anything to them, 'cause they'd freak! You know. Forget doin' their laundry ever again.

"And so Jerry started becoming abusive. He really started drinking and then I'm hearing, 'Fat slob! You never do anything! I'm the one! If it wasn't for me, you'd starve to death, you son of a bitch!' And he complained bitterly to EVERYBODY. That I don't do anything. John came up there and said, 'Why don't you panhandle, Tom, and get your own instead of sponging off of Jerry?' I jumped up and I told him, 'I'll beat your ass! Get the FUCK out of my face!' You know?"

Of course, the Bridge People used the term fuck to mean a variety of things, just as it is used in the rest of U.S. society, but here it is used quite frequently. When Tom used it to mean something like "to hell with you," he had a way of spitting the word in your face. For a second, with just that word, he let out a short, hostile hiss. It was like a little leak of frustration's caustic steam that normally simmers unnoticed deep within his soul.

"So then, Jerry and I had a fist fight. He attacked me with a knife, so I just backhanded him. He rolled down the hill. Then he had two seizures, and then I felt sorry for him. And then, he wound up drunk with Larry. Larry and Abe were living under the low bridge, by the parking lot [the northern one nearer the service station and Eddie's Market and away from Angelo's] and he could never make it up. He was so fucking drunk, he couldn't come up from the low bridge up to my bridge, and one day, he says—He sobered up and came up and got some clothes. He started coming up to get clothes 'cause he had the diarrhea so bad, he'd just shit. And he must have had twelve pairs of pants. I said, 'Jerry, this is the last clean pair of pants you've got in this bag.' I says, 'Where are your other clothes?' He says, 'In another dirty bag. We'll go do the laundry one of these days.' He says, 'I just can't make it up here.' See, Larry was workin' in the parkin' lot and makin' fifty dollars a day and keepin' everybody drunk."

"Fifty?"

"Yeah! Larry had lots of money. And Whisperin' Bill got a check for over five hundred dollars from somewhere, and, see Larry works at a parking lot downtown and he gets paid. He's a parking lot attendant. He gets paid cash money. So then Sam Robbins was gettin' food stamps and Sam would buy everybody a bottle of wine. Abe was getting a welfare check AND food stamps, so it was one big blowout party down there. So Jerry was so plastered, he could never make it up the hill. And he was gone for like six months.

"Then later, I was getting food stamps and we'd go down to the Grand Central Market. We bought up enough groceries to get enough change. I'd buy a single loaf of bread, put down a food stamp, and get back seventy-five cents. Jerry would do the same. We'd do it on a single apple. A single tomato. Then we'd go back for another single tomato. By the time we were finished we'd have ten tomatoes, ten oranges, and ten apples, and thirty dollars in cash. So I bought Jerry tobacco, I bought myself tobacco, a fifth of Cabin Still bourbon. [Falsetto voice] Ooooo!" Tom grinned and did a parody of a corny television salesman with a W. C. Fields voice. "'Five ninety-nine! On sale!' And I bought two six packs of beer and we just, just tore it up. And then, my food stamps ran out in September and I,"

Tom sighed, "I never went back, down to welfare, 'cause then I was already panhandling."

Another time, Tom called this process of getting change from small food stamp purchases, "breaking down the food stamps." It's not necessary anymore, because most liquor and grocery stores in the area will simply take food stamps for liquor and tobacco purchases although it's against the law to do so. It's really an unenforceable, cosmetic statute. There are also enterprising street people acting as food stamp brokers who will give a person cash, minus a commission, for food stamps, typically seventy-five dollars cash for ninety dollars worth of food stamps.

"Jerry said, 'How can you just go out and panhandle now, and leave our stuff up there?' I says, 'Well, Jerry, you said you could handle it. Keep me in cigarettes and beer. But you left. Where's this bullshit attitude?' I said, 'I spent my money.' I was makin' twenty a week between Richard and the laundry and unloading the truck. I said, 'I spent it on you.' 'Yeah, but that's only once a week!' See when Jerry was drunk, he'd want to fight about that. And then another reason I was glad he left. You know what it's like to lug a five gallon jug of water up that hill? And do you know what it is to have to go look for wood every day? Then have to have water to wash up dishes? I didn't care about hot food! I said, 'Fuck it!' When Jerry left, I started going to the missions, then I found out about the dumpster, from Karen and Mark."

"At Angelo's?"

"Yeah. And then they left, Karen and Mark, and John moved over. And Mack moved in there. And John would cook something up, 'Tom, you want some hot food?' I said, 'No, I don't care about hot food.' He says, 'You hungry?' I says, 'No, not really.' So I ate at the mission and I panhandled. Plus I'd buy a can of frijoles and some tortillas. So I learned where the good dumpsters were. I was panhandling three days a week. Then it was Jerry's whole attitude that he was supporting me. Well, he wasn't. Well, I suppose in a way he was, but he's the one who said, 'I have SO much. You could just sit here all day and read your books, and do your thing with Richard and Benny and unload the store two days out of the week. And the rest of the week, I can handle it.'"

"So you feel he put you into a double bind, huh? He said stay here in camp and then he groused about you being in camp?"

"Yeah. So then when I started leaving to go panhandle, Jerry would be sittin' there furious. 'Cause he went to panhandle and I went and panhandled and came back and they'd stolen his brand new Levi jacket. Plus they took the groceries that Jerry had bought. Canned goods. Jerry said, 'If you'd just BEEN HERE!' I say, 'Hey man, FUCK YOU! Give me five dollars every morning! In my pocket! And I'll baby sit.' 'Cause see, I can go out and panhandle and get more than that."

"Yeah. How come you guys don't use those lockers built into the bridge? Is it too much hassle?"

"No, it's not too much hassle. Karen and Mark had three Crescent wrenches and they got a big bolt with double nuts on it and they'd tighten it up. And I told Jerry we could do that and he said, 'Oh, better than that, we should go out and get a bunch of cheap padlocks.'"

"Yeah, you can get a cheap padlock for a few bucks."

"Yeah, but any of those cheap padlocks, if anybody really wants into them, a wine bottle will break them open."

"Yeah, I guess you'd need to buy a fairly decent padlock, maybe spend ten bucks." I caught myself and added, "but ten bucks, I guess, is a lot of money."

"Well, we can get a cheap Crescent wrench for two bucks. All it needs is two Crescent wrenches. To hold the nut. You just tighten it so tight that nobody without another Crescent wrench can ever get into it. But with me being there all the time, it was never a necessity, and then when Jerry left, I didn't care if they stole anything. See, everything I thought was worth saving, I took with me. See, the only thing to take with me were my headphones, my cigarette lighter, and my cigarettes. If they steal my clothing, I can go to the missions. If they steal the blankets. Every blanket they got after a while, and I went to Mack, owner of Mack's Market, and I said, 'Mack, somebody stole our blankets. Do you have any old blankets at home?' He says, 'Yeah.' He says, 'I'll bring some tomorrow.' He gave me four really nice blankets. So, you know, there's lots of places I can go and get things. And so I didn't care if they stole anything. They stole two of my pants. I had just got four pairs of pants that fit me. Look how fat I am. Ha, ha, ha. It's not so easy to find pants this big.

"So then Jerry moved back in after a while, up to where I was living, and then all that bullshit started, with Big Joe and Tiny coming back, and then Jerry decided that he wanted to live down there on the low bridge again because he was starting to drink heavily again. So Jerry moved down where we are all living now. So one day, it was about six o'clock and it's already starting to get dark, and they yelled up at me, 'Come on down, we've got all this extra food!' I said, 'Oh, well, I'm not hungry!' They said, 'You'll like this. It's a burrito! Plus we've got a bag of chips that's never been opened.' And they told me what it was and I said, 'All right! I'll have it in the morning!' So I went down the hill and we talked. And then about two or three days a week, Suzi would bring up stuff like that. 'Come on down! We have so much, we hate to throw it away!' They'd give John and them some food, Tiny some food. They gave John Morris some food.

"And now Suzi is sayin' that if wasn't for her, I would starve to death. Now with me living there, if they don't cook, I have nothing to eat. Like I'm just, you know, just sittin' back. And like I told Suzi the other day, she offered me some of that stuff and I said, 'I don't want it, Suzi. I don't want to hear any complaints that all I'm doing is just sponging off of you. I don't smoke your cigarettes, I sure as hell don't drink your wine and,' I says, 'I went to the dumpster too, and half of all that Jerry and I dug out, it's mine.' And some guy came over the other day and gave her these sweet rolls. And her and Jerry were fighting savagely and, um, who was it? Art was sitting there. And I had two six packs of beer and a pint of vodka; it was gonna last me a day and a half. And I'm sitting there and I said, 'Suzi, that guy's tryin' to give us some free food down at the sidewalk.' And she turned. And Jerry was calling her a bitch and a whore and everything and this guy didn't know WHAT to do. He had this bag of these big French pastries: sweet bread with cream filling in it. Kinda like a strange looking cream puff. And she brought them back and said, [witchy voice] 'What are they? Well, there's three of them. One apiece.' So she put them back and went back to their argument.

So the next morning I got up and just took one, 'cause Jerry said that any food that comes in over the fence belongs to all of us, but any money belongs, the money belongs to anyone they give it to unless they specify to divvy it up. So then Suzi got bent out of shape about that, and then, the roast beef, she was bent out of shape about that, because I found five pounds of roast beef and just took half of it and gave it to the cats. Suzi feeds the cats, but she wanted to make a stew with all them vegetables and that roast beef. Well, I said, 'I found it.' You know? And then she knows that I'm not eating, but her biggest bitch to Jerry is, 'How can he be so fat? Look how much he eats. He goes to the dumpster and comes back with six cheeseburgers. And eats them!' Well, that's why I'm fat!" Tom chuckled. "Ha, ha, ha. What the hell does she want?"

"That's certainly not her problem, though, is it."

"I KNOW! And Jerry told her fuck it, he could care less. You know, 'So Tommy's fat,' you know, and she says, 'That's worse than being a drug addict.'" Tom laughed heartily, and I joined in. "And then she launched. That was her opening to tell us that she's never done drugs. Which I honestly believe. She's of an older generation. She's ten years older than I am."

"How old do you think she is?"

"I think Suzi's fifty-one, fifty-two. She was born in '38 or '39. That would be ten years older than I am, 'cause I was born in '47. But she was very pleasant this morning....But you know, when you showed up, you must have immediately realized that they were crocked."

"Oh, yeah," I said.

"And in a hateful mood."

"Oh, yeah, I could tell."

We arrived at Tom's office, a bus stop on a busy corner in the heart of Chinatown. We just sat on a bench and continued talking. Tom didn't seem in any hurry to begin work, although there were plenty of pedestrians passing by.

"So you think the key to living under the bridge is really just to travel light. I mean not accumulate a lot of stuff and not have to hassle with cooking and that kind of thing?"

"Yeah. Yeah. See I appreciate the hot meals that Suzi cooks, but, well, everybody bitches that everybody else is bummin' off of them. I've bitched about Suzi when she comes over and picks up the butts at the end of my bed."

"'Cause that's your resource, huh?"

"Yeah, that's my resource. So now I put my butts in a little tunafish can. And she came over there and she's lookin' around for them butts. And I says, 'Suzi, I'm savin' my butts now.' You know, I said, 'Panhandling's not as good as it used to be.' Even at the first of the month, it's not as good as it used to be when I first started two years ago."

"Why do you think that is?"

"I don't know. I think maybe…I think it's 'cause I'm there so often, the novelty wore off of a White boy panhandling in Chinatown. I recognized people. I see the same people day in and day out. I recognized the same secretaries that I never bother to ask, 'cause they've never done anything. Except this one business woman. Has her own business up the street, she always wears slacks and a blouse, you know. She never gave me money, but she always smiles. Now she gives ten cents. After a year. Ha, ha, ha, ha."

"Ten cents?"

"Yeah. Ha, ha. But I don't care, 'cause she always smiles and she's very nice about it. And she speaks English, and she's got three kids, and they're all very nice kids…."

"So everybody is excited that Big Joe is gone," Tom commented. "He's on welfare and getting his check. I don't think he'd ever be coming back. He had gone and told Tiny and all of them, that since there was so much bullshit with all the Mexicans, he would stay in camp if they could keep him in liquor and cigarettes. And Dirty Mack and Tiny were doing it for a while and then Tiny left. And Mack was giving him three to five dollars every day. He was telling him, 'Mack, they'll steal everything you have.' You know, 'Nobody else will help me out, it's up to you.' So Mack was makin' all that money, you know. Mack drinks a fifth of bourbon a day plus he smokes two packs of cigarettes a day. He buys Dorals and he eats and was feeding the cats and buying them cat food. You know. So then, Joe had that going for him. And then Larry moved out, so there was no freebies coming from Larry, and then Will moved out, 'cause they opened up his stomach and they took out part of his intestines. He had a perforated ulcer. He was throwing up blood. Oh, it was ugly. The paramedics took him. So it boils down to Dirty Mack and Sam Robbins. And Sam doesn't panhandle that much. And Mack started refusing. He had to, 'cause they ran him out of his Courthouse Building spot, so all he was making was four or five dollars a day.

"He used to sit there for four hours and he would not leave. He had his watch. He would not leave until four hours had passed. And he would leave with nothing less than twenty. And he'd go get a fifth of bourbon for six fifty. A rot gut bourbon, you know. And uh, so this was when Jerry and Suzi were still sick and had diarrhea for a month and just laid there. Every morning he'd bring them cigarettes, fried eggs, and sausages. And he'd bring them two bottles of wine. Sometimes he'd apologize 'cause all he had was enough money left over to get them one jug, but he'd say, [raspy old man's voice] 'I'll be back at lunch.' So he kept them drunk and in cigarettes. Sometimes a pack of Dorals and then to kinda make the money go further, he'd throw in a pack of Bugler. So now, Mack is making so much less money, he's not drinking bourbon himself.

"And so Joe would take Sam out and let Sam do the panhandling for him. And then Joe would just sit back and help him drink it up. And then Sam Robbins took off one day. And then Joe went on this drunk and was throwin' these Molotov cocktails."

"So you think that might have had something to do with why he spun out?

"Yeah. Suddenly nobody would do anything for him."

Later Tom spoke about his relationship with Jerry again. "See Jerry and I don't argue about anything. It's just that Suzi complains. It's always something. You know, I went down. This guy brought us a whole pizza. And I told Jerry, 'We have a whole pizza that was bought for us.' They were too drunk to walk down the hill to get it. I said, 'One third of this pizza is mine and the rest belongs to you.' And he says, 'Yeah.' I took one third of it and put it in a plastic bag and went over to my bed. I read my book and ate one piece and put the rest of it away for later on. And they didn't eat. And the next morning Suzi got up and looked at that pizza, she took one bite out of it and she decided to feed it to the birds. She was already drunk. She just fed two thirds of a good pizza to the birds. Jerry freaked....Now I don't touch any of their stuff."

"Yeah."

Tom and I had been sitting on his bus bench for almost half an hour, and he had yet to begin panhandling for the day. He liked to start the day with some change, so he fished around in his pockets to find a lucky penny that he thought he had. I told him that I had some change he could start with. I reached into my pocket and came up with eleven cents. He remarked that it would bring him luck. Many panhandlers have a lucky coin or little ritual or habit that they half-heartedly believe might bring them luck, like a weekend fisherman with a lucky hat or favorite fly. Although some panhandlers walk around, most sit at the side of a steady stream of pedestrians, ply their line, and try to set the hook. Most seem to think that what they say and do only has limited effect on their income, and come to believe that luck is the major factor in their success or failure for the day. Luck in this context is as good an explanation as saying that it is the result of random events, or fate, or the work of gods. It's hard not to believe in luck or some such thing when you occasionally get a "big hit" for no apparent reason, then go weeks or months without one.

Tom continued talking about life under the bridges. "Like this morning, Jerry said, 'You want some of those vegetables, Tom?' I said, 'Sure.' He said, 'Well, don't eat them all!' I keep hearin' that."

"Yeah....So do you have any tactics for reducing conflict there?"

"Yeah, I just go out and get my own food, most of the time. But if they're gonna cook up two pots of food, and then get so drunk they're not going to eat it and then wind up throwing it out, I might as well have some. But there's a price to be paid for that."

"Yeah, I asked Jerry one time about the value of you being in camp a lot, and he refused to acknowledge that it was of any service to him at all."

"What did you say?"

"Basically I said that you're there a lot, not all the time, but a lot and I said it seemed to me that the more somebody's there, the safer it is for all the stuff, you know. But he said that it didn't really matter."

"Yeah, he's right. It doesn't really matter. There's so much shit there, what could they steal?

"Well, it seems to me that there are some things that they'd feel very badly about if they were stolen. Like radio Leo, you know. I mean they're gettin' a lot of enjoyment out of radio Leo right now."

"Suzi takes it with her."

"Oh." I hadn't realized that, but the Bridge People do take with them anything they really want to keep. Bigger items, like bedding and spare clothing, they think of as more or less disposable and replaceable.

Tom coughed for a few seconds. "You see, they asked me to move over, I didn't ask them. 'Cause I was havin' the trouble with the Mexicans."

"Yeah."

"So I just thought, sure, why not, you know. Well, any time Jerry gets drunk and he makes a big pot of stew, I help myself to a little, he says, [gruff, old man's voice] 'Well don't eat it all, Tom!' 'Cause I'm fat. So I always get—Well one day I just took and dumped every bit of it back into the pot and I said, 'Keep it.' I went back to my bed and was reading my book and Jerry brought over a bowl, and he said, 'Well, you can eat some, but you don't have to eat it all.' And I said, 'Well who in the FUCK said I was going to eat it all?' So I got up and dumped it back in the pot again."

I had to chuckle at that and Tom joined in.

"So about that time, Julio showed up and he said, 'What are you doin'? I said, 'Nothin'.' He said, 'Go to the store.' And he gave me some money and says, 'Get yourself a half a pint and a six pack of beer and bring me back a half pint of gin and two of those little tonic bottles,' he said, 'and get about five books of matches."

"Oh," I said chuckling, "we have a little rock, huh?"

"Yeah, he had some rock. A twenty dollar rock. I don't care about it. Let them smoke that rock. So Jerry watched Julio smoke that rock. He had to come up, [affected, musical voice] 'Well, hi Julio! How are ya?'

"See, Jerry won't spend his money on coke, but anybody pops a rock in a pipe and shoves it in his face, he's not gonna refuse. John spent his whole check one month in three days. His whole welfare check on rocks. It was when he was living on the other side of the street. He came up there one day and he gave me a ten dollar rock and I said, 'What's this for?' He said, 'Well, I want to sit up here and smoke my rocks, but I don't want you to say anything to anybody about it. I don't want to do it down in front of them.' 'Cause he was livin' there with—Jerry was there, Suzi was across the street by herself or with Jimmy Newby, so it was Larry, Mack, and John…and Abe. It wasn't too long ago. And I says, 'I don't care if you want to smoke this rock, but I don't want a rock.' I said, 'I'd rather have you just give me three or four dollars and I can go to the liquor store and get a cheap three dollar six pack of beer and some roll your own tobacco and maybe a half pint.'"

Tom added that he knew that Big Joe also smoked cocaine from time to time as did Luke Broder, although they would never admit it.

By this time, we had been on the bench for about an hour, but Tom had only been working for half that time. He had made a dollar. He said that he had made as much as nine dollars in an hour. His best return was eighteen dollars in an hour during Chinese New Year's. Tom alternated between talking to me and working the pedestrians. He didn't vary his line much. Some panhandlers do, complimenting people or joking around, but not Tom.

"Excuse me, sir. Can you spare some change today, sir? Can you spare some change? Thank you very much, sir!" Tom looked into his dirty, pudgy palm at the change that an elderly Chinese gentleman had given him. Then he looked up at me and grinned. "Thirty cents," he chuckled.

By eleven forty-five or so we had made a dollar and seventy cents. As the day wore on it became more smoggy. We sat chatting and smoking while Tom worked. "Spare change? Can you spare some change today, ma'am? Excuse me, ma'am, can you spare some change today? Can you spare some change for a poor person?"

Naturally, from time to time we talked about panhandling incidents.

"You never know how it's gonna go," he said. "One time Big Joe was drunk and abusive and aggressive with somebody and they wouldn't give him any money, so he called them whatever he called them, you know, a string of four letter words. And they karate kicked him in the face and went running down the street.

And he was so drunk he couldn't have chased anybody. They popped him a good one. The whole of his face was a mess. His lip was split."

I chuckled, "That's a cold shot. Ha, ha, ha, but I'm sure he deserved it."

"Yeah he did." Then Tom talked about a time when he, Jerry, and Joe had been sitting around camp talking. Jerry had told the story about when the police took his cap and threw his money out into the street. "Then Joe said, 'Well, Ah had something worse than that happen to me. It's my own goddamned fault.' He was putting all of his money in this light weight windbreaker jacket with a zipper, with two patch pockets on the side. Droppin' it in, droppin' it in. And he said that he had about twelve dollars. He would have had about fifteen, but he kept buyin' short dogs and polishing them off. So he took his jacket off, 'cause it got warm and he had it sitting there on the bench and these little Mexicans went by, [in a Mexican accent] 'Hey man, you got some monee?' And Joe called them a bunch of motherfucker Mexicans, and one of them ran around behind him and went like this," Tom demonstrated a kick, "and Joe backed off and it gave the guy the time to grab his jacket and run down the street with it. And all of Joe's money was in it.

"I put my money here." Tom patted the breast pocket of his shirt. "And now I always keep my paper money in my back pocket, in case somebody—You know, if you go up to somebody with paper money hanging out, and they could grab it and run down the street. But Joe brought that on himself. It probably never would have happened if he hadn't been so abusive with those kids."

"Yeah, I guess you can't be cussing people out for not giving you money. That's not part of the game."

"Naw. Naw. But uh," he paused for a moment, coughing, "my money's never been taken from me like that."

A few minutes later, Tom talked about Jerry's latest seizure. "He went stiff and snot ran out of his nose. And he went AHHHHHHHH! Like an epileptic. But he went rigid, he wasn't flopping. You know, he can't bite his tongue, 'cause he doesn't have any teeth. So I don't worry about that. The thing was, we kept calling the paramedics. He had four seizures in two weeks. And the paramedics would come and he would say, 'I don't wanna go to the hospital.' So finally they said, 'Don't call us for him ever again, unless he's REALLY BLEEDING!'"

I chuckled. "Yeah, I took him to the hospital on my motorcycle one time."

"Oh, you're the one on the motorcycle? I never knew who you were.—Excuse me, sir! Can you spare some change, sir. Can you spare some change, ma'am?"

"So the philosophy is that if somebody passes out and rolls down the hill..."

"It's their own damn problem."

"You just leave them there?" I asked. "Nobody feels that that's cruel or...."

"Naw. Abe felt that way. Larry said that too. 'Any asshole,' this is Larry talking, [W.C. Fields voice] 'Any asshole that gets that drunk, that can't keep from fallin' down the hill, deserves to be down the hill.' Ha, ha. And he said, 'Look Tom, we could be going down that hill five times a day to catch somebody.' He says, 'Here where we live, it's easy. 'Cause it's only about thirty feet and we're only about ten feet above the level of the sidewalk.' But, I'm a good sixty feet above the sidewalk." He was referring to his old camp under the high bridge.

"Yeah, when you were under the high bridge, that was a serious roll."

"Yeah, I would say that it was about sixty feet. That's about like a five story building. And I'll say it was about a forty-five degree angle up that hill. Now where you were sleeping last night, there was this one guy and this one bitch were fighting up there, he slapped her and she came back and hit him with an empty wine bottle and he rolled over and grabbed her hair and they both came tumbling down. I watched. They made it all the way down to the very end."

"I don't see how you'd stop if you got rolling on that slope."

"Especially if you're drunk. There's no way to stop...until you hit the fence. Ha, ha, ha, ha. If it wasn't for the fence, you'd be out on the sidewalk."

"Yeah, ha, ha, ha."

"Excuse me, sir. Can you spare some change for a poor person? Can you spare some change, ma'am?"

"How come you don't use a hat?"

"Because it's so obvious. When you go like this," he held out an imaginary hat, "and the cops see you. A hat like that means that you're panhandling. See, they just think I'm sitting here. Well, they know I'm panhandling, but they've never caught me going like this," he extended his hand with the palm up, "but once.—Excuse me, ma'am, can you spare some change for a poor person? Can you spare some change, ma'am? Can you spare some change? Can you spare some change, ma'am?"

I asked Tom to make some generalizations about his clientele.

"The basic generalities. Well, the secretaries, in Chinatown, they never give you anything. Rarely does it ever happen. And businessmen with suits, with ties, and jackets, and vests? Nothing. I don't even bother asking them. It's the older people, the housewives, and the kids. And White tourists rarely. But then I started asking them and they probably make up ten percent of what I take in. I ask everybody, here. The more people you ask, the bigger the chances you'll get something."

At about twelve thirty, Tom said that he had had enough. We had been there for about two and a half hours and he had made about four dollars and fifty cents. That worked out to about a dollar and eighty cents per hour for the day. He has been on the same schedule for almost a year, he said. His food stamps had run out last October, and he had gotten tired of going downtown to do Benny's laundry and to unload the truck at Mack's Market. That required walking through the most dangerous part of Skid Row, about a three and a half mile round trip. However, the biggest factor in his decision was that he was able to make enough panhandling.

Tom returned once again to the topic of Big Joe. He said that one time Joe and Tiny had moved back under the bridges and "within two weeks, everybody was fighting with everybody else. Within a week they had a fight between themselves about—Somebody woke up and helped themselves to somebody else's bottle. They're always going through all that shit....Joe really wanted to kill Suzi one time. Jerry and Suzi were over at Big Joe and Tiny's camp and they had been drinking all afternoon. She was whining to Jerry, [witchy voice] 'I want to go home!' Well, Jerry was having too good a time and she's too drunk to walk across the street by herself without somebody taking her. She'd get run over by a car."

"She can't see very well, huh?"

"No. So they told her, 'Just crawl in a bed, and sleep, and we'll wake you up later with something to eat and another bottle of wine.' So she did, and she pissed all over Joe's bed."

"Oh no!" I had to laugh.

"He didn't discover it until after they woke her up. They didn't have any food to eat, but they had another couple of bottles of wine. And it was time for Jerry and everybody to really go home, 'cause it was like twelve o'clock at night. Which is an extremely late night for people who are up every morning by five. Especially when they start drinking by nine [in the morning], you know. That's a long hard day."

"That's a typical pattern, huh?"

"Yeah." Tom coughed. "And so, I had gone home at eleven. I brought down a whole bunch of vegetables, and they were going to cook them up, but nothing ever happened with it, and I could have cared less. I had just gotten my food stamps. So then, I see Suzi and Jerry stagger across the street, 'cause all the street lights are on. Then in about twenty minutes, I hear Joe yellin', 'YOU FUCKIN' WHORE, Suzi! YOU PISSED IN MY BED!'

"I've been so plastered that I haven't made it up to go the bathroom; it hasn't happened now in over six months. Last time it happened, it was last September. It was on my birthday, I got so drunk. I panhandled on my birthday. It was the same day that that chick got beaten to death. And I did Benny's laundry, Richard's laundry, and I panhandled ten bucks, so I had twenty some dollars on me. And I went to Eddie's and I got grand and I bought a pint of Bacardi and two six packs of sixteen ounce Burgie [an inexpensive beer]. I came home and they told me the chick had been murdered. I thought, 'Oh my God!' And I'm up there on that hill. I sat there and cracked the seal on the Bacardi and I said, 'I'm gonna drink every bit of it in the next ten minutes.' On an empty stomach. I hadn't eaten yet. I guzzled it down. And then, I ran back to Eddie's and got another pint, before it hit. By the time I got back, it was just getting into my system. And I'll say that was about two o'clock that afternoon, I don't remember anything after that."

"Just a blackout, huh?"

"Yeah, it was. That's why—The police wanted me to remember about that chick and her boyfriend fighting all day. I said, 'I was so fucking drunk, I don't remember anything.' And then I woke up, and said, [cheery, childish voice] 'Oh, my bed is wet. Did I knock over my water jug?' I tried to convince myself I didn't piss, but then I got a whiff of it, and that was it. I took my blankets down. And the sprinklers came on, then we could turn them on by hand, so I went down and turned the sprinklers on and rinsed off every one of my blankets. It took me an hour to do it. All those blankets. I hung them up on a clothes line. Then I stripped down and put on my shoes, [W.C. Fields voice] and armed with a bar of soap, I got a bath. Ha, ha, ha, ha, ha, ha.

"Well, it's warm in September, and the water is fairly warm. In winter, the water is so COLD, you couldn't possibly—You'd have to fill a big jug and leave it in the sun and it will bring the water up to a nice temperature that you can douse yourself with."

"Now you can't turn the sprinklers on any more?"

"Naw, the overriding thing has been shut down, so the manual turn-ons won't work. Their sprinklers across the street haven't come on once. Ours comes on, but only those two."

A minute later, Tom said an interesting thing about Suzi and Jerry's deportment around camp that led me into a brief explanation of social science.

"I asked Suzi and Jerry why don't they fight in front of Jackson when he's here, like they do when he's not here. Suzi looked at me like I was crazy and she says, 'He wouldn't like that.'"

"In social science, that's called role management, and it really throws off a lot of research."

"Oh. I don't think you care if they fight one way or another—"

"No, I don't."

"—as long as they don't take to stabbing one another in your presence."

"Yeah, or me."

"Yeah," Tom said, and we chuckled together.

"Yeah, my idea is to get it the way it is, as real as possible and that's why I come down and hang out for a long time."

"Well, you ought to sneak down some time. Hee, hee, hee, hee."

"Naw, I don't want to do that. I don't want to be dishonest about it. But there's a real problem in social science, reactive research they call it. Much of the social science literature is full of nonsense based on interviews. Say like somebody comes down and interviews Jerry. He's gonna say, you know, 'I'm a very non-violent person,' you know. And he IS when he's sober, but then he gets drunk and he's a real different kind of person. So if you don't spend a lot of time with people, you get a flaky idea of what's goin' on. You'd never find out what's real by doing interviews."

"Me, when I get drunk, I just want to sit there and listen to music and want everybody to leave me alone."

Since Tom read a lot, I had assumed he was interested in social issues and was used to dealing in abstractions. He wasn't, which disappointed me a little. "When I get drunk," I said, "I just go to sleep." I chuckled. "I'm a real fun party animal, you know."

"Yeah, hee, hee, that's what they call a nip and tuck drinker. One nip and you tuck them away in bed."

"Yeah, that's me." A moment later I asked, "Is it productive to panhandle at night?"

"Well, if you wanted a pack of Bugler, for ninety cents, you can make a dollar. If you're that desperate for a cigarette, you walk all that way to panhandle just a little bit of money. I did it the other night with Art. There was nothing to smoke. I can get by without anything to drink, but I HAVE to have a cigarette. That's the worst problem that I've got going. And my little overeating problem....Ahhh.

"One of these days I'll do laundry. I've got all these blue pants and they really show the dirt. My chocolate brown corduroys, I can wear those for a week and they never look dirty."

"Yeah, corduroys are good."

"I'm gonna do laundry tomorrow."

"Yeah. Where do you do your laundry?"

"I'm gonna turn the sprinklers on. If I can get them to turn on. But Angelo's is so easy. I've got ten gallons of water sitting there, plus Suzi's got a box of Tide, I can do everything by hand."

"So you've got a basin or something to wash them it?"

"Yeah, I've got a five gallon bucket. But I like it better when the sprinklers come on, 'cause then you get all wet. I'm gonna make a pair of cutoff Levi's tomorrow too. And cool off. It's gonna be a hot summer, this year, I think."

"Yeah, and dry."

"Yeah, and we got our haircuts, that Art gave us. It's a great looking haircut. Look how even it is. I can feel that it's even." He had no mirror, of course. "Art has a cosmetology license. He went to school for a year."

"How often do you get haircuts, do you think?"

"Me?"

"Yeah."

"Twice a year."

"Really?"

"Yeah. And then one haircut is to shave it down to nothing. Like Kojak."

"Oh really? You shave it all the way down to nothing?"

"Yeah. I go down to LAMP, Los Angeles Men's Place, and Randolph has cut my hair twice, shaved it down to nothing. And my beard, but he leaves my moustache. I put on my knit cap, you know."

"So you don't get sunburned, huh?"

"Yeah. But I usually do it in the winter."

"Well, a haircut like that should last you quite a long while."

"Oh, about six months. But this is super short. My hair was already starting to come down to here," he indicated shoulder length. "Art gave one to Jerry and I said, 'Art, can you cut my hair too?' And he said, 'Sure, come over.' And Suzi was upset because she was gonna cut Jerry's hair. But Suzi's not a cosmetologist. She just lives under a bridge and she starts hacking away at your hair, you know. Ha, ha, ha."

"She seems to get upset about a lot of things, huh?"

"Yeah. She wants to be the den mother. And she wants to be Jerry's big romance. Jerry's just not interested."

I told Tom that I was going to take off for a few hours to go talk to some other people, and that I would be back later. He said that Jerry and Suzi wouldn't be back until late that day. "They won't be back for a while. This is Saturday."

"Is Saturday a better day for them?"

"Yeah, usually. They go out earlier and stay later."

It was about one o'clock when I left Tom. He was slowly walking back toward the bridge, while I headed south down Market looking for some of my other homeless friends. I walked down to Seventh and then over to my favorite burrito shop on Spring under the Senator Hotel, one of the smaller, sleazier Skid Row hotels located about a mile south of the bridges. I had one of their great bean burritos and a diet coke and relaxed for a while, immersed in loud, rhythmic Mexican jukebox music. Then I meandered back toward the bridges.

When I got there, around five thirty, Jerry and Suzi were back in camp. He was slurring badly and she had already passed out. I tried to talk to him a bit about how his day had gone and he said that he had a five dollar day canning. He soon joined Suzi in alcoholic slumber and I sat around talking with Tom until about ten when he said he was getting sleepy.

It was a bit early for me, so I decided to take another hike down Market to look for some of my other street friends. I trudged off past the Civic Center area to Market Street then headed south. I got down to the end of the area, about a mile south of the Civic Center, where my homeless friends hung out without seeing anyone I knew, and I confess I was somewhat relieved about that. I felt that I needed a break from homeless life. The poverty, drunkenness, demoralization, and filth were getting to me. I realized that I was very, very lucky to be able to simply walk away from it for a while, but it was depressing to think that millions of people like Tom and Jerry could not. Without a great deal of help and a change in national priorities, they would spend the rest of their lives in a pitiful oscillation between horrible hopeless reality and pathetic drunkenness, trying to dull the pain.

I headed to Gorky's, the Russian restaurant and brewery on the south side of Skid Row where Dana and I used to meet for forays into the field. The bright lights and noisy, arty crowd were both a shock and a solace. I had a drink called Imperial Stout, a creamy, dark brew. A blues band led by a harp player was performing. They stayed up tempo and rocked pretty well. I noticed a young cocktail waitress that, upon first glance, I immediately dismissed as an airhead, a Valley girl type. At one point she put down her tray and walked up to the microphone, strutting slightly I was prepared to be embarrassed for her, but when the band revved up, she really took off. It was a great show, reminiscent of Janis Joplin. After my little vacation that lasted for about an hour, I began hiking back to the bridge, wobbling slightly under my load of beer. I looked at my watch—it was a little after midnight.

Feeling adventuresome, I decided I'd walk through scary Skid Row by the Union Rescue Mission on my way home. It was about twelve thirty when I passed by there. There were about twenty homeless people sleeping on the sidewalk around the entrance to the building and slightly fewer on the sidewalk across the street.

There were numerous pilasters with little alcoves and niches between them along the old weathered faces of the mission building and Saint Vibiana's Cathedral next door. From each a miniature river of urine emanated, running across the grimy slickness of sidewalk and over the curb into the gutter.

There was one little campfire on the sidewalk, with several figures huddled over it. It seemed like a fairly warm evening to me, but, of course, I was full of stout. The little fire blazed, a single spot of cheer and warmth in the bleak, concrete badlands. I wondered if this might be one of the thousand points of light that President George Bush talked about in his inaugural address. There were six Black men sitting on the steps of the cathedral facing the small campfire. Across the fire from them stood a White woman, who looked to be maybe eight months pregnant. She had her back to me as I walked by, but even in the flickering light of the fire I could see that she was haggard and filthy. They were having a friendly talk around the campfire, but I didn't stop and join in.

Most of the people sleeping on the sidewalk were lying on mattresses consisting of several layers of cardboard, with blankets of some sort over them. It was common practice to pull the blanket completely over one's head. I guess it's to keep the light out of your face and to secure a modicum of privacy. Ostrich-like security seems to be a factor, although there may be some protection in covering your face. I suppose that if people can't see your head, they can't be sure you're actually asleep or know with any certainty who you are. I've asked several street folks about this behavior at different times, but their answers haven't been very informative.

As you can imagine, people used all manner of things as blankets, whatever they could get: moving van pads, mattress pads, sleeping bags, plastic tarps, scraps of canvass, and, of course, blankets.

A couple of people were sleeping in cardboard condos—cardboard boxes cut and fitted together to form a single long box. They're much more reminiscent of coffins than of condos, but cardboard condos are what they're often called on the street. There are numerous toy and trinket warehouses in Skid Row, and since these days most of these things (like most other things, it seems) are imported, there is an abundance of cardboard boxes to make into cardboard condos (along with a paucity of toy manufacturing jobs).

I walked directly to my motorcycle when I got to Angelo's parking lot and got out my parka and windpants. Then I headed back to camp. It was a little after one in the morning when I stretched out on my mattress. A Sheriff's helicopter about a mile west of camp sang me a lullaby. Its landing lights glared in the night, searching for some bad hombres no doubt.

A streetsweeper came roaring through at about one thirty. It was an industrial strength unit mounted on a large truck. It set up a merry racket. Clang, bang, rattle, rumble, CLANG, BANG, RATTLE, RUMBLE, clang, bang, rattle, rumble. Impossible to sleep through, even stoutly sedated.

Jerry had made up a bed for me next to and outboard of his. During the next couple of nights I would grow to deeply loathe this bed, although the proximity to Jerry's and Suzi's beds did facilitate observation. The main problem was the stench. Only about five or six yards away from me was the near edge of the amorphous latrine area. Most of the time, if any breeze blew at all, the latrine was directly to weather. There were dozens of individual piles of feces in various stages of decay discernable. In a couple of places, larger piles existed, suggesting that numerous bowel movements had been deposited there, one on top of another. One of these, about a foot tall, was only about five or six yards upwind of my bed. Of course, this latrine area did not have the benefit of a sprinkling of lime. No holes had been dug. Nothing had been covered up. Squadrons, if not complete air forces, of flies had been born, raised, and spent happy, productive lives here. When the breeze was just wrong, I would awake to find myself suppressing a gag reaction; otherwise, I would be aware of the smell only a few minutes out of every hour.

I guess part of my problem was that I wasn't a heavy smoker like the Bridge People, whose sense of smell had been thoroughly blunted. While I affected a pipe when in the field, I don't smoke it much at other times and never smoke cigarettes. Smoking a pipe did blunt my sense of smell, but, I found, not nearly enough.

About three, a splashing sound woke me. I looked over to find that Jerry had slid on his back toward the foot of his bed. His feet were planted firmly on the ground, wide apart. His knees were bent. From this position, he was directing a strong stream of urine away from the bed and down the hill. When he was finished, he just walked himself back to the head of the bed with his elbows like some upside down amphibian. In terms of conservation of energy, it was a rather elegant adaptation. He never really got out of bed to urinate (of course, he did urinate all over our bedroom.)

27. Canning and dumpster diving

As usual when I slept under the bridges, I awoke at first light, but this morning I went right back to sleep. After a late night like the previous one, I was a bit of a sloth. I got up at about seven thirty, just in time to see Jerry and Suzi off to work. They said they wanted to get an early start, since, according to a news report they had heard on radio Leo, it was going to be quite hot today, perhaps a hundred degrees. I made arrangements to meet them at the Six O'clock store. That would give me time to make some phone calls and discreetly grab something for breakfast. Jerry had already been to Angelo's dumpster.

When I did finally get up, I locked the parka and windpants in the saddlebags of my motorcycle and walked up State Street to the Six O'clock Store. I was a bit hung over from all the stout the night before, so I went in and bought a pint of light beer and a bag of *chicharrones* (thoroughly rendered and desiccated fragments of pig skin). I walked over to a shady curb nearby and drank my breakfast just like a genuine Bridge Person. The *chicharrones* weren't very good, so I broke a lot of them up for the pigeons just as Suzi might have done. It felt selfish to be drinking without sharing, and it would have been embarrassing to have Suzi and Jerry catch me at it, so I went back in the store and got a couple of beers for them and, because I still needed to smooth out some rough edges from the night before, I got another for myself. Then I walked down to the construction site where Jerry and Suzi usually took their breaks.

They showed up there shortly after I arrived. They were very happy to get a couple of cold beers, of course.

I noticed again that Suzi's talk was rather disjointed and disorganized. I thought that this could be attributed to several factors. For one thing she seemed so used to being interrupted by her companions that she sometimes didn't bother to finish her sentences. For another, she may just have gotten bored with statements before she finished them. But she probably had a touch of what psychiatrists call organic brain syndrome—brain damage caused by too much alcohol consumed over too many years.

We chatted about this and that for some time as we sipped our beer. Suzi mentioned in passing that Tom had given her the cigarette papers I had given him the day before, which made me happy. Jerry launched into a defense of bridge life, emphasizing the skills required to stay alive in that environment.

"So many people don't realize how it is. Actually, if you could take some of these people out and throw them underneath the bridge, and come back ten days later, they'd be dead. Because they couldn't figure out how to survive."

"Where to get food, or how to get water, or, you know, everything," Suzi said.

"I'm not embarrassed to say that I eat out of a dumpster," Jerry said.

"Me neither," Suzi said.

"Oh, there's a lot of good stuff," I agreed. I wasn't being completely honest, however, and I wouldn't have dared to eat what they ate. I would be one of those found dead after ten days.

"I mean, after all, Angelo's is not a sleaze ass little restaurant," Jerry said.

"You know what I came home yesterday with?" Suzi interjected. "I came home yesterday with four—Well we were pickin' through the thing, and Jerry said, 'Aah, there's nothin' else there.' I said, 'Well, I want to go check this side.' I went to the side and there was a whole mess of cabbage leaves, right? So I'm just kinda pushing it to the side and I saw this foil. And it looked like one of those foils, you know, covered up with paper? And I pulled it out, and it's a din-din. So I shoveled some more. I found four of them. That was our supper last night," she concluded.

"Oh, that's right, Tom told me about it," I said.

"Mashed potatoes and broccoli and, and, and, and roast beef with gravy, that was underneath this thing. There was not a damn thing wrong with it. They just threw it out."

"And this morning, hee, hee, hee, I celebrated a firm turd," Jerry said.

"A firm turd?" I chuckled, "well, all right!" Despite their protestations about the quality of their diet, all bridge people were constantly plagued by lower gastro-intestinal infections. By my observation it was a rare week under the bridge when at least someone wasn't suffering from a bout of diarrhea. As Jerry's comment demonstrates, a firm bowel movement was cause for minor celebration.

Suzi reported that they had harvested their first tomato. There were some volunteer cherry tomato plants in the area that got watered by the sprinkler next to camp. The year before, they'd planted a fairly extensive garden, but it was destroyed by Caltrans workers, who periodically chopped down small trees and shrubs and poisoned the ivy and annuals with herbicides, presumably as a solution to the homeless problem. It was a senseless and cruel policy. The passersby did not want to see the homeless people and the homeless people did not want to be seen, so why chop down the vegetation that helped both groups of people feel more comfortable? The purpose, I suppose, is to make the homeless people feel uncomfortable in hopes that they will leave, but there is no place for them to go. Every agency and town, it seems, thinks that homeless people are transients from somewhere else, and that they should go back there. But perhaps it is beginning to dawn on people that the homeless are not transients. They are our local, homegrown poor people with no place to live. None of the Bridge People were recent arrivals to Los Angeles. Caltrans might have modified their scorched earth policy recently, since they hadn't been around poisoning and chopping things down for many months.

Suzi and Jerry told me that when Caltrans came through recently, they had made the noisy Hispanics clear out of their camp. Some of them had moved back in, but they had been much quieter. Caltrans left John Moe's little plywood shack intact, and they thought that was fine. Jerry said that some time ago they had even taken pictures of it. I thought that I should do the same. A guy named Gene had built it, but he was now on SSI for mental health problems and living in a Toyota camper. On this trip through the bridge area, Caltrans did not bother Jerry's camp.

A few days earlier, Jerry and Suzi had found another five pound box of frozen cocktail hot dogs and taken some to John Moe in his shack. "We brought a whole mess of them over to Mack," Suzi said. "'Cause Mack eats hot dogs. And we gave—Sam Robbins wasn't around, so we left his bag over there. And then we walked over, and Jerry, he had to knock on the door, because there's a lock on the door."

"I felt like an Avon lady," Jerry said. We all laughed.

"Yeah, selling door to door, or would that be bridge to door?" I said.

"I told to John Moe, I said, 'God damn,' I said, 'I'm delivering hot dogs,' and I said, 'I feel like an Avon lady. Would you like to buy some lipstick?'" We all chuckled. "I heard a clink. I knocked on the door, and I know he thought it was Sam Robbins. And then I heard the clink, and I said, 'Oh, it's just me, John Moe.' I said, 'It's Jerry.' And he goes, 'Oh!' And he opened up the door and he, he said, 'Oh, I thought it was Sam.' But he polished off his bottle before he opened the door. Just to make sure. Hee, hee, hee, hee." We all laughed.

The talk turned to Dirty Mack. "I gave him a sweater once," Jerry said, "a nice cardigan sweater. This was last winter when it was COLD. And we'd found it and I took it over to him and I said, 'Here Mack,' I said, 'Sleep, you know, sleep with this sweater on underneath your blankets and you'll stay warm.' I went over the next day,"—Suzi, who had heard this story before, was already chuckling—"and here the sweater was half way down the hill in the dirt. And I said, 'Mack. Why don't you wear the sweater?' And he said, 'It's not dirty enough.' 'Oh.'"

Suzi talked about Oriental people she had met. "Well, I just call them all just Orientals," she said. "I don't even classify them, 'cause there's too many different kinds. But, I'll tell ya, they are nice people. We've got some nice Oriental people on our route. This one gal, she came out, it was hot as hell, and she came out, and I checked three dumpsters, and Jerry usually gets us some water, and we take a break there, and she came out and she said, 'Hot, hot, hot.'" Suzi used a very clipped voice to indicate an Oriental accent. "And he says, 'Yes it's hot.' And she came out with two cans of soda. The other day she cut up a mango and sliced it for us. And it was ice cold. 'Cause I'd never eaten one. I really don't particularly care for them. But this one, I don't know. She had it all sliced up and it was ice cold. Man, it hit the spot."

"And then the young girl come out and handed me two sodas, and some potato chips," Jerry said. "Oh yeah, we get a lot of chips we can't eat, you know. They're hard, you know." Recall that they have no teeth.

"Well, we never refuse, because, I always say, 'If I refuse....'"

"We take them back to Tommy," Jerry said.

"And we can always find somebody to eat it," Suzi said.

"Yeah, Tom's got teeth," I said.

"Well, he's got, I think he's got three molars left," Jerry said.

I gathered that the Bridge People always graciously accepted whatever was offered to them, then distributed to other people what they didn't want or couldn't use.

I noticed that Suzi had acquired a new canning stick. It was once a broom or mop handle painted robin's egg blue, that now had a six penny finish nail in its proximal end. I asked about the finish nail and she said that it wasn't as good as one with a head on it (a box nail).

"You should see us when we get a can over there," Suzi said, pointing to the other side of a chain link fence. "And he hauls it over, and then he brings it up and then I hook it with my....Hee, hee, hee, hee, hee."

"We call them a two sticker," Jerry added.

"Well, I'll tell ya, it beats a hanger any day," she said.

"Yeah, those people that run around with hangers, I can't understand them. That's stupid," Jerry said. Nonetheless, Jerry assured me, there were plenty of canners who used coat hangers instead of canning sticks.

I looked up as we were walking along and noticed that all three of us were wearing visors.

Jerry told me that there was often a cold beer waiting in the shade for him near a dumpster that he hits regularly. And there was another household where, if they saw him, they would offer him a cold beer.

On Sunday, Monday, and Wednesday, there was another can truck at Five Corners. The operator didn't offer as much money for aluminum as their regular can man, and he rounded weight down while the guy they usually went to rounded up. But they did sometimes sell to him. That day Jerry said that they would see about selling the cans they had collected so far at this truck. When we got there, he took the bag of cans from Suzi and trudged off toward the truck, while Suzi and I investigated the trash cans and dumpsters of a nearby alley. Jerry returned shortly with the cans. This guy was offering only seventy-five cents, and the other guy usually paid eighty cents. Jerry said that he didn't think it was worth it to sell to this guy.

They were tempted to sell early because Suzi's bag of food and other things was getting heavy. She and Jerry had a discussion and decided that they would stash the bag under some bushes. These decisions about whether or not to cache some things were very important corporate decisions and were usually discussed at length before action was taken. Suzi usually carried everything until she just could not carry any more, then Jerry would consent to carry some things. At that point, he might broach the topic of caching something.

We hit a dumpster behind a large coin-operated laundromat and I asked if it was a good place to find clothing. Suzi said that it was, and in fact I noted several pieces of clothing on that occasion, as I had on previous visits to this dumpster.

"OOOOOH! Oooooh!" Suzi screamed.

I was startled and looked over at her.

"I gotta get outta here! That's enough for me," she said, suddenly backing away from the dumpster. Her hand was in front of her face. "There's a dead cat in there! Oooooh!"

Suzi grabbed her bundles and quickly walked away from the dumpster. We moved further down the alley.

Suzi found a serviceable thermos while we were canning. Later, we hit a dumpster behind an apartment house and happened upon a major find of frozen food. She dug through the garbage like an expectant kid at Christmas digs through the wrapping paper. It was like a glimpse into homeless heaven.

"Oh my GOD! I don't believe it! Fish fillets, ten of them. Ha, ha, ha, ha, ha," she cackled. "Stuffing! Oh, we can make stuffing! Ha, ha, ha. Oh, my God. Oh well, I know we're not going any further than the Safeway." (That is, we'd be ending the canning route early.) "Oh, my God! Gizzards, like the ones we had to get rid of the other day. Oh my goodness! What a score! What a score! Somebody cleaned out the refrigerator."

"Frozen solid," Jerry said. "There's nothing wrong with that."

"Yeah," I said, although I was pretty sure he was saying this for the benefit of Suzi and himself. He and Suzi engaged in discussions of the utility of a find each time they encountered something, weighing the potential value of an item against the hassle and work of carrying it home. They discussed whether to carry or stash the item and finish the canning route, or to quit canning and forfeit any money they would have made. They considered the necessity of preparation and preservation of food items and the possibility of repairing non-food items. They seemed to be talking just to each other as I stood a couple of yards back from the dumpster and observed.

"Nope. Not a damn thing," Suzi agreed. "We might have to ask Jackson to carry a bag for us." Suzi chuckled and shot me a glance as if embarrassed a bit to suggest such a thing.

"Yeah, sure, I can carry some stuff," I said.

"Oh, look at this! Honest to God! That's all kinds of chicken."

"Frying chicken." Jerry scoured off the frost with the palm of his hand and squinted at the label. "Family pack. Frying chicken leg quarters," he read.

"Looks like you guys are going to have a party tonight," I said. "When you find a bunch of stuff like this, do you—Oh there's a big fish. What is that thing? A perch or something?"

Jerry held the package up, trying to make out the label. "Capelin," he said.

"What's that other word there?"

"I think that's a Spanish word," he said, handing the big packaged frozen fish to me.

I tried to decipher the faint, frost damaged label. "Mojarra," I read. "I've heard of mojarra. Fish, I think it means. Generic fish." We all had a little chuckle. "Well, it looks good. Well, what a score. When you find a bunch of stuff like this, do you stop your canning and go back, or do you shorten it down, or...."

"It depends. Like now, like I said, we're not going any further than Safeway. I'm not going all the way to the bingo place," Suzi said. Suzi had actually answered my question before I had thought to ask it. They tended to stay flexible and adapt to changing situations along the canning route.

Suzi and Jerry discussed what to do with the frozen food they had found when they got back to camp. "We'll stack that meat in the brown bags," Suzi said, "and put it in that cooler [a styrofoam cooler that belonged to Tom]. And with the froze food on top of each other that'll keep 'em. And we'll use the food that's gonna spoil fastest. Fish, chicken. 'Cause the other stuff won't spoil. And we're gonna eat plenty hardy, I know that." Suzi was as ebullient as a quiz show winner.

"What we should do," Jerry said to Suzi, "when we get home, is just start cooking and cook it all up."

"Oh, you can't cook it all up," Suzi replied.

"It'll last longer," Jerry said.

"Well, yeah, but you know, I'll be damned if I'm gonna cook up all of our food just so Tom can eat it when we turn our back. It'll last longer, but I'd rather see it spoil than see him get fatter and fatter on us."

We got their catch of the day bagged up and continued trudging along the canning route. Later, I again observed Jerry "enriching" his aluminum load. He pulled a couple of AA batteries from his pocket, dropped one each into a couple of cans, and then crushed the cans as usual by stomping them with his heel. "Down and dirty," Jerry said grinning.

"Well, we use them [the batteries] until they're used up and then we use them again," Suzi said. "Why waste them? Hee, hee, hee, hee. That ought to help out that white bag," she said, referring to the weight of the plastic grocery bag that was not yet full of cans.

"Yeah, that'll help that white bag. A LITTLE bit," Jerry said.

We sat down and took a break at the customary place near the school. Since we had made a major discovery of frozen food, that topic was foremost in their minds. "I was gonna say," Jerry said, "we ought to bypass the vegetable dumpster. No, no, huh uh. That thing's like a magnet to me. Well, we can fix up a big pot of vegetables, to go with this stuff. Carrots, zucchini, onions…."

"Zucchini, carrots, onions, and celery," Suzi said.

"Fixed that the other day. Tommy devoured it," Jerry said scowling.

"That night we debated three times what we were gonna eat for super," Suzi said. "Because we kept coming up with new finds and changed our minds." She grinned, and let out a jubilant cackle.

"Well, it sure beats going down to the L.A. Mission and gettin' a tray full of grub," Jerry said.

"And then we found some uncooked pizza, and then Tom said, [breathless falsetto] 'Oh, I'll eat the pizza!' I said, 'Well, you've gotta cook it first.' 'Oh well, I don't want to bother with that.' So….Ha, ha, ha, ha."

"But I cooked it for him," Jerry said

"So how did you cook the pizza?" I asked.

"We take a tray," Suzi said, "put water in it, and then—Those flat trays we find at Angelo's?"

"Yeah."

"You put your pizza on that, and then take another one and put it upside down. And when the water boils it cooks the pizza."

"Oh, I see, it steams it a little bit."

"It cooks it. It actually cooks it. It don't burn. It actually cooks it," Suzi said.

"And that was a good pizza," Jerry said. "It had that thin crust too. It's not like Angelo's pizza. Angelo's pizza, the crust is that thick." He held his hand in front of him, his index finger about an inch and a half above his thumb.

"I like those thick pizzas," I said.

"Oh, you like them? I like the thin, crispy ones," Jerry said.

"I like the dough. Give me dough, bro'," I said. Jerry and I chuckled.

While we were at the school, Jerry and Suzi continued their discussion of the day's agenda. It was decided that Suzi should take the cans we had accumulated to the can truck at the Safeway, while Jerry and I checked a few trash cans in the alley and then rested. They had collected what I estimated to be at least ten pounds of frozen meat: bacon, pork chops, chicken, and fish. They decided they had to head home right away.

We got on the topic of former jobs, and Jerry said he had had lots of different jobs. At one time he worked as a bill collector for Aetna Financial Services. "I didn't really like it, to tell you the truth, because a lot of those people, they just fell on hard times. And you go up there and you knock on their door and you know damn good and well that it's like the coroner coming to visit. I was NOT the bearer of good news. You know, like, 'Oh, hey, your job is back in order, you know, come on back to work.' It was, it was hard."

Suzi said that she had worked in a factory for BSR making turntables and eight-track tape players. Larry, Little Joe, and John Moc had also done factory work.

As we walked, I asked Suzi about her burden bags. In order to keep things organized, she usually carried things in several small, different colored plastic bags inside a bigger, grocery-sized plastic bag. That day, for example, she had a black bag in which she carried packets of salt, pepper, and other condiments. She had a light blue one with forks, spoons, and a knife. In a grey one, she carried her manila envelop of important documents.

We made it home by twelve forty that day. There had been a stop at the Six
O'clock store, during which a couple of jugs were purchased. It had been my
impression that they spent, on average, about fifteen minutes on each of their
breaks, but the time varied a great deal. That day I had finally had the presence of
mind to time the breaks and found that they ranged from no break to twenty-eight
minutes.

We had collected six pounds of cans at eighty cents a pound for a total of four
dollars and eighty cents. Jerry said, "That's not bad for as short a route as we went
today. And not having that much to start out with." They had worked for about
five hours and had each had earned about ninety cents an hour, but they had also
found several dollars worth of frozen foods.

When we got home, I sat around chatting with Jerry and Suzi for a while, then,
like a real bridge person, I took a siesta. At about four thirty that afternoon I got up
and took a walk around Downtown to talk with other street friends.

When I got back, at about eight o'clock that evening, I found everybody in their
usual places. I walked over to where Tom was reclining on his mattress and
chatted with him about his day. Larry had come by and paid Tom to make a run to
the store for him, then they had spent most of the day talking and drinking. Larry
had run into Big Joe, who had disappeared again.

"Big Joe. He's livin' at the Weingart and on welfare. And he's doin' his
[work] project and the minute he gets his first check, and his first food stamps, he
said he's going to Portland. And Larry said, 'Don't come back to the bridges,
'cause nobody wants ya.'"

"That's pretty candid of him," I said.

"Well, Joe's an asshole."

"Yeah? What makes him an asshole?"

"Well, he wants to argue. And he's very dogmatic about his opinion. If you
don't believe him, you ARE the enemy. So he, therefore, will slap you down and
kick you. He's very physically aggressive."

"How about reciprocity? Is that a factor?"

"Yeah. He's a sponge. A parasite. He CAN go out and make ten dollars a
day, he says, but he'd rather sit back and let everybody bring it to him. 'Cause he
was the big time wrestler on television and we don't have to fear for anybody

stealing from us. The thing we have to fear is HIM stealing from us. I mean that's the way it works. He talks a great deal about having guns. And when push comes to shove, I'll say, 'You got a .38? An Uzi machine gun, a .45, a 9 millimeter?' You know. 'I want to see it. What's it look like? I've never seen a gun, you know. I have nothing to do with guns.' And he's just a line of shit, you know. I said, 'Well you ain't got one. You ain't got even a 22.'"

"I think someone like him would be very dangerous if he actually happened to have one. 'Cause instead of throwing Molotov cocktails around, he could be shooting people."

"Well, that's about all he can do. And then he fucked up. He threw three of them and they didn't do anything. He was so stupid, he didn't know enough to make a Molotov cocktail."

"How did he do it?"

"Well, he took a dry piece of tee shirt and shoved it in and lit the tee shirt with a butane lighter. But there was no alcohol or gasoline or even wine on it. And when he threw it, the force of him throwing it extinguished the wick, but if he had gasoline on it, it would have never gone out. So it didn't happen for him. He was very upset. He was DISTRAUGHT!"

"Distraught over his failure as a Molotov cocktail maker."

"He complained bitterly, you know, that life was not going the way he thought it should be."

I asked Tom about the run he had made for Larry and the function of such runs in the under bridge economy. I asked if sending people on runs was a major way of redistributing and sharing wealth, but I didn't explain my thesis well enough for him to really understand it. In my defense, Tom was a little drunk.

"Well, no," Tom said. "Larry doesn't know anything about redistributing wealth. All Larry knows about is he's sittin' in the chair you were sitting in, and it's hotter than hell. It's reaching ninety degrees and he's too tired and don't give a fuck about walkin', but if somebody will? I mean, it's like, if you can afford to pay somebody else to do it, why not? If you don't want to do something yourself, what is the going rate to pay somebody else to do it? That's all it is. I mean I've done it. I've paid for people to go to the store for me, I give them two dollars and have them bring me back about nine dollars of...JUICE."

"How much do you have to have, in your pocket, before it's worth it to you to send somebody? Twenty bucks?"

"No, oh, not at all. I can give Jerry, right now, a dollar to go to the store, and that dollar will buy him a short dog. Thunderbird. I might give him a dollar to bring me five cents of penny candy. I mean it doesn't matter what I buy. The run is a dollar. Always will be."

"The basic run, huh?"

"Yeah."

We sat and watched the cats and smoked. Three fire trucks came charging by one after another, separated by about a hundred yards. The animated earnestness of the fire trucks, lights flashing, engines roaring, contrasted with our indolence and detachment. Sitting up under the bridge, you kind of watch life go by. There is a separation from the street, since you are some thirty yards away and above it. You have sort of a God's eye view of what goes on from there. For the most part, there are just working-class people walking past, and middle-class people driving by, but occasionally there is a little moment of drama, like the fire trucks, or a fender bender, or someone walking by that the Bridge People know.

There had been a major event under the bridges involving the kittens. Since Big Joe's departure, Jerry, Suzi, and Tom had acquired seven kittens. They had all been named several weeks before, based partly upon gender identifications performed by Big Joe. Well, while playing with Margret, Tom found that "she" was a he. This called into question the gender of the rest of the kittens, so he had held each one upside down in his big arms, one at a time, and found that Elizabeth was a male too. Squeeky and Patches were still females. In Joe's defense, I should point out that it is much easier to determine cats' gender as they get older. Tom often remarked upon how much fun it was to watch the kittens play.

"Well, we don't have any rats running around anymore. The kittens are fun. I love 'em. There's something about them. I feel like a human being. I didn't at first. I felt less than a human being, you know. Like a cave person. You really don't feel like you're part of civilization when you live down here. I don't want to be a troglodyte," he said, adopting the term I had introduced.

"There's a grand tradition of troglodytes though, like the gypsies of Spain, you know, flamenco dancing—"

"I don't want to be a troglodyte. I remember when I had a great apartment and a Volkswagen, I was a rich clerk working for Bob's Grocery Store. And then I started doing drugs and this is the aftermath. I played, and God knows, I've paid. 'Cause if you play, you WILL have to pay one day."

"So why do you think you live down under the bridge? You seem to be an intelligent, capable guy, and you're not an alcoholic or a drug abuser now."

"I'm just a moderate heavy drinker."

"I wouldn't even say you're a heavy drinker."

"You don't think so?"

"Naw. A half-pint of vodka a night? That's not so much. I've known you for over a month now, and this is the first time I've seen you with a buzz. A righteous buzz."

"I HAVE a buzz! HAAA, haa, haa. That's true. But I have had a buzz, when you were here and you didn't know about it."

"Well, that's...interesting. Yeah. I don't think a buzz is detectable, but like a righteous buzz, a double buzz, or something, when you start slurring and wobbling, or...."

"Yeah, I'm double buzzing. I woke up this morning with nothing. And Larry came by with food stamps. And Art gave me five dollars. He said, 'Go get yourself something.' You know, I ran down to the liquor store. You KNOW I did. A FAT person weighing three hundred pounds, I could have outdistanced that new Corvette. I mean! I could have thrown my hip into an RTD bus and flipped it over on its side. But I juice it up, you know, about once a week. I go into Chinatown about, I think the average is about five days out of seven."

"Yeah. But you don't spend a long day down there. Three or four hours, something like that?"

"No, an hour, hour and a half."

"Oh, is that all?"

"Yeah. All I need is four dollars and seventy cents. And that gets me a six pack of Old Milwaukee's best. A dollar ninety-nine plus tax. Plus a half pint of Fleischman's Vodka for a dollar fifty-nine and Top's tobacco for eighty-five cents. So all that adds up, plus the tax, to four seventy."

"But Top's went up to ninety cents with the new tax, so your total would be four seventy-five now....Would you consider yourself demoralized?"

"Ha, ha, ha, ha. Well, what are morals these days? You know. I don't kill anybody, or stomp on anybody."

"No no. Demoralization means being depressed about your opportunities, and society, and uh, that kind of thing. No confidence. Hopelessness...." (I looked it up later and the first definition was indeed lack of morals, like Tom thought, but I had never heard it used that way nor is it used that way in social science.)

"Yeah. Yeah, I'm pretty demoralized then. My whole thing is if I can hang out under this bridge, when I'm sixty-five I can get SSI and social security. Ha, ha, ha. I haven't worked, I haven't had uh, I haven't had a job in ten years. And for ten years I was a retail clerk, a journeyman, making seven, eight, and nine dollars an hour. It doesn't seem like much now, but at the time it was. Minimum wage was two fifty."

"Yeah."

Tom lapsed into silence for a few moments. Then he said, "Well, I'll just do my thing. What I want to do is get out from underneath this bridge."

"You do?" I was surprised. I thought that Tom, in his hopelessness and apathy, was pretty resigned to bridge life. "What is it about this bridge you don't like?"

"It's not the bridge, it's Suzi and Jerry. Fighting and screaming and all that. I've got such a hostility thing going against him, I just want to slap him and beat the shit out of him. For what he does to Suzi, but then I understand his point of view. She's just a whiner. She whines and whines and carries on."

"I think she's probably been doing that her whole life, though, not just with Jerry, but probably every man she's been with. It's pretty sad," I said.

"Yeah. A search for Mr. Goodbar. Her whole life has been a search for a man who will beat the shit out of her." Tom paused for a moment. "My daydream is that I'm sitting here on my bed and the Brink's truck hits the Cadillac, flips over, and bags of money are everywhere. I grab it up, grab my cat Squeeky, and I figured, if that happened to me, how many cats would I leave with? I'd take Squeeky and Boots. And then get myself an apartment. And then, uh, come back and grab the rest of the cats, go to a doctor, get some speed, and get skinny. Get all my teeth jerked. Buy a brand new Toyota. And go back to the Valley and sell real estate."

"And sell real estate, huh?"

"Yeah, well...."

"Yeah, you could probably do that."

"I think anybody in real estate is probably makin' fifty thousand a year. You don't even need a high school diploma. I know the San Fernando Valley. I was born and raised there. I could try to sell real estate and have my cats."

"What would it take besides the Brink's truck? I mean, is there a more realistic way to start?"

"Maybe a lottery ticket? Naw, I don't have anything realistic," Tom said sadly. "I'm just here for the duration."

"So do you have any plans for moving to another bridge or anything?"

"No, I can't go for another bridge. If Suzi and Jerry moved out, I'd be happy. I'm just tired of their arguing. I'm very much a loner. Everybody knows it. Everybody freaked that I moved over here."

"Why did you do it?"

"Well, the Mexicans WERE crazy. This one was going around with a hatchet chopping up the trees. And he woke me up one night and said something in Spanish, and I don't know THAT much Spanish, but he had a raised hatchet in his hand. And I picked up a stick and I told him, 'I'll kill ya, you motherfucker!' And he seemed to understand what that meant. And then he came back about three hours later, had no clothes on, and he asked me if I had a can of beer. It was crazy. They're all nuts. I'm crazy enough, but I don't need that kind of bullshit, you know." Tom let out a heavy sigh and looked out into the eerie green penumbra that surrounded the bridges at night. He said despondently, "I'm just here 'til I die."

Then he cheered up a bit. "Hopefully I'll make my social security. I'm forty-two years old, this coming September twenty-second. If I get my check, I'll move back to the Valley, North Hollywood, across from the park. Get a bus pass. Old senior citizen, you know."

Jerry and Suzi had passed out that night at about seven. I hadn't interacted with them much, since they were sloppy drunk and intent on loudly abusing one another. They had had a thoroughly meaningless fight, about rolling cigarettes of all things. I was surprised at how much it saddened me and I just tuned it out.

Tom and I retired at about nine. I stuffed my sweater inside my shoulder bag to use as a pillow and put my parka over me. It wasn't cold at night at that time of year in Los Angeles—July—when the nighttime temperatures are usually in the lower sixties or upper fifties.

I stretched out on the bed that Jerry had made for me near his. It was definitely a political move to make my bed near his to assure that I would interact more with him than with Tom. Jerry and Art were sleeping together on Jerry's bed. As I closed my eyes and drifted off to sleep, the slight north breeze occasionally wafted over me, carrying the horrible heavy smell of stale feces, like waves from middle-class, Protestant hell.

28. The last resort

I slept late again and awoke just after six o'clock with the long rays of sunshine that slanted through the eucalyptus trees tickling my face. It was a Tuesday, not that it mattered much under the bridges. As usual, Jerry and Suzi were smoking cigarettes and talking quietly. Jerry showed me a real brass alarm clock that he had found in a dumpster some time earlier. It was an old time wind up piece, Swiss made, with a seven jewel movement and brass bells on top. It lost about a minute a day, but Jerry set it to radio Leo or the chimes from the Music Center. The key for adjusting the alarm was missing but, as Suzi pointed out, "We don't need no alarm anyway."

"For heaven's sake," Jerry said, pointing at the sun, "there's our alarm right there."

Tom had diarrhea that morning and didn't join our conversation. I complained that I was still a little sleepy and the talk turned to sleeping under the bridges.

"The most sleep I've had was when I was in the hospital," Suzi offered.

"You always sleep with one eye open, sort of?" I asked.

"Yeah. Ya have to."

"Guys think this is the Holiday Inn or something," Jerry said.

"Yeah, like this is a resort, you know," Suzi said sarcastically. "This is a resort?"

I thought to myself, 'Yeah, I'm afraid it's definitely the last resort,' but I only asked, "Do you just tell them to keep movin'?"

"Yeah. And so—It's just like the other day, here comes this scruffy guy. And I was just tellin' 'em, I was sayin', [deep gravelly voice] 'Over there in the corner!'" She re-created the scene by pointing to the hole in the fence. "I'm tryin' to be stern, but then, you know me. Yeah. Right. Five foot two, big eyes, you know, I'm in big trouble, hee, hee. But, you GOT to do it! That's the only way you can keep sons a bitches outta here. You gotta REALLY act tough. I was standin' around with that goddamned big pipe over there that we smash the damn firewood with. I stood there! And looked tough! And I meant it. Because I figured, 'I'll kill you off! You might kill me, but I'm gonna kill you first!'" She paused for a moment. "You've got to be tough," she added grimly and quietly. She scowled for a couple of seconds and then laughed, breaking the tension. She sounded like a Hollywood version of a witch when she laughed—the friendly, good witch.

The talk turned to Dirty Mack.

"Have you actually seen him roll in the dirt?" I inquired.

"Yeah. Like a sow in a waller," Jerry replied.

"Yeah."

"And I asked him, I said, 'Mack, what are you doin'?'" Jerry continued. "'Cause I thought maybe he'd slipped a cog or something like that, you know. And he goes, 'Oh, I'm too clean for work.' He said, 'I gotta get dusted up for work.'" We all chuckled. "And you know, actually, if you're too neat—If you go out panhandling in a three piece suit, forget it. You're gonna starve to death. So, uh, put on your cleanest dirty clothes, and uh, uh, muss your hair up and look a little disheveled and pitiful, and everything else. That's when the bucks start coming in."

"Do you ever look purposefully more pitiful when you, when you go out panhandling?"

"Oh, definitely," Jerry said. "Yes. When I did panhandle. Right now, I'm on a hiatus for a while, because, you know, five warrants out for my arrest is enough. So now I'm a canner and let me assure you being dirty enough is NO problem when you dig in dumpsters all the livelong day. So now I walk around with my canning stick, my staff, and I look like Moses. Ready to part the trash," Jerry quipped.

"I guess Moses was a canner, huh?" I said.

"He must have been. Why would he carry a canning stick. I think he must have collected cans when he lost his job in Egypt."

We all chuckled.

"There's a bunch of mechanics on our route, and they drink a lot of beer, and one of 'em collects the cans. Like he needs that money," Jerry added sarcastically.

"Yeah."

"He's probably makin' eighteen, twenty dollars an hour. So he collects cans so he can have some extra change. Haa! Now please, do me a favor. Move underneath the bridge and live off of four dollars a day. And what you can find in a dumpster. See what it's like. And you can take your twenty dollars an hour and cram it up your ass!" Jerry said bitterly. "Appreciate what you've got!"

"Yeah," I said, thinking what an important maxim that really was. "Appreciate what you've got," I repeated.

"There's one guy up there," Suzi said, "one guy up there. And he's good, I don't know what—"

"Yeah, but he's like the custodian or something," Jerry said. "He finds cans and hides them for us, once or twice a week or something like that."

"Yeah, he sees me," Suzi said, "and he goes, '¡Señorita! Uno momento.' You know. Oh boy, I don't even wait to squish em, I just say to Jerry, I say, 'Jerry! We got cans. Let's go across the street and squish 'em across the street," she laughed.

Jerry said that he wanted to listen to the radio. "After all, we have to know what's happening in the world today," he said cheerily. I had an appointment at UCLA, so I told them I had to be going. They said they would need to get to work pretty soon, too. It was about seven thirty.

I got back to the bridges a couple of weeks later, toward the end of July. From Angelo's parking lot I could see that the camp where Jerry had been living was a charred, melted mess. No one was there, so I went across the street to Dirty Mack's camp and talked briefly to Larry, who had moved back under the bridges after an absence of several months. He told me a little about the fire and said that Jerry was now living under the northeast bridge, another low one. It was about four in the afternoon when I walked up Cardenas the short distance to Jerry's new camp. He was sitting on his mattress reading. He was wearing a burgundy MacDonald's visor, a nice burgundy window pane print, short sleeve sport shirt, and khaki shorts. He had black, over the calf socks and sandal style house slippers. I was struck by how thin his legs were and by their shocking pink color, the result, in part, of their being quite clean. Almost everything outside and everybody on the street in downtown Los Angeles is covered with dust and road grime. When I occasionally saw a really clean street person in clean clothing, the brightened colors were rather startling. Within a few hours, however, they were thoroughly dusted and dulled down to normal.

I had only very rarely seen street people wearing shorts. In fact, Jerry is the only one I have ever seen wearing them as far as I can recall. Tom mentioned to me that he was going to cut off some pants to make them into shorts, but I never saw the result, if in fact he ever did it. It would have been a memorable sight. Tom carries his weight well, though, and has pretty good muscle tone. Even an inactive camper gets a fair amount of exercise compared to house dwellers.

"Well, pull up a space and sit down," Jerry said, offering me a bare place on the ground near his mattress. He quickly spread out a couple of sheets of newspaper in the same way that someone in better circumstances would pull out a chair for a guest.

"Well, how's things?," I said, grunting as I lowered myself to the newspaper chair.

"Considerably more skimpy than they were the last time," Jerry said, motioning around his camp. "But other than that, I cannot complain."

"Well, good. Good."

His camp now consisted of a solitary double bed mattress with a tattered, filthy comforter on it and a small pile of clothing and food spilling out of a couple of white plastic grocery bags near the head. Within arm's reach was a piece of newspaper on which sat a couple of paper plates of food with other paper plates as covers. There were some cookies on the newspaper too. Ants were swarming over all them. A couple of magazines and other sections of newspapers lay nearby. Suzi was passed out on a mattress next to Jerry, on the side away from me. I couldn't help noticing her figure through her black sweatpants. I was shocked at how bloated her abdomen was and how her legs seemed to lack muscles. Her thighs were atrophied and her ankles swollen, making them nearly the same diameter. She looked like a piece of lab equipment under a cover. Her body was a small spherical tank. Her legs were a couple of pieces of four inch diameter pipe with knobby pipe unions for knees.

"So what," Jerry said, "this is only the third time, in three years."

"The third time you've been burned out?"

"Yeah, in three years. Yeah, if it doesn't happen once a year, I don't know it's a new year. Ha, ha, ha. The calendar hasn't turned over yet."

The frequency with which fires occurred under the bridges was truly remarkable. One wouldn't think there would be much to burn at a homeless person's camp, but there was. And since virtually everybody smoked and many drank to wild excess, I guess I should have been surprised that there weren't more accidental fires. However, two of the three that I knew about were the result of anger not accident.

"How did the fire start?" I asked.

Jerry shook his head silently, as if to say tsk, tsk. He pointed to the lifeless shape in the bed next to him.

"Somebody had a cigarette," I said. I had already learned from Larry how the fire had started.

"And in the same condition she is in right now. And Art and I, we were sitting over on Tommy's mattress eating peanut butter and crackers and talking, and I went," he wrinkled up his nose. "'Art,' I said, 'I smell plastic burning.' And his head snapped and he looked over at the couch. Flames were leaping this high up

over the arms of the couch." Jerry held his hands about a yard apart. "And Suzi
was laying in the middle of it."

"In it? Oh my God!"

"I went over and I YANKED her up off the damn couch and Art helped me.
She kept tryin' to go back to lie back down on it, that's how drunk she was. So
finally, we got her half way down the hill, and I told Art, I said, 'I'm callin' the fire
department.' I said, 'You get her the rest of the way down the hill.' So I go up
and call the fire department, this IDIOT at the fire department wants to play forty
questions with me. 'What's on fire?' I said, 'EVERYTHING I own is on fire!
Get your ass OVER here!' 'Well, are there any dangerous chemicals?' and la-de-
da, and 'Is this an exact address?' I said, 'Drive down Cardenas Street, when you
see the black smoke and the flames you will find the exact address.'" Jerry delivered this in his Jack Benny deadpan, and I had to laugh. "And finally," he paused
for the laughter to die down like any good comic, "I bet I was on the phone ten
minutes, and I stepped out of Angelo's and I looked up and at this time, Jackson,
the flames were leaping so high, coming up and over the side of the bridge, that
people on the freeway were stopping. And the smoke was just horrendous."

"Oh, my God."

"All that plastic and the clothing and especially the plastic. All the milk crates
that we had and everything. The fire was so hot, it MELTED our pots and pans.
Cast aluminum pots and pans literally exploded. Nothin' left. Absolutely nothin'.
And so," he said with a sigh, "it's time to rebuild."

"So the, uh, Mexicans don't live over here anymore?"

"Uh, yeah. Upstairs," he nodded up a path to the upper bridge. "But they're
not the loud ones. There are four of them that live up by John Moe. And they're
REAL nice. They wave and they're pleasant and stuff like that. And they're quiet.
And they don't bother anything, because when I leave, you know, leave to do my
canning, and, and, to do my business for the day, and I come back and uh,
nothin's bothered at all. And, of course, Gary kinda keeps an eye on things for
me." Gary was the attendant at the parking lot adjacent to the northeast low bridge.

I asked about Tom.

"Tommy's not back from panhandling yet, and we're worried."

"Oh, you think he mighta got arrested?"

"I think maybe he got snagged, because he's never ever this late. Never ever."

Next to Jerry's mattress were a pair of almost new Nike running shoes. "Are those new shoes?"

"Art got those shoes for me."

"Those are nice."

"And they are so spongy and comfortable. I want to tell you, I almost just bounce up and down the sidewalk."

"Yeah, ha, ha." After a short pause I told Jerry, "That's a nice visor. Nice shirt too." (I'm partial to visors. So is Jerry. The disadvantage, he pointed out once, is that you can't use one to panhandle because there's nothing for people to put money into.)

"I ran into this lady, her name's Beth. And uh, she's been coming over and, and, she brought me some stuff and then I've been going out to church with her and stuff like that. They have a DYNAMITE minister. I want to tell you," Jerry said, "I can't remember her name right now, she's a Black lady, and she's about mid-fifties to sixties. And I want to tell you, it is hell fire and brimstone. And she dances around, stuff like that. She's good. She's from Philadelphia. And we went out Saturday and went to services. She preached, and I told Beth, I said, 'I enjoyed that.' No use going to church and going to sleep. And there's no way in the world you can go to sleep listening to this lady. NO WAY."

I asked Jerry about his current daily schedule, since earlier in our conversation he had said something that made me suspect that there were some changes. He said that he had made seventy-five cents yesterday. I asked what his day had been like.

"I walked all the way up, past The Four Dumpsters, over here, you know, then we walked over where we take our first break at the school thing, and then Suzi, she went on and then I headed on downtown and did canning down there and got my lunch."

"Got your lunch? Where'd you get your lunch?"

"Oh, I didn't tell you about that?"

"Huh uh."

"Well!" He paused dramatically. (Come to think of it, Jerry can sound a LOT like Jack Benny.) "I went to court, you know, on January seventh, on this murder thing, and I went up to get my witness fees and Bonnie said it was continued again to August the eleventh."

"Uh huh."

"And this was, well, the fire happened January sixth—"

"July sixth," I said.

"July sixth. And so I had nothing. And Bonnie says 'How's it goin'?' and I must have smelt like Smokey the Bear's first cousin, or something like that, you know. And she goes, 'You smell like smoke.' 'W-e-l-l, we had a little bit of an accident.' And she goes, 'What's that?' And I said, 'Well, we had a fire.' And she goes, 'Well, what happened?' I said, 'EVERYthing is gone.' And she goes, 'Well, you've gotta have at least lunch.' And so she gave me a voucher for lunch and she said, 'You know what? You're entitled to lunch EVERY day, until court.' She said, 'As a matter of fact, would you like to be put up into a hotel?' And she said, 'That way we'll give you breakfast, lunch, and dinner.' And I thought, 'Oh, in a hotel they can keep too much track of you.' I thought maybe I'd get to the Weingart where you have to be in at ten thirty at night. And you can't leave until seven and all that crap. So I just took the lunch voucher and so now I go down and have lunch every day."

"At the Courthouse?"

"At the Criminal Court Building. They have real good food, good specials down there. All of their soups are homemade. It ranges anywhere from creamed chicken noodle soup to uh, New England clam chowder. Potato soup. Vegetable beef. And so, I, I get soup. And uh, Bonnie, the detective for the prosecutor, says, 'Now Jerry. Don't go down there and get a dollar seventy-nine sandwich.' She says, 'Spend it all!' And I said, 'Well, Bonnie,' I said, 'If I run over, over the five dollars, then I have to pay out of my pocket.' And she always reaches in, she hands me fifty cents and says, 'Here's fifty cents leeway.'"

I asked Jerry again about this severnty-five cents he had made.

"I had left Suzi, and I was walking back, and there's a parking lot near the Hall of Administration. I call it my religious parking lot. The guy who runs it is very religious and always hands me tracts and stuff like that. And, uh, so anyway, I waved at him, and he waved at me and handed me a tract. Well usually when he hands me a tract, he also hands me a quarter. But I didn't get the quarter, I just got the tract. So I went past the bus stop and there's a trash can there. And I got five cans out of the trash can and I was smooshin' 'em; somebody tapped me on the shoulder. This young man, a blond haired kid, handed me a quarter, and I thought, 'Oh, well, five cans and a quarter. Why not? Good stop.' So then I went down through the mall and I got a few more cans, and then I headed down toward the uh, uh, Hall of Records. And I was going through the trash can there, and this lady comes up and taps me on the shoulder and SHE hands me a quarter. So I thought, 'Well! Fifty cents. Wow!' So I go and I get my voucher for my lunch and I go up and I eat it. And I do a little more cannin' and I'm coming home and I go past the religious parking lot again, and he waved at me and I waved at him and he come running up behind me and he said, 'May the good Lord bless,' and he handed me a quarter. And so that was seventy-five cents. And like I told you, I can't panhandle any more 'cause the cops all know me, but I had people just give me money out of the clear blue sky. I'm gonna fight it tooth and nail? I mean after all, seventy-five cents is a pound of cans."

"Really! So what's your route like now? You get up at the same old time, five thirty, six?"

"Yeah. And usually Larry comes by and Will, and they'll holler up, 'Let's go have coffee!' And so we'll walk down to Giotto's and have coffee."

"Giotto's huh?"

"Yeah. Twenty-one cents for two cups. You can't beat it. So then I go down and get two cups of coffee. Any more than two cups and I, then, I can't handle the caffeine. And then I come back and I meet Suzi."

"So Suzi's not sleepin' here mostly, huh?"

"No, huh uh. She's still over there with Tommy. She might come over here. We have to find her a mattress and stuff like that. The only thing she's sleepin' on over there is a little piece of foam. You know, one of those little pieces of foam like I had underneath my bed over there before. Before the holocaust.

"I've lost everything. Everything. I have this that I have on. And I have one more change of clothes that is SO filthy, 'cause I wore it for three weeks. And I don't know if it's salvageable or not. But, uh, then I go canning with Suzi. I go with her to the stations, and The Four Dumpsters, and then over to the school. And then she goes on over that way, and by that time it's like about nine thirty and then by the time I make it back downtown, with my quirky, little ole bird legs, uh, it's about ten thirty and if I'm lucky, I can find, maybe the front page of the *Times* or the *Herald*, so I can do my news reading. You know, I'm crazy about that."

"So then, you can a little through the mall between the Music Center, and...."

"Yeah, and uh, in early morning it's not real good. Maybe ten, twelve cans, but then, that's a third of a pound. Why not. So then I swing all the way and up around and then I go to the fifteenth floor of the Criminal Courts Building. People going in there don't realize that there's ashtrays in there so there's shorts all smashed all over the sidewalk. So then I pick up all the shorts off the sidewalk. He paused and grinned, then said dramatically, "This is MY day! Hee, hee, hee. And then I ride to the fifteenth floor, that's where the courts are. And hopefully I have found a short that's long enough, and I sit there and I pretend to smoke the short, you know, like a cigarette cigarette. And I always sit next to the ashtray that has the longest shorts in it. Because, you know, people come out of the court, take two puffs off the cigarette and then put it out and jam back in. So I sit next to THAT ashtray."

"Ah haaa."

"And as I'm nonchalantly smoking my cigarette, I'm going like this." He made a motion like he was rapidly picking berries.

"Ho ho," I chuckled. "Pickin' 'em up and putting them in your pocket, huh?"

"Yeah. And so I get my cigarettes. And then if there's another good ashtray, I nonchalantly pick up whatever newspaper I've got, *Downtowner*, I don't care what it is. And I move over to that ashtray, and pick all them up. And then I end up, I've got tobacco for the day."

"So you've harvested your day's tobacco, huh?"

"Yeah, re-harvested. And the only thing I have to do is get my voucher and then go and get my meal. And the meals they put out are...well, I'm still not hungry now. Well, I'm not a big eater anyway. You know, Suzi and I are neither one big eaters. And so, it's plenty for me and so I eat my noon meal and then I walk around and I can some more. Uh, I might get two and a half pounds of cans up there and that's for Suzi to start off the morning. I just dump them in her sack with hers. 'Here, Babe. Go up and sell 'em.' Because for me to go down and around and everything else and then walk all the way up to the can man, you know, to sell them, I'd never make it up there by three o'clock."

There are other aluminum recycling places, Jerry pointed out, but they are even further away. He's usually back home at about two thirty or three, about the same as his old canning routine.

"I like to stay down to the mall to the last nth degree. You know, one of them things. Just maybe somebody will come out on break, 'cause they get their break between three and three fifteen. And if they come out on break and I see 'em sippin' a soda then I nonchalantly sit down, you know, and pretend I'm doing something, and, uh, for fifteen minutes, and then they throw the cans away and I go get the cans then I come home."

"It sounds pretty good."

"Well, it's, it's not too bad. I told Suzi, I said, 'We're covering both ends of the route. And we've been averaging—We've been very, very lucky. The last week, week and a half, uh, seven to eight pounds a day." (About two and a half to three dollars a day per person.)

"Really? Things are pickin' up, huh. Do you think it's the hot weather?"

"Well, it's a lot better than doing three and four pounds a day."

"Do you think the hot weather has something to do with it?"

"Oh yeah. The hot weather. Also the price of cans has dropped. It's dropped a dime. It's down to seventy cents."

"At one time it was up to eighty-five cents, wasn't it?"

"Uh huh. And that's when EVERYBODY was cannin'. Everybody and their grandmother. I don't care if the old grandmother was in a wheelchair, they had her out there pickin' up cans, you know. It's ridiculous. Every other person you met on the street had a bag of cans in their hand. And they don't realize—These people that are doin' it, well, they're doin' it for extra money. But we're doin' it for REAL money! I mean, this lets us survive from day to day.

"That's another thing that TICKED me off about the fire. The canned goods that I had stashed away, and the macaroni and the lima beans and everything else. That was all perfectly good. KA-POW! All the cans exploded. And then, I had seven cigarette lighters. They blew up. Everything went. Absolutely everything.

And by this time, Art had her over to Will and Larry's place. And she's sittin' in the dirt, comatose. Just staring around. Couldn't figure out where she was at."

"She was still really drunk, huh?"

"Oh, she had three fifths of wine in the couch that she had stashed, that burned."

"Now that's a real tragedy. Now we're talkin' major tragedy," I chuckled.

"I mean, I want to tell you, you think the Lindberg baby kidnapping was bad?" We chuckled. "The kidnapping of that wine was a MAJOR social development. And, uh, she had stashed it, and I KNEW that she had stashed it, because Big Joe and Little Joe were buying the wine and Suzi would wink at me and shove a bottle down into the couch."

"Oh, so Big Joe came back for a couple of days, huh?"

"Aah, yeah, for a little bit. He was spending most of his time over there because Little Joe was having a 'social relationship' with Suzi."

"Ooooh....How's your health been lately?"

"Oh, not too bad. My legs are gettin' better. They're not so puffy. They're little puffy now. But I've been doin' a lot of walkin'."

"Have you had any diarrhea lately?"

"No, I've been eatin' that good food from the cafeteria, and stuff like that, and then Beth's been bringing me up good food and stuff, so....Well, it depends what you mean by diarrhea. To me, diarrhea is when you can shit through a screen door at forty paces. I haven't had that for the longest time. My stool isn't real firm, though. I have celebrated a few REAL genuine turds. I mean, when I get a firm turd, I almost want to stick a candle in it and light it and have everybody over. But, uh, no, I haven't been having any problems, lately. Knock on wood."

"For a couple of months, there, you were sick the whole time, huh?"

"Oh yeah. Yeah. With fever and cramps and, well, I couldn't even get out of bed. And, and, of course, living in the dirt and stuff like that, it's impossible to get over it because it just reacts, and reacts, and reacts. You can't wash your hands. You can't stay clean. I mean, if I would try to stand up to clean something, like even if I had sheets for my bed, I would've shit my pants before I had a chance to lay back down again. You know, the sanitary conditions underneath the bridge, well they're not the worst, but they are DEFINITELY not the best."

Although I couldn't get Jerry to estimate how often he got serious gastrointestinal infections, in my judgment, most of the Bridge people seem to have problems at least six or eight times per year, but rarely as bad as the bouts Jerry and Suzi had suffered that year. Homeless people who eat at missions or those who can afford to buy their food probably don't get really sick more than a few times per year.

I looked down to the street and noticed Larry headed south back to his camp pushing a shopping cart full of pieces of boards, firewood that he probably got at the lumber yard a couple of blocks away. He looked up and I waved. He waved back and continued pushing the cart toward his camp.

It was getting late, so I told Jerry that I had to be going. I walked toward Market to check on some of my other street friends at about five thirty.

I wanted to get Tom's perspective on the fire under the bridge, so at about eight o'clock I began walking back to his camp (where the fire had been). He still wasn't in. Since he so thoroughly enjoyed smoking tobacco, I had bought him some prime rolling tobacco and papers at the Tinder Box, a fancy tobacco shop in West Los Angeles. I didn't want to carry the tobacco around any longer, so I stuffed it into his blankets and hoped that he would end up with it. It was about eight thirty and quite dark under the bridge when I left.

A few days later, I headed toward Jerry's old burned out campsite under the south bridge. It was only about six thirty, but already getting a little dark under the bridges. From the sidewalk it was always hard to see if anyone was in that camp, but it was even harder because of the fresh coating of soot. Tom hailed me. I was in luck. I climbed through the hole in the fence and saw him on his mattress. I asked him about where he had been the last time I had come by to say hello.

"Fisher. He finally couldn't handle it anymore, seeing me there panhandling. So I was there, and a lot of it is my own damn fault. He came this way, I guess that way's north, toward Dodger Stadium. And there I was, and he saw me and he slowed down. So I just got up and walked away. So I'm halfway down to Lee's and I saw that he continued on up. So I ran back and was panhandling. I had just made three bucks, and I needed four dollars and seventy cents, and that gets me everything I need at the liquor store. And I had just gotten about four pounds of roast beef for the cats, so I didn't have to worry about buying cat food. They're eating better than I am, as usual." He laughed.

"So I'm sitting there and Fisher comes back the other way. And he saw me. He turned on his lights, and pulled this big dramatic U, and made everyone come to a screeching halt. And there was no place for me to go. I, I can't run down that alley and up Oak Street, 'cause he'll chase after me, you know. You're just there. He says, [raspy voice] 'I'm gonna give you a ticket for panhandling! What's your name?' So I gave him my name reversed," Ken Thomas instead of Tom Kinkaid, "but I forgot I did that a year ago for a jay walking ticket, so there was a warrant for me. So I got arrested anyway; he gave me a ticket. He took me down. I was lucky it was during the week." If you get arrested on a Friday night or a weekend, you will wait until Monday to be arraigned.

"He took me down on a Wednesday. Around eleven o'clock. I sat in City Jail, you know, the Glass House. And then they took me to court on Hill and Thirtieth or Twenty-Eighth, somewhere out there. And I didn't even go to court. The guy said, 'Anybody who's here just for warrants, might as well plead guilty right now. We're gonna read your names. You'll get time served and we'll take you back, either at twelve o'clock or five o'clock back to County.' So they took me back at twelve o'clock. So from one o'clock they're starting to process me out. I didn't get out of that jail until twelve thirty that night!

"So I'm sitting in jail, and I have a dollar fifty, so I'm buying cigarettes for a quarter apiece. I'm having a nicotine fit. And there's an old guy sitting next to me, a White guy, and he's about sixty. And I says, 'You want the rest of this cigarette?' I had bought this cigarette from a guy, and he handed it to me so fast I didn't notice it was a menthol, and I don't like menthols. So he was happy to get that. And I got this other guy to give me two cigarettes for a quarter, 'cause he was desperate to make just one more quarter. So this guy says, 'Do you suppose I can have some of that cigarette?' And I says, 'Sure. I'm getting out, I'm not going to the pen.' He says, 'When we get out, if we get out together, I'll buy you a pack of cigarettes.' And I said, 'Great.'

"When you get out, you go through this one room, and once they push the buzzer, you're in this lobby area, where there's canteen machines, and bathrooms, and people waiting. And once you're out of that door, you're free. And there's windows like at a bank teller, and there's a woman that is the cashier. Whatever you've got on the books, she pays it to you. Plus you go to this other window, the property window. So this guy I've been givin' cigarettes to, he's an old guy and he was sayin' [raspy old man voice, but loud] 'I got three hundred dollars!'

"E-V-E-R-Y-BODY looks over, 'OHHH?' And you know where County is, to walk though there at night, it's rough. And this one Black guy latched onto him like he was a parasite. And he's got forty coming. The old White guy got his money first, 'cause this Black guy was having a problem on the computer, getting it okayed for his payment of forty dollars. So we went running out the door. So I said, 'Look, there's six of them waiting for us. Just up, around the corner, onto Beech Street, and you're gonna get rolled. I'm not walkin' with ya, and get a beating for somebody else's money.' And he says, 'Well, we'll take a cab.' So we went over, and there's all kinds of cabs there. Off duty cabs, and for twenty bucks, they'll run you to Hollywood. We couldn't find a cab that would run us to Cardenas and Buena Vista, to drop me off, because they want to make the big money, you know. This one cab driver says, 'By law, they have to take you, whether they want to or not, on a short run.' He says, 'They're not even running their meters, they're just pocketing the money.' And so the old guy hands me three bucks, and he says, 'I'll take a cab into Hollywood.' I said, 'Good.' So he paid the twenty and the guy said it was no sweat to drop me off, 'cause there's really no way to catch the freeway in Chinatown, so he had to come here anyway. So we drove by the vultures! And this one guy began chasing the cab, 'Where's my THREE HUNDRED DOLLARS?'"

"Did he say that really?"

"Yeah!"

"That's amazing."

"And you know, the cab driver had his windows rolled up, and when we got in he said, 'Lock your doors and keep those windows up 'til we get into Chinatown and away from the jail.' A lot of people have been robbed right there. Not everybody has money, but this guy was running his mouth about the three hundred he had on him."

We continued to chat, Tom sitting on his mattress, and I on a scorched and twisted kitchen chair. He said that he was down to one cat. The cats used to romp and play in the parking lot, and people would think they were strays and pick them up and take them home. Now he just had the little crippled kitty, Beulah.

Some time before he had mentioned that he might apply for food stamps or general relief, so I asked him about it.

"I went down there, and I didn't have any I.D. I forgot and left my wallet here with my food stamp card and my metal plate for the County General Hospital. And so it was going to be an eight hour thing, so I just said, 'Oh, to hell with it.' So I just went over and did Benny's laundry for him and made a couple of bucks. But I don't really want to be on welfare. I don't want to live downtown in one of those hotels. And have to get up here every morning and have to go down and sign a voucher. I might do it for one check, though."

Tom said that Big Joe was back, which he thought was an unfortunate development. Larry had left again. Will and Larry didn't get along well, and Will had basically run Larry off. Will supported himself canning and glassing (recycling glass). He left camp around four in the morning and got back around noon, a seven or eight hour workday. Tom said that he'd been making thirty to forty dollars a day (three dollars and seventy-five cents to five dollars and seventy-one cents an hour) and that he'd been supporting a friend, an old White guy named Rick. Will made considerably more than Jerry and Suzi make canning, of course. Will, like Jerry, was handicapped (virtually all the Bridge People were handicapped). He suffered from paranoid schizophrenia and had some serious gastrointestinal problems that had not been completely solved even after a couple of surgical procedures. But those problems didn't seem to have debilitated him the way alcohol abuse had Jerry and Suzi.

Tom said that Larry was "sending me to the store every day, almost, for a while. Givin' me a dollar to buy a bottle of wine for myself. I just buy tobacco with it. I haven't panhandled but one day, and that was last Saturday. I had no tobacco, and Art was here. I said, 'Art, let's go up and get some sandwiches at the church, and then we'll walk down Beech, and you sit on the bus bench with me. And the minute I panhandle one dollar, that's gonna be it. And you keep an eye out for the cops.' So I panhandled two bucks and invested in two dollars worth of tobacco. So now I'm panhandling this little parking lot over here [Angelo's] at seven o'clock in the morning. I was there this morning at six. Between six o'clock and seven, I made, uh, I made three dollars and sixty cents.

"That's pretty good."

"Well, that gets me my tobacco. And I got a couple of cans of beer out of it. So I haven't been drinking, really. And I invest my money in tobacco. And I bought a can of cat food. And the cat came back smelling like fish. I went over to the dumpster, and there were all these crab legs and this big chunk of albacore. Her stomach was just so swollen. I thought maybe she had, you know, some disease or something. But she'd just made a little pig of herself. The albacore was JUST over the hill. Cooked."

"It was cooked, though?"

"It was cooked. But for a human to eat it, it was maybe just one day too late. But for a cat, it's no problem. They can eat something that's a little gamey like that."

"Yeah. Sure they can," I said.

"Yeah. But every time I eat something that's just gone off, I wind up on the hillside seven times a day with the revenge of Montezuma. And I just can't go through that. I went through that flu, two weeks ago. Where I was coughing up my lungs. They put Art in the hospital."

"Oh no!"

"Yeah. He was in the hospital for five days. He had partial pulmonary edema, they said. But, I just laid here. I thought I was gonna die one day. I told Jerry and Suzi to come by and see how I feel later, and if I don't feel so good, call the paramedics and have them take me to the hospital. I felt much better that evening. I found a bottle of Pepto Bismol I forgot I had, so I chuggalugged that, and it helped with the diarrhea and the nausea and the gas. Oh, it was terrible. I was living on water."

"How are you getting along with Jerry and Suzi these days?"

"Oh Jerry and I are getting along fine."

"Suzi's away now, so she doesn't bother you so much now, huh?"

"No. She doesn't come over much. After this burned down, Jerry was living over on Buena Vista. Where that grey apartment building is on Buena Vista, just before you get to Grand, there's a great big concrete wall."

"Oh yeah."

"Well, he was living there underneath a tree, and Suzi was here for a couple of days. Then Jerry moved under that low bridge, and Suzi went over there, and she came back and picked up a few things, and went over, and eventually she moved over there. Then she and Jerry had an argument, so she moved in with Will and Dirty Mack and those guys over there. Then Will caught her stealing his wine when he was asleep...."

Tom stopped and looked down at the street below us where a young man in shabby clothing with long blond beard was walking down Cardenas. He was shouting at the very top of his lungs at his voices. His anguish and anger echoed eerily off the bridges like some horror from the time of Dickens. We had to stop talking for a moment to watch.

"He walks by here maybe three times a week," Tom said quietly, "but he's never been like that before. Talkin' shit to the devil!

"So anyway, Suzi packed up her shit and went running back to Jerry. I told her she could never live over here with me. She said, [witchy voice] 'Well, look at the pig pen that it is!' I says, 'I DON'T CARE!' See all that trash over there? That was in an orange sack. I went panhandling and some guys had come here and dumped it 'cause they wanted the plastic sack. Then I picked it up. And then the wind came up and blew all that shit around and I said, 'Fuck it. I don't care. I…just…don't…care!'"

"It is a bit overwhelming. If you did care it would take an awful long time to get it squared away." Since the fire, with the exception of Tom's mattress, the entire area under the bridge was a mass of burned and charred clothing, twisted frames of furniture, and bare blackened bed springs.

"Yeah. And the nice thing about it, is that no one has tried to move in with me, 'cause look at that mess. I'm not gonna try to clean it up. Except yesterday. I was here half asleep, and suddenly there's somebody talking to me with a heavy Spanish accent. A Mexican guy. 'Can I move in here with you?'

"I said, 'No!' He said, 'I clean all this up.' I said, 'No.' I said, 'I like livin' alone.' I said, 'If you want that mattress, there's three other bridges down there you can live under. And I don't want nobody livin' here with me. I like livin' alone.'"

Tom and I continued talking about the exigencies of bridge life for quite a while. Then he told me about the Fourth of July.

31. Independence Day

Tom said, "Joe came back on the Fourth of July. Remember, he deliberately set his bed on fire. He came back and told us. He didn't want anybody else sleeping there. Went down and got on welfare. And was there for a month and got his first check, which was some three hundred dollars, and then came back here and wanted to stay here. It was hot on the Fourth of July. He says, 'I'm gonna spend a lot of this money, Jerry, so you don't have to do anything, and neither does Suzi, the old whore!' So, I went out panhandling and came back with this six pack of cheap beer. I made five dollars. Four dollars and seventy cents is my tobacco, my half pint, you know, and a six pack of cheap beer. Joe doesn't particularly like me anyway. We just kind of avoid each other.

"I went down there [Chinatown]. I was just wringing with sweat when I got back. Turned on the sprinklers, changed clothes and got a bar of Dove, got all washed up. And then Joe wants me to go down to the store and get two cases of beer and he's gonna give me a buck and a half. And so I did. And then he went down himself and came back. They must have gone through four cases of beer and he's got this Mexican hanging around him, this Chicano. So Joe gave him twenty dollars to go downtown to buy some weed, and the guy came back and said he got beat out of the money. Yeeaah," Tom said with exquisite sarcasm.

"He bought everybody cigarettes. Jerry and them. And then a couple of times, he'd say, 'Why don't you go to the store and I'll buy you a beer. Here's two dollars for yourself.' So I'd go to the store. But I did my panhandling. Then he wanted to argue with me that I didn't want to come over there and talk with him. He gets lonely when everybody's passed out. Frankly, there isn't a great deal that we can talk about. And then the Mexican stole his radio. And Joe was [deep Southern accent] 'gonna keel 'em!' And the Mexican came back two days later with no radio, and Joe said, 'Aw fuck it.' This is a twenty-five dollar GE AM/FM.

"So Will was living over there, and Larry was living over there, and they were all fighting back and forth. And Big Joe said one day, 'Well, I guess we wore out our welcome around here, didn't we?' And Larry says, 'Yeah! And you brought it on yourself. Nobody was glad to see you come back even with a lot of money in your pocket.'

"So they took off again [Big Joe and Little Joe]. And they've been gone since Fourth of July. He went up to Salt Lake City and he said the minute he left with Little Joe, his luck changed. Everything he had was stolen. And so I asked Joe—Big Joe gets a disability check from Salt Lake City for something—I says, 'Well why'd you come back?' He said he was drunk and fell on the train and wound up back here. I says, 'Well, when you gonna go back on welfare here?' He says, 'I can't go back on welfare here until October.' I don't understand that," Tom said.

"Well, usually it's a sixty day penalty," I said.

"Yeah, August, September, then it would be October. Yeah. But he's been quiet. The first day back he got into an argument with Larry. Then one morning he comes over here with a bottle of wine and he says, 'Everybody's passed out over there and asleep and I'm lonely.'

"I says, 'Well, get a book, right there, and go read.'" Tom chuckled. "He just barges in on you and demands that you visit with him. I just can't be bothered. Then he threw it in my face, about 'Well, Ah certainly paid for a lot around here on the Fourth of July!' I mean, I says, 'Yeah, and that's the problem. That's why I didn't want anything from you. You go tell that to Suzi and Jerry.' He threw that in their faces already. The day he showed up he wanted a drink and they didn't have one. He said, 'Well Ah certainly paid a lot on the Fourth! Ah spent mah whole check on you people!' He was spending his money on Ross and Little Joe and this Mexican and himself. There's some people you just don't want to do anything for you, 'cause you'll never hear the end of it."

"That's really true. Really true," I said.

Tom told me that Dirty Mack had been arrested recently for panhandling. He had been working the courthouse area, but Tom didn't know where. They put him in jail over night. Mack said that it's getting much tougher because there is so much competition now. Tom agreed. "There's, there's five panhandlers on every corner," he said.

After a while, the subject of Jerry's teeth came up.

"He got his teeth all straightened," Tom said, "and he had a beautiful smile and then over a period of six months he was having pains and eruptions. So they went in and did a biopsy and found he had cancer of the jaw bone. So they had to jerk all of his teeth, cut down into the bone and dig out the cancer. Cobalt treatments and all that." Jerry had told me that this occurred when he was only nineteen years old.

Tom got to reminiscing about when he had all the kittens. He missed them a lot, though he did still have Beulah, the crippled runt of the litter. I thought of the irony of a crippled kitty for the crippled Bridge person. A match made in heaven. He asked me if I could remember when they were born. I couldn't. My mind seemed so overloaded with professional obligations and the daily grind in a contemporary megalopolis, that I needed to take notes to remind myself of everything. In fact, I did have notes about the arrival of the kittens, but not with me.

"I think they are about nine months old by now," Tom said. "I was just asking Jerry and he thought that's about when it was. You lose track of time down here. I used to remember things better when I got my food stamps every month. I couldn't even tell you what today's date was."

"Well, I guess it doesn't have much importance."

"No it doesn't. The only time Jerry remembers the date, was when Jerry was making all that money as a witness. Oh did you hear about that guy who killed the chick? Did Jerry tell you about it? He was getting a five dollar voucher for lunch at the cafeteria. He was getting eighteen dollars every day he showed up in court. They finalized it. What do you think happened to the guy? He killed her, you know. He beat her in the face with that piece of re-bar until she was dead. He changed his story three times. What do you think he walked with? His sentence?"

"I can't imagine."

"All right," Tom said, leaning toward me intently and warming to his subject. "He changed his story three times. He was gonna defend himself, and he did that for a while, then he wanted to get an attorney. Then he got rid of that attorney and wanted another one. So they got so tired of this thing, the judge told him, this was a week ago, 'Right now, you can plead guilty or no contest to manslaughter, involuntary manslaughter. Four years in jail suspended and four years probation and no fine."

"So he walked."

"He walked. And he killed her. There were no eyewitnesses, but everybody knows he did it and there was good circumstantial evidence. They arrested him originally on murder one. Then they dropped it to murder two. But he didn't even get voluntary manslaughter. It was involuntary. That's even less. And then to get just four years suspended jail time."

"That sounds pretty sleazy. That's awful....So Jerry's not on the lunch wagon any more, huh?"

"No. That all came to a screeching halt. The last day Jerry showed up in court, he was there on a Tuesday and Wednesday. And then he showed up Thursday with Jimmy Newby. They were each getting eighteen dollars. They got their eighteen dollars Wednesday and they had enough money left over when they got up that morning to go to the Six O'clock Store, and they showed up in court plastered. So drunk they wouldn't let them into the courthouse. The prosecuting attorney, this chick that was handling it, she got them some coffee and told them to sit in her office." (Of course, the drunkenness of the witnesses for the prosecution may have been a factor in the lenient sentence.)

"Why did he go there with Jimmy Newby?"

"Jimmy Newby was living there when the murder happened. He was a witness, Will was a witness, Sam Robbins was a witness."

I asked if Tom knew where Jimmy Newby was staying now.

"He gets six hundred and forty a month, so he's got a motel over near County General Hospital....He's still a mess. He's still a drunk. He fell asleep with a cigarette and it burned down and he was so passed out it burned down past his fingers, so his fingers are swollen twice their size. 'Cause he's dirty. He doesn't keep his bandages on and he gets falling down drunk rolling down these hills, you know. And he gets dirt in them and they get reinfected. They told him they would have to amputate his arm if he didn't keep it clean. It took SIX MONTHS for all those burns to heal. When he was drunk and fell into the firepit. 'Cause he kept getting it reinfected. His arms were swollen twice their size."

"Jeez. He's such a self destructive guy."

"Yeah. And stupid. He got ripped off for his food stamps last month. He went down with Larry, to buy something, I don't know. And a guy just took his money away from him. He was so plastered."

"Yeah. Seems like he's always getting victimized."

"He gets really drunk...and violent. He trashed their camp over there."
(Across the street, where Dirty Mack, Big Joe, Larry, and others live.) "Just threw
everything down the hill. On a drunk. He didn't know why he did it. He just did
it. And then a couple of times he attacked Jerry, 'Let's wrestle!' Well Jimmy
Newby is...what? About six six and weighs probably two twenty. Look at Jerry.
He's a string bean. Jerry's ribs were just black and blue. He [Jimmy] grabbed
Suzi one day by the arm and left a handprint. When he was drunk and she was
drunk. When he got that drunk, I'd stay away from him."

We went on to talk about food stamps.

"Anything you buy with food stamps, you have to pay a commission."

"Yeah. It's like black market currency."

"Yeah. And then one day I had a tooth that was just killing me. And all I had
was my food stamps. I paid my rent. So I went over to the Hard Rock Cafe and
said, 'Anybody got any codeine? Any fours?' And a guy said, 'Yeah! Come on
over. I got some fours.' I said, 'I got this tooth.' He said, 'Yeah. I can see a little
swelling there.' I said, 'All I got is food stamps, man, but I need two fours.' I
said, 'I can pay a dollar more with the stamps than the going rate.' The going rate
was two dollars. And he said that was fine with him. He has to buy groceries too.
So I popped that four, and a half hour later I felt it working. That tooth was strange
for about two days. I was living on fours for about two days and then it went
away. Then about six months later I had to go to County General and they pulled
it."

"How did you decide that it was the time to go to County?"

"My tooth kept hurting."

"Oh. And you weren't able to get any more fours, huh?"

"Well, I was running out of money. There were hundreds of fours out there,
but I didn't have any more food stamps. I thought this tooth would just flare up for
three or four days and then it would go away. And it did do that, but like I said,
about four or five months later it flared up again, but it stayed flared. So I went up
to County, to the dental clinic. I got there at seven o'clock in the morning, and by
ten thirty it was pulled. I had my prescription by twelve. Just about the time the
Novocaine was wearing off. And I popped three of them." We chuckled. "This

was years ago. I don't even know what kind of pain pill it was. But I took three of them and about an hour later—WOW! I was flying. I been up there, let me see, three times now to get teeth pulled. I just went about four months ago. They gave me these things, ibee bouferins, bufferins or something."

"Oh ibuprofin." I asked for more details about Tom's dental history. He said that a poor person couldn't get dental work done anywhere, so what you had to do is let things go until the tooth needed to be pulled. They will pull teeth at the County/USC Hospital, but will not do fillings or other dental work.

After a moment's pause, Tom said, "It's so quiet here, now. No arguing."

"Yeah. That's nice."

"Joe wanted to move in with Suzi and Jerry, and he started to bring it up, and Jerry said, 'No. There's no room here.' So he's over there with Will."

A while later I asked, "Did you ever live in one of those cardboard condos?" At that time, I had seen plenty of them, but hadn't talked to people about them much and hadn't slept in one.

"Yeah. I had to. I only had one lightweight blanket. And once you get into a cardboard condo, the cardboard retains all your body heat. So, I had to take my blanket off because I was starting to sweat. And I had to take my jacket off and used it as a pillow. And in the dead of winter, you can sleep with just your clothes. If it's made well enough. I'm so big and put out a lot of body heat, I would be heating up so badly in there, I had to cut a little trap door vent. Yeah. I lived in a cardboard condo for about two months in State Park.

"How long do you think Jerry's been on the street," Tom asked.

"I don't know. I don't think you can believe him, you know," I said.

"I can't believe some of the things he's told me anymore," Tom said. "I heard him tell you he never knew how to panhandle until Tex taught him, about two years ago, three years ago. When Tent City was there. That's when I met Jerry. Tent City. And then just the other day, he was complaining to Suzi that he's been panhandling for over twenty years."

"Yeah," I said. "He's told me that too, that he's been on the street for twenty years. I find it difficult to believe a lot of what he says. I mean, I can't even figure out how old he is, for instance."

"Yeah. I don't know. I believe he's been on the street for twenty years, but I don't know. I'm starting to worry about him because he's getting to the point where he can't concentrate on a conversation. His mind spaces out. But he's drinking a lot less."

"Is he?"

"Yeah. 'Cause they don't make but six or seven dollars canning. And then half of that goes to Suzi. So, when he was panhandling, I know he was making ten, fifteen dollars a day at the State Building. And then when his check rolled in, look out. He got checks for about six months. He was on a disability. He had to go to Hollywood Mental Health Clinic. He had to talk to a doctor. They gave him bus tickets. And then they gave him a bus pass. And as long as he kept his appointments, he was getting his disability, so he didn't have to do a work project or anything like that."

"It was a mental health disability?"

"Yeah. You can have a physical or a psychiatric disability, and until the doctors determine one way or another, on our welfare, you don't do a work project and you don't have to do a job search. Of course, as soon as they see that, they rush you up to Cardenas and Ninth, and they file for your SSI. (Naturally, the county would like to get everyone possible off their rolls and into federal programs.) So Jerry went up there and did that. And I don't know where he was having his check sent."

"He never was getting SSI, though?"

"He never fulfilled. He never went though with it. He got to such a point that he was drinking so much he couldn't keep any appointments."

"Oh, that's too bad."

"Yeah. Well, you've seen Jerry and Suzi here."

The conversation drifted along. Tom reminisced about Skid Row in the late 1970s and early '80s.

"Listen, when I was at the El Rey, which is now the Weingart, the rent was eighty-five dollars a month. And my check was one hundred eighty-one. So I had almost a hundred dollars in cash. And food stamps were fifty-five bucks.

"So you could actually afford a place to live on welfare then?"

"Yeah. Everyplace was so cheap. Yeah. You really could. 'Cause you had almost a hundred dollars in cash, after you paid your rent. Now your whole check goes for rent. And like when I was working at Mack's Liquor, I had it made. I had a pretty good room at the old Johnstone for eighty bucks. A room like that would go for three or four hundred dollars now, you know, like at the Cecil or the Pacific Grand. Most of those little old hotels are history and now the rents are crazy. You know all those little parking lots all over the older part of downtown? Well, there used to be cheap hotels there. But they decided they could make more money parking cars. That's the way it goes, ha, ha, ha, ha."

We talked for a few minutes more about Jerry. "It's like I told Jerry the other day about his drinking. He was up here plastered. I don't know how he made it up here. I guess he was going to the dumpster 'cause he didn't have any food. And he brought back these meatballs. And Jerry's sense of smell is so bad, I said, 'The cat won't even eat it, Jerry, that's how bad it is.' And he was plastered. I said, 'You know, Jerry, about your drinking? It's just suicide on the installment plan.'"

"Yeah."

"He said, 'Thanks a lot, Tom.' Jerry would like to think I drink like he does, but I don't."

"No. And I also think he knows that he's committing suicide, but...."

"I keep telling him, I say, 'Look how bad you're getting. You can't even walk without that stick, anymore.' He doesn't even read anymore. He used to read and he used to do lots of things. We used to play cards, and he'd always have a couple of paperbacks going. He used to eat. He doesn't even do that anymore," Tom said.

I had also noticed Jerry's decline and found it troubling, but Tom knew him much better than I did, of course. A few minutes later, the topic of Jerry's age came up again.

"I doubt that he's any older than you and me," I said.

"Well, I'm forty-two, and Jerry has said so many times—Well once he told Suzi he was born in something like 1938. Well that would be eleven years older than I am, so he'd be fifty-two, fifty-three."

"I don't think he's that old."

"I think Jerry'd be too old for Viet Nam. How long did Viet Nam run for?"

"Well, it's hard to say, but it began in something like '66 and it ran until about...."

"Wasn't it earlier than that?"

"Well, yeah. But it didn't start heating up until about then. I was in the Army from '63 to '66, but I was in Germany. And I thought it was starting to get kind of hot in say '65 and '66."

We were both getting sleepy. We never returned to the topic of Jerry's age, but we had talked about it before and always ended up wondering. I had really intended to talk to some street people in the Civic Center area that night and to sleep there, but it was already late and I was tired. I told Tom that I'd brought a small hammock with me, and I'd just sling it between a couple of trees next to his bridge instead of sleeping on Suzi's old mattress. He said fine and lay down to sleep. I didn't bring it up, but the condition of the camp was steadily deteriorating, and the spare mattress was much the worse for wear. I suppose I would have slept there if I REALLY had to. I walked a few yards to the north and found a couple of eucalyptus trees about three yards apart and tied the hammock, made of light netting, tightly between them at about chest heighth. Then the hammock and I wrestled in the weird greenish light for a few minutes. Eventually I was able to get situated. It was quite a comfortable alternative to the ground. I slept a little cold, but otherwise had a fine night. It must have been about eleven o'clock when I went to sleep, very late for a Bridge person.

33. Jerry's depression

I awoke at about six. Since Tom and I had talked late into the night, I didn't feel much like getting up. An Hispanic guy in work clothes walked by below me on Cardenas Street. He waved and grinned as we made eye contact. Something about seeing someone in a hammock makes people grin. Unfortunately, I couldn't spend the entire morning cheering up the neighborhood that way, so I climbed out and untied my bed from its twin trees. I wanted to administer the Present States Examination (PSE), a psychiatric diagnostic instrument, to Jerry first thing that morning for the AHMI Project. I gathered up my old day pack and headed down the hill. I was going to wish Tom a good morning and tell him I was off to work, but he was still asleep, so I left without saying anything.

As I said, at that time Jerry was living under the northernmost bridge on the east side of Cardenas. To get to it and all the other campsites there, you had to crawl through a hole in the fence and walk up a fairly steep pitch of bare dirt. This northernmost bridge was the lowest of all, and the easiest to get to. As I approached, I noted that Suzi was sleeping there with Jerry. This campsite received early morning sun, unlike the old camp where Tom still was, and besides, Jerry was usually an early riser. Nevertheless, Jerry and Suzi were still asleep. I stood at the foot of his bed and called out to him. He awoke with a start, sat up, and was immediately ready to talk. He was glad to see me, he said, and asked how I had been. I said that I had been fine and told him that I wanted to take him to Giotto's for coffee and to conduct a formal interview with him. He said that would be fine with him. Suzi asked if she should stay and I said that she should.

Jerry slipped on his shoes and was ready to go without further ado. We walked east toward Chinatown. As I said, there are a few blocks of vacant lots there where mansions had stood. As we walked along he pointed out his old campsite under what looked like a large, old pepper tree. It was set back from Buena Vista something like forty yards. He pointed out other campsites of homeless people here and there under the trees.

"Is there a little level place there?" I asked.

"A VERY little level place," Jerry chuckled. "One day a tractor came through and cut all the weeds and everything, and when I come home, half of my bed was buried underneath the dirt, so I had to—That's when Art got pissed off and says, 'You're not staying here anymore.' So that's when I ended up back underneath the bridge—OOOH!"

Startled, I turned to see what was wrong with Jerry. He had knelt down as if he was having a stroke or something, but then I saw that he had reached for an almost complete cigarette that was still smoldering on the sidewalk. "How about that, the motor's runnin'." He laughed. "Now, THAT'S finding a snipe."

I asked about Art, and Jerry said that the last thing he knew, he was staying at the King George Hotel. He was still on SSI, but from time to time he stayed under the bridges. In my experience, a lot of the people on SSI with mental health disabilities occasionally lost their entitlements through bureaucratic bungling when they moved. I was glad to hear that Art was still receiving his and apparently doing okay. He was a very generous guy and a good friend to Jerry and the others.

As we walked along, Jerry found another nice snipe or two. "Waste not want not," he said once as he knelt down to pick up the butt.

Although Jerry's legs were much better, he still walked rather slowly and needed his walking stick. "Now it only takes me a half a block to get limbered up, instead of two blocks. So, I, I, I'm coming along on them. A lot better than when I first had my stroke."

Eventually we got to Giotto's. We stood at the counter. We both ordered coffee and I ordered a bran muffin for myself. Jerry didn't want anything to eat. He asked if we needed a booth, and I said that we did want a little privacy, so he led the way to a secluded area in the back. After we had seated ourselves and had a sip or two of coffee, Sam Robbins came over and gave Jerry a bag of muffins. He was looking more presentable than I had ever seen him. His clean wavy hair, whitened with the snow of time, cascaded over the collar of a clean plaid flannel shirt. He just dropped off the bag quickly and went back to a table across the room where he was sitting with a couple of other older men.

I explained the PSE to Jerry and assured him that it was strictly confidential. He seemed to appreciate the consideration, but said that he was not in the least concerned about such things. I recorded his responses on the PSE form, of course, but I also taped the session. His responses supported my earlier diagnosis of major depression. Occasionally during the interview we hit upon some topics that interested me. Like getting colds.

"How often do you get colds?" I read.

"I get two a year. One lasts from January first until the end of June, and then one starts at the first of July and ends around December thirtieth. I continually get—You can't help but have colds and sinus problems in this weather. I mean, the smog is bad enough, and then living underneath the bridge with freeway traffic on top of you and Cardenas in front of you. And that extra exhaust that you get. And then livin' in the dirt ain't too awful nifty either. And then with the pollen and everything else. I don't know if they'd really call it a COLD cold; it's congestion. Continually. If I don't end up with emphysema, it'll be the Lord's wonder."

I asked about his most serious bout with depression. It had taken place some fifteen years ago when he had an apartment.

"It just comes. It just comes, but this time when it came, it was...." He looked down and shook his head as if to say no. "I locked my doors. Pulled all my window shades down. Went so far as to unplug my T.V. and radio and I just sat there. And Jimmy Johnson had a key to my apartment, and he used to come and bring me food. The only thing I did was sit on my bed. And that went on, it went on for about two weeks, and that's when Jimmy Johnson finally called my family and my family came and then next thing I knew I woke up and I was in a padded cell—in a strait jacket no less—dying for a cigarette and no way to smoke it. I looked on my bed table beside me, and there were cigarettes sitting there."

"How did you become unconscious?"

Jerry did a pantomime of giving himself an injection. "I don't know what they shot me with, but BOY, they shot me. And I went and kicked the door to my room. I was locked in a rubber room, a padded cell, I should say. It had mattresses all around. I mean, how could anybody hurt themselves when they're in a hospital gown, depressed, and in a strait jacket to boot? I mean, and I need to be in a padded cell? If that doesn't reinforce your depression, nothin' does. You know, that they've got that much confidence in you. You know, your confidence level gets about minus four."

I asked for his views on his drinking.

"The reason I drink is to KEEP calm. I don't drink nearly as much when I'm on my medication, 'cause my medication keeps my nerves down. When I don't have them, which I can't get them, because I don't have I.D. and all this other crap that you have to go through to get it, so then I drink. And I drink wine because it keeps me calmer than beer does. If I had to drink beer to stay calm, Eddie would be making a fortune selling me beer. I'd be drinking three or four cases of beer a day, easily."

34. Giving a damn

Toward the end of September, 1989, I was walking down the sidewalk across from the Music Center on my way to the bridges, when I ran into Dirty Mack. It was about eight thirty in the morning. He was so clean, I almost didn't recognize him. He was panhandling, of course, and was only about forty yards north of Jerry Jenson, another homeless friend of mine. Dirty Mack recognized me and said hello in his quiet manner. He is quite reserved when sober, but loud and incoherent when drunk. Not an ideal field consultant. He was wearing a dark brown polyester pullover, dark dirty slacks, and some dirty running shoes. I asked him about his location, and he said that this was one of his normal spots. He had a couple different ones, he said. He said that Caltrans had come by and "wiped everybody out under the bridge." There were only a couple of fellows living at his camp now. There had been as many as six at one time.

Some fellows in suits came walking up the sidewalk toward us, and Mack turned to me seriously and said, "Excuse me, I've gotta panhandle."

I said, "Oh, okay. I've gotta be going anyway. Take care, Mack." I dropped a little change into his hand and walked away.

"Thanks, Jackson," he said and smiled briefly before turning his attention to his potential benefactors coming down the sidewalk. He was among the most dedicated panhandlers I'd met.

I continued toward the bridges. As I crawled through the fence, Tom yelled a hello from his bed. I yelled hello back and trudged up the little hill to where Tom was lying on his side, braced up on one elbow. The area around his bed was still encircled by trash. I fished around in my shoulder bag and pulled out a large can of Top's cigarette tobacco. "I brought you a birthday present."

"You bought ME a birthday present?" Tom said. Then he saw what I had in my hand. "Oh my God! THANK YOU! I didn't know Top's had this [a can]. Are there papers in here?"

"I think so."

He began looking at the label. "Two hundred of them!"

He scooted over and made a place for me to sit on the foot of the mattress. All the chairs and crates had burned long ago, of course, and Tom had never replaced them. There was no other place to sit. I told him that I didn't have much time because I had a meeting scheduled. He said that he'd seen my motorcycle over in the parking lot. He had been panhandling in Angelo's parking lot lately and had been making fair money at it, he said. I joked that he had an enviably short commute to work: fifty or sixty yards, mostly downhill. We had a little chuckle about that.

Virtually everyone who parked in Angelo's lot worked for the county or the Los Angeles Department of Water and Power. Right after payday, Tom typically made five or six dollars. His take tapered off to three or four as the last payday became a fond memory, and people begin to tighten their belts until the next one. Tom said he had developed regulars. One woman regular usually gave him three dollars a week. Another woman gave him a dollar a day. These were the only regulars that he mentioned, but he may have had others. It was interesting to me that they were both women. However, both Jerry and Tom have told me that, in their experience, women aren't necessarily more generous than men.

One problem Tom was having, he said, was that he didn't have a watch, and he had to be at work in the parking lot by about six to intercept the first wave of employees on their way to work.

He said that Caltrans had come about two weeks before and cleaned up the place, as Mack had told me. He had only a little foam mattress at the time and had dragged it over into the foliage to get it out of the way while they worked. They had told him that he could keep anything he took with him. Of course, he didn't have much to take. When they were finished, he dragged the mattress back and that was all there was to setting up housekeeping again. Later that same day, a Mexican guy had come up and asked him if he wanted a mattress. He said sure, and so he and the Mexican walked over to the Mexican's apartment near Buena Vista and Cardenas, perhaps one hundred and fifty yards north of Tom's camp, and lugged the mattress back.

Tom was now working for the parking lot attendant at Angelo's parking lot from time to time. They gave him a dollar or two to clean up the area around the dumpsters and around the parking attendent's shack. Some dumpster divers, he said, threw trash around and left the area a mess. One time, when the place had been especially trashed, he'd worked for half an hour and the guy had given him three dollars. If there was just a small amount of trash thrown around, it took him only a few minutes and he made a dollar. He had been getting hired like this two or three times a week.

He also had a job chopping garlic at a Thai restaurant in Chinatown near his old panning office. Once a week he'd go down there and chop garlic for an hour or two and they'd stuff him with Thai food and give him a couple of dollars. He laughed and said he'd never seen so much garlic in his life. It was their week's supply. He smelled like an Italian sausage for days, he said.

Tom said that all the cats were now gone. The last one, little Beulah, had recently been taken home by somebody in the parking lot. Since then, the rats had again become a force at Tom's camp. He said that for a while, he'd been trying to clean up his camp about once a week and put trash in huge orange plastic bags that Caltrans left for him. But the rats came out in the night and ate through the bags and spread the trash all around. He expressed surprise that they would do this. I was surprised that he was surprised. A plastic bag is nothing for a rat. I had seen them gnaw through drywall, plywood, and even the insulation on electric wiring and plastic pipe. Their tenacity and industry is truly admirable, though little else about them is.

He hadn't tried to keep his camp clean for very long, he said. It was just too much trouble because of the rats. Of course, that didn't explain the deep ring of trash around his bed, but in my view, his depression and demoralization did.

"Well, if it was immaculately clean around here, people would come into camp and steal stuff. If I leave it trashed, nobody's tempted. My things, I don't really have anything worth stealing anyway, but my radio, and I take that with me. But my things are really pretty safe. I mean, look at this mess," he said with a wince.

Tom really liked having a little radio with headphones. It was one of the only thing he cared about besides eating and smoking. Despite his keeping them with him at all times, they still got ripped off and I had seen him go through several different sets. One thief grabbed Tom's radio and headphones from him one day while he was taking a siesta in his bed and actually wearing the headphones. Another set was taken by a trusted campmate. It is almost impossible to keep anything when you're homeless. I'm sure the trashed camp did indeed discourage potential thieves and in that regard, it was a clever adaptation to a very harsh reality. But I thought that Tom would have taken better care of himself, his things, and his camp if it weren't for his depression and deep demoralization.

Tom said that a few days before a couple of drunks had come up through the hole in the fence and were so plastered that they had passed out in the bushes, right next to the fence. The next morning they got up and went on their way.

"So I thought, sometimes when I lay down on my mattress, the change falls out of my pockets, so I better go check the bushes. I couldn't believe it, I found eighty cents in change, half a pack of Winston 100s, and an unopened short dog of Night Train. It was, I must tell you," he paused dramatically, "a most memorable event in my life. A major score. Ha, ha, ha, ha."

We continued to talk, but I had to go to my meeting at UCLA. I told Tom so and left at about ten thirty. Later that day, I returned downtown and talked with other homeless people in Skid Row proper. I had planned to camp with some of my street friends who sleep on the sidewalks near the missions in Skid Row, but that didn't work out, so I thought I'd camp with Tom under the bridge. It was about eight that evening when I left Market Street and headed back to the bridges. Tom was there on his mattress just where I had left him that morning.

We chatted for a few moments, then I suggested that we walk down to Eddie's and get a couple of quarts of beer. That was agreeable to Tom, so he fumbled around in the deep rubbish surrounding his bed, found his filthy nylon court shoes, and put them on his filthy bare feet. We got up and picked our way down the short, steep slope to the hole in the fence and then walked north toward Eddie's. We got a cold six pack of pints, a *National Enquirer* and a bar of soap for Tom, and a small bag of *chicharrones* for me. As we walked back toward his camp, I offered Tom some of the *chicharrones*, but he declined. His teeth weren't up to it, he said.

Tom said that one of the main benefits of living under a low bridge, as opposed to a high bridge, was that during the holidays, people would bring gifts and drop them off. Last year he had gotten lots of canned goods—cheese ravioli, potted meat, tuna, a couple boxes of crackers, and cookies. "It was nice," he said. At that time, Tom had been camping under the low bridge to the northeast of his present campsite, where Jerry, Suzi, and Rubio were now. One of the reasons that Jerry didn't want to move to a high bridge, he said, was that Thanksgiving and Christmas were coming. I was a little surprised that the Bridge People would plan ahead to the holidays back in September.

There is a lot written in social science about the "present time orientation" of poor people being a cause of poverty. From what I saw, however, a present time orientation is mostly a result rather than a cause of poverty. The people I knew on the street were certainly capable of planning ahead when there was some practical value to it, but their experience on the street was "use it or lose it." The reason I seldom saw them saving or planning was that it didn't usually work for them. There were few real opportunities for planning or saving in their environments. Daily life for the very poor consists of being bounced from one crisis to the next. They have virtually no control over the timing or direction of the bounce. The rich and powerful hold the racket and the best adaptation for the very poor is to be resilient and ready to respond to whatever they come up against.

In a moment, Tom continued to talk about Jerry's decline. We both found it troubling. "He's really a lot more disabled than when I first met him. He's gone down the tubes physically. You know, he really needs that stick to walk with now. Before, it used to be a prop for sympathy when he was panhandling. Now it's become a real necessity."

"Well, he seems like he's walking better than right after his stroke, but still he can't walk well. Right after his first stroke, he couldn't do much better than a shuffle," I said.

"He had a couple of seizures just a couple of weeks ago."

"Did he really?"

"Yeah, he had one on his canning route, and he had another when he got back. And when I saw him, I asked where Suzi was, and he said that she had gone to the liquor store. He just had a seizure and he wanted a drink." Tom shook his head as if he couldn't believe it. I'm sure he really cared about Jerry. He was saddened to see his old friend fading away.

John Moe crawled through the hole in the fence, came up the hill, and chatted with us for a few minutes. He was staying in the campsite just up the hill. After he turned in, Tom and I talked for a while longer. Tom said again that reading takes his mind off "all this shit around here." He said that Big Joe and Jerry read a bit too, when they were sober enough. Tom typically went through three or four books per week. Mostly adventure or science fiction. "Anything but romances," he said wincing. "I like to read the *National Enquirer*, too. I know it's full of bullshit, but it IS truly amusing, ha, ha, ha. It's entertaining, you know. They're always getting sued over stuff they make up about movie stars, but who cares. It doesn't matter. Nothing matters, ha, ha, ha."

Tom told me that an Oriental woman had been stopping by three times a week to drop off the *Los Angeles Times* for him. She wrapped it in a plastic bag and threw it over the fence. Tom, Jerry, and the others were much better informed about current affairs than I had expected them to be. They had frequent access to newspapers, usually secondhand like most things in their lives, and read them rather often.

It was about nine thirty when Tom began to yawn and stretch. Being ever the keen observer, it finally dawned on me that I was keeping him up. I said good night and picked my way through the ivy north of the bridge for a few yards then slung my hammock between the two young eucalyptus trees. I put on my windpants and parka and wrestled with the hammock for a couple of minutes trying to get arranged and comfortable. It was about nine forty-five when I dropped off to sleep.

I awoke several times during the night, of course. Besides the occasional loud car or truck on the freeway above or Cardenas below, there were rats scurrying around in the leaves and brush under my hammock proving, as Tom had told me, that since the kittens were no longer in camp, the rats were back in force. Their fussing around was so loud that it woke me several times. It sounded like they were playing football on a field covered with corn flakes. There would be silence for a few minutes, and then CRUNCH! Crunch-crunch-crunch! Then silence again, like they were in between plays, then CRUNCH! CRUNCH! Crunch-crunch-crunch! It went on like that much of the night, but I was able to sleep through most of it. I was certainly glad I was not sleeping on the ground.

At about six A.M., when John Moe came down the hill past me to go panhandling, I was facing the other way and not fully awake yet, so I didn't say anything to him. I saw Tom leave to go panhandle in the Angelo's parking lot at about six ten, pretty much as he had said he was going to do. I didn't stir until about six thirty or so, well after both "bums" had gone to work. A lot of the time, these guys went to work two or three hours before us respectable, middle-class folks do. Will was really an early bird. He used to go to work canning at four in the morning, and that beats most farmers.

I packed up my windpants, parka, and hammock and headed to the parking lot to lock this gear in the motorcycle saddlebags. While I was at the motorcycle, I saw Tom near the dumpster, some thirty or forty yards away. He shouted a greeting and waved. I finished up at the bike and met him as he was walking toward me. He talked to me about his panhandling business, just like any other proud businessperson. He pointed out various cars in the lot and told me how much the people who owned them typically donated to him.

"See that brown pickup with the sun shade? The cardboard sun shade?"

"Yeah," I said.

"That's forty-five cents. See that little Honda car, that silver one, by where the guy is standing?"

"Uh huh."

"That was a quarter."

"Uh huh. Well, all right."

"My dollar lady, let's see, what does she drive? Oh, see that little gold car with the crunched fender?"

"Uh huh."

"She's good for a dollar, three days a week.

"That's not too bad."

"Naw. Payday's not yet. I used to have a schedule for the paydays for the county."

I looked at my watch. "Today's the twenty-ninth," I said. I realized that I wouldn't have known the date either were it not for my watch.

"Oh, well then they should have gotten paid. Oh, well, v-e-r-y nice. And Monday should be gangbusters. I have trouble remembering dates and things. The further away it gets, it's just a blur. Not that I don't understand or remember, but I can't keep track of stuff like that. So much of my life is just day to day. So many days are the same. I wake up and I honestly don't know what day it is. And the only way I can keep track, if I don't go up to the newspaper machine and look at the date. Well, the date REALLY doesn't mean anything to me. I know the day of the week. They dump the trash at Angelo's Restaurant on Mondays, Wednesdays, and Fridays. If I find the trash cans empty, it's gotta be Monday, Wednesday, or Friday. And when there's nobody there to panhandle, it's the weekend. Ha, ha, ha. You know, that's my time keeping schedule."

Tom said that he had washed up that morning at a faucet he had shown me about forty or fifty yards north of his camp on the same side of Cardenas. It was a leaky Caltrans hydrant used to irrigate the vegetation around the freeway bridges. It had a handle that could be turned manually (most require a wrench). The discovery of this hydrant had improved Tom's quality of life considerably, since he could readily clean himself and his clothing without hauling water up the hill by hand. He no longer had the large plastic containers for carrying water anyway; they had been destroyed in the fire. The hydrant was quite leaky, and there was a miniature marsh of a few square yards just downslope from it. I thought that this must be the water source that supported the small, but vicious mosquito population that had been making a sharp inpression on me lately.

When I thought about it, I was amazed at how an apparently insignificant event, like the discovery of a leaky hydrant, could alter the lifestyle and quality of life of a homeless person. Their lives seemed to be hugely effected by little events like these over which they had no control.

That made me think of another homeless friend of mine who had been living in a downtown doorway for a couple of years. He was careful to leave before the people who worked there showed up in the morning and he didn't return until well after they had gone. He liked the doorway because it sheltered him from the wind, the rain, and the gaze of passing pedestrians. It was also quite close to his panhandling place and the cheap coffee shop where he spent a lot of his time drinking coffee and talking to his friends. He kept a very low profile, kept the area clean, and tried to avoid causing anyone any trouble. I had visited him in this rather pleasant little nook several times, talking together for hours about homelessness. He had made friends with the security officers that patrolled the area and police didn't bother him there.

Then the owners of the building changed security companies. One night the new security officers woke him up and dragged him out of his doorway and into the gutter. A few nights later, a female friend of his tried to sleep there and resisted when they dragged her into the gutter. She got a broken thumb for her trouble. He tried to sleep in the doorway again a couple of times, but was caught each time and had to give up and move. Like most homeless people I know, he just shrugged it off. Street people were completely powerless and couldn't afford to give a damn. It was just too painful and pointless to care about anything. It was a lesson they quickly learned through repeated painful failure and disappointment. After a while, it was even tough to give a damn about themselves.

Tom mentioned that when he had washed up that morning, he'd used the soap I had bought him the night before. His previous bar of soap had been in a plastic bag that also contained some empty beer cans he was saving for Jerry. Caltrans had taken the bag when they came to clean up the burned out camp some two weeks before. Tom said he was going to take a bath and wash his pants today too. We chatted for a couple more minutes, then I told Tom that I had to be going. He went back to work near the dumpster, and I began walking toward the northern bridges looking for Jerry. I wanted to finish giving him the PSE.

As I searched, I thought about my few days on the street. I had gradually gotten dirtier and dirtier. It took a tremendous effort to stay even somewhat clean if you were sleeping under bridges, in bushes around public buildings, on the sidewalk, or in any of the other nooks and crannies of the city that street people find to sleep in. As my personal appearance deteriorated, I began to notice that some of the people that I met on the sidewalk looked through me as though I wasn't quite there. Of course, a lot of well-dressed, affluent, apparently competent people in the city were thoroughly alienated from their fellow human beings. They didn't smile or make eye contact with one another anyway. But even downtown, there were occasions where, in close quarters, if there weren't too many people on a sidewalk, people might nod and smile. But when I was dirty, it was different. I experienced the difference between being Dr. Underwood and being Mr. Homeless, and the contrast was stark and troubling. If I, as a poor and dirty Bridge person, had the audacity to say good morning to someone, as Jerry often did, people pretended they didn't hear and stared straight ahead like palace guards. But I could see them startle and freeze at my callous disregard of their obviously superior status. They behaved as though they risked the immediate disintegration of our great democracy if they recognized me as a fellow human being. When that happened to me, I felt insulted, sad, and angry all at the same time. The anger and insult eventually evaporated, leaving bitter salts of disgust for these clean, respectable people, my fellow responsible citizens. But I began to understand that the aversion they have for the poor and dirty is a veneer over deeper fear, guilt, and ignorance. I deeply believe that knowledge is the antidote to fear; justice the antidote to guilt.

As I walked along from Tom's camp toward Jerry's current one, I noted that the trail from the lower northeast camp to the upper northeast camp had nice steps carved in it. Later I found out that Gene had originally carved them with a crutch and Larry had recently recarved them with a stick. I climbed them and joined Jerry at his latest camp. Big Joe was there too. They both expressed their frustration with the fact that Rubio was back. They said with him around there was a constant threat of violence.

"Violence is the only thing he knows. And what's gonna happen is that it's gonna end up—Suzi, you know Suzi and her mouth. She'll egg him on and WHAPPO," Jerry said.

I gave Jerry a pack of Top's cigarette tobacco I'd brought for him. He and Joe had gone panhandling the previous day at the Courthouse together. Evidently they'd formed a partnership.

"He made eighty cents yesterday," Joe said, chuckling.

"I made, hee, hee, hee, eighty cents," Jerry said.

"Ah made about ten dollars," Joe said proudly.

"Well, ha, ha, ha, he's got me stuck up against this wall and then he goes into this breezeway where there's all the traffic. In and out, in and out, in and out. And here I am sittin' on the fuckin' wall. Everybody that walks by me, he's already hit! Ha, ha, ha, ha," Jerry said.

"It don't matter none," Big Joe said. "It don't matter if he makes it or Ah make it, it goes to the same place anyway."

"Yeah, we just turn it into wine, you know, like Jesus and the loaves and fishes. Ha, ha, ha, ha." Jerry laughed.

"Did Larry go canning or anything yesterday?" I asked.

"Yeah, he set up here and watched the camp," Big Joe said.

"And you didn't mind that he was just watching the camp while you were working?"

"No, huh uh," Jerry said. "That's just as much of a job as anything else. That's the way I look at it, anyway. This stuff about this is mine and that is yours business. That doesn't work underneath the bridges."

"Larry helps out when he gits somethin. He gits food stamps. He gits down, he gits down and does his share," Big Joe said.

"Oh, so he shares the food stamps with you when he gets those, huh?" I asked.

"He shore does," Joe said.

Despite how sanguine they sounded about sharing and reciprocity, it was a major source of strife as well as a solace. They did share an enormous percentage of their resources with each other. But sharing had large social costs, as illustrated by the problems that had clouded the camp that Jerry shared with Tom and Suzi. This situation with Larry watching the camp sounded to me like the partnership that Tom and Jerry had had some two years before, when Jerry gradually came to deeply resent Tom for watching the camp just as he had requested. Partnerships, friendships, and the composition of camps changed constantly among the Bridge People.

As among traditional hunters and gatherers, friction between campmates was often resolved by group fission. The offending person might be asked to leave, as in the case of Luke Broder. Or the group might dissolve and reform in a different combination. For example, a while back Will threw Larry out of their camp at the lower southeast bridge. Larry then moved to an upper bridge by himself, where Big Joe joined him, and finally Jerry joined Larry and Joe. Right after the fire, Jerry had moved to an open camp under the big pepper tree by himself; then he'd moved to the northeast low camp, also alone; then Suzi joined him; then Rubio joined them; then Jerry moved up the hill to join Larry and Big Joe. The Bridge People constantly formed new camp combinations. There were no formal means, like arbitration or courts, of solving interpersonal problems. There was just argument, which could quickly escalate into violence and avoidance. While avoidance usually meant moving to another camp, it could mean moving away from the bridges altogether, as Abe and Luke had done, or it could mean going away for a time, as Big Joe, Little Joe, and Tiny had done.

I asked about what they did to keep people from stealing their belongings when they went to work.

"About alls you can do is jest keep whatever you want to keep with you. People WILL come through the camps and they WILL go through your belongin's and take whatever they want. That's jest the way it is. You can try to stash things in the bushes, but people will sometimes find that too. But, you know, Larry is in camp most of the time these days." He nodded at the sleeping figure on a mattress nearby.

A couple of weeks before, while Jerry and Suzi were gone canning, Caltrans had come into their camp and cleaned them out again. By that time they had acquired a couple of swivel-base armchairs, an end table, and a nice seagrass mat for a carpet. Caltrans took it all. Joe and Larry were in their camp, above Jerry's place, but Big Joe thought the Caltrans people were just picking up paper, or, he said, he would have gone down to Jerry's camp and asked them not to remove Jerry's things. That sounded a little funny to me, since it would be difficult not to notice someone carrying off armchairs. Of course, Joe and Larry may have been thoroughly drunk and not capable of paying attention.

The urge to acquire some furniture and belongings to make life a little more comfortable had to be balanced not only against the possibility of difficulties with Caltrans, but also against the problem of trying to keep people from stealing what you had. It reminded me of an old saying from the 1960s: "Everything you own, owns you."

The situation with Caltrans had evolved into a futile, meaningless cycle under the bridges. The Bridge People would accumulate furniture and try to fix up their camps so they could live more comfortably. But the furniture that, from their perspective, provided them a minimal level of comfort was also, in the view of some nearby office workers, an eyesore. The office workers would lodge complaints with Caltrans, and Caltrans would come and clean up the area. At times, the camps of the Bridge People were almost as clean as a Boy Scout's, but typically, there was a substantial amount of trash in the area. Of course, there was also a great amount of variation in how clean camps were among the Bridge People. Larry was at the clean end of the continuum and Tom was at the other. For a while, the Hispanics living at the upper northeast camp had virtually covered the hill near their camp with paper and trash.

Regardless of how clean the camps were, I could certainly understand why people would be offended at the sight of people camping under a freeway bridge. It was something I never thought I would see in this great country. The problem, I thought, was that people complained to the wrong parties and viewed the problem much too superficially. The problem could never be solved by cleaning up the area and running off this or that group of homeless people. It could only be solved by providing housing, health services, and jobs for the very poor. People should be outraged about the misguided policies that, in a little over a decade, have turned our great American cities into scenes from Calcutta or London at the time of Dickens. Instead of complaining to Caltrans or some other hapless agency about the homeless as eyesores, it seemed to me they should complain to Congress, to the Secretary of Housing and Urban Development, and to the President about horribly failed housing and economic policies.

A few moments Jerry raised me from my cheery reverie as he looked forward to the holiday season.

"Well, with the holidays coming up, and stuff like that, we could start making out pretty good. That's the reason why, that's the only reason, I hated to leave the low bridge [where Suzi and Rubio were]. Because when we were over there last year, people were bringing us over stuff right and left. Driving by throwing bags of clothes at us, and everything else. That's when one of the owners of Angelo's come over with them two big pans of quiche. Lobster quiche and crab quiche. Well, you know, you can eat only so much quiche. And there it was. There was three of us. And we had these HUGE pans of quiche. And they were still hot. They said, 'We made too much, for a party. So I thought you guys would like it.' Then he delivered a pan over across the street too. He come over here and then delivered some over here too. He didn't want us to feel like we were getting a handout or something like that. But he's a nice guy. One of the few left in the world. I wouldn't be at all surprised if Angelo's doesn't feed us on Thanksgiving. Wouldn't amaze me in the least."

About eight thirty Big Joe woke up Larry to ask him how much money he had. Joe wanted to get up enough for a bottle. While this was going on, I asked Jerry again about panhandling.

"When you go out panhandling with Joe, how do you decide who gets to sit where?"

"It don't make no difference really. Like I said, when we make it, we make it. That's it. Who makes what doesn't matter."

"A lot of them lawyers know me," Joe said, "down there where we been goin'. They give me money all the time. That's the reason we been goin' down there."

"Yeah, he's been going there. He's got regulars, like I used to have at the State Building. I had my regulars. And that makes a hell of a difference. It really docs. Because they get to know ya, and they trust ya. And they know you're not out to harass 'em or anything else, like a lot of the panhandlers do. You know, they'll panhandle somebody, and if they don't give them money, they'll cuss them out." Jerry scoffed, "That's real good business sense. But when you get your regulars," Jerry continued, "that's when you get it."

"How do you cultivate regulars? I mean, uh, do you cultivate regulars?"

"Well, they git to seein' you sittin' there ever' day," Joe said. "Maybe give you a quarter today, and then they might end up givin' you a dollar, after they git to know you for a while, ever' time they see ya."

"So you just try to be friendly?"

"Yeah," Big Joe said, "talk to 'em nice."

"Yeah, down at the State Building, I even got to know them by name," Jerry said.

"How did you get to know their names?" I asked.

"Well, sometimes they'd sit down and talk to you and stuff. And eventually you just get to know their names."

"Oh," I said, "I saw an expression in the paper the other day, and someone was talking about Skid Row, and the wines that they're gonna pull off Skid Row, and somebody said that they call short dogs, shorties. Well, I never heard you guys call them shorties."

"Well, there's an expression that goes, if you're panhandling and stuff, and you're down around there, you walk up to somebody that you kinda half-assed know, and say, 'I need a quarter to get Shorty out of jail.' And that's, 'I need a quarter for a short dog.'"

"Yeah?"

"The first time they did that, I didn't know what they were doin'. I didn't know Shorty. Hee, hee, hee. And I thought, 'Get him outta jail? Then that takes twenty-five dollars or something like that, and he needs a quarter?' And I'm sittin' there tryin' to get enough to get my own short dog."

After a while, Joe, who was unsuccessful in prying any change out of Larry, said, "Well, since nobody has any money, we'd better be off to work. Ah gotta panhandle me up a bottle, so's Ah can git well."

Jerry, Big Joe, and I got up and picked our way down the steep trail to the fence and Cardenas Street. Then we walked slowly, because of Jerry's bad legs, toward the Civic Center. Big Joe stayed at his panhandling area near the mall entrance to the County Court House, while Jerry and I continued on to the Winchell's so I could finish administering the PSE to Jerry.

36. Big Joe gets well for his birthday

After we had dropped off Big Joe, we ran into Raleigh, a young Black homeless man I knew, near the County Court House. He was looking healthier and cleaner than usual and was wearing clean clothing. Raleigh called Jerry, Red. I was surprised that they knew each other. Looking back, I shouldn't have been, since they'd panhandled about a block away from one another for a couple of years or so. Raleigh told Jerry about me. "Hey man, this guy is really good people, man! Really a nice guy, man."

Evidently I had made a very good impression when, one night not long before, I'd bought him a burger. He had just gotten out of jail that afternoon and had no bedding, no place to sleep, no money, and hadn't eaten since that morning. He was wearing just a tee shirt when he thanked me for the burger and went wandering off to look for a place to sleep. I remembered that a shudder had gone through me when I watched him walking away and I thought of how cold he was probably going to get that night.

We exchanged greetings briefly and then Jerry and I continued on our way. I remarked that I was surprised that Jerry knew Raleigh.

"Street people is a society within a society," Jerry responded. "You get to know everybody that's on the street. And you know about their families, and stuff like that."

We arrived at the Winchell's and walked up to the counter. I wanted to get Jerry something to eat, but, as usual, he wouldn't accept anything but coffee. We sat and sipped our coffee while we finished the PSE. A bit later I asked Jerry if he used to stay in the Skid Row hotels, as Tom had.

"Well, yeah, but mostly I was just in the street down there. It costs too much money to go down to them hotels. Even though they are 'cheap hotels,' but uh they're still really expensive. Well, like when I found this sweat shirt, there was a bunch of papers in the pocket."

"Uh huh."

"And I was lookin' through them, and whoever this belonged to, had stayed at a hotel for one week—a hundred and fifty dollars!"

"Yeah."

"I could live a month on a hundred and fifty dollars. And I mean that's food, booze, and everything else. It doesn't take much."

"Yeah, that's about what you do live on. If you made five dollars a day, and it was a thirty day month, that would be a hundred fifty dollars. And when you're canning, there are some days when you don't make five bucks."

"No. Huh uh. One day last week, before Rubio come back, Suzi and I, we went all the way to Third and Burlington. And ended up with three pounds."

"Three pounds, huh. What's that, two seventy five or something?"

"Two and a quarter," Jerry said. Then in his flat, Jack Benny voice, he said, "Whoopee," and paused dramatically. Then he chuckled. "And to have to walk all that way, too." He smiled at the irony and shook his head.

After a while, Joe joined us at the Winchell's. He said that there hadn't been much foot traffic at the Courthouse, so he'd thought he'd come over and sit with us. He was looking worse and worse. He said that he had thrown up a couple of times this morning after he drank some water. He thought he would have been better off without the water. Despite the project rules about not giving people money, I gave Big Joe a couple of dollars and told him to consider it his birthday present. Jerry was not in the least under the weather, even though yesterday he had been significantly drunker than Joe. He had told me on several occasions that he did not get hangovers. I was skeptical, but, I have to say, after camping with him, that it is indeed the truth. I'd seen Jerry pass out after being sloppy, falling down drunk and then wake up the next day as if he'd gone to sleep over nothing stronger than camomile tea. We chatted and sipped our coffee. Big Joe came back about twenty minutes later.

"Ah turned it up and drank about a fourth of it before Ah come back in here," Big Joe said, pulling open his old Army fieldjacket just enough to show Jerry and me the neck of the short dog. Jerry giggled.

"Yeah? Well that should help, huh?" I asked.

"Yeah. It'll help settle my stomach," Joe said. He did look a lot better.

We continued chatting, and a bit later I asked about sharing. "How do you decide about sharing? Like, how do you decide what's fair?"

"You use what you can use, and then you give the rest, like we go up to Joe. If it's more than what Joe can use, Joe goes down and gives it to John Moe or Sam Robbins or somebody. That's the way you do it."

"Is it kinda like having favors in the bank?"

"Yeah. 'Cause everybody does it."

"What if somebody doesn't do it?" I asked. "Let's say somebody named X came into camp and seems like a nice guy to you, so you let him stay there. And you share with him. You know, like you give him some food, maybe give him a little wine, over a period of a week or something, and he never gives anything back."

"That's happened before," Big Joe chuckled. "We tell them to git the hell outta there."

"Hee, hee, hee, we politely tell them to go get a new address," Jerry said.

"And how long does it take for somebody leeching like that before you do something?"

"About a week," Big Joe said.

We continued to chat about this and that for another half hour. When we got up from the table, Jerry gathered up the extra napkins, as he often did, and pointed out, "It's not for writing home to mother." I noticed that Big Joe did not bother picking up his napkins. It seemed there was some variation in how rugged rugged individuals are. It was about ten fifteen.

I left the field for a while, got my camera, and returned to take some photos of Tom's camp after the Caltrans cleanup. Then I left the bridge, locking up the camera in the motorcycle saddlebags and heading downtown again. I regretted not having the camera with me a short time later when I ran into Big Joe and Jerry again at State and Market. With their long full beards and floppy tee shirts, they looked like dirty, delinquent elves hiding out from Snow White.

Big Joe wore a huge, dirty, dark green tee shirt and Levi's that were too short by about ten inches. He was about six feet four and weighed two hundred and fifty pounds. He had a big round belly and moved like a big, friendly bear.

Jerry wore a floppy, dirty, light blue tee shirt and dirty, baggy, grey chinos. He stood six feet tall and weighed about a hundred and forty pounds. He was

hunched over, concave to Big Joe's convex, and moved like a frail old man. Big
Joe had a long, full, brown beard; Jerry had a similar one in red.

They were a classic pair of happy drunks; laughing, staggering, and only able
to remain relatively vertical by holding each other up from time to time. Evidently,
they had met with enough panhandling success to buy a fifth. As they waited for
me on the corner, they swayed around like a pair of defective gyroscopes. This
was a busy area in the middle of the Civic Center, and I was concerned they might
get run over, or arrested or beaten up by L.A.'s finest. When I got across the
street, I urged them to be careful and to get home at their first opportunity. "You
guys are too drunk to panhandle now, anyway," I said. They laughed and howled
their agreement at this, but I don't know if they took my advice or not. At the time,
it didn't occur to me to intervene and try to drag them home.

I conducted some research with some of my other street friends for the rest of
the day and then, deciding to camp again with Tom for the night, headed back to the
bridge. Tom was under the bridge on his mattress when I arrived. He told me that
he had had a six dollar day panhandling in Angelo's parking lot, which set a new
personal record. He had made as little as a dollar, but never more than six.

Tom started talking about the kittens. He was really a pet lover. He had told
me several times how much he missed the kittens and how they had made him feel
more like a real human being. He loved to just lie on his mattress and watch them
play and explore around camp. Their liveliness and curiosity contrasted vividly
with the dull apathy and deadening drunkenness of bridge life. He really loved it
when they'd curl up next to him while he lay there reading. They didn't care that he
was homeless, depressed, dirty, and fat; they just cared. But they were gone, so he
had started feeding some mice that lived under a nearby cardboard box. He'd given
them some scraps of pizza that evening.

"They're cute," Tom said. "I don't like the rats. The rats are stupid, man, they
just crawl right over you. They don't seem to understand to go around. The thing
about the rats is that they piss as they go along. And they shit as they go along. I
was sleeping a couple of nights ago, lying flat on my back, and I felt two little
paws, a little pressure on my shoulder. And I turned, and sure enough that was a
rat. The problem is, if I have any surplus food, they're over here getting it. So
now I just throw everything over in that direction." He pointed down the hill

toward the street. "A little bit of a hot dog, or a scrap of bread, or something. I usually save a few empty beer cans and fill them with up with water, then if they wake me up at night, I can throw them. 'Cause an empty beer can, you can't throw very far. Put a little weight in it with some water, though. I got one rat right up along side the head."

"Ho, ho. Really?"

"It was a lucky shot, I have to tell ya. I'll admit to that. I can usually come within a foot of them, one way or the other."

"I heard them in the bushes where I was sleeping off and on all night."

"Oh, did you?"

"Yeah."

Tom and I continued to talk until about nine thirty. I always kept him up past his bedtime when I came to visit. I slept in my hammock again in the trees a few yards north of Tom. During the first part of the night, I was cold. I lay there half dozing with my mind at a fast idle, like a motor with a stuck choke. I half-pretended to be asleep, waiting for the night to be over as I thrashed around in the hammock trying to get comfortable. After a couple of hours of that I finally admitted to myself I was not asleep and not going to get any sleep unless I somehow got a little warmer. I sat up and, with the hammock swinging wildly, wrestled with my nylon poncho until I got it wrapped around me. Then I slept pretty well for the rest of the night.

I awoke in the morning about seven, very late for a bridge person. I eventually got up and walked the few paces to Tom's camp. He was awake, reclining on his mattress, reading and smoking cigarettes. We chatted briefly, then I walked up to the Winchell's near the Civic Center area where I ran into Dirty Mack. It was about seven thirty. He was sitting on the sidewalk drinking coffee that he'd bought at the Winchell's a couple of doors down. He said that since it was a weekend, he was going to walk out State three or four miles and work there. He said that he needed twelve dollars and fifty-five cents that day. He showed me his grocery list: some barely legible scribbles on a scrap of brown grocery bag with the items he wanted in one column and prices in another. He calculated his cash requirement and then panhandled until he got it, he said. I knew that Tom did the same thing, but his list was very, very short and he didn't need to write it down. He got discouraged more easily than Mack, too. Mack worked much longer hours than any of the other Bridge People, with the possible exception of Will, the canner, and had a higher standard of living. He also had the worst drinking problem and the worst personal hygiene of any of the Bridge People. He was very friendly to me that morning, which I thought was a little out of character. I had given him a little change yesterday, and perhaps that was a factor. I moved on to talk to some of my other street friends and left the field later that day.

Because of other research, I didn't get back to the bridges until the day after Thanksgiving. I looked in at Tom's camp, but he wasn't there. Then I proceeded to what I thought was Jerry's current camp. I thought he had moved back to the low one on the northeast where Rubio, Suzi, and Larry had been living. There I saw Suzi and Larry and talked to them for a few minutes. I asked them how they'd been getting along, and they said about the same. The canning business was only fair. They canned every day, but now only cashed the cans in every week or two. In the preceding two week period, they'd cashed in eighty-eight pounds of cans or about seventy dollars worth, so they were still making approximately four dollars a day per person.

"There's a lot of people canning, these days," Suzi said. "It's a lot harder than it used to be, you know."

"Yeah," I said sympathetically. "Well, you look pretty prosperous. The camp looks REAL nice." They had their mattresses neatly lined up against the abutment and had a dilapidated couch and a couple of old kitchen chairs arranged nicely around a hearth made of concrete blocks. There were a couple of milk crates with plastic bags in them. There was no trash at all in the area. Larry kept a clean camp.

"Well," Larry said, "so long as it looks decent, Caltrans won't bother us. So we try to keep it cleaned up."

"The last time Caltrans cleaned us out, those people over there must have bought new furniture," Suzi said, pointing north to some small, run down houses, "so they were throwing out all the old stuff, and mattresses, hee, hee, hee, hee, hee."

"Oh, so you were able to refurnish right away, huh?" I asked.

"Yeah. It's nice to have real mattresses, 'cause we were sleepin' on cardboard and blankets."

We continued to talk for a while, then they told me that Jerry was home. I thought at first they meant that he was above us in the upper camp, but it turned out that Jerry was living with Dirty Mack and the guys directly across Cardenas from Tom.

Jerry was indeed home, along with Dirty Mack. As usual for Bridge People, they were lounging on their mattresses. Jerry's mattress was near the south end of camp, then Mack's about a yard away from his, then a gap of perhaps three yards, then a couple of empty mattresses. Beyond that was a large, loose collection of garbage where the ivy began at the north edge of camp.

After we exchanged greetings, I asked Jerry how he had spent Thanksgiving. He regaled me with the menu. He gloried in describing food and how he acquired and cooked it, but after camping with him and talking to other Bridge People, I knew that he seldom cooked or ate much. His meal descriptions were entertaining, as much to Jerry as to any listener, but were shamelessly romanticized.

"We had chicken breast with uh, uh, orange sauce. Rice pilaf, salad, dressing."

"You did a lot better than I did," I chuckled. "My Thanksgiving dinner consisted of a MacRib sandwich at MacDonald's with one of my homeless friends who lives on Market Street."

Jerry said that one of Rubio's regulars had come by and taken Rubio to the grocery store. Then Rubio cooked Thanksgiving dinner for all the Bridge People at his camp. John Moe, Sam Robbins, Larry, Rubio, Suzi, and some others attended, in addition to Jerry. Eight or ten total, Jerry said. Dirty Mack was invited, but hadn't gone.

Jerry continued to bring me up to date on recent bridge life. He was still panhandling in the mall at the Courthouse. The police hadn't been bothering him there and his income had steadily increased as he developed regulars. He'd had a good day Wednesday and made twenty-four dollars. I had observed that he typically didn't work the day after a good day like that, though he often insisted that he worked every day.

While Jerry and I talked, Mack began singing, but I couldn't recognize the tune or understand the words. Perhaps howling would be a more apt description of it. Jerry told me that Tom had been up singing all night the previous night. All of a sudden it had gotten rather musical under the bridges. Jerry had seen Tom heading north on Cardenas sometime that morning and hadn't seen him since. He had been invited out to Thanksgiving dinner by one of his regulars from Angelo's parking lot. He'd gone to this guy's house, spent the day, eaten, and done his laundry.

Tom was still having trouble getting shirts that fit, but now had gotten some. He'd said he was going to bring some shirts over for Mack, but he hadn't done it yet, Jerry said.

While we talked I sat on a milk crate, the ubiquitous, all-purpose furniture of bridge folk. Jerry was on his mattress, either sitting or lounging at different times. I could look over his shoulder toward the edge of the abutment to the north, past the other mattresses. Several times during our conversation, I saw three or four fat rats scampering through the collection of garbage near the dripline. I noticed that I had gotten quite used to seeing them and they didn't offend me much anymore. I wondered to myself if I might be "going native."

I reminded Jerry that the last time I had visited him, he, Big Joe, and Larry had been staying in the upper northeast camp (adjacent to and above Rubio and Suzi's current camp). I asked him how it had happened that Larry was now with Rubio and Suzi.

"Well, because uh, Big Joe beat the shit out of Larry."

"Oh. Humm. And what was that about?"

"I have, really, I don't have any idea. There's all kinds of arguments and fights underneath the bridges, and none of it makes any sense to me. It's a bunch of dumb, miserable people gettin' drunk to forget their troubles, then they get in a fight and beat the shit out of each other. Then they get drunk again to forget that and it starts out all over again. It sure doesn't make any sense to me. But there's a whole lot on God's earth that doesn't make sense to me, so what the hell."

By this time we had walked past Rubio's and Suzi's camp and had gotten to the parking lot to the north of the bridges. As we went past Rubio's and Suzi's, I'd asked Jerry if he wanted to stop and say hi, and he'd said no. As we crossed the parking lot, we met Tom. From the brown paper bag cradled in his arms, it looked like he was returning from Eddie's. He was wearing a very large black short sleeve shirt and had headphones on. He had an ear to ear grin as he greeted us.

"Well, theeeere's Tommy!" I announced loudly like Ed McMahan introducing Johnny Carson, when we were twenty or thirty yards apart in the parking lot.

"Ooooo!" he yelled back in falsetto. "Well, aren't you the grand ones! So happy Thanksgiving." He reached into the bag and gave Jerry and me each a cold beer.

"Well, thanks. I got you a little prize too." I fished into my bag and got him a box of Tops rolling tobacco.

"Well, thank you," Tom said.

"Good to see you. You're looking really cleaned up and good!"

"Yeah, well I went out to Tujunga, I got an invitation from one of my panhandler regulars. I had a happy Thanksgiving."

"Well, I heard you singing," Jerry said.

"Yes. That's what John Moe said." Tom looked at me sheepishly and confessed, "I was singing last night. I got blitzed. And I came back with two fifths."

"Fifths of what?"

"One of Bacardi and one of gin. I came back at nine o'clock, and then by about four o'clock this morning, I don't remember too much."

We all chuckled.

"So anyhow, I'm just getting blitzed," Tom said. "And Fisher, whew! I was walking down Beech [in Chinatown]. I went to the church and got a dollar. So, I'm bopping down the boulevard and suddenly here comes Big Joe and Tiny. And Tiny's got bad feet. And I never saw Tiny move so fast. I said, 'What's going on?' Big Joe said, 'Fisher! He ran us out, man. He was shaking his stick, "GET OUTTA HERE!" I don't think he really wanted to arrest us as long as he saw us move in a direction AWAY from Chinatown.' So suddenly there was Fisher in the parking lot at Beech and Market and so I ran around the corner, and Joe and Tiny took off, and they said that Fisher has been walking the beat."

"Walking?" I asked.

"WALKING. They're walking the beat. Are you ready for that?"

Tom told me that a week before he'd gotten a fifty dollar hit panhandling. He'd bought a carton of Pall Malls, a fifth of Bacardi, and case of beer. Then he bought himself a burger for dinner and he went to a movie. (There are several cheap movie theaters on Market where you can get in for under three dollars. One is an all-night theater that houses some three hundred homeless people on a typical night.) He'd taken a couple of days off; then, while he still had a little beer, cigarettes, and Bacardi left from his spree, he'd decided to panhandle anyway in Angelo's parking lot.

"So I made three dollars. And Mel pulled up, 'I've been looking for you!' I said, 'Oh, well, here I am!' He said, 'You want to come to my house for Thanksgiving?' And I said, 'Well, what's that gonna be like?' You know? 'Old tired relatives? I'm not even a Christian, and I'm a faggot.' He said, 'That's all right! We're Jewish!'"

We all chuckled.

"So anyway," Tom continued, "I said, 'I stink, you know. My clothes are nasty.' He said, 'Well, that's all right. We've got a washing machine and a dryer in the garage.' You should see their house. It's magnificent. It's a quarter acre estate in Tujunga Canyon overlooking the wash and the mountains. It's breathtaking, just breathtaking. With a hot tub and a golden retriever in the back yard.

"They had two twenty-pound turkeys and thirty people showed up. But they don't smoke and they don't drink. Except Mel's mother. So her and I are out in the backyard sitting by the hot tub chain smoking! [Gravelly falsetto] 'I'm the only one in the family who smokes, Tom!' I said, 'Yeah, here, light me up would ya?' Ha, ha, ha. So anyway, she smokes Winston 100s, ultra light," Tom winced. "And Mel bought me a pack of cigarettes, Pall Malls, and they had three bottles of wine, for thirty people. I thought, 'Oh my God!' Mel's mother said, her name is Bessie, she said, 'They don't even drink in this family! But I saw two bottles of wine, let's go get a drink!' So, we boogied off into the den. So Bessie and I knocked off a bottle of wine. You know, but I was sober, that does nothing for me. It was white. Johannesburg Riesling, you know. It was nice. So anyway, I had a good time, you know. I porked out. Ate a lot of turkey."

Tom said he also got a lot of clothes, but none fit him. He offered a jacket to Jerry, and said he'd bring it over. Mel had given him a bunch of paperback thrillers, too. He got on a scale at Mel's. He thought he was approaching three hundred pounds, but he turned out to be only two seventy. He was happy about that.

At that point, Jerry was having trouble standing up and slurred that we had to be off to get some coffee at Giotto's. Tom said that he'd heard that you have to spend at least a dollar there now. You couldn't just buy ten cent coffee like you once could unless you bought something else too. In his best imitation of an upper class Englishman, he said, "It's...to keep out the vagrants."

We all had a nice chuckle. As we parted, Tom wished Jerry and me a good day, and then he leaned over to me and whispered, "Get Jerry a bottle of wine, would ya. He's in bad shape."

"Okay. Yeah, he's in trouble."

In fact, Jerry was not in good enough shape to walk to Giotto's, about a half mile from where we stood, so we decided not to bother with the coffee. It appeared to me that if he didn't get something alcoholic to drink soon, he would be quite sick. Despite what he said, even Jerry could occasionally get a serious hangover. I went over to Eddie's while he sat on the curb. I ran into Rubio on the way and said hi. He was canning. I got Jerry a fifth of Thunderbird and bought myself a couple of tall beers.

On the way back to the bridge, Jerry talked about Rubio and Suzi. "As much as we've had our falling outs and stuff like that, and differences of opinion, when it comes down to it, they say, 'All right Jerr, come on. Let's go up and have a hot meal.' Rubio's always good for that. ALWAYS good for that. I can't say too awful much more about him that's good," Jerry chuckled.

Jerry and I walked slowly back to his campsite. After we'd sat down and he'd had a few gulps of wine, he seemed to feel better and we continued to chat. I knew that the Bridge People were not "transients" and none were recent immigrants to Los Angeles, but I wanted to get an idea of the overall stability of the Bridge People as a subculture, so I asked Jerry how long he had known the various campers. He said that he had known Larry eight or nine years; Suzi only three or four years; Rubio three or four years too, he had showed up about the same time as Suzi; Big Joe and Little Joe about six years; Tiny about two and one half years; John Moe, Sam Robbins, and Dirty Mack about five years; and Tom over twelve years.

Jerry told me that he and Big Joe had recently dissolved their panhandling partnership.

"Well, it got to the point where I was doing the panhandling and he was doing the spending."

"You mean, you guys weren't walking up there together?"

"Oh, yeah, we were walking up there together. Of course, I couldn't even fart without him coming over to smell it. But it just got to the point that I was makin' the money, and he wasn't doin' nothin'. It just happened gradually." They were partners, Jerry said, for eight or nine months.

I told Jerry that I wasn't sure about his age because he had told me several different ages at different times.

"Nobody ever knows my real age. You want to know my real, real age?"

"Yeah. Uh huh."

"I was born January sixteenth, nineteen thirty-eight."

If that was true, and it jibed with what he had told Tom, that made Jerry fifty-five years old. I still wasn't sure I could believe him. From his talk, he seemed several years younger; from his appearance, several years older.

He said he had been hospitalized on the order of twenty times for depression. The staff at Hollywood Mental Health wanted him to get into an outpatient program on several occasions, but he didn't follow through with it. He didn't think it would do any good. (He was probably too depressed to follow through with anything.) It had been a long time since he had been to Hollywood Mental Health, maybe three or four years he thought. He'd had a mental health evaluation when he was in County/USC Hospital after his major stroke. He hadn't been hospitalized for mental health problems for about six years or so.

While we were having this conversation, Dirty Mack was lying on his mattress slurring out a running commentary. I asked Jerry about what kinds of medication he has been on for mental health problems and Mack piped up, "He has got as much medication as I can give him today." I chuckled. Jerry said that he had been on all kinds of medication: lithium, Thorazine, Valium, and a variety of others.

"Those three are the ones that stick in my mind. The Thorazine turns you right into a fuckin' zombie. You take a pill, and, and it would turn you into a vegetable. You couldn't think. You couldn't feel. You couldn't do nothin'."

"How is that different from wine? Does wine turn you into a vegetable?"

"Oh no, no, no. Wine is a, a, catalyst. There are extents where wine will wear you out, stuff like that. But shoot, it's not like what Thorazine does. And then Thorazine combined with Valium on top of it. You turn into a vegetable. And, and, all you do is just sit there looking stupid. And that's the only thing you CAN do, is look stupid."

I looked up and saw Tom coming across the street with the jacket that he had told Jerry about.

"Oh, here he comes," Jerry said.

"He looks too nice to come up here, doesn't he?" I said chuckling.

"Yep. Really. Hee, hee, hee. What IS this bullshit? Ha, ha, ha."

Tom arrived at the top of the little hill puffing. "Heeer is zee frock from Monsieur De Beeg Stomach." He bowed deeply and held out a nice, brown ski parka. The Bridge People shared my appreciation for earth tones.

"Thank you, Monsieur Tommy. Thank you. Hey, this is pretty nice! You have exquisite taste, Monsieur." Jerry gave Tom a dramatic drunken bow while still seated and almost fell out of his chair. We all chuckled. I didn't know if Jerry was acting or really drunk. Whatever, it was a great gag.

Still trying to get a better idea about camp to camp movements, I asked Tom about Larry and Will, guys who had once lived at Dirty Mack's camp.

"Will got run out of here," Tom said.

"Well, he ran out Larry, at one point didn't he?" I asked.

"Yeah. Well, he ran off Larry, and then everybody ganged up on Will. And then also Will didn't want to be here anymore. I don't know, Will has all kinds of stories about owning a plantation or something?" Tom looked at Jerry for confirmation.

"Yeah," Jerry answered.

This got my attention because I have found that tales of wealth like this on the street are usually delusions, suggesting paranoid schizophrenia.

"In Louisiana or something. And there's natural gas or oil. And he's got a crazy sister-in-law. I just say, 'Yeah, yeah, Will. Sure.'"

Street people, like the rest of United States society, had only a very foggy idea of what mental illness was like, but unlike the rest of us, they had a very high level of tolerance for deviance. They typically accepted delusional stories and fabricated personal histories, albeit halfheartedly and with a large grain of salt. They had little to lose by tepid belief. They tended not to confront one another when they suspected the truth had been stretched or snapped, partly because they didn't really care or count on the truth and partly because even mild confrontation could escalate into violence. Craziness, to street people, typically referred to meaningless and unpredictable violence, like the behavior of Jimmy Newby or Rubio, for example. They did notice if someone constantly talked to his or her hallucinations, but they didn't understand this as florid schizophrenia. They referred to such a person as someone who was "not wrapped too tight" or "playing with a light deck" or some other such expression. There was little stigma attached to such behavior.

We continued to talk about bridge life. I was engrossed in the conversation and was surprised when I looked up and realized that it had gotten dark and was beginning to get cool. It was approaching Tom's bed time, too. I told him that I had to be going. I told him how much I had enjoyed talking to him, and he thanked me again for the tobacco. We walked together across the street, then I continued on to Angelo's parking lot. It was about seven o'clock when I left.

I didn't get down to see my friends under the Cardenas bridges again until the day after Christmas. I had spent Christmas with some of my other street friends and had come by the bridges to visit, but the only one home was Dirty Mack, and he had been very drunk and quite incoherent so I didn't stick around.

I approached Tom's camp. He shouted hello. I shouted hello back as I crawled through the hole in the fence and then trudged up the short steep slope to where his mattress lay in his halo of rubbish. He sat up and we exchanged greetings.

"Christmas was a bummer. Last year, there were so many people, they would pull up in vans, cars, 'Hey guys! Merry Christmas!' and hand us bags of groceries, cooked dinners, shopping bags full of clothes, which none of them fit me. I never got a thing, well, the only thing that fit me out of about thirty pieces of apparel was my knit cap. But everybody else made out. I got three pairs of corduroy Levi's, brand new, never been worn, with the price tags still on them. I gave them to Big Joe. He was so overwhelmed, 'cause he knows I don't particularly like him. And he doesn't particularly like me. But we can get along. We can listen to the radio, 'cause he knows all the music I know. So anyway, this Christmas, it didn't happen like that. It was DISMAL." Tom's face wrinkled up as though he'd just bitten lemon peel.

"Friday, this truck pulled up, a Toyota, with a Mexican family. And they had a thirty gallon trash can in the back loaded with sodas and ice. And you got one little paper sack, like you take to school when you're a kid with your lunch. Two hot dogs, ketchup packets were in it. And then, we got all this good stuff."

He reached behind him and fished around in the discarded food wrappers, brown paper bags, and crushed tobacco boxes. He really just lived on his mattress. Everything he needed he could reach from there: his tobacco, his beer, and his few items of spare clothing. And what he didn't want he just tossed away from there too. Food scraps he tossed down toward the fence because of the rats. While his filing system had some very obvious drawbacks, it did work, and he soon came up with the bag he was looking for.

"Uh huh!" he said and turned back toward me. "They're Christians." He winced and showed me the bag. It had a green, construction paper bell that proclaimed "Jesus Loves you!"

"I got a toothbrush. My teeth are rotting, and I never use it. You want a toothbrush? Take it. You've got teeth."

"Sure I'll take it. Yeah, I've got teeth." We chuckled. Then he continued his inventory.

"I got a little plastic razor. It would take twenty-seven of these to get rid of this beard. And I got this really fancy bar of soap. Do you speak French?"

"No."

"It smells nice." He held it to his nose and then passed it to me. It smelled a little strong for me, but I don't like perfumes. After a few minutes he leaned over and got a brown paper bag and pulled a Burgie out. "You wanna beer? It's cold."

"Sure." He handed me one and reached in for another for himself.

"And then, you wouldn't believe the ripoff. The ripoff of the century for the bridges. This couple pulled up, you know, in a new Honda Accord, really nice looking. And I see them pull up in the parking lot over there," he said pointing to the northeast, toward the camp where Rubio and Suzi now lived. "Rubio runs down there. He obviously knows them, 'cause they're going, 'Hi!' I can't hear what they're sayin' from here. But they pull three big shopping bags and two cardboard boxes and another shopping bag and they go marching up the hill to Rubio's camp. I go, 'Oh, well somebody brought something.' He scored, you know. Somebody he's panhandled in the parking lot is bringing something to their camp. Which I think is wonderful.

"I'm sitting here picking up all the cigarette butts I can lay my hands on. Breaking them up and re-rolling them. The tobacco is bone dry, and you know. I thought I'd put it in a plastic bag and put in a spritz of water and shake it up to moisten it up a little, you know."

"Yeah. That helps a little, huh."

"Yeah, 'cause when it's that dry, it burns so fast, and it's harsh and hot. Plus when you roll it, it breaks up into powder. Then you can't really smoke it. Ugh! So anyway, there were these four Chicanos, well, they're Hispanics, they're not Chicanos. They weren't born and raised here. And they're walking by, and I yell,

'HEY! Can you spare some change?' And they're very young. There are two guys and these two chicks. This one chick had a body like Sophia Loren. I mean, va-va-voom. She's only five foot two. They kept walking and by the time they got to the hole in the fence they finally decided to stop. 'Cause I kept going on, you know. 'Any change at all? Anything?' And this guy came back and gave me four quarters. It was around four o'clock. I didn't know this at the time. Saturday. So I rushed down there and got the four quarters, and thought, 'Ah ha! Tobacco!' I go rushing off to Eddie's and the couple are still up at Rubio's camp with all the food. And I made sure they saw me come out of the hole in the fence down there [just across from Rubio's and Suzi's]. You know how I jump on the fence and it weaves back and forth?"

"Yeah."

"Well, I went, 'OOOOOH!' I gave a great performance: 'Watch the fat person lose his balance climbing through fence!' Lawrence Olivier couldn't have done better. And then I looked, and they all saw me. And I boogied on up and cut across the parking lot by his camp." Normally Tom didn't walk through that lot to get to Eddie's. "And then I hear, [gruff, gravelly voice] 'Tommy! We have some food for you!' You should have heard the disdain in his voice. I said, [pretending to shout] 'All right! Well, great! I'm going to the store. I just got a dollar so I can buy some tobacco. I'll be right back! [Under his breath] Don't think I WON'T be back.'

"So I go over to Eddie's. I get the tobacco and I'm coming back through the parking lot, and down to Cardenas, and up through the hole in the fence. They built steps, you know. I went charging up the steps. They have got—This is it."

He swiveled around on the bed, fumbled around in the rubbish again, and came up with a large, empty styrofoam plate with a lid.

"This styrofoam dinner, it's a big one, too," he said excitedly. "This side," Tom pointed with a dirty, pudgy finger, "was filled with ham, off of one of those ham loaves that was sliced. Good quality ham, but it was rectangular shaped. Cut that thick." He held up his fingers to indicate about half an inch. "And this was a mound of white rice with gravy, and this side was sweet potatoes or yams. After you cook 'em, you can't tell one from another. And this over here was pork and beans.

"They had about seventy of these. All those shopping bags and crates were full of these dinners. Really, there was enough so that everybody under the bridges could have had two or possibly three. I didn't say thank you, 'cause he didn't give it to me, it was those other people. And he never would have brought it over here. They kept all of them, ha, ha, ha, ha."

"So that was Christmas. No, that was Friday, so then Saturday, I woke up again with no tobacco. And I thought, 'Oh Christ. Do I really want to go into Chinatown, before Christmas, and get caught by Fisher and Miller, and get arrested again?'" For a person who can't make bail, a holiday weekend is the worst possible time to get arrested, because he will be in jail until court convenes next, perhaps several days later. "So, I thought I'll go up to the church. Claim another loose tooth and I have to go to the hospital and I need bus fare. So I went up that way. I had a quarter in my pocket. A Mexican guy at the corner gave me a quarter. And then there were two guys coming out of Eddie's. And one guy gave me seventy-five cents. I said, 'Screw it.' You know. I had a bag of bread from the bread man."

"What's the bread man?"

"Oh, the bread man is the guy that stops at Angelo's. I don't even know what his name is."

"Oh, and he gives you stale bread if you're there at the right time?"

"No, it's not stale, it's fresh. Right of the truck. Baked that day. He gives me whatever I want. The minute he shows, I run down there, [friendly, musical voice] 'HI! How's it goin' guy?' One day he gave me twenty-four English muffins."

"What did you do with twenty-four English muffins?"

"I ate 'em. I sat down and I ate about six of them. I put ketchup on them. That was my breakfast, and then for lunch, I had three of them. And then the rest I ate for dinner. And I had a six pack of beer and a half-pint of vodka.

"So anyway, I went into Eddie's and got my tobacco. And then Sunday, the sweatshop was working. I couldn't BELIEVE it! Christmas Eve. So my little Mexican lady, she who goes by. She's given me three dollars. That's all she's ever given me. But she smiles and waves, and that is really nice."

"Yeah, I remember seeing her go by and you waved at her."

"Yeah. And she had her son with her. He's real cute. He'll probably look like Fernando Lamas when he gets older. Anyway he's real cute." He lowered his voice, "She's kinda old to be having a young kid like that. She's got to be forty at least. He's about two years old. She doesn't really speak much English. Her English is about like my Spanish. Which isn't all that much. Anyway, they had a party at the sweatshop, so she gave me a bag of donuts. There was like, two apple fritters, a cream puff, and then a chocolate old fashioned. And then I got one lemon filled and a raspberry filled. I was in hog heaven."

"And then her friend, who always walks with her. The sex kitten. She's got this body like you wouldn't believe. Like Raquel Welch. I mean, hot pants six inches above the knees, stockings, heels, and a halter top with a leather vest. She gave me this quart container of Chinese barbecue. So I got that food, and I'm just going nuts. And so then Christmas came, and I figured that somebody is going to show up here loaded down. I said, 'Don't go into Chinatown. I have enough tobacco, plus the butts that are spread throughout the area. Anywhere I toss them.'"

"So you're not saving them in a can anymore?"

"Naw. I got over that. Then I thought I should quit being so lazy and get a can. I don't have a can anymore. Caltrans got that." Of course, beer cans were quite plentiful, but he didn't have knife or can opener for cutting them open. "So I went to the Catholic Church up there Sunday morning, but I missed the mass and all the Christians were gone. And there was nobody to panhandle. I've never made any money panhandling at the church, but I figured Christmas morning I should at least make five or six bucks. It's Christmas! Come on! But it was too late. So I got two sandwiches [at the back door], and Lucy the housekeeper gave me these two of these expensive bakery cookies. So I came back home. Anyway, so at about three fifteen, I didn't know what time it was really 'cause I don't have a watch. I'm gonna try to talk you out of your watch."

"I'll get you a watch." (Later I bought him a cheap digital that he had his eye on at Eddie's.)

"Ha, ha, ha, ha. All right. I said, 'I don't think anybody's coming around with any food.' I said, 'Fuck it, I'm going back to the church.'"

"Is that the place where you pick up the sandwiches?"

"Yeah. So I thought, well, I'll go up there. And I'm sober. I haven't had any money. My drinking is way down. So anyway, I'm going up to the church, and I'm about ten feet away, and the head priest comes pulling out in his Buick. These are not Lutherans driving cheap Chevies, these are Catholic priests. There was the old one, who's really hateful, and there's another old one and a young one. The young one is very nice. He even slips me in a soda and a couple of bucks sometimes. He gave me five bucks once. I just freaked.

"I ring the door bell. Nothing. Absolutely nothing. And I'm sitting there and I say, 'Oh shit. Well so much for that.' I still got some bread left over, you know. I can eat that. So I went around to the front of the church and I think, 'Look at all these Chinese people.' But of course, they're out shopping. It's not a big to-do for them, 'cause they're not Christian. You know, I panhandled three dollars and eighty-seven cents," he paused dramatically, "in thirty minutes."

"Wow," I said. (Later I figured that was seven dollars and seventy-four cents per hour.)

"I couldn't believe it! I was freaked! Just totally freaked! It's happened to me three other times. I've tried it there time and time again, and nothing. Absolutely nothing. But suddenly, I'm making money. And then the worst happened. There was all these White people. All these older White people. Ho, ho, ho. And they went up and tried to open the doors of the church. And I said, 'I'm sorry, it's closed. You're much too late for mass.' [Falsetto] 'Oh thank you.' And they came down the steps. And I'm on the edge of the steps by the big juniper bush. 'Can you spare any change?' [Haughty, caustic falsetto] 'We don't HAVE any change.' This bitch, she said, 'We don't have any change.' I said, [soothing, saccharin voice] 'Well, thank you...in the name of Jesus. And have a nice Christmas.'"

"Oh good! I'm glad you said that! Ha, ha, ha!"

"Ha, ha, ha. Yeah! And they looked at me. Such hatred I've never seen. You know, I loved it."

"Yeah, in the name of Jesus. The hypocrisy of a stingy Christian."

"And then they were still standing there, and this Chinese woman was coming down the sidewalk, 'Excuse me, ma'am, could you spare some change?' She flipped out a fast fifty cents right on the spot. I just looked at the Christians and smiled, 'Guess who's going to take over the world one day.' You know? Ha, ha, ha, ha."

"Ha, ha, ha. That's great."

"So anyway, I bopped off to Eddie's, you know. I got a half pint and a sixpacker. I didn't have enough to get tobacco. Paid for EVERYTHING, but I was like forty cents short. Came back home, listened to my headphones. The batteries died, so that was the end of that. I have no batteries."

"Oh, I've got batteries." I carried spares for my tape recorder and the flash for my camera.

"Oh, great! Double A?"

"Yeah. Go on."

"So anyway, I finally go to sleep, 'cause I've got Steven King's *Christine*. And I read a few pages, and it's getting dark, so that's it. I'm not gonna go sit on the grass in the spill light from the freeway, you know. So I'm asleep, and I wake up and Jerry's going, 'You tired, ass punk motherfucker, old man!' Well, that's everybody over there. Hee, hee, hee. So that didn't give me a clue to who it was. And then Mack STREAKED up the street. Naked. Buck naked. With his little box and a bag. And he sat down in the fucking middle of the street on the yellow line."

"On Cardenas?"

"Yeah! Right here!" Tom pointed down to the bustling, four lane street. "And I got up, put on my shoes, and slapped on my jacket, you know, and I went through the fence, you know. [Pretending to shout] 'Get outta the street! You'll get killed, you tired-ass son of a bitch! Ha, ha, ha, ha! And he told me to fuck myself in my ass. And I said, 'You can't get it up if you WANTED to.' Ha, ha, ha. And he said, 'I want to panhandle. FUCK these people!' And I said, 'You're crazy, man!' And I reached down and grabbed him, and he slapped me off. I said, 'Oh fine, motherfucker. Die!' The cars are just whizzing by, and he's got his hand out. I heard he made a bundle at Christmas. He was making about forty or fifty dollars a day, and drinking it as fast as he can, and chain smoking. They say he's going through about four packs a day. Dorals. So, I say, 'Well, fine Mack.' So I went charging up their hill, 'What's wrong with this crazy old man?' And John Moe is going, 'The senile son of a bitch!' You know. And I said, 'Whose mattress got set on fire? Mack's?' He said, 'Naw, Jerry.' Jerry set his mattress on fire a couple of days ago. Flames were shooting up. And they dragged him off so he wouldn't burn to death."

"Oh, he passed out with a cigarette, I guess."

"Oh yeah. Yeah. Madness. Just madness, you know. So all that's been going on. They're all fighting." He reached around behind him near his mattress and came up with a length of steel pipe about an inch in diameter and two feet long. "This is Paula Pipe. It's just for display. I'm not going to use it. They're all old men over there. But I'm going to just go over there and slam this into that crate, and make a lot of noise with her, and yell, 'SHUT UP! I'm tryin' to sleep, you motherfuckers!' Somewhere I've got her friend, Stella Stick." He turned around again and fumbled in the rubbish. "Here's Stella Stick!"

"Oh, now that's an impressive unit."

He slapped it into his palm with a loud smack. "It's a shovel handle, you know. Paula and Stella. Stella would make an impression, you know, but Paula? Paula is heavy duty. She's a hard core Communist bitch. Ha, ha, ha."

"Ha, ha, ha. Yeah, really. An Impressionist and a Communist."

"Ha, ha, ha. I love 'em. We've been sleeping together for a lot of years under these bridges."

"Have you really?"

"Oh, I take them from bridge to bridge. I never leave them at home. So, anyway, I go over there and Jerry's sitting by the campfire, hunched up. Looking so frail. He's so fucking frail. I'm really upset about that. He's huddled there. Little thin, bony shoulders. Little knobby knees. He's so scrawny. I think Jerry will probably die under these bridges. Probably won't be too long. I hope not. He seems to have plateaued out. He's not getting any worse. But he ain't getting any better either, you know. And, he was sitting there by the fire, and there was a crate there, and so I sat down next to him. And he jumped about a foot.

"I told Jerry that he's getting even worse looking than Mack. Jerry's been very nice to me. And there've been times when he's been very vicious. And uh, you know, it goes back and forth. So I talked to Jerry for a while, and then Mack came back and settled down and put his clothes back on. He gave me a pack of cigarettes and a pull on his bottle, and then I was able to go back home and get some sleep. And that's my Christmas."

"Well, all right. That's not such a bad Christmas."

"Well, it was pretty depressing, though, at times."

Tom and I continued to chat. The research period was nearing an end and I wanted to know about some of the changes that he'd seen people go through under the bridges. I started with Jerry's weight, and he said that he thought he weighed about a hundred and forty. I find that heavy people tend to be good at estimating weight. It's something they tend to be rather conscious of. He said that Jerry'd lost about twenty to twenty-five pounds since he'd known him, and he was thin to start with. He said that Jerry told him he should weigh about a hundred and seventy. That made sense to me, since we were the same height, six feet, and I weigh about a hundred sixty-five.

He thought Sam Robbins had lost ten or fifteen pounds since he'd met him, too. "He used to be funny when he was drinking. He'd talk about this spaceship that would come down and rescue all the drunks under all the bridges and take them all to the great big winery in the sky. You know, he had all kinds of funny quips and stories. We used to just sit there and giggle. We'd actually howl 'cause he was so nutsy. But now he's just hateful. Just hateful. And he doesn't even read anymore. But he's compulsive about stealing books for us. Ha, ha, ha. That's where I got this." He held up the Steven King book, *Christine*. "But Sam's not a fun person to talk to anymore. The only time we ever converse is when I'm panhandling the parking lot and he walks by going to the Six O'clock Store. I'm there at six thirty panhandling, 'Don't tell me where you're going Sam. I know, you're going to the GROCERY store to get a quart of milk for the baby.' And he cracks up. But then after that, his face just collapses, and he just kinda walks by. He's really depressed.

"And Suzi's getting worse. Her mind. She's getting dumpier looking, and her mind is going. She's just kinda—She spaces out more often. She doesn't read. Finally they got a radio and she sat there for three or four hours, drinking her wine, chain smoking, staring at the traffic, and listening to the music. You could never talk to her and it would be fine. I sat here one day with Suzi for eight hours when Jerry was gone, and I was reading and she was just staring off into space. But I know what it's like to just sit here and listen to music on my headphones and chain smoke, but Suzi, when you talk to her, she doesn't hear you.

"So it's very quiet now that Big Joe and Little Joe and Tiny are gone. When they were living here, it was miserable. I was never so glad to see people leave."

We continued our quiet conversation.

"Oh, you wouldn't believe what the vicious rats have done."

"Yeah, I just saw one duck into a hole a couple of yards behind you."

"Yeah, I know. There's some big mothers." Tom rummaged around in the trash behind his bed. "I'm looking for a Dixie cup. Not a styrofoam one, a paper cup. Remember that bar of soap you bought me for my birthday? When we went down to the liquor store?"

"Uh huh."

"Look. This is all that's left of it. Look at the rat teeth marks."

"Oh, they chewed it."

"They EAT it. Look at that. Those are rat teeth marks. Look at that! It was a brand new bar of soap. Can you imagine? They eat soap! The fucking dog over there used to eat soap, and once she ate a Brillo pad, and swallowed it. Can you believe it? We had to hide our soap. I told Larry, I said, 'Well, maybe we'll get lucky and she'll fart bubbles like Lawrence Welk.' So I have to put the soap in here to keep the rats out of it. Look at that! I'd say they took a third of that, maybe half. Look at those little teeth marks. I mean, I do feed the little ingrates, ha, ha, ha. What I don't eat, I just toss out there. They don't bother me much. Live and let live."

A bit later, Tom described his world view.

"You're born, you live, and you croak. And I'm just putting in my time. That's what you do between being born and croaking. It's all very meaningless to me. Who cares?"

He spoke of loneliness. "Joe used to come up here and wake me up. 'Everybody's asleep.' And I said, 'Well, what are you wakin' me up for? To tell me that everybody—that Tiny's asleep, John Moe is asleep, and Jerry and Sam Robbins and Mack?' You know what he said? He looked me straight in the eye. And he was upset. 'I'm lonely. Would you talk to me?' So anyway, I looked at him, and I said. 'All right. I'll talk to you. I'll give you an hour, and then you go over there and kick somebody's ass and get THEM up to talk to you.'

"That's the only time I've felt sorry for him. And at times I HAVE enjoyed his company. He's a very lonely man; a very lonely man, but he's so rowdy and he's dangerous. Why do you think I've got Stella Stick and Paula Pipe?"

We continued to chat for quite a while. Since I had gotten Tom's description of Christmas, I decided to move along. I had spent a lot more time there than I had planned. It was about two thirty when I wished him well and headed back to Market Street.

I had been looking for Jerry, but had been missing him. In mid-January 1990, I found him at his new office in the breezeway near the Courthouse. I had an AHMI Personal History Interview that I needed to conduct with him. He was very drunk and very dirty. He had snot dripping down his shaggy red moustache and into his beard. He was really filthy, even by bridge standards. I asked him if he had done anything special the day before.

"Aaaa, yeah. Oh yeah, yesterday was good. It was my birthday."

"I was wondering if you remembered." As soon as I said it, I knew that it was an insult. I thought I had been put off by Jerry's sloppy drunkenness and filthy appearance, but then I realized I was really angry at Jerry, angry at him for drinking himself to death. I didn't say anything about it. It didn't seem appropriate for an ethnographer. "So what'd you do for your birthday?"

"Aaaa. I got drunker 'n ten thousand Indians."

"Yeah? Seems like you've got a little buzz right now."

"Aaaa, yeah I do."

"Do you have a jug with you?"

Jerry reached around behind him and produced a half-empty fifth of Thunderbird. He looked me right in the eye for a moment with a straight face. Then he burst into a loud laugh. "Ha, ha, ha, ha, ha."

"Ha, ha, ha. There it is," I said. "All right. Just checkin'. Just checkin'. I noticed a sheriff just walked by. He doesn't bother you here, huh?"

"No, they don't bother me here."

He panhandled a couple of pedestrians. It was pathetic. He was so drunk he could hardly utter his lines.

"Hit ever'body up," he slurred. "I was just thinkin' about going home. It's COLD!"

"Yeah it is cold. Been sleepin' warm enough?"

"Yeah. When I get underneath my covers and stuff like that, I'm warm enough. But comin' out here and goin' to work? You have to go to work. Have to. Have to do it."

"How much you made today so far?"

"About sheven dollars."

"Well that's much better than canning, huh?"

"Oh yeah, much better.—Pardon me, ma'am, could you schpare a little bit of shange today? Hello sir, could you schpare a little bit of shange?"

His performance spurred me to ask, "Is there a point of drunkenness beyond which people quit giving you money?"

"I don't...think so."

I asked which camp he was in. He was still in the lower, southeastern camp along with Dirty Mack, John Moe, and Sam Robbins. Since he could barely talk, I didn't see much point in staying. I wished him a happy birthday and left at about twelve thirty.

I tried to touch base with Jerry a few more times in ensuing months, but I had other work to do and I didn't run into him until the middle of March, 1990. When I rounded the corner of the breezeway at the Courthouse and looked at the bench that was now Jerry's office, I was surprised to see Big Joe dwarfing Jerry on the bench. I was glad to see Big Joe. We all said our howdys. Joe said that he'd been back from Salt Lake City for about a month. I asked him if it was a little cold up there, and he said, "Are you kiddin'? It was snowin' like hell when I left there! Ha, ha, ha, ha."

I asked how he'd gotten there and he said, "I went up there on the rails, but I got a disability check up there and I caught me a Greyhound back. I said, 'To hell with this,' you know." (It is very, very cold riding a freight train in winter because of the windchill factor of a fifty or sixty mile per hour wind.)

I excused myself to go inside the Courthouse and use the bathroom. I also took the opportunity to tape some notes to myself. Big Joe now had hair down to his shoulders and a very long, full beard reaching to the middle of his chest. Both hair and beard were a dark brown color streaked with a lot of grey. There had been no grey at all when I first met him.

While some people age gradually with a long graceful middle age, there is a time in the lives of many people, typically in the mid-forties, when time swiftly transforms them. Within just a few years a person can go, like my friend Big Joe, from being a fairly young man with brown hair and a robust, weathered face, to being a grey, wrinkled old man. It's as though someone's life had rounded its buoy and had tacked from an exuberant and youthful close reach to the quiet downwind tack of old age. I hadn't seen Joe for a long while and I was startled at the change he had gone through. I had also begun to see the streaks of silver in my own beard and was a little shocked to realize that Father Tme had yelled "Ready about!" in my own little voyage, but perhaps not yet, "Helm's a lee!"

Joe was looking cleaner and healthier than I had ever seen him, despite the tack of Father Time. He looked like the kind of guy you see in a little ski town running a snow plow or towing somebody out of a ditch. He was wearing a heavy, plaid wool shirt over a tee shirt, both untucked and hanging loose over dirty Levi's. He had on some rather new hiking boots with Vibram soles.

Joe's apparent good health was in sad contrast with my friend Jerry's. Jerry had been slipping steadily the last couple of years. He was wearing some very nice black penny loafers and a nice tan corduroy suit topped off with a gray wool driving cap. But the suit was really filthy. There were great splotches where sweet Thunderbird had splashed and then attracted dirt over days and days of drinking in the dirt. Dark grime surrounded the collar, cuffs, fly, knees, and seat of the suit. Black, shiny dirt had accumulated on his skin to the point where it was beginning to have measurable depth in richer areas like his neck and hands.

His friend Art had given him the clothes and shoes. Dirty Mack had given him the driving cap. Jerry said Art now "has a real nice little place up in Hollywood. And uh, he drug me up there. Dressed me up. Made me take a shower."

"The audacity of some people."

"Trimmed my beard, cut my hair."

"Yeah, you're lookin' real good." I lied shamelessly. I didn't think it would do either of us any good to confront the reality of Jerry's decline. He was determined to drink himself to death and it made me very sad. I was sure there was nothing I could say to change his life, so I didn't bring it up. Maybe I was just being a coward, but I didn't want to make him feel worse about himself than I knew he already felt. I realized that we really had become good friends across our many economic and cultural differences. As between any friends, there was a lot left unsaid between us, but perhaps more in our case because of those differences.

"You got any cigarettes?" Big Joe asked.

"Yeah. I do. I've got Marlboros and Camels. What kind do you want?"

"What kind do I want? Ha, ha, ha, ha. I don't hear that very often. A Camel'll work. A Camel."

I thought to myself, beggars really cannot be choosers, at least not very often. I tossed him the pack. "Why don't you guys split those."

"Sure. Thanks. Thanks a lot," Big Joe said.

"Hello sir! Could you spare some change today?" Jerry said to a passerby. He was fairly drunk today, but not so bad that he couldn't talk. Turning back to Joe and me, he held the cigarette up in front of his face and smiled at it. "Oh, goody, good, good. A Camel. It don't have a hump in it? Ha, ha, ha."

"We can roll it around in the dirt a little bit so you'd feel more at home," I said, trying to make a joke, but I realized it was cruel. Over the last couple of years, I had grown to like him a lot. I realized it was silly, but I felt somehow he was letting me down as he slowly killed himself with wine.

"Yeah, make it like a real Camel with a hump in it, ha, ha, ha," Big Joe said.

"Oh thanks a lot you guys. Ha, ha, ha." Jerry lit the cigarette and took a long lungful. After he let out the smoke, he smiled and turned to me. "Well, we're sixty-five cents short of our goal," he said seriously. "And it's probably gonna be the hardest sixty-five cents I've ever made."

"I'll give you sixty-five cents to answer all these questions." I held up a bulky interview schedule. "It's a long damn thing. You ought to get something for suffering through it."

"Okay," Jerry said.

"It still might be the hardest sixty-five cents you ever made, ha, ha, ha, ha."

"Ha, ha, ha, ha. Yeah, really. Like that last one we did at Giotto's."

"Yeah." I turned off the tape recorder, and Jerry and I waded into the Personal History Interview for the AHMI Project. We covered topics like demographics, subsistence, employment history, and benefits history.

After we finished, Jerry told me that he had been in the hospital again. He had had yet another stroke. He was not walking well. According to Big Joe, he'd fallen down and hurt himself when the seizure hit and his problems with walking had resulted from the fall. I thought he was just trying to put the best possible face on an increasingly grim situation. It seemed to me that Jerry's problems with walking were more a result of the stroke itself. Now Jerry could again only take very slow shaky steps. This was about the same condition he'd been in after his first stroke, maybe a little worse. He didn't have a cane. He certainly needed one, but he had Big Joe to lean on. The seizure had taken place a couple of days ago. His campmates had called the paramedics, and they had come and taken him to the hospital. He had been released from the hospital the next day.

In his way, Jerry had been a good friend and campmate. Even sadder to me than his deteriorating personal hygiene and physical health, was alcohol's work on his mind. Once an avid reader of light fiction and newspapers, up on the affairs of the day, he now no longer even looked at the headlines. In conversation, his mind drifted and turned like a rudderless skiff before an alcohol tide. He could scarcely keep on a subject for more than a sentence at a time and was becoming more and more forgetful. His sardonic wit and word play seemed gone forever. The warm eyes that used to twinkle merrily while he pointed out a paradox were dull, deep red and desolate. A year or two ago he had some insight into his life and his physical and social surroundings. Now he often couldn't tell the difference between his wishful wine dreams and what had actually taken place. My friend Jerry was one of the walking dead. A booze zombie waiting for the final seizure and doing everything he could to hurry it along. He loved his bottle more than his life.

He smothered himself in the wine to shut out the pain, filth, and failure he would have to wake up to, if he ever really woke up. He couldn't throw off the blanket of booze and wake up sober. He struggled to wrap himself tighter and tighter in wine's warmth. He had completely given up on the painful, senseless reality of extreme poverty in the land of plenty. Deep in this alcoholic cocoon, he would soon realize the only hope not shredded by the winds of fortune or driven on the shoals by his own shortcomings. He would soon attain the only status he had left to strive for: to be permanently dead drunk. In his way, he had been a good friend and he was already gone.

We finished the interview schedule and I gave him the sixty-five cents he needed. He hobbled away toward the north leaning on Big Joe with every shaky step, frail, sick, and pathetic. They were on their way to Eddie's to get another bottle. I watched them make their slow, wobbly way across the lush green courtyard. They looked out of their element among neatly dressed attorneys and bureaucrats rushing between appointments.

Jerry and the Bridge People were caught in a dark dismal eddy while the rapid river of progress roared along without them. Their lives recall a time when human beings led technologically simpler, but more connected lives; when we tried to help lame friends walk to the next waterhole; when we hunted, gathered, and scavenged; when we lived in little camps where we knew everybody and shared whatever came our way, both the good and the bad. In a way, I envied the social connectedness of the Bridge People. They got to spend as much time as they wanted with their friends, sometimes much more than they wanted. Their friendships were certainly problems for them too, but they did offset some of the misery, sickness, and hopelessness of their horrible poverty.

As Jerry and Big Joe hobbled away, I knew that I would continue to visit them and the others under the bridges from time to time for as long as they lived there. I also knew there was little I could do that would significantly improve their lives. I couldn't bring them social justice, economic opportunity, or hope for a better life. It was the hopelessness that got to me, not the filth or drunkenness or poverty. Hopelessness was a heavy smog that darkened the lives of the Bridge People. It dimmed the enlightenment that did exist in greater society. Without hope, they would continue to live like they were serving a life sentence; as though they were just doing their time. They looked forward only to having their sentence commuted by the great warden in the sky. There were perhaps a couple of million other extremely poor, very flawed, homeless people in somewhat similar straits. I sighed and brushed away a couple of tears.

As I rode my BMW toward the coast, I knew that soon I would be at my favorite watering hole on the Pacific Coast Highway, watching the surf pound into the rugged rocks just below the sundeck. To unwind, I'd probably have an overpriced glass of cold Chardonnay that might cost as much as Jerry and Suzi made in a day of canning. As I relaxed in the comfortable bar filled with clean, well-dressed strangers, I'd be wondering, as I have been for years now, what can a responsible, civilized society do about people like Tom and Jerry, Big Joe, and the others.

It is important to realize that there are many adaptations to extreme poverty in the United States. Some people double up with friends or relatives, some stay in missions or shelters, some camp near missions or in various other urban nooks and crannies, some stay in all-night theaters, and many live in SRO hotels in between stays on the street. Most homeless people in my acquaintance stay in some combination of these places over the course of a year, and, as you have seen, most of the Bridge People have used most of these different adaptations at some time or other. Living in a camp the way Tom, Jerry, and the others do is only one way of being homeless.

The Bridge People, like members of any subculture, share the vast majority of their beliefs and values with members of the mainstream culture, but their lives are being shaped in distinctive ways by the ecocultural niche that they occupy. Here I review some of the beliefs, values, habits, and practices of the Bridge People and their way of life in general, emphasizing those aspects which distinguish them from mainstream American society. All of the possible adaptations to homelessness should be studied ethnographically in order to piece together a valid view of extreme poverty in the United States today.

In general, the camps under the bridges seemed roughly representative of the dozen or so other homeless camps I have visited in the downtown area of Los Angeles, and in Venice and Santa Monica, coastal towns west of Los Angeles. These camps are typically inhabited mostly by White middle-aged males, many of whom (but certainly not all) are heavy drinkers. These men are similar in many respects to the "Skid Row bums" of the 1950s and 1960s, although they are younger. These days, there are often Blacks, Hispanics, and women also living in homeless camps. (Although there are an increasing number of children among the homeless, I did not see any in the camps that I visited.) Besides the camps in Los Angeles with which I am familiar, there are camps of homeless people in other ethnic neighborhoods of the city, camps of the rural homeless, and camps of Hispanic undocumented workers. The people in these camps undoubtedly differ from the Bridge People in significant ways, but I am not familiar with them.

In my experience, homeless camps vary in size from one individual to about ten, with two or three being somewhat typical. When camps get large, interpersonal friction eventually heats up and leads to group fission. Many people who camp out prefer to camp alone to avoid interpersonal conflicts.

————•————

There is a myth in the United States that many of the homeless have fallen from high level positions as professors, bankers, physicians, and the like. So widely spread is this myth that it is even believed by many of the homeless themselves. It was rumored among the Bridge People, for instance, that Dirty Mack had been a college professor. He told me, however, that he, like Tom, had been a retail clerk before becoming homeless. The Bridge People, like the vast majority of homeless people I have gotten to know, had histories of employment in unskilled or semi-skilled positions. Many had been factory workers years ago. In general, their level of educational attainment was low. Rubio was completely illiterate, and several others, including Tom, did not have high school diplomas.

————•————

While the Bridge People spent time primarily in the company of other homeless people, they did have some contact with mainstream middle- and working-class Americans. They occasionally read the L.A. *Times*, supermarket tabloids, and news magazines, and heard the news on the radio, so they knew a fair amount about the world beyond the bridges. Their principal interaction with the outside world took the form of patron–client relationships in the context of panhandling. Their next most frequent form of contact with the nonhomeless was with service providers and agents of formal social control, viz., social workers, care providers at public hospitals, paramedics, policemen, and judges. In their interactions with these people, the Bridge People generally felt exploited and abused. Police and welfare workers in particular were viewed with trepidation, fear, and some loathing.

————•————

As you saw in the body of this report, the people who lived under the bridges were subject to frequent bouts of dysentery, occasionally of such severity as to require hospitalization. They also suffered frequently from colds and influenza. They often were injured, sometimes as a result of intoxication, sometimes as a result of attacks by robbers or of fights among themselves. Because of their filthy living conditions, injuries often become infected. Since it was difficult for them to obtain routine medical care (as you saw, it can take many hours to see a nurse or physician), they often put off dealing with initially minor health problems until they became life threatening and required the use of paramedic ambulances and emergency room care. This situation resulted in a great amount of unnecessary suffering on their part and an increased tax burden for all citizens. Similarly, since they could not get routine dental care, they put off dental problems until severe, chronic pain occurred and the offending tooth had to be pulled.

—•—

Keeping clean was a serious challenge for the Bridge People, one that often defeated them. They washed up occasionally by hauling water to camp in plastic water jugs or by taking bird baths at hose bibs in the vicinity. They also occasionally cleaned up in the bathrooms in public buildings in the Civic Center and in fast food restaurants on Market Street. The public bathhouses they once used are now closed because of the AIDS epidemic. There are shower facilities in missions in Skid Row, but taking a shower there requires spending a lot of time standing in line, and they felt that it was a lot of trouble. It is also somewhat dangerous to go there, and they didn't feel that getting a shower was reason enough to risk it. They did not brush their teeth, brush their hair, shave, or get haircuts, except on a very occasional basis. Part of the reason for their poor personal hygiene were their filthy living conditions and poor access to bathing facilities. But in my judgment, a large part of it was their hopelessness, demoralization, and depression.

Sanitation was as much, if not more, of a problem as hygiene. The Bridge People relieved themselves in the bushes only a few steps away from their mattresses. Over time, this resulted in numerous exposed piles of feces in close proximity to their living areas. The combination of poor personal hygiene and open latrines contributed to the frequent gastrointestinal tract infections and other illnesses that they suffered. They did have two ways of disposing of garbage—the nearby dumpsters and the orange bags left, and sometimes picked up, by Caltrans.

Finding a place to go to the bathroom was a problem all over Skid Row, where people camp on sidewalks and in parking lots. This constitutes a growing public health hazard for homeless people and for the community at large as well. While some homeless people have limited access to toilets in missions, public buildings, or in fast food restaurants, many do not. In fact, one downtown alley is called, by the street people, "Shit Alley." I have been to Shit Alley and I assure you it more than lives up to its charming name. Rather than provide toilet facilities for the poor, the city recently fenced off Shit Alley as its way of denying that a public health problem exists. As a stop-gap measure until the problem of homelessness can be resolved by a national program to provide economic opportunity and low cost housing for the poor, cities like Los Angeles need to provide plentiful public toilets and showers for the destitute in the areas, like Skid Row, where homeless people are found in large numbers.

—•—

I found little of the specialized vocabulary that used to be associated with the tramps and bums of an earlier era among the Bridge People. For example, they had but few terms for people like themselves: bum, tramp, bridge person, drunk, alcoholic, homeless person, panhandler or panner, and canner. With the exception of panner and canner, these terms are also in common usage among the general United States population; none of them holds an esoteric meaning for the Bridge People. By way of contrast, in the late 1960s, Spradley (1970) found some 15 different names distinguishing tramps of various kinds, most of which were exclusively used by tramps themselves. I take this lack of a distinctive lexicon as a indication of increased demoralization and devolution of the subculture of tramps.

Bridge People did employ nicknames and epithets extensively. Nicknames and epithets such as Big Joe, Tiny, Dirty Mack, Mack With The Cans, and Moustache Moe were based on physical traits or behavioral attributes. They were typically conferred by others; at least I didn't encounter any self-conferred nicknames. The extensive use of nicknames may be related to the fact that last names were only rarely used or known among the Bridge People and could not be invoked to distinguish between several people of the same name.

Some places had been given nicknames as well. These names—such the Six O'clock Store, Plasma Park, Raggedy Hill, and Five Corners—referred to the physical attributes of the location or to behavior associated with it and held more meaning for the street people than the official names for these locations.

The Bridge People frequently told stories as an entertaining way to pass the time. Of course, they preferred to pass the time drinking as well, but storytelling occurred even in the absence of drinking. Sometimes storytelling took on the characteristics of a friendly competition in which storytellers tried to top one another. The stories they told often involved drinking exploits or fights that the narrator had witnessed or participated in, often as the hero of the piece. Sexual escapades were also related, but much less often. They also told many stories of life on the streets.

Like middle- and working-class people, the Bridge People also exchanged the news of the day and "talked shop." This included stories about their experiences while panhandling or canning, their encounters with the police, their problems with the welfare system, and the like. In these stories, the narrator or some other protagonist usually figured as a trickster who outwitted some more powerful adversary, like a social worker, a store keeper, or a police officer. I am relatively confident that, when I wasn't present, they told stories about how they tricked the visiting anthropologist.

———•———

The time orientation of the Bridge People was largely day-to-day, because existence was a day-to-day struggle for them. When there was some justification for it, as when Tom and Jerry anticipated the coming of Christmas, the Bridge People were certainly capable of planning for the future. However, for the most part, thinking and talking about the future had little psychological, social, or economic value for them. They could do little enough to influence their present, let alone their future.

Existing as they did in an eddy far to the edge of the mainstream, where the seasons went slowly around, the months and years drifted by, and no progress existed, they tended to view time as cyclical rather than linear. The Bridge People knew when it was the weekend, and when it was near the first of the month, because these made a difference in their panhandling and canning businesses, but they did not generally note the day of the week nor the date. When a specific date had some particular significance—for example, when someone was getting foodstamps or expecting a G.R. check—they kept pretty good track of it.

———•———

Getting enough to eat was not too much of a problem for the Bridge People and only occasionally was it a great cause of concern. Most of them were opportunistic feeders and ate whatever they could get from whatever source was available. Their primary source was the nearby dumpsters. Some people, like Tom, sought handouts and also worked for food, and everyone bought some food some of the time, if only for special occasions. Others, such as Dirty Mack, typically bought all of their food with the proceeds of their panhandling. In general, the Bridge People brought food back to camp and cooked it if necessary. They occasionally preserved fresh food by cooking, which extended its shelf life a day or two in cool weather. In general, delaying consumption of food for any amount of time was not particularly prudent, because it was often nearly rotten before they got it. Sometimes cans of food were found and saved for a crisis, but there were no cash reserves.

There were no regular meal times under the bridges, and even the number of meals varied from day to day. Most Bridge People did not have a morning meal. For the wine drinkers, wine was the preferred beverage first thing in the morning as it was throughout the day. Sometimes some of the Bridge People would walk to a fast food joint or cafe and buy a cup of coffee. On rare occasions they would make coffee at camp. In the majority of camps, most meals were taken together by most of the residents, but some campers, like Dirty Mack and Tom, generally ate their own food on their own schedule. To me, the situation seemed quite similar to how roommates behave with one another.

More elaborate meals were prepared collectively on an occasional and sporadic basis, as a festive occasion somewhat analogous to a dinner party among middle-class family or friends. The more frequent basis for a social get-together was the acquisition of a supply of alcoholic beverages, however. I noticed that outstanding meals were often discussed and recounted, but some of this talk was surely for my benefit. The Bridge People, like most people I have met, try to make the best of a bad situation when presenting themselves to others. They highlight the aspects of their lives that made them feel—and seem to others—more competent, comfortable, and successful. Only infrequently did they let down their guard and talk about, and think about, how miserable their lives really were.

Alcoholic beverages were usually consumed right away, sometimes before returning to camp. Part of this was a desire for immediate gratification, but part was a fear that the bottle might be stolen. As you recall, having bottles stolen by campmates created considerable friction from time to time. I rarely saw or heard of food being actually stolen, the misunderstandings between Tom, Jerry, and Suzi over food notwithstanding. Some of the heavy drinkers among the Bridge People would occasionally go for two or three days with hardly any food if they had sufficient alcohol.

———•———

Smoking cigarettes was an important part of the life under the bridges. Cigarettes were smoked during virtually every social interaction. The informal exchanges of tobacco provided something of a social bond between the campers, although conflicts occasionally arose regarding reciprocity. The Bridge People had three basic means of acquiring tobacco—buying cheap, ready-made cigarettes as Dirty Mack did, buying pouches of loose tobacco and rolling their own as Tom did, and sniping (picking up butts) as Jerry did. Dirty Mack spent the most money, Jerry spent the most time, and Tom probably got the best tobacco. Most Bridge people utilized all three of these methods from time to time, but they bought roll-your-own tobacco most often. They would have preferred to buy ready-made cigarettes if they could have afforded it. When they smoked snipes, they frequently utilized a crutch (a piece of matchbook rolled around the butt of the cigarette to form a cigarette holder) in order to smoke them down to the last few millimeters. Most Bridge People smoked the equivalent of between 15 and 25 cigarettes per day, but if they had had an extra good day's panning or canning, they smoked more.

———•———

Among the Bridge People, there was no difference between the clothing worn by women and men. Everyone wore Levi's or trousers, tee shirts, sport shirts, casual jackets, cheap ski parkas, and the like. Clothing was often found in dumpsters, but occasionally it was brought to the bridges or given to the Bridge People as they walked along the street. Clothing was also available at missions and second hand stores about half a mile away, but the Bridge People didn't often avail themselves of these sources. They wore whatever clothing come their way, although they preferred dark work clothes since they held up well and did not show dirt. Except for Dirty Mack, most of the Bridge People tried to keep up their personal appearance to some degree. Given the difficult, dirty conditions in which they live, keeping themselves and their clothing even somewhat clean was a considerable challenge. Canning, which requires extensive and sustained dumpster diving, is an especially filthy occupation. On the other hand, appearing too clean and neat could be a liability in panhandling, and this too was a factor in their poor personal hygiene and the condition of their clothing.

Because Tom had problems getting clothes that fit him, he washed or rinsed out his clothing about every two or three weeks (though he said he did it more often). Most other people talked about washing clothes, but what I observed was that they usually discarded clothing when it got too dirty. It required much less money and effort to discard dirty clothing and acquire fresh than it did to wash it. It cost about two dollars to wash and dry a single load at a laundromat, plus another fifty or seventy-five cents for the soap. That amounted to as much as a third of a Bridge person's typical daily income. To translate it into middle-class terms: for someone making $24,000 per year, that would be like a load of wash costing about $33.

—•—

Ownership of various things was problematic for the Bridge People. Campsites were "owned" by whomever happened to be currently occupying the site. When newcomers showed up, they typically respected that and asked if they could stay. If a person, newcomer or not, was deemed undesirable as a campmate, he was asked or told to leave, with the request backed up by the threat or the actual application of force. This was typically done by individual argument and action, not by a group decision. I witnessed and heard about people getting "thrown out of camp" for some of same kinds of things we middle-class people would have problems with in a roommate—failing to do a share of the chores, failing to reciprocate favors and assistance, and generally being difficult to get along with.

Panhandling places were also owned in a way, but rights were much less definite. Every day desirable panning places were theoretically up for redistribution on a first come, first served basis. Panhandlers knew where the good panhandling places were and who had been working them. They typically tried to stay away from one another. However, with ever-growing numbers of panhandlers have come increasing problems of overcrowding. I observed that if a panner came to his favorite panning spot and found someone else already there, he would find another place for that day. He would probably feel imposed upon and gripe about it, but direct discussions and confrontations about panning places were avoided.

Canning routes were also thought of as owned and talked about as if they were, but exclusive rights were even less enforceable than for panning sites, and ownership was not remotely possible. Canners had little knowledge of one another's canning routes, but most tended to avoid one another's areas when they did know about them.

—•—

The economy of the Bridge People was based primarily upon panhandling. They deemphasized the dependency aspects of panhandling and thought of themselves as independent business persons, which, in a way, they were. There are obviously very strong similarities between what Tom, Jerry, and the others do and what we middle-class people do on a much larger scale when we "pass the plate," practice grantsmanship, or conduct fund raising activities.

Tom made about seventy-five to a hundred dollars per month, and his income was below average for the Bridge People. He didn't make as much per day as Jerry or Big Joe did when they worked, but he worked more days per week. It was not uncommon for Jerry or Dirty Mack to make ten to fifteen dollars on a decent panning day, while Tom typically quit after taking in three to six dollars. Dirty Mack made between two hundred and three hundred dollars per month, the most of anyone under the bridges by far, but he often worked a seven day week.

There are occasionally reports in the news media about panhandlers making considerable sums of money. Of course, these are based on self-report and self-report alone has limited scientific validity (see Bernard, Killworth, Kronenfeld, and Sailer 1984). I have been told the same kind of tale from time to time, but after observing dozens of panhandlers in action over a period of about three years, I greet such tales with great skepticism. In my experience, panhandlers tried to put the best face on things and often talked about the exceptional twenty or fifty dollar day as if it were typical. From what I saw, such a day was far from typical.

Canning was next in importance among the economic activities of the Bridge People. It was dirtier, required more physical exertion and longer hours, and netted less money than panhandling. For many, it was what they fell back on during times they could not panhandle. For others, like Will and Suzi, it was their main occupation.

Besides panning and canning, the Bridge People did several other kinds of work to earn money. At times, someone might be paid to stay in a camp and act as a security guard or domestic hand, but these arrangements usually didn't last long because of misunderstandings and jealousies. Tom and others supplemented their income from panhandling by cleaning up a parking lot or doing some other small odd job. A few, like Larry, found occasional employment in the formal economy.

Alcohol and cigarettes were media of exchange and often the most valued possession that people had, more important than money. Sometimes when I asked Bridge Person how much they made panning or canning, they would reply, "Oh, I made two bottles this morning," or "Only enough for some tobacco."

—•—

The Bridge People walked where they needed to go in town. They seldom took a bus, although some of my other homeless friends did from time to time. Big Joe, Little Joe, and Tiny hitchhiked, rode freight trains, and took buses when they traveled across the country. They seemed to come and go a couple of times a year. However, the vast, vast majority of the homeless people I met were not transients. With the exceptions noted above, all of the Bridge People had lived steadily in downtown Los Angeles for many years and even Big Joe and the others who traveled had been in Los Angeles off and on for many years. We middle-class people like to use the term "transients" because it puts distance between us and the poor. It is a term that implies an explanation for extreme poverty that doesn't require serious examination of our economic system. There is also a notion that many homeless people travel north for the summer and south for the winter like the retired "snowbirds" do in their motorhomes. The homeless people who I knew that travel around the country did not do that, although weather was a factor in their itinerary. Their traveling seemed spurred as much by getting tired of being where they were, or by having worn out their welcome there, as by the weather.

The panners among the Bridge People rarely walked more than a mile or so from the bridges, although Dirty Mack did sometimes walk several miles west of the Civic Center area on Sundays. Canners walked some three to five miles away from the bridges in their daily search for cans. If they had a reason to do so, Bridge People did occasionally walk several miles in a day, as when Jerry walked home from County/USC Hospital. I knew one street person that occasionally walked from downtown Los Angeles to Santa Monica, a distance of about 20 miles, to spend a day or two at the beach before walking back to downtown Los Angeles.

———•———

Life under the bridges was largely egalitarian. Some minor fluctuations in status occurred on the basis of who had money for the purchase of drink and tobacco, but these changes were quite temporary. People were generally classified as either a "nice guy," or an "asshole." A nice guy was someone who shared and reciprocated; an asshole was someone who didn't. Competence and work were respected, but sharing the rewards of one's efforts seemed to be more important than the work *per se* in terms of status. Women appeared to have somewhat low status, but under the bridges, I witnessed only the treatment of Suzi and heard about a few others. Suzi was taken advantage of as a worker and a liquor-store runner while she was sober enough to walk. She was frequently in arguments, where she often held her own, and in physical fights, which she always lost. When she passed out, she was occasionally raped. Other street women that I know about fared a bit better than Suzi, although all women on the street live under the dark shadow of physical abuse, assault, and rape.

———•———

Research suggests that learned helplessness is one of the main etiological factors in depression. People feel helpless when they are unable to affect the outcome of situations in their lives. If they attribute this inability to factors that obtain over a wide variety of situations, feelings of helplessness can become chronic. Attributing such failure to internal factors such as personal traits rather than to external factors such as the economic system leads to lowered self-esteem. This learned helplessness produces the flat affect and lack of motivation characteristic of depression. Combined with extremely low expectations of goal attainment, it results in a deep, chronic hopelessness (Alloy, Abramson, Metalsky, and Hartlage, 1988; Garber and Seligman, 1980; Seligman, 1975). It seems clear that this view of depression is relevant to the Bridge People. Their repeated failures in the formal economy and other social problems, often exacerbated by self-destructive habits like alcohol abuse, had led to a sense of helplessness which had led in turn to demoralization and hopelessness.

Economic deprivation itself has been shown to be directly associated with mental health and social problems. Mental illness, for example, is found more often among the poor (Horwitz 1984). Koegel, Burnam, and Farr (1988) found vastly more mental illness and antisocial personality among the homeless in Los Angeles than among a demographically similar sample of people with places to live. During times of increased unemployment, there are increases in reported depression and other symptoms of stress such as fear, loneliness, and anxiety. Unemployment leads to losses in self-esteem and self-confidence and to a decline in morale. (See Horwitz 1984 for a review of this literature.)

There was little *esprit de corps* under the bridges and among other homeless people that I knew. There was little of the pride and independence that was seen among tramps and bums in the early 20th century. There was little sense of class consciousness, or political consciousness, and little antagonism toward the rich and powerful. Bridge People seldom had any goals other than immediate survival, which was defined in large part as obtaining the day's supply of alcohol and tobacco. Having a capacity for work and being competent at it were respected as ways of procuring food, tobacco, and alcohol for the day, but work was not seen as a way of improving one's life. There was little hope for the future. There were, in fact, very few viable opportunities to improve one's condition by working harder. They had almost no chance of getting a real job in the formal economy that would pay enough and be steady enough to enable them to get off the street. The situation was quite overwhelming for the Bridge People and they were thoroughly demoralized by it. They despaired of ever getting off the street, and in fact, the subject rarely came up in conversation. They had almost completely resigned themselves to life under the bridges and, in their own ways, tried to make the best of it.

—•—

Cheap, fortified wines were consumed in prodigious quantities by many of the Bridge People. Typical favorites were Thunderbird, Night Train, and white port, which are 18 to 19% alcohol by volume, or 36 to 38 proof. At the end of the study period, they cost about $2.85 per fifth in downtown liquor stores near the bridges (but were only $1.99—30% less—at a discount liquor store in Brentwood, a fashionable, upper-middle-class area of Los Angeles). This heavy consumption of alcohol compounded the problems of learned helplessness, demoralization, and hopelessness that afflicted the Bridge People.

Getting solid quantitative data on alcohol consumption is quite difficult because self-reports regarding drinking are of little value. (This is also true for middle-class people, see Rathje 1977). In addition, most wine drinkers shared their wine at least some of the time, and since they drank directly out of the bottle, neither they, their fellow drinkers, nor I knew how much a particular person in a drinking circle consumed. Measuring what each person drank would have upset the natural flow of events, and would therefore have been of little research validity from my perspective. Participant observation led me to believe that wine consumption varied from one to three or, at the most, four fifths per day per person. On several occasions, I observed Jerry and Suzi drink two fifths within a few hours and pass out, and I assume that they could complete that cycle at the most only a couple of times in a day. Bridge people and other street people told me that they consumed as much as five or six fifths of wine in a day, but I feel that these reports were highly romanticized.

In general, the amount the Bridge People drank was a direct function of how much money they had been able to take in during the day of panhandling or scavenging. Their economic priorities were succinctly summarized by Jerry when he noted, "Cash is for wine." Some of the Bridge People, however, did not as a rule drink wine. Dirty Mack drank whiskey, Tom, Abe, and Larry preferred beer, and Tom habitually drank a little vodka with his beer. Frequent drunkenness was the rule, but even judged by middle-class American standards John, Red, and Tom actually imbibed only moderately.

In the early stages of a drinking episode, interaction among the Bridge People was convivial, but as people got drunker, arguments often ensued. There were virtually no social controls on drunkenness. People did occasionally express concern about the high level of one another's drinking or about their own and they usually attempted to get a passed out drinking partner safely home, but they were not interested in intervening as they saw a companion proceeding toward irrational violence or drunken oblivion. In general, they had a *laissez faire* philosophy towards matters of drinking. It was well understood that heavy drinking would ultimately kill them, but the heavy drinkers did not seem to have a problem with that. In fact, I got the impression that some of them felt the sooner, the better. . . .

Heavy drinking contributed greatly to social conflict among the Bridge People and in the long run exacerbated their problems. The purchase of alcohol used up most of their meager resources. Nonetheless, their alcohol consumption had several positive aspects. Getting enough money to get drunk served as incentive for getting up and going to work, much as the goals of buying a house, raising a family, and accumulating material goods lend a sense of meaning and direction to the lives of many Americans. The social consumption of alcohol provided a forum for exchanging news and gossip and a sense of comaraderie. Tales of alcoholic exploits and drunken disasters provided a major source of entertainment. The reciprocal purchase of alcoholic beverages provided a mechanism for the redistribution and sharing of what little money people had. The camaraderie of the drinking circle provided one of the only emotionally positive aspects of lives otherwise characterized by failure, stigma, sickness, and misery. It helped bolster their battered sense of self and provided some sense of social solidarity and common purpose. The consumption of alcohol was not an unmitigated evil.

Demon Rum was certainly a big problem, but he was standing on the broad shoulders of Demon Poverty.

———•———

Alcohol obviously played a very important and mostly destructive role in the lives of most of the Bridge People. There is a vast scientific literature on drinking that might help us understand some of the deeper reasons why people abuse themselves with alcohol. It is certainly unreasonable to dismiss these people as "worthless drunks," as if putting a pejorative label on them explains anything. Alcoholism, like all self-destructive behaviors, is most productively viewed as a symptom of other problems of self and society. It is primarily a medium of expression and the message is one of anxiety and despair.

It has been shown that the expectation of a reduction of pain and tension is often a factor in heavy drinking, although tension is not actually reduced (Mendelson and Mello 1979; Peele 1985). Among men heavy drinking is associated with a need for a feeling of power (Boyatzis 1976; McClelland, Davis, Kalin, and Wanner 1972). In a study of alcoholics that bears directly on the situation of the Bridge People, McGuire, Stein, and Mendelson (1966) found that the consumption of alcohol tended to temporarily increase feelings of self-confidence, feelings of social adequacy, and sociability. Peele (1985) found that drinking led to a perception of reduced life complexity. Research has also shown that stress, and especially uncontrollable stress leading to ingrained pessimism about the possibility of improving conditions, caused or encouraged a wide variety of addictive, self-destructive behaviors, like the alcoholism we saw under the bridges (Marlatt 1982; Peele 1985; Shaefer 1976).

Findings of this kind lead me to endorse a psychosocial model of alcoholism, which looks at alcoholism as a self-destructive, habitual way an individual has of coping with his or her environment (Peele 1985). Heavy drinking starts as a way of dealing with situations that are perceived as stressful or overwhelming. Drinking may even be adaptive at first, but it gets out of hand and can become a very self-destructive, ingrained habit. Changing the self-destructive habit, or addiction if you will, requires changing the outlook of the alcoholic. However, because alcoholism is primarily a reaction to the environment of the alcoholic, the single most important requirement is reducing the stresses of that environment. While this psychosocial model of alcoholism contrasts with the popular notion that alcoholism is a disease, there is a vast body of scientific evidence which suggests that alcoholism and other addictive behaviors do not have the characteristics of a disease (for excellent reviews, see Fingerette 1988 and Peele 1985).

—•—

Friendship was a profoundly important, yet problematic aspect of life for the Bridge People. There was a tremendous amount of sharing. Small amounts of money were constantly being loaned and borrowed. People frequently shared food, cigarettes, and alcohol. Friends were often hired to go to the liquor store, providing them a chance to earn a dollar. While the absolute amounts of money involved in all these transactions were quite small, usually only a few dollars at most, the transactions were very important. The Bridge People often lent one another something on the order of 50% of a typical day's income—two or three dollars. For a middle-class person who made $25,000 per year, a day's income would be a little over $100 and an equivalent loan would be $50. The Bridge People loaned, borrowed, and shared much more, and more frequently, than you and I do.

Under the bridges, friendships provided a little economic and social margin. When people had an occasional surplus, they generally shared it with a friend. It worked like putting favors in the bank. Bridge People had no cash reserves and little food was ever stockpiled, but they did have each other. When they did favors for others and shared with them, they were investing in a little cushion against setbacks that they would otherwise not have. For example, Dirty Mack took care of Suzi and Jerry when they had one of their very serious episodes of dysentery. The favor bank was not without flaws, of course. Luke Broder, Sam Robbins, Suzi, Jerry, and Big Joe all violated a trust or fell in arrears in reciprocity at one time or another. All of them were eventually forgiven, as you will recall, with the exception of Luke Broder, who was told to leave the area. Animosity and ill-will did not seem to last long under the bridges. Although there was considerable grumbling, there were no lasting grudges. Even Rubio was allowed back into the bridge community despite a history of unprovoked assaults with deadly weapons on other Bridge People.

The Bridge People lived in close proximity to their friends and interacted with them many times throughout the day. They often sat around drinking and gossiping together in the early morning before going off to panhandle and in the afternoon after returning from work. Like most social talk, the camp conversations tended to be superficial in content, but significant in terms of satisfying social needs and a sense of identity. However, on occasion there was open discussion of important feelings, as when Big Joe broke down in tears as he told Jerry and Suzi about his childhood.

While the friendships of homeless people have been characterized as temporary by some researchers, I did not find that to be the case under the bridges. People did come and go, but most of the people under the bridges had known one another for several years. Some of the older literature also suggests that homeless people are disaffiliated, that is, that they are out of touch with their kin and lack economic and fraternal ties to the larger society. I found that to be generally true for the Bridge People. They had little or no contact with parents or siblings. Parents and siblings were outside the street culture and generally lacked the means for understanding the lives of street people. Moreover, some Bridge People had exploited their kin to the extent that they refused to have anything further to do with them. However, if you look at the Bridge People as members of a distinct subculture rather than focusing on their marginality with respect to the broader culture, they appear quite affiliated. They saw their friends quite frequently, shared information about economic or political developments that affected them (like the behavior of the police regarding panhandling), discussed their emotions to some degree, expressed concern for one another, and frequently shared money, bottles, and food. I view friendship as the main social institution sustaining the bridge subculture.

The problems of people like Jerry and the rest of the Bridge People have occupied my thoughts for some five years now, and I have read extensively about the problems of homelessness and extreme poverty in the United States. In conclusion, I offer some of my thoughts about the causes of homelessness and suggest some solutions to the problem of housing the hundreds of thousands or even millions of our fellow citizens who are now without adequate housing. As a result of my anthropological training, I have come to believe that social and cultural issues should be approached holistically, so I range far beyond the freeway bridges of Los Angeles to consider as well the underlying trends in American society which my experience and reading suggest have produced the widespread extreme poverty you see on American street corners today. The causes of something like homelessness can never be "proved" to the degree that causality can be proved in physics and certainly never to the satisfaction of a closed mind. But some reasonable inferences can be made from what we have seen among the Bridge People and from what we find in the research literature if we approach the enterprise with a respect for empiricical research and with high regard for reason and common sense.

—•—

I should begin by emphasizing that although the Bridge People obviously have severe problems and self-destructive habits, these problems did NOT cause their homelessness. Homelessness is a housing problem, and a poverty problem, and it can only be solved by providing housing and decent jobs at a living wage for all Americans, even those with handicaps, self-destructive habits, and/or limited capabilities.

I find the housing situation in America today similar to a game of musical chairs. In that child's game, those who are talented and swift get the chairs; those who are slower are left standing. So it has been in the housing market of the 1980s and early 1990s. As a result of gentrification, misguided tax laws, and a severely reduced federal budget for low cost housing, there are increasingly fewer and fewer cheap places where poor people can live, and the poorest, slowest, and most handicapped, those with mental health and substance abuse problems, are left standing in the street.

—•—

Changes in tax and domestic policy during the Reagan years were a major cause of homelessness. For example, we of the middle and upper classes now benefit from almost 55 billion dollars in homeowner's tax write-offs and low cost home improvement loans every year, while housing assistance for the poor now stands at just under 14 billion dollars. Some deride programs to house the poor as welfare, but, in fact, the vast majority of welfare in this country goes to the well-off. Eighty cents of every federal housing dollar, in the form of tax write-offs, goes to home-owners. The well-off even get homeowner's tax write-offs for vacation houses, while the typical family at the poverty line spends 65% of their monthly income for rent (Center on Budget and Policy Priorities 1984).

Federal taxes for families at the poverty line went up approximately 300% during the early Reagan years, while a wide spectrum of programs that benefit the poor were slashed: education was cut 57%, social services were cut 37%, employment training was cut 73%, health care was cut 42%, community development was cut 66%, and housing was cut 70%. The Department of Housing and Urban Development (HUD) budget has gone from a high of 31.7 billion dollars in 1979 to 7.5 billion in 1989. The number of new housing units has dropped from a high of 516,721 (under President Ford) in 1976 to only 5,223 in 1983. In 1989, the level was back up 86,501 new units (Ford Foundation 1989).

If we had continued to build low cost housing at roughly the rate of the Ford and Carter administrations, we would have had approximately 2.35 million more units by 1993 than the Reagan and Bush administrations actually built. It is informative to compare the number of lost low cost housing units to the estimates of the total number of homeless people in the United States. A controversial HUD study estimated that there were only 250,000 to 300,000 homeless Americans in 1984, while other estimates have run as high as 3 million. Homeless people are obviously very difficult to count, but whatever the total population of homeless people, those 2.35 million lost low cost units would have made a big difference in the availability of housing for the poor and for the extremely poor people who are left out in the streets today.

These changes in federal policy contributed to homelessness by severely reducing the availability of cheap places to live and virtually destroying the programs that helped unskilled poor people get the jobs and job training that allowed them to afford housing. If alcoholism, drug abuse, and other handicaps actually CAUSED homelessness, and if, for the sake of illustration, there were 2 million homeless persons in the United States, then logic would suggest that there should be approximately 2 million empty low cost rooms that these alcoholics, drug abusers, mentally ill, and handicapped people voluntarily abandoned when they "chose" to live in the streets and pursue their bad habits. Likewise, there should be some 2 million jobs that these people refused to accept when they "chose" to live in the streets. But, of course, there are no such rooms. They have been torn down in the course of urban renewal or turned into expensive condos by gentrification. There are no such jobs. They have been automated out of existence or moved offshore largely because of misguided tax and tariff codes.

Low cost housing and jobs for the lower skilled are being held in drastically short supply primarily as a matter of governmental policy. As long as we cling to these misplaced, misinformed national priorities, we can be assured that some millions of Americans will be left out in the streets. We should not be surprised to find out that they are the halt, the lame, and the otherwise handicapped.

—•—

We should relax building codes to allow for the new construction of single room occupancy (SRO) hotels. As Tom said, about 10 years ago you could readily get a room on Skid Row (not a great room, but a room) for about $85 per month. I have stayed in several of these sleazy Skid Row hotels, and in many of them rooms now cost $350 to $400 per month. Across the United States, we lost something on the order of a million cheap rooms between 1970 and 1979 to gentrification and urban renewal (Green, n.d.). The rate of loss had slowed by the the 1980s, but cheap rooms are still being lost. In the Los Angeles Skid Row some 7,000 cheap hotel rooms were lost between the 1950s and the 1970s, and no new cheap hotels have been built there in 40 years (Hamilton, Rabinovits, and Alschuler 1987). Again, it is informative to compare these 7,000 lost rooms to the estimates of the number of homeless persons in the downtown area. Koegel, Burnham, and Farr (1988) found estimates of the number of homeless people in the downtown area ranging from 7,000 to 15,000. Cheap hotels were where most extremely poor people used to live in the days before homelessness became a household word. Four new SRO hotels were recently constructed in San Diego, and they are thought to have eased the homelessness problem there to some degree.

Without a place where one can be safe and clean, and get a decent night's sleep, it is almost impossible to obtain conventional employment and maintain regular work hours. It is time that we middle-class people who set the building codes realize what the REAL choices are for the very poor. You will recall that Jerry complained that the hotel rooms he had stayed in were roach infested, dingy, depressing, and lonely. He would rather live under a bridge than live in such a room. After staying both under the bridges and in Skid Row hotels, I would agree that this kind of room can be little or no improvement over life in the street. But it also seems quite possible to design and construct SRO hotels that would be relatively cheap to build, easy to maintain, and at the same time user friendly.

——•——

Ownership is one of the foundations of responsible citizenship and a major element of self-identity in America. In other cultures, one's sense of identity is linked to family, clan, lineage, village, and the countryside itself, but here it is not. To a regrettable degree, in America as we approach the 21st century, you are defined by what you own and what you do for a living. If you own nothing and don't have a job, you are no one. If you own nothing and have little hope of ever owning anything, you have little to lose by irresponsible, antisocial, or even criminal behavior, and indeed, you might have something to gain. Aristotle understood this notion well when he said, "Poverty is the parent of revolution and crime." To avoid the type of civil unrest seen in Los Angeles just this past summer, we need to seriously rethink the real world of rewards and punishments at work in the barrios, ghettos, and Skid Rows of America. To really get tough on crime, you must get tough on poverty. Anything else is just political repression. My experience suggests that all Americans would be well served by introducing rewards for responsible behavior by the very poor and by allowing them to earn a small stake in America. Low cost housing programs of the federal government should focus primarily on ownership, not rental projects.

While home ownership is a major part of the mainstream American pie, fewer and fewer people can afford their first piece. As discussed above, large tax interest incentives go to owners, not renters. We should consider building the equivalent of cheap hotels with the rooms available FOR SALE to the very poor—SRO condos, if you will. To help the very poor, units like this should sell for $100 down and the mortgage payments should be about 25% of the monthly take home pay for a full-time minimum wage job, that is, about $170 per month. Currently, an income of at least $18,000 a year is required to qualify for low cost housing in Los Angeles (it varies for different programs), but full time minimum wage workers (in California) gross about $8,500. Shouldn't there be some relationship between the minimum wage and the cost of minimum housing?

If we designed programs like some low cost housing plans in Europe, the owner could sell any time, but the price would be linked to the rate of inflation, plus a few points for profit, so that the units would remain relatively low cost as they changed hands over the years. Rather than having SRO condos restricted to low income individuals, I would stipulate only that the buyer has to actually live there. To encourage interaction and to help develop social skills and an appreciation for participatory democracy, SRO condo owners could be given a discount for attending and participating in monthly condo association meetings.

Everybody in this great country should have the opportunity to own a place to live, even if it is a tiny place. Perhaps it could be an eight by twelve foot room with a sleeping loft or a captain's bed, a small sideboard instead of a kitchen, and a bathroom down the hall. My experience with small sailboats, vans, and campers suggests that talented designers can make comfortable and inexpensive accomodations out of tiny spaces. For example, the sideboard in a Volkswagon Westphalia camper is less than three feet long, but it contains a small refrigerator, a two burner stove, a small sink, and some storage space. Certainly with all our American ingenuity and technical expertise we could design something like that for user friendly SRO condos.

Owning a place to live is a major part of the American Dream, but it is a dream buried by years of misguided, irresponsible housing policy. A program for building SRO condos which incorporated ethnographic research and innovative designwould be of great benefit to society in trying to learn how to deal with housing for the very poor and how housing ownership might interact with other social problems and self-destructive behaviors that are often associated with poverty— alcoholism, drug abuse, and crime.

————•————

People occasionally ask me why homeless people don't "get a job." The answer is complex, of course, but there are two basic reasons. From what I could determine from interacting with people living on the street (as opposed to those living in shelters or welfare hotels), most of the homeless do have jobs of some kind. Panhandling is a job. Canning is a job. Cleaning up a parking lot is a job. It's not that homeless people don't want to work, or that they don't work. It's that most of the jobs they are able to get are informal ones that pay very poorly and aren't recognized as jobs by the members of the middle class. Some Bridge People pursued their jobs with considerable dedication, despite their handicaps. As you will recall, Jerry lay in the pigeon feces to get a single can; Will typically began canning at four A.M. Some 20 to 30% of homeless people actually do have conventional jobs in the formal economy, but still can't afford a place to live (Coalition on Human Needs 1990).

On the street, just getting by is a time and energy consuming job. Going to a mission to get a shower can take an hour and a half (and there's a chance you might get mugged or get in a fight). Seeing a physician might take six to eight hours, as it did when I took Jerry to County/USC Hospital. Seeing a social worker can take a very frustating half a day or even a couple of days. Life on the street saps people's energy and emotional strength. Just taking care of basic survival needs—finding wholesome food, clothes, water, money for alcohol and cigarettes—leaves little energy for improving one's condition, even for someone who isn't immobilized by the insidious web of hopelessness, depression, and drunkenness.

There are very few jobs available in the formal economy for people with handicaps and few skills, and there is tremendous competition for low skill jobs in

Los Angeles. Homeless people are at a big disadvantage in getting a conventional job, and they know it. They typically have no address or message phone, so even if someone wanted to hire them, it would be hard to make contact with them. It is quite difficult for them to keep themselves and their clothing and paperwork clean and to keep anything at all safe from thieves. For these reasons, homeless people do not perceive the formal economy as a source of opportunity. However, they are routinely resourceful and successful in finding opportunities in the informal economy, as you saw in the case of Jerry, who, despite his extreme drunkenness, was sensitive to changing conditions on the street and switched from panning to canning and back to panning as circumstances warranted.

I noted another example of the resourcefulness of the Bridge People on a visit after the research period ended. The canners among the Bridge People, Will, Larry, Suzi, and Rubio among them, realized that the number of cans available on the street was steadily declining, primarily, they thought, due to the ever increasing numbers of people on the street. So they began collecting glass. Glass is much, much heavier and had to be sorted into colors when it was cashed in, so until that point Bridge People hadn't bothered with it. In the face of changing conditions, however, they began using "tramp trucks" and getting enough glass to make up for the declining supply of aluminum cans. Glassing eventually became as important as canning as an occupation among the Bridge People.

The important point to note here is that when presented with real economic opportunities, without hidden bureaucratic barriers, street people responded appropriately and took advantage of those new opportunities. Despite their physical and mental handicaps and their self-destructive habits, most were capable of shifting their subsistence strategies to adjust to changing conditions. It seems to me that if American society wants to eliminate homelessness, an essential step must be to provide real job opportunities in the formal economy for homeless people to respond to.

———•———

My research among the homeless, both the Bridge People and others, leads me to believe that the welfare system needs a complete overhaul. It is now a punitive system that exacerbates learned helplessness and dependence and alienates the very people it is supposed to help. I think most citizens would prefer a system that helps people get on their feet and become reasonably productive and responsible citizens. That's just what many of the people I know who are on welfare would prefer too.

In Los Angeles and many other places, the current approach to developing good work habits among welfare recipients is to have all able-bodied people do a "work project" consisting of eleven days of work per month. They receive their checks at the end of the month by mail. Since many of these people can't afford rooms in even the cheapest hotels for the whole month and therefore have no mailing address, their checks are sent to liquor stores and check cashing agencies. In order to participate in this "workfare," people must go through a complicated qualifying procedure. This procedure is viewed by applicants that I have talked to—Tom, Jerry, Dirty Mack, John Moe, and Sam Robbins among many others—as unnecessarily lengthy, demeaning, and punitive. They feel that the system is purposefully designed to discourage people from applying.

In my judgment, a better approach would be to do away completely with the qualifying procedures for able-bodied people. Why not simply provide community hiring halls where people could show up to work at minimum wage, contracted and supervised by the county. Pay workers at the end of the day, rather than at the end of the month. Psychological research suggests that better results in modifying behavior are achieved if rewards closely follow successful task completion. If mainstream society believes that impoverished people need help in associating rewards with working, then we should make work readily available and follow work with immediate and meaningful rewards.

We should make half-day work available for those who can't work a whole day. If the program weren't punitive and authoritarian, and if the job weren't a lot of hassle to get to, even someone as demoralized and unmotivated as Tom would probably prefer to show up for a few hours of work and make minimum wage than to panhandle. Remember, he often got little jobs like picking up trash in Angelo's parking lot and chopping garlic at the Thai restaurant. At the present minimum wage, he would be making about seventeen dollars for four hours of work, compared to his average daily income from panning of about four or five dollars. He might be even more encouraged to work if he knew he could buy an SRO condo for about forty dollars a week.

Job training, childcare, and formal education should be fundamental components of any program intended to help people get on their feet. We could work out a system of incentives to encourage people to move up to private sector jobs. Private sector employers could be encouraged to participate through tax incentives and matching funds.

In my view, a welfare system based on incentives rather than punishments would go a long way toward defeating the cycle of learned helplessness and hopelessness we see among many poor and homeless Americans today. As a society, we need to realize that just as people can learn helplessness, so too can they learn industriousness. However, industriousness cannot be learned by hopeless, demoralized poor people through the additional punishment, humiliation, and regimentation they meet in the current welfare system. If we Americans believe in work, and I believe we do, we need to encourage and reward work and we must provide every possible opportunity for people to get at least minimal work, no questions asked.

—•—

We should significantly increase the minimum wage. The minimum wage is curently at the lowest in inflation adjusted dollars since the 1950s. This in itself would be bad enough, but in the face of steep increases in housing costs, it is a national disgrace. Twenty to thirty percent of homeless people are employed in the formal economy and still can't afford a place to live. Median rents for all Americans increased at about twice the rate of the median income over the last twenty years.

Coupled with an increase in the minimum wage should be tax relief for the poor. Income taxes for a poverty level family of four are five times what they were in the 1970s (Coalition on Human Needs 1987). An increase in the minimum wage might be irrelevant to some homeless people, like Jerry, Dirty Mack, and Suzi, because of the ravages of advanced alcoholism. But others, like Rubio, Larry, and Tom, already work in the conventional economy from time to time. Unfortunately, there is little incentive for them to seek out steady, conventional employment if they can't even afford to rent a decent room on the wages that are available to them.

———•———

At the same time, we need to increase the number of stable, good jobs in the private sector for less skilled, less talented Americans. During the 1980s, manufacturing jobs, where people could earn decent middle-class wages, declined by approximately 9%. America lost about 1.8 million American manufacturing jobs during this period in a process often called deindustrialization (see Bluestone and Harrison 1982; Wallace and Rothschild 1988). The vast majority of these jobs, some 1.2 million, were moved to other countries (Bartlett and Steele 1992; Suskind 1992). At the same time, the population of workers (people over 16 years of age) increased by 11%. It's no wonder that perhaps 2 or 3 million Americans are left on the street with no work. We have no room here for a discussion of deindustrialization and the reasons that factories are being moved offshore. Suffice it to say that this movement is largely through holes in tax codes and tariff structures—ruptures created by the heavy pressure of lobbyists for corporate elites. Indeed, it seems quite reasonable to view the deindustrialization of America as class warfare: the corporate elites who increase their profits by moving factories overseas against the workers and the middle class who lose their jobs. (About 40% of the lost jobs are white collar [Wallace and Rothschild 1988]). While some U.S. industries have lost their edge in productivity, in general these factory jobs were not lost because of the inefficiency of American workers, and they certainly were not moved out of the U.S. by "the invisible hand of the market" operating on a "level playing field" (for a good discussion, see Bartlett and Steele 1992). Taxes on corporations that offshore American jobs should increased to reflect the true social costs to the taxpayer of such socially irresponsible, unpatriotic behavior.

Perhaps a modest tariff (10% for example) should be assessed on all products made offshore or partly made offshore by American companies. Perhaps the same tariff should be assessed to all goods imported from countries who pay a less than our minimum wage (adjusted to the cost of living there) to encourage those countries to provide a decent living for their workers as well. And we should assess these tariffs on all goods from countries that don't allow free labor unions. These levies could help pay for unemployment benefits, subsidize the retraining and educating of displaced American workers, provide matching funds to help private sector employers of the unskilled, and grants, loans, and training for American workers who want to start their own businesses. Finally, such tariffs would lighten the load on the citizen taxpayer who currently has to pick up the tab for irresponsible corporations who move American manufacturing jobs offshore.

Likewise, we must look upon the hiring of a worker as a prosocial activity and find ways to encourage it. Currently, there are significant paper and financial burdens on employers when they hire someone. The so-called "benefits" associated with employment in the U.S., that is, health insurance, childcare, unemployment insurance, and workman's compensation, are disincentives to hiring. They make American products more expensive and therefore less competitive on the world market. They should not be funded as taxes upon employment, but rather, since they greatly increase the quality of life and reduce suffering and crime in the entire society, they should be paid for by general tax revenues. We need single payer national health insurance, universal access to childcare, workman's compensation, and unemployment insurance funded by all taxpayers, not just employees and employers in the formal economy. We need to encourage employment by making it as simple and cheap as possible to hire someone. Hiring an American is a patriotic act. Shipping a factory out of the country or causing an employer to ship a job overseas through burdensome bureaucracy or excessive employment taxes is an unpatriotic, antisocial act.

The issues surrounding the creation of stable, decent paying jobs are complex. It is certainly not as simple as reducing taxes on corporations. In the 1950s, when more manufacturing jobs were being created than at any time in our history, corporations paid some 39% of all taxes paid to the federal government. Now they pay only 17%. (In 1950, individuals accounted for 61% of all taxes paid to the federal government, now they pay 83% [Bartlett and Steele 1992]). There are probably many worthwhile approaches that might be taken, but clearly our goal should be decent, stable employment for all Americans.

—•—

Taxes on real property should be progressive. Presently, in California and other places in the United States, property taxes are based on a percentage of the value of the property. While the wealthy pay more taxes on their residences, they pay at the same tax rate as the poor, and they pay a much smaller percentage of their income. Progressive property tax rates would result in higher taxes for mansions and very low taxes for minimal housing units, like SRO condos and, presumably, lower rents and mortgages for low cost units. Lower taxes would also help spur the construction of low cost housing and make low cost apartment buildings more attractive investments, since the overall operating costs would be lower. And they would lower the overall cost of small houses for the low and moderate income buyer. Progressive property taxes on commercial property should also be a great help to small business, and most jobs in America are in small business. They would also be a help to people trying to start new businesses. Progressive property taxes would not necessarily be a tax increase, but would simply shift the tax burden to those most able to bear it. Research should be conducted to find other ways to encourage private sector builders to focus more of their activity on providing low and moderate income housing.

---•---

We should generously increase the federal housing budget for new low cost housing construction and for education and job training and drastically reduce military spending. It seems that to solve increasingly serious social and economic problems in the United States, we must begin by a return to the budget priorities of the Ford and Carter Presidencies. Defense spending under Presidents Ford and Carter, during some of the darkest days of the Cold War, was about 100 billion dollars; now after some modest reductions from the peak of the Reagan years, it is still over two and one half times that amount, despite the fact that the Warsaw Pact has dissolved and the Soviet Union no longer exists.

In a direct sense, with our dramatically increased military spending and our dismantling of domestic programs, we have purchased homelessness, gang violence, the "drug crisis," the decline of American education, the decline of American manufacturing, and a variety of other social problems. The Reagan–Bush years could be viewed as a vast experiment to test the hypotheses that social programs were unnecessary, and that taxes on corporations and the rich were too high. You can view part of the ragged, wretched results on the streets of urban America today. It is now time for an experiment on a grand scale to test the

Aristotlean hypothesis that by dramatically reducing poverty we would also dramatically reduce drug and alcohol abuse, other self-destructive and irresponsible behaviors, and crime.

—•—

The crisis of homelessness in America brings into sharp focus the overall incapacity of government at all levels to deal rationally and reasonably with the complex problems of contemporary society. Public discourse on important policy issues of the day is often dominated by theatrical posturing, sound bites, and photo opportunities. Out of such lofty public debate, we are often offered political candidates representing the full range of abilities from the mediocre to the wildly incompetent. We have people in the highest positions of leadership in the country who can scarcely put words together into a coherent sentence, let alone create informed, rational policy. The electorate, not amused by non-choices, are expressing their increasing frustration with the electoral process by voting with their feet. Curtis Gans of the Committee for the Study of the American Electorate calculated that presently only about 36% of those eligible actually vote in general elections, and presidential elections have only a slightly better turn out. This means that in a close race, only a little more than 18% of the electorate would have voted for the winner. A big winner might garner the votes of 25% of the electorate. If, as Thomas Jefferson suggested, the only legitamate basis of government is the consent of the governed, these figures raise serious questions. They seriously compromise any claim that elected officials might make about representing the will of the people and ruling by the consent of the governed.

People of moderate means and, of course, the poor are completely shut out of the electoral process because of the ever increasing importance of campaign money. It now costs an average of over 4 million dollars to win a U.S. Senate seat. Campaign spending went up on the order of 470% between 1976 and 1989, increasingly fueled by money from corporate political action committees and not from constituents (Johnson 1990). It is certainly conceivable that some women and men of moderate means have the ideas, abilities, and energy America needs to help solve her problems and to provide leadership as we approach the 21st century, but the avenue to public office is blocked by huge bags of special interest money. The vote itself is of little value if the overwhelming majority of citizens are effectively barred from elected office. The sad fact is that the democratic process in America is rigged. Our democracy is sliding toward plutocracy on skids of irresponsible campaign spending, greased with money from irresponsible corporate elites.

A particularly egregious example of how democracy works in Southern California can be found in the defeat of two measures on the ballot in the city Burbank which would have limited the growth of major entertainment studios. Spending records reveal that the committee against the measures, supported by NBC, Warner, and Disney, spent at least $544,692 and may have spent much more, while the committee supporting the proposals spent $16,045 (Braxton 1991). That is, the opponents of the proposals outspent the proponents by a ratio of 30 to 1. They bought the election as surely as if they had hired thugs to stuff the ballot box. Regardless of the merit of the proposals (and of course they may have been quite flawed), this sort of thing makes a mockery of the democratic process.

Major election reform, including some combination of public financing of elections, spending limits, donation limits, and guaranteed access to television time and newspaper space for all points of view, is required to put the democratic process on a level playing field, to give all citizens access to public office, to allow a broader range of ideas to be presented on television, in our major newspapers, and in other public forums. While some may suggest that public financing of elections would be expensive, the true cost of our current system of elections financed by corporate elites seems to be ever increasing incompetence and corruption on the part of elected officials, and alienation and cynicism on the part of the electorate. A good example of the cost of corporate elite funding of elections is the de-regulation of savings and loan institutions and the resulting epidemic of savings and loan failures that have cost the public some 500 billion dollars so far (Barlett and Steele 1992).

The Declaration of Independence was written by Thomas Jefferson, in consultation with Benjamin Franklin, John Adams, and others, and adopted in less than a month in 1776. The Constitution was framed in five months in 1787. In contrast, the elected officials that our current money-driven political system produces hasn't even been able to balance a federal budget since 1969, and it has gotten much, much worse during the reign of Reagan and Bush (Johnson 1991).

We select people for higher office now more for their ability to raise money for election than for their ability to comprehend our culture, our history, and our social and economic systems. We must encourage reasoned debate of issues, based upon the empirical findings of social science and history, if we are to deal with challenges like homelessness on a rational basis.

—•—

There are various ways to solve the problem of homelessness and extreme poverty. The most just and reasonable long term solution is to provide extremely poor Americans with better opportunities to earn a living and to provide them opportunities to buy a tiny piece of the mainstream American dream—a place of their own to live. This will be challenging. It will probably be expensive in the short term, but a great investment for the future. It could be accomplished in a variety of ways, not just the ways I have outlined here. The path I would choose leads through election reform toward a government more responsive to the needs of all Americans, toward increased democracy, toward reduced crime, and toward greater justice for all. It is a course that requires some sacrifice by those who have gained the most from America and it asks that they give a little more back to the society that made their great success possible. It is a course that requires empathy and compassion for those who have it a lot tougher than we do, and it requires greater tolerance of those who are different from us or who live in ways we would not choose for ourselves.

Empathy and tolerance are the foundations of a democratic civilization, and their absence most characteristic of barbarism. Understanding what other people go through and caring about it is what prevents a democracy from decaying into a tyranny of the majority or an outright oligarchy. In a democratic society, it is empathy and tolerance, not fear, punishment, and police power, that prevent the Hobbesian war of all against all. The problem of homelessness ultimately raises the serious question of what kind of society we wish to become. Are we to be the land of opportunity or the land of opportunism? Do we Americans have the courage, character, and conviction to reform our political and economic systems to become a truly democratic civilization with liberty and justice for all, even for its least able citizens?

———•———

Although the existence of widespread extreme poverty in America must be addressed at the level of national policy, there are some things that a private individual can do to help. We can all write or call our representatives at all levels of government to express our concern about housing and jobs for the very poor. Demand that the root causes of homelessness—lack of housing and jobs—be addressed in homelessness policy, and not the construction of shelters and missions. As Tom and Jerry pointed out, life in missions and shelters is often more dangerous and more demeaning than living under a freeway bridge. A policy of building more missions and shelters for the extremely poor deals with the problem in the most cosmetic way and completely ignores the causes of homelessness. It institutionalizes and legitimizes extreme poverty and misery as a way of life. It ignores the needs of the housed poor and the moderate income citizens who also face a very difficult housing situation, many of whom may be only one paycheck from the street.

If you want to do something at a more personal level, you can, in a sense, "adopt" a poor person. That's what I have done, with Tom and Jerry, and a couple of other homeless people.   I now go by the bridges from time to time and bring them what I can afford, typically some ibuprofen and peroxide for the unkind cuts and pains of street life, some tobacco because that's what they want, perhaps some clothing and old running shoes because that's what I have.

Before beginning this research with homeless people, I used to resent the panhandlers I saw. I was irritated when I read in newspapers that some of them said they liked being homeless or bragged about how much money they made from panhandling, or what a good life they lead. After spending three years conducting research among various homeless people, I came to understand that this kind of talk was simply a forlorn attempt to put the best face on failure. Braggadocio and denial will help keep a battered self afloat even when it is awash in woe and misery.

May I suggest that, instead of resenting panhandlers, we all try to say hello and give a poor person a little change when we can. You can't help everyone, but perhaps you might pick out a panhandler or two in the area of your work or somewhere else that's convenient. Become a regular, as Tom and Jerry would call it. You will surely get a warm smile and a "God bless you, Sir! or a "Thank you so much, Ma'am!" Of course, you won't be making a major difference in their lives, but a warm smile and a "God bless you" is really not a bad bargain for a few coins. It will make you both feel better for a few moments about life in these United States.

Appendix: Field methods

This book is an experimental form of report that has been called dialogical ethnography (Dwyer 1982) or narrative ethnography (Rose 1990). It contrasts with more traditional research reports and ethnographies by allowing the reader to hear what the ethnographer said to the people being researched, field consultants I call them, and by allowing the field consultants to tell the story of their lives pretty much in their own words. I chose this relatively untried genre because I thought it important for the reader to actually get to know some individual homeless people rather than read some generalized account of how they lived. I also thought it would be more engaging and readable for the general public, who, as voters, must ultimately come to terms with homelessness as a social problem.

The tradition of anthropological fieldwork suggests that the researchers should live full time among the people they study. I felt this was impractical for work with the homeless, mainly because there was no way to safely store the tools of the trade (books, laptop computer, transcriber, tape recorder and camera). I did try to document all facets of their existence—eating, sleeping, working, socializing and so on—to get a well-rounded and valid view of their lives. Boswell anticipated these common sense underpinnings of anthropology when he said, "Nobody can write the life of a man, but those who have eat and drunk and lived in social intercourse with him."

I began by taking short field trips during the day, then longer daytrips, and then I stayed in some Skid Row hotels for a few days. Many homeless people spend a few days in these hotels from time to time, and I wanted to document what life in them was like. After I got to know Jerry pretty well, I stayed with him and his campmates under the bridges for a few nights at a time. Altogether, I spent some 30 nights on the street with various homeless people, half with Bridge People and half in SRO hotels. I have also spent approximately 200 days in the field with various homeless people since the AHMI Project began in October 1987.

Days in the field typically consisted of what anthropologists call participant observation. In this case, that just meant hanging out with people in their natural habitat with my tape recorder on. I informed everyone I talked to (for longer than a couple of minutes) that I was an anthropologist from UCLA and I asked for and received permission to tape them. I would ask questions and observe what they did as they went about what I hoped were their typical daily and nightly lives. What I asked about was somewhat subjective, of course, but that is true of all human endeavor, including the physical sciences. It was determined by a number of factors, but particularly by my education as a medical and psychological anthropologist and my interests in substance abuse.

Transcribing tape recorded conversations and typing up other notes took three or four long days at the computer for every full day in the field. When I had spent four days in the field, for example, I might spend three weeks at home working on fieldnotes, perhaps sixteen workdays, before returning to the world of the homeless. Much of the fieldwork consisted of day trips of only a few hours, and sometimes I would spend hours walking the streets searching for my homeless acquaintances. These occasions would produce many fewer notes than a full day and night of interaction, of course. Altogether, I probably spent some 600 days transcribing and notetaking.

The verbatim material presented here is accurate, but I deleted many of the grunts, stutters, and false starts of real talk to make it readable. I attempted to do this in a consistent manner. That is, I tried to smooth out the rough spots in the talk of all my field consultants (and myself) to a similar degree. My aim was to make available to the reader the actual pace, the full flavor, and the real words of the interactions. This material is sanded and lightly oiled, but it is unvarnished.

In preparing this book, I had to boil down thousands of pages of detailed, mostly verbatim field notes into a few hundred pages that contained the essence of bridge life. This process required that I constantly make subjective decisions about what to leave in and what to leave out. I attempted to include passages that I felt explained, clarified, and epitomized the existence of the Bridge People. My agent, Laurie Harper of the Sebastian Agency, was very helpful in the later phases of this process. The order of events and conversations is essentially accurate. However, in order to reduce redundancy, some topics that came up many times have been presented in a single representative episode containing portions of several different discussions of that topic. Of course, I had to leave many, many conversations out entirely.

No report can be truely objective and complete, and this is no exception. But one can try to be as explicit as possible about the way the research was done and attempt to be fair to others and to other points of view. These are worthwhile goals and the basis of modern, postpositivist scientific understanding (Lincoln and Guba 1985). A complete record of what transpired would be empirically impossible on the one hand, and impossible to publish on the other. This report was my best effort at a fair, honest, and open interpretation of what happened, presented in a way I thought would be accessible to a wide audience. It was composed, like a photograph is composed, out of what was really out there, but it is taken from a particular perspective and through my own ethnographic lens. Of necessity, any perspective will leave much outside the field of view and bring some things into focus while leaving others blurry. To form a clear, broad, and coherent picture, other ethnographic lenses should be focused on other scenes of extreme poverty in the United States today.

References

Alloy, L. B., L. Y. Abramson, G. I. Metalsky, and S. Hartlage
    1988 The Hopelessness Theory of Depression: Attributional Aspects. British Journal of Clinical Psychology 27:5-21.

Barlett, Donald L. and James B. Steele
    1992 America: What Went Wrong? Kansas City: Andrews and McMeel.

Bernard, H. Russell, Peter Killworth, David Kronenfeld, and Lee Sailer
    1984 The Problem of Informant Accuracy: The Validity of Retrospective Data. Annnual Review of Anthropology 13:495-517.

Bidinotto, Robert J.
    1991 Myths About the Homeless. Reader's Digest, June, pp. 98-103.

Bluestone, Barry and Bennett Harrison
    1982 The Deindustrialization of America: Plant Closings, Community Abandonment, and the Dismantling of Basic Industry. New York: Basic Books.

Boyatzis, Richard
    1976 Drinking As A Manifestation Of Power Concerns. In Cross-Cultural Approaches to the Study of Alcohol. M. W. Everett, J. Waddell, and D. Heath, eds. The Hague: Mouton.

Braxton, Greg
    1991 Studios in Burbank Outspent Anti-Growth Plan Backers 30 to 1. Los Angeles Times, August 3, p. B3.

Center on Budget and Policy Priorities
    1984 End Results: The Impact of Federal Policies Since 1980 on Low Income Americans. Washington, D.C.: Interfaith Action for Economic Justice.

Coalition on Human Needs
    1987 Campaign for Common Sense. Washington D.C.: Coalition on Human Needs.

Dwyer, Kevin
    1982 Moroccan Dialogues: Anthropology in Question. Baltimore: Johns Hopkins University Press.

Eisenberger, Robert, Denise C. Park, and Michael Frank
    1976 Learned Industriousness and Social Reinforcement. Journal of Personality and Social Psychology 33:227-232.

Fingerette, Herbert
    1988 Heavy Drinking: The Myth of Alcoholism as a Disease. Berkeley:
          University of California Press.

Ford Foundation
    1989 Affordable Housing: The Years Ahead. New York: Ford Foundation.

Garber, J., and M. E. P. Seligman
    1980 Human Helplessness: Theory and Applications. New York: Academic
          Press.

Green, Cynthia
    n.d. Housing Single, Low Income Individuals. New York: Setting Municipal
          Priorities.

Hamilton, Rabinovitz, and Alschuler, Inc.
    1987 The Changing Face of Misery: Los Angeles' Skid Row Area in
          Transition. Los Angeles: Community Redevelopment Agency.

Horwitz, Allan V.
    1984 The Economy and Social Pathology. Annual Review of Sociology
          10:95-119.

Johnson, Haynes
    1991 Sleepwalking Through History: America In the Reagan Years. New
          York: W. W. Norton.

Jonas, Steven
    1989 Is the Drug Problem Soluable? American Behavioral Scientist 32:295-
          315.

Katz, M. B.
    1986 In the Shadow of the Poorhouse: A Social History of Welfare in
          America. New York: Basic Books.

Koegel, Paul, M., Audrey Burnam, and Roger K. Farr
    1988 The Prevalence of Specific Psychiatric Disorders Among Homeless
          Individuals in the Inner City of Los Angeles. Archives of General
          Psychiatry 45:1085-1092.

    1987 The Epidemiology of Alcohol Abuse and Dependence Among Homeless
          Individuals: Findings from the Inner-City of Los Angeles. Rockville,
          MD: National Institute of Alcohol Abuse and Alcoholism.

Lincoln, Yvonna S., and Egon G. Guba
    1985 Naturalistic Inquiry. Newbury Park, CA: Sage.

Marlatt, G. A.
    1982 Relapse Prevention: A Self-control Program for the Treatment of
          Addictive Behaviors. *In* Adherence, Compliance and Generalization in
          Behavioral Medicine. R. B. Stuart, ed. New York: Brunner/Mazel.

McClelland, D. C., W. Davis, R. Kalin, and E. Wanner
    1972 The Drinking Man. New York: Free Press.

McGuire, M. T., S. Stein, and J. H. Mendelson
    1966 Comparative Psychosocial Studies of Alcoholic and Nonalcoholic
          Subjects Undergoing Experimentally Induced Ethanol Intoxication.
          Psychosomatic Medicine 28:13-25.

Mendelson, J. H., and Mello, N. K.
    1979 One Unanswered Question about Alcoholism. British Journal of
          Addiction 74:11-14.

Peele, Stanton
    1985 The Meaning of Addiction: Compulsive Experience and Its
          Interpretation. Lexington, MA: D.C. Heath.

Rathje, William L.
    1977 Archaeological Ethnography. . . Because Sometimes It Is Better to Give
          Than to Receive. *In* Explorations in Ethnoarchaeology. Richard A.
          Gould, ed. Albuquerque: University of New Mexico Press.

Rose, Dan
    1990 Living the Ethnographic Life. Newbury Park, CA: Sage.

Seligman, M. E. P.
    1975 Helplessness: On Depression, Development and Death. San Francisco:
          Freeman.

Shaefer, James M.
    1976 Drunkenness and Cultural Stress: A Holocultural Test. *In* Cross-
          Cultural Approaches to the Study of Alcohol. M. W. Everett, J. O.
          Waddell, and D. B. Heath, eds. The Hague: Mouton.

Spradley, James P.
    1970 You Owe Yourself a Drunk: An Ethnography of Urban Nomads.
          Boston: Little, Brown and Company.

Suskind, Ron
    1992 Tough Vote: Threat of Cheap Labor Abroad Complicates Decisions to
          Unionize. Wall Street Journal, July 28, pp. A1, A6.

Turnbull, Colin
  1972 The Mountain People. New York: Simon and Schuster.

Wallace, Michael and Joyce Rothschild
  1988 Deindustrialization and the Restructuring of American Industry. *In* Research in Politics and Society, Vol. 3. M. Wallace and J. Rothchild, eds. Greenwich, CT: JAI Press.

Wielawski, Irene
  1991 Patients Giving Up On Emergency Rooms. Los Angeles Times, August 28:pp. A3, A20.

Index